T0178677

Advanced Backend Code Optimization

*To my parents who gave deep human foundations to my life.
I am proud to be their son.*

– Sid TOUATI

Series Editor
Jean-Charles Pomerol

Advanced Backend
Code Optimization

Sid Touati
Benoit Dupont de Dinechin

WILEY

First published 2014 in Great Britain and the United States by ISTE Ltd and John Wiley & Sons, Inc.

ISTE Ltd
27-37 St George's Road
London SW19 4EU
UK

www.iste.co.uk

John Wiley & Sons, Inc.
111 River Street
Hoboken, NJ 07030
USA

www.wiley.com

Library of Congress Control Number: 2014935739

British Library Cataloguing-in-Publication Data
A CIP record for this book is available from the British Library
ISBN 978-1-84821-538-2

Printed and bound in Great Britain by CPI Group (UK) Ltd., Croydon, Surrey CR0 4YY

Contents

INTRODUCTION xiii

PART 1. PROLOG: OPTIMIZING COMPILATION 1

**CHAPTER 1. ON THE DECIDABILITY OF PHASE
ORDERING IN OPTIMIZING COMPILATION** 3

1.1. Introduction to the phase ordering problem 3
1.2. Background on phase ordering 5
1.2.1. Performance modeling and prediction 5
1.2.2. Some attempts in phase ordering 6
1.3. Toward a theoretical model for the phase ordering problem 7
1.3.1. Decidability results 8
1.3.2. Another formulation of the phase ordering problem 11
1.4. Examples of decidable simplified cases 12
1.4.1. Models with compilation costs 12
1.4.2. One-pass generative compilers 13
1.5. Compiler optimization parameter space exploration 16
1.5.1. Toward a theoretical model 17
1.5.2. Examples of simplified decidable cases 19
1.6. Conclusion on phase ordering in optimizing compilation 20

PART 2. INSTRUCTION SCHEDULING 23

CHAPTER 2. INSTRUCTION SCHEDULING PROBLEMS AND OVERVIEW . 25

2.1. VLIW instruction scheduling problems 25
2.1.1. Instruction scheduling and register allocation in a code generator . 25
2.1.2. The block and pipeline VLIW instruction scheduling problems . . . 27
2.2. Software pipelining 29
2.2.1. Cyclic, periodic and pipeline scheduling problems 29

2.2.2. Modulo instruction scheduling problems and techniques 32
2.3. Instruction scheduling and register allocation 35
    2.3.1. Register instruction scheduling problem solving approaches 35

**CHAPTER 3. APPLICATIONS OF MACHINE SCHEDULING TO
INSTRUCTION SCHEDULING** 39

3.1. Advances in machine scheduling 39
    3.1.1. Parallel machine scheduling problems 39
    3.1.2. Parallel machine scheduling extensions and relaxations 41
3.2. List scheduling algorithms 43
    3.2.1. List scheduling algorithms and list scheduling priorities 43
    3.2.2. The scheduling algorithm of Leung, Palem and Pnueli 45
3.3. Time-indexed scheduling problem formulations 47
    3.3.1. The non-preemptive time-indexed RCPSP formulation 47
    3.3.2. Time-indexed formulation for the modulo RPISP 48

**CHAPTER 4. INSTRUCTION SCHEDULING BEFORE
REGISTER ALLOCATION** 51

4.1. Instruction scheduling for an ILP processor: case of a
    VLIW architecture 51
    4.1.1. Minimum cumulative register lifetime modulo scheduling 51
    4.1.2. Resource modeling in instruction scheduling problems 54
    4.1.3. The modulo insertion scheduling theorems 56
    4.1.4. Insertion scheduling in a backend compiler 58
    4.1.5. Example of an industrial production compiler from
        STMicroelectronics 60
    4.1.6. Time-indexed formulation of the modulo RCISP 64
4.2. Large neighborhood search for the resource-constrained modulo
    scheduling problem 67
4.3. Resource-constrained modulo scheduling problem 68
    4.3.1. Resource-constrained cyclic scheduling problems 68
    4.3.2. Resource-constrained modulo scheduling problem statement 69
    4.3.3. Solving resource-constrained modulo scheduling problems 70
4.4. Time-indexed integer programming formulations 71
    4.4.1. The non-preemptive time-indexed RCPSP formulation 71
    4.4.2. The classic modulo scheduling integer programming formulation . 72
    4.4.3. A new time-indexed formulation for modulo scheduling 73
4.5. Large neighborhood search heuristic 74
    4.5.1. Variables and constraints in time-indexed formulations 74
    4.5.2. A large neighborhood search heuristic for modulo scheduling ... 74
    4.5.3. Experimental results with a production compiler 75
4.6. Summary and conclusions 76

CHAPTER 5. INSTRUCTION SCHEDULING AFTER
REGISTER ALLOCATION 77

5.1. Introduction 77
5.2. Local instruction scheduling 79
    5.2.1. Acyclic instruction scheduling 79
    5.2.2. Scoreboard Scheduling principles 80
    5.2.3. Scoreboard Scheduling implementation 82
5.3. Global instruction scheduling 84
    5.3.1. Postpass inter-region scheduling 84
    5.3.2. Inter-block Scoreboard Scheduling 86
    5.3.3. Characterization of fixed points 87
5.4. Experimental results 87
5.5. Conclusions 89

CHAPTER 6. DEALING IN PRACTICE WITH MEMORY
HIERARCHY EFFECTS AND INSTRUCTION LEVEL
PARALLELISM 91

6.1. The problem of hardware memory disambiguation at runtime 92
    6.1.1. Introduction 92
    6.1.2. Related work 93
    6.1.3. Experimental environment 94
    6.1.4. Experimentation methodology 95
    6.1.5. Precise experimental study of memory hierarchy performance . . . 95
    6.1.6. The effectiveness of load/store vectorization 100
    6.1.7. Conclusion on hardware memory disambiguation mechanisms . . . 103
6.2. Data preloading and prefetching 104
    6.2.1. Introduction 104
    6.2.2. Related work 105
    6.2.3. Problems of optimizing cache effects at the instruction level 107
    6.2.4. Target processor description 109
    6.2.5. Our method of instruction-level code optimization 110
    6.2.6. Experimental results 116
    6.2.7. Conclusion on prefetching and preloading at instruction level . . . 117

PART 3. REGISTER OPTIMIZATION 119

CHAPTER 7. THE REGISTER NEED OF A FIXED
INSTRUCTION SCHEDULE 121

7.1. Data dependence graph and processor model for register
    optimization 122
    7.1.1. NUAL and UAL semantics 122
7.2. The acyclic register need 123
7.3. The periodic register need 125

7.3.1. Software pipelining, periodic scheduling and cyclic scheduling . . 125
7.3.2. The circular lifetime intervals 127
7.4. Computing the periodic register need 129
7.5. Some theoretical results on the periodic register need 132
    7.5.1. Minimal periodic register need versus initiation interval 133
    7.5.2. Computing the periodic register sufficiency 133
    7.5.3. Stage scheduling under register constraints 134
7.6. Conclusion on the register requirement 139

CHAPTER 8. THE REGISTER SATURATION 141

8.1. Motivations on the register saturation concept 141
8.2. Computing the acyclic register saturation 144
    8.2.1. Characterizing the register saturation 146
    8.2.2. Efficient algorithmic heuristic for register saturation computation . 149
    8.2.3. Experimental efficiency of Greedy-k 151
8.3. Computing the periodic register saturation 153
    8.3.1. Basic integer linear variables 154
    8.3.2. Integer linear constraints 154
    8.3.3. Linear objective function 156
8.4. Conclusion on the register saturation 157

CHAPTER 9. SPILL CODE REDUCTION 159

9.1. Introduction to register constraints in software pipelining 159
9.2. Related work in periodic register allocation 160
9.3. SIRA: schedule independant register allocation 162
    9.3.1. Reuse graphs 162
    9.3.2. DDG associated with reuse graph 164
    9.3.3. Exact SIRA with integer linear programming 166
    9.3.4. SIRA with fixed reuse edges 168
9.4. SIRALINA: an efficient polynomial heuristic for SIRA 169
    9.4.1. Integer variables for the linear problem 170
    9.4.2. Step 1: the scheduling problem 170
    9.4.3. Step 2: the linear assignment problem 172
9.5. Experimental results with SIRA 173
9.6. Conclusion on spill code reduction 175

CHAPTER 10. EXPLOITING THE REGISTER ACCESS
DELAYS BEFORE INSTRUCTION SCHEDULING 177

10.1. Introduction 177
10.2. Problem description of DDG circuits with non-positive distances . . . 179
10.3. Necessary and sufficient condition to avoid non-positive circuits . . . 180
10.4. Application to the SIRA framework 182

10.4.1. Recall on SIRALINA heuristic 183
10.4.2. Step 1: the scheduling problem for a fixed II 183
10.4.3. Step 2: the linear assignment problem 184
10.4.4. Eliminating non-positive circuits in SIRALINA 184
10.4.5. Updating reuse distances 186
10.5. Experimental results on eliminating non-positive circuits 187
10.6. Conclusion on non-positive circuit elimination 188

CHAPTER 11. LOOP UNROLLING DEGREE MINIMIZATION
FOR PERIODIC REGISTER ALLOCATION 191

11.1. Introduction 191
11.2. Background 195
11.2.1. Loop unrolling after SWP with modulo variable expansion 196
11.2.2. Meeting graphs (MG) 197
11.2.3. SIRA, reuse graphs and loop unrolling 200
11.3. Problem description of unroll factor minimization for
unscheduled loops 204
11.4. Algorithmic solution for unroll factor minimization:
single register type 205
11.4.1. Fixed loop unrolling problem 206
11.4.2. Solution for the fixed loop unrolling problem 207
11.4.3. Solution for LCM-MIN problem 209
11.5. Unroll factor minimization in the presence of multiple
register types 213
11.5.1. Search space for minimal kernel loop unrolling 217
11.5.2. Generalization of the fixed loop unrolling problem
in the presence of multiple register types 218
11.5.3. Algorithmic solution for the loop unrolling
minimization (LUM, problem 11.1) 219
11.6. Unroll factor reduction for already scheduled loops 221
11.6.1. Improving algorithm 11.4 (LCM-MIN) for the
meeting graph framework 224
11.7. Experimental results 224
11.8. Related work 226
11.8.1. Rotating register files 226
11.8.2. Inserting move operations 227
11.8.3. Loop unrolling after software pipelining 228
11.8.4. Code generation for multidimensional loops 228
11.9. Conclusion on loop unroll degree minimization 228

PART 4. EPILOG: PERFORMANCE, OPEN PROBLEMS   231

CHAPTER 12. STATISTICAL PERFORMANCE ANALYSIS:
THE SPEEDUP-TEST PROTOCOL   233
    12.1. Code performance variation   233
    12.2. Background and notations   236
    12.3. Analyzing the statistical significance of the observed speedups   239
        12.3.1. The speedup of the observed average execution time   239
        12.3.2. The speedup of the observed median execution time, as well as
            individual runs   241
    12.4. The Speedup-Test software   244
    12.5. Evaluating the proportion of accelerated benchmarks by a confidence
        interval   246
    12.6. Experiments and applications   248
        12.6.1. Comparing the performances of compiler optimization
            levels   249
        12.6.2. Testing the performances of parallel executions of OpenMP
            applications   250
        12.6.3. Comparing the efficiency of two compilers   251
        12.6.4. The impact of the Speedup-Test protocol over some observed
            speedups   253
    12.7. Related work   253
        12.7.1. Observing execution times variability   253
        12.7.2. Program performance evaluation in presence of variability   254
    12.8. Discussion and conclusion on the Speedup-Test protocol   255

CONCLUSION   257

APPENDIX 1. PRESENTATION OF THE BENCHMARKS USED IN OUR
EXPERIMENTS   263

APPENDIX 2. REGISTER SATURATION COMPUTATION ON
STAND-ALONE DDG   271

APPENDIX 3. EFFICIENCY OF SIRA ON THE BENCHMARKS   279

APPENDIX 4. EFFICIENCY OF NON-POSITIVE CIRCUIT ELIMINATION
IN THE SIRA FRAMEWORK   293

APPENDIX 5. LOOP UNROLL DEGREE MINIMIZATION:
EXPERIMENTAL RESULTS   303

APPENDIX 6. EXPERIMENTAL EFFICIENCY OF SOFTWARE DATA PRELOADING AND PREFETCHING FOR EMBEDDED VLIW 315

APPENDIX 7. APPENDIX OF THE SPEEDUP-TEST PROTOCOL 319

BIBLIOGRAPHY 327

LISTS OF FIGURES, TABLES AND ALGORITHMS 345

INDEX 353

Introduction

An open question that remains in computer science is how to define a program of *good quality*. At the semantic level, a *good* program is one that computes what is specified formally (either in an exact way, or even without an exact result but at least heading towards making a right decision). At the algorithmic level, a good program is one that has a reduced spatial and temporal complexity. This book does not tackle these two levels of program quality abstraction. We are interested in the aspects of code quality at the compilation level (after a coding and an implementation of an algorithm). When a program has been implemented, some quality can be *quantified* according to its efficiency, for instance. By the term "efficiency", we mean a program that exploits the underlying hardware at its best, delivers the correct results as quickly as possible, has a reasonable memory footprint and a moderate energy consumption. There are also some quality criteria that are not easy to define, for instance the clarity of the code and its aptitude for being analyzed conveniently by automatic methods (worst-case execution time, data-flow dependence analysis, etc.).

Automatic code optimization, in general, focuses on two objectives that are not necessarily antagonists: the computation speed and the memory footprint of the code. These are the two principal quality criteria approached in this book. The computation speed is the most popular objective, but it remains difficult to model precisely. In fact, the execution time of a program is influenced by a complex combination of multiple factors, a list of which (probably incomplete) is given below:

1) The underlying processor and machine architecture: instruction set architecture (ISA), explicit instruction-level parallelism (very long instruction word – VLIW), memory addressing modes, data size, input/output protocols, etc.

2) The underlying processor micro-architecture: implicit instruction-level parallelism (superscalar), branch prediction, memory hierarchy, speculative execution, pipelined execution, memory disambiguation mechanism, out-of-order execution, register renaming, etc.

3) The technology: clock frequency, processor fabrication, silicon integration, transistor wide, components (chipset, DRAM and bus), etc.

4) Software implementation: syntactic constructs of the code, used data structures, program instructions' order, way of programming, etc.

5) The data input: the executed path of the code depends on the input data.

6) The experimental environment: operating system configuration and version, activated system services, used compiler and optimization flags, workload of the test machine, degradation of the hardware, temperature of the room, etc.

7) The measure of the code performance: experimental methodology (code loading and launching), rigor of the statistical analysis, etc.

All the above factors are difficult to tackle in the same optimization process. The role of the compiler is to optimize a fraction of them only (software implementation and its interaction with the underlying hardware). For a long time, compilation has been considered as one of the most active research topics in computer science. Its importance is not only in the field of programming, code generation and optimization, but also in circuit synthesis, language translation, interpreters, etc. We are all witness of the high number of new languages and processor architectures. It is not worthwhile to create a compiler for each combination of language and processor. The core of a compiler is asked to be common to multiple combinations between programming languages and processor architectures. In the past, compiler backends were specialized per architecture. Nowadays, backends are trying to be increasingly general in order to save the investment cost of developing a compiler.

In universities and schools, classes that teach compilation theory define clear frontiers between frontend and backend:

1) *High-level code optimization*: this is the set of code transformations applied on an intermediate representation close to the high-level language. Such intermediate representation contains sophisticated syntax constructs (loops and controls) with rich semantics, as well as high-level data structures (arrays, containers, etc.). Analyzing and optimizing at this level of program abstraction tends to improve the performance metrics that are not related to a specific processor architecture. Examples include interprocedural and data dependence analysis, automatic parallelization, scalar and array privatization, loop nest transformations, alias analysis, etc.

2) *Low-level code optimization*: this is the set of code transformations applied to an intermediate representation close to the final instruction set of the processor (assembly instructions, three address codes, Register Transfer Level (RTL), etc.). The performance metrics optimized at this level of program abstraction are generally related to the processor architecture: number of generated instructions, code size, instruction scheduling, register need, register allocation, register assignment, cache optimization, instruction selection, addressing modes, etc.

The practice is not very attractive. It is not rare to have a code transformation implemented at frontend optimizing for a backend objective: for instance, cache optimization at a loop nest can be done at frontend because the high-level program structure (loops) has yet to be destroyed. Inversely, it is possible to have a high-level analysis implemented at assembly or as binary code, such as data dependence and interprocedural analysis. Compilers are very complex pieces of software that are maintained for a long period of time, and the frontiers between high and low levels can sometimes be difficult to define formally. Nevertheless, the notion of frontend and backend optimization is not fundamental. It is a technical decomposition of compilation mainly for easing the development of the compiler software.

We are interested in backend code optimization mainly due to a personal inclination towards hardware/software frontiers. Even this barrier starts to leak with the development of reconfigurable and programmable architectures, where compilers are asked to generate a part of the instruction set. In this book, we have tried to be as abstract as possible in order to have general results applicable to wide processor families (superscalar, VLIW, Explicitly Parallel Instruction Computing (EPIC), etc.). When the micro-architectural features are too complex to model, we provide technical solutions for practical situations.

I.1. Inside this book

This book is the outcome of a long period of research activity in academia and industry. We write fundamental results in terms of lemmas, definitions, theorems and corollaries, and in terms of algorithms and heuristics. We also provide an appendix that contains some experimental results. For future reproducibility, we have released most of our experimental results in terms of documented software and numerical data.

Although we did not include all of our mature research results in this book, we think that we have succeeded in summarizing most of our efforts on backend code optimization. In the following, we briefly describe the organization of this book.

Section I.3, on basic recalls on instruction-level parallelism (ILP) in processor architectures, starts with explaining the difference between superscalar and VLIW architectures. ILP processor architectures are widely covered in other books, so this section will be a brief summary.

Part 1: introduction to optimizing compilation

Chapter 1 is entitled "On the Decidability of Phase Ordering in Optimizing Compilation": we have had long and sometimes painful experiences with code optimization of large and complex applications. The obtained speedups, in practice, are not always satisfactory when using usual compilation flags. When iterative compilation started to become a new trend in our field, we asked ourselves whether such methodologies may outperform static compilation: static compilation is designed for all possible data inputs, while iterative compilation chooses a data input and therefore, it seems to simplify the problem. We studied the decidability of phase ordering from the theoretical point of view in the context of iterative compilation.

Part 2: instruction scheduling

This part of the book covers instruction scheduling in ILP. The chapters of this part (Chapters 2–6) use the same notations, which are different from the notations used in the following part. The reason why the formal notations in this part are slightly different from the notations of Part 3 is that the instruction scheduling problems are strongly related to the theory of machine scheduling. In this area of research, there are some common and usual notations that we use in this part but not in Part 3.

Chapter 2, entitled "Instruction Scheduling Problems and Overview", is a reminder of scheduling problems for ILP, and their relationship with register optimization. Special attention is given to cyclic scheduling problems because they are of importance for optimizing the performance of loops.

Chapter 3, entitled "Applications of Machine Scheduling to Instruction Scheduling", is an interesting chapter that discusses the relationship between theoretical scheduling problems and practical instruction scheduling problems. Indeed, although instruction scheduling is a mature discipline, its relationship with the field of machine scheduling is often ignored. In this chapter, we show how the theory of machine scheduling can be applied to instruction scheduling.

Chapter 4, entitled "Instruction Scheduling before Register Allocation", provides a formal method and a practical implementation for cyclic instruction scheduling under resource constraints. The presented scheduling method is still sensitive to register pressure.

Chapter 5, entitled "Instruction Scheduling after Register Allocation", presents a postpass register allocation method. After an instruction scheduling, register allocation may introduce spill code and may require making some instruction rescheduling. This chapter presents a faster technique suitable for just-in-time compilation.

Chapter 6, entitled "Dealing in Practice with Memory Hierarchy Effects and Instruction-Level Parallelism", studies the complex micro-architectural features from a practical point of view. First, we highlight the problem with memory disambiguation mechanisms in out-of-order processors. This problem exists in most of the micro-architectures and creates false dependences between independent instructions during execution, limiting ILP. Second, we show how to use insert instructions for data preloading and prefetching in the context of embedded VLIW.

Part 3: register optimization

This part of the book discusses register pressure in ILP, which can be read independently from Part 2. In order to understand all the formal information and notations of this part, we advise the readers not to neglect the formal model and notations presented in section 7.1.

Chapter 7, entitled "The Register Need of a Fixed Instruction Schedule", deals with register allocation. This is a wide research topic, where multiple distinct problems coexist, some notions are similarly named but do not have the same mathematical definition. Typically, the notion of the register need may have distinct significations. We formally define this quantity in two contexts: the context of acyclic scheduling (basic block and superblock) and the context of cyclic scheduling (software pipelining of a loop). While the acyclic register need is a well-understood notion, we provide new formal knowledge on the register need in cyclic scheduling.

Chapter 8 is entitled "The Register Saturation": our approach here for tackling register constraints is radically different from the usual point of view in register allocation. Indeed, we study the problem of register need maximization, not minimization. We explain the differences between the two problems and provide an efficient greedy heuristic. Register maximization allows us to decouple register constraints from instruction scheduling: if we detect that the maximal register need is below the processor capacity, we can neglect register constraints.

Chapter 9, entitled "Spill Code Reduction", mainly discusses schedule independent register allocation (SIRA) framework: this approach handles register constraints before instruction scheduling by adding edges to the data dependence graph (DDG). It guarantees the absence of spilling for all valid instruction schedules. This approach takes care not to alter the ILP if possible. We present the theoretical graph approach, called SIRA, and we show its applications in multiple contexts: multiple register file architectures, rotating register files and buffers. We present SIRALINA, an efficient and effective heuristic that allows satisfactory spill code reduction in practice while saving the ILP.

Chapter 10, entitled "Exploiting the Register Access Delays before Instruction Scheduling", discusses a certain problem and provides a solution: until now, the literature has not formally tackled one of the real problems that arises when register optimization is handled before instruction scheduling. Indeed, when the processor has explicit register access delays (such as in VLIW, explicitly parallel instruction computing (EPIC) and digital signal processing (DSP)), bounding or minimizing the register requirement before fixing an instruction schedule may create a deadlock in theory when resource constraints are considered afterward. The nature of this problem and a solution in the context of SIRA are the main subject of this chapter.

Chapter 11 is entitled "Loop Unrolling Degree Minimization for Periodic Register Allocation": the SIRA framework proves to be an interesting relationship between the number of allocated registers in a loop, the critical circuit of the DDG and the loop unrolling factor. For the purpose of code size compaction, we show how can we minimize the unrolling degree with the guarantee of neither generating spill code nor altering the ILP. The problem is based on the minimization of a least common multiple, using the set of remaining registers.

Part 4: Epilog

Chapter 12, entitled "Statistical Performance Analysis: The Speedup-Test Protocol", tends to improve the reproducibility of the experimental results in our community. We tackle the problem of code performance variation in practical observations. We describe the protocol called the Speedup-Test; it uses well-known statistical tests to declare, with a proved risk level, whether an average or a median execution time has been improved or not. We clearly explain what the hypotheses that must be checked for each statistical test are.

Finally, the Conclusion describes some open problems in optimizing compilation in general. These open problems are known but do not yet have satisfactory solutions in the literature. Here, we conclude with a general summary.

I.2. Other contributors

This book is the outcome of long-term fundamental, experimental and technical research using graph theory, scheduling theory, linear programming, complexity theory, compilation, etc. We had great pleasure and honor collaborating with many talented people with high-quality backgrounds in computer science, computer engineering and mathematics. Table I.1 provides a list of collaborators for each chapter, whom we would like to thank very much.

Chapter	Contributor	Nature of the contribution
Chapter 1	Pr Denis BARTHOU	Formal proofs and modeling of phase ordering problems
Chapter 6	Dr Christophe LEMIET	PhD work, implementation, experiments, performance analysis of memory disambiguation mechanisms.
	Dr Samir AMMENOUCHE	PhD work, implementation, experiments, performance analysis of instruction scheduling under cache effects on VLIW processors.
	Pr William JALBY	PhD direction
Chapter 9	Dr Christine EISENBEIS	Initial intuition and formal description of the SIRA framework, PhD direction
	Dr Karine DESCHINKEL	SIRALINA heuristic proposal, software implementation
	Dr Sébastien BRIAIS	Software implementation of SIRALINA, experiments
	Mr Frederic BRAULT	Integration of SIRA framework inside an industrial compiler for VLIW processors, experiments and performance analysis
Chapter 10	Dr Karine DESCHINKEL	Iterative method for eliminating non-positive circuits in data dependence graphs
	Dr Sébastien BRIAIS	Formal proofs and algorithms, implementation and experiments
Chapter 11	Dr Mounira BACHIR	PhD work, formal proofs, implementation and experiments
	Dr Albert COHEN	PhD direction
	Dr David GREGG	Contribution on algorithms
	Mr Frederic BRAULT	Experimental study with an industrial compiler for VLIW processors
Chapter 12	Dr Julien WORMS	Parametric statistics, statistical testing
	Dr Sébastien BRIAIS	Speedup-Test implementation
	Dr Abdelhafid MAZOUZ	Experimental study of program performance variability

Table I.1. *Other contributors to the results presented in this book*

I.3. Basics on instruction-level parallelism processor architectures

Today's microprocessors are the powerful descendants of the Von Neumann computer [SIL 99]. Although various computer architectures have been considerably changed and rapidly developed over the last 20 years, the basic principles in Von Neumann computational model are still the foundation of today's most widely used computer architectures as well as high-level programming languages. The Von Neumann computational model was proposed by Von Neumann and his colleagues in

1946; its key characteristics result from the *multiple assignment*s of variables and from the *control-driven* execution.

While the sequential operating principles of the Von Neumann architecture are still the basis for today's most used instruction sets, its internal structure, called micro-architecture, has been changed considerably. The main goal of the Von Neumann machine model was to minimize the hardware structure, while today's designs are mainly oriented toward maximizing the performance. For this last reason, machines have been designed to be able to execute multiple tasks simultaneously. Architectures, compilers and operating systems have been striving for more than two decades to extract and utilize as much parallelism as possible in order to boost the performance.

Parallelism can be exploited by a machine at multiple levels:

1) *Fine-grain parallelism*. This is the parallelism available at instruction level (or, say, at machine-language level) by means of executing instructions simultaneously. ILP can be achieved by architectures that are capable of parallel instruction execution. Such architectures are called *instruction-level parallel architectures*, i.e. *ILP architectures*.

2) *Medium-grain parallelism*. This is the parallelism available at thread level. A thread (lightweight process) is a sequence of instructions that may share a common register file, a heap and a stack. Multiple threads can be executed concurrently or in parallel. The hardware implementation of thread-level parallelism is called *multithreaded processor* or *simultaneous multithreaded processor*.

3) *Coarse-grain parallelism*. This is the parallelism available at process, task, program or user level. The hardware implementation of such parallelism is called *multiprocessor machine* or *multiprocessor chips*. The latter may integrate multiple processors into a single chip, also called multi-core or many core processors.

The discussion about coarse- or medium-grain parallel architectures is outside the scope of this book. In this introduction, we provide a brief analysis of ILP architectures, which principally include static issue processors (e.g. VLIW, EPIC and Transport Triggered Architectures (TTAs)) and dynamic issue processors (superscalar).

Pipelined processors overlap the execution of multiple instructions simultaneously, but issue only one instruction at every clock cycle (see Figure I.1). The principal motivation of *multiple issue* processors was to break away from the limitation on the single issue of pipelined processors, and to provide the facility to execute more than one instruction in one clock cycle. The substantial difference from pipelined processors is that multiple issue processors replicate functional units (FUs) in order to deal with instructions in parallel, such as parallel instruction fetch, decode, execution and write back. However, the constraints in multiple issue processors are the same as in pipelined processors, that is the dependences between instructions have to be taken into account when multiple instructions are issued and executed in parallel. Therefore, the following questions arise:

– How to detect dependences between instructions?

– How to express instructions in parallel execution?

The answers to these two questions gave rise to the significant differences between two classes of multiple issue processors: static issue processors and dynamic issue processors. In the following sections, we describe the characteristics of these two kinds of *multiple issue* processors.

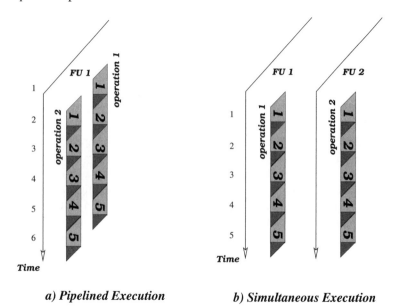

a) Pipelined Execution   **b) Simultaneous Execution**

Figure I.1. *Pipelined vs. simultaneous execution*

I.3.1. *Processors with dynamic instruction issue*

The hardware micro-architectural mechanism designed to increase the number of executed instructions per clock cycle is called *superscalar execution*. The goal of a superscalar processor is to dynamically (at runtime) issue multiple independent operations in parallel (Figure I.2), even though the hardware receives a sequential instruction stream. Consequently, the program is written as if it were to be executed by a sequential processor, but the underlying execution is parallel.

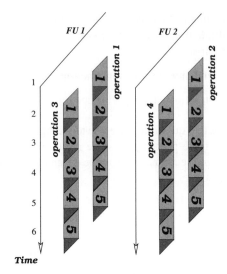

Figure I.2. *Superscalar execution*

Again, there are two micro-architectural mechanisms of superscalar processors: *in-order* execution and *out-of-order* (OoO) processors. A processor with an in-order issue sends the instructions to be executed in the same order as they appear in the program. That is, if instruction a appears before b, then instruction b may in the best case be executed in parallel with a but not before. However, an OoO processor can dynamically change the execution order if operations are independent. This powerful mechanism enables us to pursue the computation in the presence of long delay operations or unexpected events such as cache misses. However, because of the hardware complexity of dynamic independence testing, the window size where the processor can dynamically reschedule operations is limited.

Compared with VLIW architectures, as we will soon see, superscalar processors achieve a certain degree of parallel execution at the cost of increased hardware complexity. A VLIW processor outperforms a superscalar processor in terms of hardware complexity, cost and power consumption. However, the advantages of a superscalar processor over a VLIW processor are multiple:

1) *Varying numbers of instructions per clock cycle*: since the hardware determines the number of instructions issued per clock cycle, the compiler does not need to lay out instructions to match the maximum issue bandwidth. Accordingly, there is less impact on code density than for a VLIW processor.

2) *Binary code compatibility*: the binary code generated for a scalar (sequential) processor can also be executed in a superscalar processor with the same ISA, and vice versa. This means that the code can migrate between successive implementations even

with different numbers of issues and different execution times of FUs. Superscalar processors constitute a micro-architectural evolution, not an architectural one.

3) *Different execution scenarios*: superscalar processors dynamically schedule the operations in parallel. Then, there may be more than one parallel execution scenario (dynamic schedule) because of the dynamic events. However, VLIW processors always execute the same ILP schedule computed at compile time.

For the purpose of issuing multiple instructions per clock cycle, superscalar processing generally consists of a number of subtasks, such as parallel decoding, superscalar instruction issue and parallel instruction execution, preserving the sequential consistency of execution and exception processing. These tasks are executed by a powerful hardware pipeline (see Figure I.3 for a simple example). Below, we illustrate the basic functions of these pipelined steps.

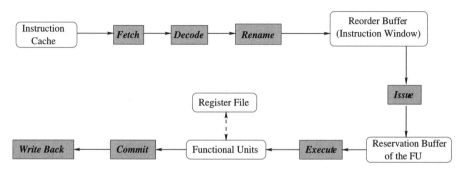

Figure I.3. *Simple superscalar pipelined steps*

Fetch pipeline step. A high-performance micro-processor usually contains two separate on-chip caches: the Instruction-cache (Icache) and Data-cache the (Dcache). This is because the Icache is less complicated to handle: it is read-only and is not subject to cache coherence in contrast to the Dcache. The main problem of instruction fetching is control transfers performed by procedural calls, branch, return and interrupt instructions. The sequential stream of instructions is disturbed and hence the CPU may stall. This is why some architectural improvements must be added if we expect a full utilization of ILP. Such features include instruction prefetching, branch prediction and speculative execution.

Decode pipeline step. Decoding multiple instructions in a superscalar processor is a much more complex task than in a scalar one, which only decodes a single instruction at each clock cycle. Since there are multiple FUs in a superscalar processor, the number of issued instructions in a clock cycle is much greater than that in a scalar case. Consequently, it becomes more complex for a superscalar processor to detect the dependences among the instructions currently in execution and to find out the instructions for the next issue. Superscalar processors often take two or three more pipeline cycles to decode and issue instructions. An increasingly used method to overcome the problem is *predecoding*: a partial decoding is performed before effective decoding, while instructions are loaded into the instruction cache.

Rename pipeline step. The aim of register renaming is to dynamically remove false dependences (anti- and output ones) by the hardware. This is done by associating specific *rename registers* with the ISA registers specified by the program. The rename registers cannot be accessed directly by the compiler or the user.

Issue and dispatch pipeline step. The notion of *instruction window* comprises all the waiting instructions between the decode (rename) and execute stage of the pipeline. Instructions in this *reorder buffer* are free from control and false dependences. Thus, only data dependence and resource conflicts remain to be dealt with. The former are checked during this stage. An operation is *issued* to the FU reservation buffer whether all operations on which it depends have been completed. This issue can be done statically (in-order) or dynamically (OoO) depending on the processor [PAT 94].

Execute pipeline step. Instructions inside the FU reservation buffer are free from data dependences. Only resource conflicts have to be solved. When a resource is freed, the instruction that needs it is *initiated* to execute. After one or more clock cycles (the latency depends on the FU type), it *completes* and therefore is ready for the next pipeline stage. The results are ready for any *forwarding*. This latter technique, also called *bypassing*, enables other dependent instructions to be issued before committing the results.

Commit and write back pipeline step. After completion, instructions are *committed* in-order and in parallel to guarantee the sequential consistency of the Von Neumann execution model. This means that if no interruptions or exceptions have been emitted, results of executions are *written back* from rename registers to architectural registers. If any exception occurs, the instructions results are canceled (without committing the result).

We should know that current superscalar processors have more than five pipeline steps, the manual of every architecture can provide useful information about it.

I.3.2. *Processors with static instruction issue*

These processors take advantage of the static ILP of the program and execute operations in parallel (see Figure I.1(b)). This kind of architecture asks programs to provide information about operations that are independent of each other. The compiler identifies the parallelism in the program and communicates it to the hardware by specifying independence information between operations. This information is directly used by the hardware, since it knows with no further checking which operations can be executed in the same processor clock cycle. Parallel operations are packed by the compiler into instructions. Then, the hardware has to fetch, decode and execute them as they are.

We classify static issue processors into three main families: VLIW, TTA and EPIC processors. The following sections define their characteristics.

I.3.2.1. *VLIW processors*

VLIW architectures [FIS 05] use a long instruction word that usually contains a fixed number of operations (corresponding to RISC instructions). The operations in a VLIW instruction must be independent of each other so that they can be fetched, decoded, issued and executed simultaneously (see Figure I.4).

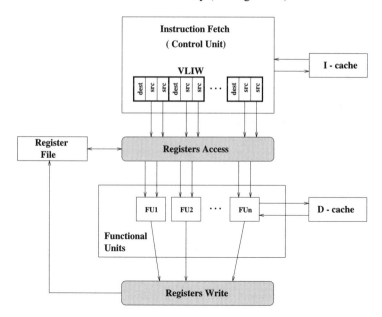

Figure I.4. *VLIW processors*

The key features of a VLIW processor are the following [SIL 99]:

– VLIW relies on a sequential stream of very long instruction words.

– Each instruction consists of multiple independent operations that can be issued and executed in one clock cycle. In general, the number of operations in an instruction is fixed.

– VLIW instructions are statically built by the compiler, i.e. the compiler deals with dependences and encodes parallelism in long instructions.

– The compiler must be aware of the hardware characteristics of the processor and memory.

– A central controller issues one VLIW instruction per cycle.

– A global shared register file connects the multiple FUs.

In a VLIW processor, unlike in superscalar processors, the compiler takes full responsibility for building VLIW instructions. In other words, the compiler has to detect and remove dependences and create the packages of independent operations that can be issued and executed in parallel. Furthermore, VLIW processors expose architecturally visible latencies to the compiler. The latter must take into account these latencies to generate valid codes.

The limitations of VLIW architectures arise in the following ways.

First, the full responsibility of the complex task for exploiting and extracting parallelism is delegated to the compiler. The compiler has to be aware of many details about VLIW architectures, such as the number and type of the available execution units, their latencies and replication numbers (number of same FUs), memory load-use delay and so on. Although VLIW architectures have less hardware complexity, powerful optimizing and parallelizing compiler techniques are required to effectively achieve high performance. As a result, it is questionable whether the reduced complexity of VLIW architectures can really be utilized by the compiler, since the design and implementation of the latter are generally much more expensive than expected.

Second, the binary code generated by a VLIW compiler is sensitive to the VLIW architecture. This means that the code cannot migrate within a generation of processors, even though these processors are compatible in the conventional sense. The problem is that different versions of the code are required for different technology-dependent parameters, such as the latencies and the repetition rates of the FUs. This sensitivity of the compiler restricts the use of the same compiler for subsequent models of a VLIW line. This is the most significant drawback of VLIW architectures.

Third, the length of a VLIW is usually fixed. Each instruction word provides a field for each available execution unit. Due to the lack of sufficient independent operations, only some of the fields may actually be used while other fields have to be filled by *no-ops*. This results in increased code size, and wasted memory space and memory bandwidth. In order to overcome this problem, some VLIW architectures use a compressed code format that allows the removal of the no-ops.

Finally, the performance of a VLIW processor is very sensitive to unexpected dynamic events, such as cache misses, page faults and interrupts. All these events make the processor stall from its ILP execution. For instance, if a load operation has been assumed by the compiler as hitting the cache, and this unfortunately happens not to be the case during dynamic execution, the entire processor stalls until the satisfaction of the cache request.

I.3.2.2. *Transport triggered architectures*

TTAs resemble VLIW architectures: both exploit ILP at compile time [JAN 01]. However, there are some significant architectural differences. Unlike VLIW, TTAs do not require that each FU has its own private connection to the register file. In TTAs, FUs are connected to registers by an interconnection network (see Figure I.5). This design allows us to reduce the register file ports bottleneck. It also reduces the complexity of the bypassing network since data forwarding is programmed explicitly.

However, programming TTAs is different from the classical RISC programming style. Traditional architectures are programmed by specifying operations. Data transports between FUs and register files are implicitly triggered by executing the operations. TTAs are programmed by specifying the data transports; as a side effect, operations are executed. In other words, data movements are made explicit by the program, and executing operations is implicitly done by the processor. Indeed, TTA is similar to data-flow processors except that instruction scheduling is done statically.

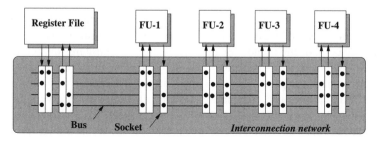

Figure I.5. *Block diagram of a TTA*

I.3.2.3. *EPIC/IA64 processors*

EPIC [SCH 00] technology was introduced to the IA64 architecture and compiler optimizations [KNI 99] in order to deliver explicit parallelism, massive resources and inherent scalability. It is, in a way, a mix between VLIW and superscalar programming styles. On the one hand, EPIC, like VLIW, allows the compiler to statically specify independent instructions. On the other hand, EPIC is like superscalar in the sense that the code semantics may be sequential, while guaranteeing the binary compatibility between different IA64 implementations.

The philosophy behind EPIC is much more about scalability. OoO processors get their issue unit saturated because of the architectural complexity. EPIC incorporates the combination of speculation, predication (guarded execution) and explicit parallelism to increase the performance by reducing the number of branches and branch mispredicts, and by reducing the effects of memory-to-processor latency.

The key features of the EPIC technology are:

– *static speculative execution of memory load operations*, i.e. loading data from memory is allowed for issue before knowing whether it is required or not, and thus reducing the effects of memory latency;

– *a fully predicated (guarded) instruction set* that allows us to remove branches so as to minimize the impact of branch mispredicts. Both speculative loads and predicated instructions aim to make it possible to handle static uncertainties (what compilers cannot determine or assert);

– *specifying ILP explicitly in the machine code*, i.e. the parallelism is encoded directly into the instructions as in a VLIW architecture;

– *more registers*: the IA-64 instruction set specifies 128 64-bit general-purpose registers, 128 80-bit floating-point registers and 64 1-bit predicate registers;

– *an inherently scalable instruction set*, i.e. *the ability to scale to a larger number of FUs. But this point remains debatable.*

Finally, we must note that VLIW and superscalar processors suffer from the hardware complexity of register ports. The number of register ports depends on a quadratic function of the number of FUs. Thus, both architectures do not scale very well since increasing the ILP degree (i.e. the number of FUs) results in creating a bottleneck on register ports. Consequently, the time required to access registers increases. An architectural alternative to this limitation is *clustered-processors* [FER 98]. Clustered architectures group FU into clusters. Each cluster has its own private register file: registers inside a cluster are strictly accessed by the FUs belonging the this cluster. If an FU needs a result from a remote register file (from another cluster), an intercluster communication (move operation) must be performed. Then, clustered architectures offer better scalability than VLIW and superscalar processors since the additional clusters do not require new register ports (given a fixed number of FUs per cluster). However, inserting move operations into the program may decrease the performance since more operations must be executed. Furthermore, the communication network between clusters may become a new source of bottleneck.

To take full advantage of ILP architectures, compiler techniques have been continuously improved since the 1980s [RAU 93b, FIS 05]. This book presents advanced methods regarding instruction scheduling and register optimization.

PART 1

Prolog: Optimizing Compilation

On the Decidability of Phase Ordering in Optimizing Compilation

We are interested in the computing frontier around an essential question about compiler construction: having a program $\mathcal{P}$ and a set $\mathcal{M}$ of non-parametric compiler optimization modules (also called phases), is it possible to find a sequence s of these phases such that the performance (for instance, execution time) of the final generated program $\mathcal{P}'$ is *optimal*? We proved in [TOU 06] that this problem is undecidable in two general schemes of optimizing compilation: iterative compilation and library optimization/generation. Fortunately, we give some simplified cases when this problem becomes decidable, and we provide some algorithms (not necessarily efficient) that can answer our main question.

Another essential problem that we are interested in is parameter space exploration in optimizing compilation (tuning optimizing compilation parameters). In this case, we assume a fixed sequence of compiler optimizations, but each optimization phase is allowed to have a parameter. We try to figure out how to compute the best parameter values for all program transformations when the compilation sequence is given. We also prove that this general problem is undecidable and we provide some simplified decidable instances.

1.1. Introduction to the phase ordering problem

The notion of an *optimal* program is sometimes ambiguous in optimizing compilation. Using an absolute definition, an optimal program $\mathcal{P}^*$ means that there is no other equivalent program $\mathcal{P}$ faster than $\mathcal{P}^*$, whatever the input data be. This is equivalent to stating that the optimal program should run as fast as the longest dependence chain in its trace. This notion of optimality cannot exist in practice: Schwiegelshohn *et al.* showed [SCH 91] that there are loops with conditional jumps for which no semantically equivalent time-optimal program exists on parallel machines, even with speculative execution[1]. More precisely, they showed why it is

---

1 Indeed, the cited paper does not contain a formal detailed proof, but a persuasive reasoning.

impossible to write a program that is the fastest for any input data. This is because the presence of conditional jumps makes the program execution paths dependent on the input data; so it is not guaranteed that a program shown faster for a considered input data set (i.e. for a given execution path) remains the fastest for all possible input data. Furthermore, Schwiegelshohn *et al.* convinced us that *optimal* codes for loops with branches (with arbitrary input data) require the ability to express and execute a program with an unbounded speculative window. Since any real speculative feature is limited in practice[2], it is *impossible* to write an optimal code for some loops with branches on real machines.

In our result, we define the program optimality according to the input data. So, we say that a program P^* is optimal if there is not another equivalent program P faster than P^* considering the same input data. Of course, the optimal program P^* related to the considered input data I^* must still execute correctly for any other input data, but not necessarily in the fastest speed of execution. In other words, we do not try to build efficient specialized programs, i.e. we should not generate programs that execute only for a certain input data set. Otherwise, a simple program that only prints the results would be sufficient for fixed input data.

With this notion of optimality, we can ask the general question: how can we build a compiler that generates an optimal program given an input data set? Such a question is very difficult to answer, since until now we have not been able to enumerate all the possible automatic program rewriting methods in compilation (some are present in the literature; others have to be set up in the future). So, we first address in this chapter another similar question: given a finite set of compiler optimization modules M, how can we build an automatic method to combine them in a finite sequence that produces an optimal program? By compiler optimization module, we mean a program transformation that rewrites the original code. Unless they are encapsulated inside code optimization modules, we exclude program analysis passes since they do not modify the code.

This chapter provides a formalism for some general questions about phase ordering. Our formal writing allows us to give preliminary answers from the computer science perspective about decidability (what we can really do by automatic computation) and undecidability (what we can never do by automatic computation). We will show that our answers are strongly correlated to the nature of the models (functions) used to predict or evaluate the program's performances. Note that we are not interested in the efficiency aspects of compilation and code optimization: we know that most of the code optimization problems are inherently NP-complete. Consequently, the proposed algorithms in this chapter are not necessarily efficient, and are written for the purpose of demonstrating the decidability of some problems.

---

2 If the speculation is static, the code size is finite. If the speculation is made dynamically, the hardware speculative window is bounded.

Proposing efficient algorithms for decidable problems is another research aspect outside the current scope.

This chapter is organized as follows. Section 1.2 gives a brief overview about some phase ordering studies in the literature, as well as some performance prediction modelings. Section 1.3 defines a formal model for the phase ordering problem that allows us to prove some negative decidability results. Next, in section 1.4, we show some general optimizing compilation scheme in which the phase ordering problem becomes decidable. Section 1.5 explores the problem of tuning optimizing compilation parameters with a compilation sequence. Finally, section 1.6 concludes the chapter.

1.2. Background on phase ordering

The problem of phase ordering in optimizing compilation is coupled with the problem of performance modeling, since performance prediction/estimation may guide the search process. The two sections that follow present a quick overview of related work.

1.2.1. *Performance modeling and prediction*

Program performance modeling and estimation on a certain machine is an old and (still) important research topic aiming to guide code optimization. The simplest performance prediction formula is the linear function that computes the execution time of a sequential program on a simple Von Neumann machine: it is simply a linear function of the number of executed instructions. With the introduction of memory hierarchy, parallelism at many level (instructions, threads and process), branch prediction and speculation, multi-cores, performance prediction becomes more complex than a simple linear formula. The exact *shape* or the nature of such a function and the parameters that it involves have been two unknown problems until now. However, there exist some articles that try to define approximated performance prediction functions:

– *Statistical linear regression models*: the parameters involved in the linear regression are usually chosen by the authors. Many program executions or simulation through multiple data sets make it possible to build statistics that compute the coefficients of the model [ALE 93, EEC 03].

– *Static algorithmic models*: usually, such models are algorithmic analysis methods that try to predict a program performance [CAL 88, MAN 93, WAN 94c, THE 92]. For instance, the algorithm counts the instructions of a certain type, or makes a guess of the local instruction schedule, or analyzes data dependences to predict the longest execution path, etc.

– *Comparison models*: instead of predicting a precise performance metric, some studies provide models that compare two code versions and try to predict the fastest one [KEN 92, TRI 05].

Of course, the best and the most accurate performance prediction is the target architecture, since it executes the program, and hence we can directly measure the performance. This is what is usually used in iterative compilation and library generation, for instance.

The main problem with performance prediction models is their aptitude for reflecting the real performance on the real machine. As is well explained by Jain [JAI 91], the common mistake in statistical modeling is to trust a model simply because it plots a *similar* curve compared to the real plot (a proof by eyes!). Indeed, this type of experimental validation is not correct from the statistical science theory point of view, and there exist formal statistical methods that check whether a model fits the reality. Until now, we have not found any study that validates a program performance prediction model using such formal statistical methods.

1.2.2. *Some attempts in phase ordering*

Finding the best order in optimizing compilation is an old and difficult problem. The most common case is the dependence between register allocation and instruction scheduling in instruction level parallelism processors as shown in [FRE 92]. Many other cases of inter-phase dependences exist, but it is hard to analyze all the possible interactions [WHI 97].

Click and Cooper in [CLI 95] present a formal method that combines two compiler modules to build a *super*-module that produces better (faster) programs than if we apply each module separately. However, they do not succeed in generalizing their framework of module combination, since they prove it for only two special cases, which are constant propagation and dead code elimination.

In [ALM 04], the authors use exhaustive enumeration of possible compilation sequences (restricted to a limited sequence size). They try to find if any *best* compilation sequence emerges. The experimental results show that, unfortunately, there is no winning compilation sequence. We think that this is because such a compilation sequence depends not only on the compiled program, but also on the input data and the underlying executing machine and executing environment.

In [VEL 02], the authors target a similar objective as in [CLI 95]. They succeed in producing *super*-modules that guarantee performance optimization. However, they combine two analysis passes followed by a unique program rewriting phase. In this chapter, we try to find the best combination of code optimization modules, excluding program analysis passes (unless they belong to the code transformation modules).

In [ZHA 05], the authors evaluate by using a performance model the different optimization sequences to apply to a given program. The model determines the profit of optimization sequences according to register resource and cache behavior. The optimizations only consider scalars and the same optimizations are applied whatever the values of the inputs be. In our work, we assume the contrary, that the optimization sequence should depend on the value of the input (in order to be able to speak about the optimality of a program).

Finally, there is the whole field of iterative compilation. In this research activity, looking for a good compilation sequence requires compiling the program multiple times iteratively, and at each iteration, a new code optimization sequence is used [COO 02, TRI 05] until a good solution is reached. In such frameworks, any kind of code optimization can be sequenced, the program performance may be predicted or accurately computed via execution or simulation. There exist other articles that try to combine a sequence of high-level loop transformations [COH 04, WOL 98]. As mentioned, such methods are devoted to regular high-performance codes and only use loop transformations in the polyhedral model.

In this chapter, we give a general formalism of the phase ordering problem and its multiple variants that incorporate the work presented in this section.

1.3. Toward a theoretical model for the phase ordering problem

In this section, we give our theoretical framework about the phase ordering problem. Let $\mathcal{M}$ be a finite set of program transformations. We would like to construct an algorithm $\mathcal{A}$ that has three inputs: a program $\mathcal{P}$, an input data I and a desired execution time T for the transformed program. For each input program and its input data set, the algorithm $\mathcal{A}$ must compute a finite sequence $s = m_n \circ m_{n-1} \circ \cdots \circ m_0$, $m_i \in \mathcal{M}^*$ of optimization modules[3]. The same transformation can appear multiple times in the sequence, as it already occurs in real compilers (for constant propagation/dead code elimination, for instance). If s is applied to $\mathcal{P}$, it must generate an optimal transformed program $\mathcal{P}^*$ according to the input data I. Each optimization module $m_i \in \mathcal{M}$ has a unique input that is the program to be rewritten, and has an output $\mathcal{P}' = m_i(\mathcal{P})$. So, the final generated program $\mathcal{P}^*$ is $(m_n \circ m_{n-1} \circ \cdots \circ m_0)(\mathcal{P})$.

We must have a clear concept and definition of a program transformation module. Nowadays, many optimization techniques are complex toolboxes with many parameters. For instance, loop unrolling and loop blocking require a parameter that is the degree of unrolling or blocking. Until section 1.5, we do not consider such parameters in our formal problem. We handle them by considering, for each program

---

3 ∘ denotes the symbol of function combination (concatenation).

transformation, a finite set of parameter values, which is the case in practice. Therefore, loop unrolling with an unrolling degree of 4 and loop unrolling with a degree of 8 are considered as two different optimizations. Given such finite set of parameter values per program transformation, we can define a new compilation module for each pair of program transformation and parameter value. So, for the remainder of the chapter (until section 1.5), a program transformation can be considered as a module without any parameter except the program to be optimized.

To check that the execution time has reached some value T, we assume that there is a performance evaluation function t that allows us to precisely evaluate or predict the execution time (or other performance metrics) of a program $\mathcal{P}$ according to the input data I. Let $t(\mathcal{P}, I)$ be the predicted execution time. Thus, t can predict the execution time of any transformed program $\mathcal{P}' = m(\mathcal{P})$ when applying a program transformation c. If we apply a sequence of program transformations, t is assumed to be able to predict the execution time of the final transformed program, i.e. $t(\mathcal{P}', I) = t((m_n \circ m_{n-1} \circ \cdots \circ m_0)(\mathcal{P}), I)$. t can be either the measure of performance on the real machine, obtained through execution of the program with its inputs, a simulator or a performance model. In this Chapter, we do not make the distinction between the three cases and assume that t is an arbitrary computable function. Next, we give a formal description of the phase ordering problem in optimizing compilation.

PROBLEM 1.1 (Phase ordering).–   Let t be an arbitrary performance evaluation function. Let $\mathcal{M}$ be a finite set of program transformations. $\forall T \in \mathbb{N}$ an execution time (in processor clock cycles), $\forall \mathcal{P}$ a program, $\forall I$ input data, does there exist a sequence $s \in \mathcal{M}^*$ such that $t(s(\mathcal{P}), I) < T$? In other words, if we define the set:

$$S_{t,\mathcal{M}}(\mathcal{P}, I, T) = \{s \in \mathcal{M}^* | t(s(\mathcal{P}), I) < T\}$$

is the set $S_{t,\mathcal{M}}(\mathcal{P}, I, T)$ empty?

Textually, the phase ordering problem tries to determine for each program and input whether or not there exists a compilation sequence s that results in an execution time lower than a bound T.

If there is an algorithm that decides the phase ordering problem, then there is an algorithm that computes one sequence s such that $t(s(\mathcal{P}), I) < T$, provided that t always terminates. Indeed, enumerating the code optimization sequences in lexicographic order always finds an admissible solution to problem 1.1. Deciding the phase ordering problem is therefore the key finding the best optimization sequence.

1.3.1. *Decidability results*

In our problem formulation, we assume the following characteristics:

1) t is a computable function. $t(\mathcal{P}, I)$ terminates when $\mathcal{P}$ terminates on the input I. This definition is compatible with the fact that t can be the measured execution time on a real machine.

2) Each program transformation $m \in \mathcal{M}$ is computable, always terminates and preserves the program semantics.

3) Program $\mathcal{P}$ always terminates.

4) The final transformed program $\mathcal{P}' = s(\mathcal{P})$ executes at least one instruction, i.e. the final execution time is strictly positive.

The phase ordering problem corresponds to what occurs in a compiler: whatever the program and input given by the user (if the compiler resorts to profiling), the compiler has to find a sequence of optimizations reaching some (not very well defined) performance threshold. Answering the question of the phase ordering problem as defined in problem 1.1 depends on the performance prediction model t. Since the function (or its class) t is not defined, problem 1.1 cannot be answered as it is, and requires to have another formulation that slightly changes its nature. We consider in this work a modified version, where the function t is not known by the optimizer. The adequacy between this assumption and the real optimizing problem is discussed after the problem statement.

PROBLEM 1.2 (Modified phase-ordering).–   Let $\mathcal{M}$ be a finite set of program transformations. For any performance evaluation function t, $\forall T \in \mathbb{N}$ an execution time (in processor clock cycles), $\forall \mathcal{P}$ a program, $\forall I$ input data, does a sequence $s \in \mathcal{M}^*$ exist such that $t(s(\mathcal{P}), I) < T$? In other words, if we define the set:

$$S_{\mathcal{M}}(t, \mathcal{P}, I, T) = \{s \in \mathcal{M}^* | t(s(\mathcal{P}), I) < T\},$$

is the set $S_{\mathcal{M}}(t, \mathcal{P}, I, T)$ empty?

This problem corresponds to the case where t is not an *approximate* model but is the real executing machine (the most precise model). Let us present the intuition behind this statement: a compiler always has an architecture model of the target machine (resource constraints, instruction set, general architecture, latencies of caches, etc.). This model is assumed to be correct (meaning that the real machine conforms according to the model) but does not take into account all mechanisms of the hardware. Thus in theory, an unbounded number of different machines fit into the model, and we must assume the real machine is any one of them. As the architecture model is incomplete and performance also depends usually on non-modeled features (conflict misses, data alignment, operation bypasses, etc.), the performance evaluation model of the compiler is inaccurate. This suggests that the performance evaluation function of the real machine can be any performance evaluation function, even if there is a partial architectural description of this machine. Consequently, problem 1.2 corresponds to the case of the phase ordering problem when t is the most precise performance model, which is the real executing machine (or simulator): the real machine measures the performance of its own executing program (for instance, by using its internal clock or its hardware performance counters).

In the following lemma, we assume an additional hypothesis: there exists a program that can be optimized into an unbounded number of different programs. This necessarily requires that there is an unbounded number of different optimization sequences. But this is not sufficient. As sequences of optimizations in $\mathcal{M}$ are considered as words made of letters from the alphabet $\mathcal{M}$, the set of sequences is always unbounded, even with only one optimization in $\mathcal{M}$. For instance, fusion and loop distribution can be used, repetitively, to build sequences as long as desired. However, this unbounded set of sequences will only generate a finite number of different optimized codes (ranging from all merged loops to all distributed loops). If the total number of possible generated programs is bounded, then it may be possible to fully generate them in a bounded compilation time. Therefore, it is easy to check the performance of every generated program and to keep the best program. In our hypothesis, we assume that the set of all possible generated programs (generated using the distinct compilation sequences belonging to $\mathcal{M}^*$) is unbounded. One simple optimization such as strip-mine, applied many times to a loop with parametric bounds, generates as many different programs. Likewise, unrolling a loop with parametric bounds can be performed an unbounded number of times. Note that the decidability of problem 1.2 when the cardinality of $\mathcal{M}^*$ is infinite while the set of distinct generated programs is finite remains an open problem.

LEMMA 1.1.– [TOU 06] Modified phase-ordering is an undecidable problem if there exists a program that can be optimized into an infinite number of different programs.

We provide here a variation on the modified phase ordering problem that corresponds to the library optimization issue: program and (possibly) inputs are known at compile-time, but the optimizer has to adapt its sequence of optimization to the underlying architecture/compiler. This is what happens in Spiral [PÜS 05] and FFTW [FRI 99]. If the input is also part of the unknowns, the problem has the same difficulty.

PROBLEM 1.3.– Phase ordering for library optimization.– Let $\mathcal{M}$ be a finite set of program transformations, $\mathcal{P}$ be the program of a library function, I be some input and T be an execution time. For any performance evaluation function t, does a sequence $s \in \mathcal{M}^*$ exist such that $t(s(\mathcal{P}), I) < T$? In other words, if we define the set:

$$S_{\mathcal{P},I,\mathcal{M},T}(t) = \{s \in \mathcal{M}^* | t(s(\mathcal{P}), I) < T\}$$

is the set $S_{\mathcal{P},I,\mathcal{M},T}(t)$ empty?

The decidability results of problem 1.3 are stronger than those of problem 1.2: here the compiler knows the program, its inputs, the optimizations to play with and the performance bound to reach. However, there is still no algorithm for finding out the best optimization sequence, if the optimizations may generate an infinite number of different program versions.

LEMMA 1.2.– [TOU 06] Phase Ordering for library optimization is undecidable if optimizations can generate an infinite number of different programs for the library functions.

Section 1.3.2 gives other formulations of the phase-ordering problem that do not alter the decidability results proved in this section.

1.3.2. *Another formulation of the phase ordering problem*

Instead of having a function that predicts the execution time, we can consider a function g that predicts the performance gain or speedup. g would be a function with three inputs: the input program $\mathcal{P}$, the input data I and a transformation module $m \in \mathcal{M}$. The performance prediction function $g(\mathcal{P}, I, m)$ computes the performance gain if we transform the program $\mathcal{P}$ to $m(\mathcal{P})$ and by considering the same input data I. For a sequence $s = (m_n \circ m_{n-1} \cdots \circ m_0) \in \mathcal{M}^*$, we define the gain $g(\mathcal{P}, I, s) = g(\mathcal{P}, I, m_0) \times g(m_0(\mathcal{P}), I, m_1) \times \cdots \times g((m_{n-1} \circ \cdots \circ m_0)(\mathcal{P}), I, m_n)$. Note that since the gains (and speedups) are fractions, the whole gain of the final generated program is the product of the partial intermediate gains. The ordering problem in this case becomes the problem of computing a compilation sequence that results in a maximal speedup, formally written as follows. This problem formulation is equivalent to the initial one that tries to optimize the execution time instead of speedup.

PROBLEM 1.4.– Modified phase-ordering with performance gain.– Let $\mathcal{M}$ be a finite set of program transformations, $\forall k \in \mathbb{Q}$ be a performance gain, $\forall \mathcal{P}$ be a program and $\forall I$ be some input data. For any performance gain function g, does a sequence $s \in \mathcal{M}^*$ exist such that $g(\mathcal{P}, I, s) \geq k$? In other words, if we define the set:

$$S_{\mathcal{M}}(g, \mathcal{P}, I, k) = \{s \in \mathcal{M}^* | g(\mathcal{P}, I, s) \geq k\},$$

is the set $S_{\mathcal{M}}(g, \mathcal{P}, I, k)$ empty?

We can easily see that problem 1.2 is equivalent to problem 1.4. This is because g and t are dependent of each other by the following usual equation of performance gain:

$$g(\mathcal{P}, I, m) = \frac{t(\mathcal{P}, I) - t(m(\mathcal{P}), I)}{t(\mathcal{P}, I)}$$

1.4. Examples of decidable simplified cases

In this section, we give some decidable instances of the phase ordering problem. As a first case, we define another formulation of the problem that introduces a monotonic cost function. This formulation models the real existing compilation approaches. As a second case, we model generative compilation and show that phase ordering is decidable in this case.

1.4.1. *Models with compilation costs*

In section 1.3, the phase ordering problem is defined using a performance evaluation function. In this section, we add another function c that models a cost. Such a cost may be the compilation time, the number of distinct compilation passes inside a compilation sequence, the length of a compilation sequence, distinct explored compilation sequences, etc. The cost function has two inputs: the program $\mathcal{P}$ and a transformation pass m. Thus, $c(\mathcal{P}, m)$ gives the cost of transforming the program $\mathcal{P}$ into $\mathcal{P}' = m(P)$. Such cost does not depend on input data I. The phase ordering problem including the cost function becomes the problem of computing the best compilation sequence with a bounded cost.

PROBLEM 1.5.– Phase-ordering with discrete cost function.– Let t be a performance evaluation function that predicts the execution time of any program $\mathcal{P}$ given input data I. Let $\mathcal{M}$ be a finite set of optimization modules. Let $c(\mathcal{P}, m)$ be an integral function that computes the cost of transforming the program $\mathcal{P}$ into $\mathcal{P}' = m(P), m \in \mathcal{M}$. Does there exist an algorithm $\mathcal{A}$ that solves the following problem? $\forall T \in \mathbb{N}$ an execution time (in processor clock cycles), $\forall K \in \mathbb{N}$ a compilation cost, $\forall \mathcal{P}$ a program, $\forall I$ input data, compute $\mathcal{A}(\mathcal{P}, I, T) = s$ such that $s = (m_n \circ m_{n-1} \cdots \circ m_0) \in \mathcal{M}^*$ and $t(s(\mathcal{P}), I) < T$ with $c(\mathcal{P}, m_0) + c(m_0(\mathcal{P}), m_1) + \cdots + c((m_{n-1} \circ \cdots \circ m_0)(\mathcal{P}), m_n) \leq K$.

In this section, we see that if the cost function c is a strictly increasing function, then we can provide a recursive algorithm that solves problem 1.5. First, we define the monotonic characteristics of the function c. We say that c is strictly increasing iff:

$$\forall m, m' \in \mathcal{M}, \quad c(\mathcal{P}, m) < c(s(\mathcal{P}), m')$$

That is, applying a program transformation sequence $m_n \circ m_{n-1} \cdots \circ m_0 \in \mathcal{M}^*$ to a program $\mathcal{P}$ always has a higher integer cost than applying $m_{n-1} \cdots \circ m_0 \in \mathcal{M}^*$. Such an assumption is true for the case of function costs such as compilation time[4] and number of compilation passes. Each practical compiler uses an implicit cost function.

---

4 The time on an executing machine is discrete since we have clock cycles.

Building an algorithm that computes the best compiler optimization sequence given a strictly increasing cost function is an easy problem because we can use an exhaustive search of all possible compilation sequences with bounded cost. Algorithm 1.1 provides a trivial recursive method: it first looks for all possible compilation sequences under the considered cost, then it iterates over all these compilation sequences to check whether we could generate a program with the bounded execution time. Such a process terminates because we are sure that the cumulative integer costs of the intermediate program transformations will certainly reach the limit K.

As an illustration, the work presented in [ALM 04] belongs to this family of decidable problems. Indeed, the authors compute all possible compilation phase sequences, but by restricting themselves to a given number of phases in each sequence. Such numbers are modeled in our framework as a cost function defined as follows: $\forall \mathcal{P}$ a program,

$$c(\mathcal{P}, s) = \begin{cases} 1 + c(\mathcal{P}, (m_{n-1} \circ \cdots \circ m_0)) \ \forall (m_n \circ \cdots \circ m_0) \in \mathcal{M}^* \\ 1 \hspace{4.5cm} \forall m \in \mathcal{M} \end{cases}$$

Textually, it means that we associate with each compilation sequence the cost which is simply equal to the number of phases inside the compilation sequence. The authors in [ALM 04] limit the number of phases (to 10 or 15 as an example). Consequently, the number of possible combinations becomes bounded which makes the problem of phase ordering decidable. Algorithm 1.1 can be used to generate the best compilation sequence if we consider a cost function as a fixed number of phases.

Section 1.4.2 presents another simplified case in phase ordering, which is one-pass generative compilation.

1.4.2. *One-pass generative compilers*

Generative compilation is a subclass of iterative compilation. In such simplified classes of compilers, the code of an intermediate program is optimized and generated in a one pass traversal of the abstract syntax tree. Each program part is treated and translated to a final code without any possible backtracking in the code optimization process. For instance, we can take the case of a program given as an abstract syntax tree. A set of compilation phases treats each program part, i.e. each sub-tree, and generates a native code for such part. Another code optimization module can no longer re-optimize the already-generated program part, since any optimization module in generative compilation takes as input only program parts in intermediate form. When a native code generation for a program part is carried out, there is no way to re-optimize such program portions, and the process continues for other sub-trees until finishing the whole tree. Note that the optimization process for each sub-tree is applied by a finite set of program transformations. In other words, generative compilers look for a local optimized code instead of a global optimized program.

Algorithm 1.1. Computing a good compilation sequence in the compilation cost model

Require: a program $\mathcal{P}$
Require: a cost $K \in \mathbb{N}$
Require: an execution time $T \in \mathbb{N}$
Require: 1 a neutral optimization: $1(\mathcal{P}) = P \wedge c(\mathcal{P}, 1) = 0$
  /* we first compute the SET of all possible compilation sequences under the cost limit K */
  $SET \leftarrow \{1\}$
  $stop \leftarrow$ **false**
  while $\neg stop$ **do**
    $stop \leftarrow$ **true**
    for all $s \in SET$ **do**
      $visited[s] \leftarrow$ **false**
    end for
    for all $s \in SET$ **do**
      if $\neg visited[s]$ **then**
        for all $m_i \in \mathcal{M}$ **do** {for each compilation phase}
          if $c(\mathcal{P}, s \circ m_i) \leq K$ **then** {save a new compilation sequence with a bounded cost
          if the cost is bounded by K}
            $SET \leftarrow SET \cup \{s \circ m_i\}$
            $stop \leftarrow$ **false**
          end if
        end for
      end if
      $visited[s] \leftarrow$ **true**
    end for
  end while
  /* now, we look for a compilation sequence that produces a program with the bounded execution time */
  $exists\_solution \leftarrow$ **false**
  for all $s \in SET$ **do**
    if $t(\mathcal{P}, s) \leq T$ **then**
      $exists\_solution \leftarrow$ **true**
      $return\ s$
    end if
  end for
  if $\neg exists\_solution$ **then**
    print *No solution exists to Problem 1.5*
  end if

This program optimization process as described by algorithm 1.2 computes the best compilation phase greedily. Adding backtracking changes complexity but the process still terminates. More generally, generative compilers making the assumption that sequences of best optimized codes are best optimized sequences fit the one-pass generative compiler description. For example, the SPIRAL project in [PÜS 05] is a generative compiler. It performs a local optimization to each node. SPIRAL optimizes FFT formula, from the formula level, by trying different decompositions of large FFT. Instead of a program, SPIRAL starts from a formula, and the considered optimizations are decomposition rules. From a formula tree, SPIRAL recursively applies a set of program transformations at each node, starting from the leaves, generates C code, executes it and measures its performance. Using the dynamic programming strategy[5], composition of best performing formula is considered as best performing composition.

Algorithm 1.2. Optimize_Node(n)

Require: an abstract syntax tree with root n
Require: a finite set of program transformations $\mathcal{M}$
  if n is not leaf **then**
    for all u child of n **do**
      optimize_Node(u)
    end for
    /*Generate all possible codes and choose the best one*/
    $best \leftarrow \phi$ {best code optimization}
    $time \leftarrow \infty$ {best performance}
    for all $m \in \mathcal{M}$ **do**
      if $t(n, m) \leq time$ **then**
        $best \leftarrow m$
        $time \leftarrow t(n, m)$
      end if
    end for
    apply the $best$ transformation to the node n without changing any child
  else {Generate all possible codes and choose the best one}
    $best \leftarrow \phi$ {best code optimization}
    $time \leftarrow \infty$ {best performance}
    for all $m \in \mathcal{M}$ **do**
      if $t(n, m) \leq time$ **then**
        $best \leftarrow m$
        $time \leftarrow t(n, m)$
      end if
    end for
    Apply the $best$ transformation to the node n
  end if

As can be seen, finding a compilation sequence in generative compilation that produces the fastest program is a decidable problem (algorithm 1.2). Since the size of

---

5 The latest version of SPIRAL use more elaborate strategies, but still does not resort to exhaustive search/testing.

intermediate representation forms decreases at each local application of program transformation, we are sure that the process of program optimization terminates when all intermediate forms have been transformed into native codes. In other words, the number of possible distinct passes on a program becomes finite and bounded as shown in algorithm 1.2: for each node of the abstract syntax tree, we apply a single code optimization locally (we iterate over all possible code optimization modules and we pick up the module that produces the best performance according to the chosen performance model). Furthermore, no code optimization sequence is searched locally (only a single pass is applied). Thus, if the total number of nodes in the abstract syntax tree is equal to $\tilde{n}$, then the total number of applied compilation sequences does not exceed $|\mathcal{M}| \times \tilde{n}$.

Of course, the decidability of one-pass generative compilers does not prevent them from having potentially high complexity: each local code optimization may be exponential (if it tackles NP-complete problem for instance). The decidability result only proves that, if we have a high-computation power, we know that we can compute the "optimal" code after a finite compilation time (possibly high).

This first part of the chapter investigates the decidability problem of phase ordering in optimizing compilation. Figure 1.1 illustrates a complete view of the different classes of the investigated problems with their decidability results. The largest class of the phase ordering problem that we consider, denoted by C_1, assumes a finite set of program transformations with possible optimization parameters (to explore). If the performance prediction function is arbitrary, typically if it requires program execution or simulation, then this problem is undecidable. The second class of the phase ordering problem, denoted by $C_2 \subset C_1$, has the same hypothesis as C_1 except that the optimization parameters are fixed. The problem is undecidable too. However, we have identified two decidable classes of phase ordering problem that are C_3 and C_4 explained as follows. The class $C_3 \subset C_2$ considers one-pass generative compilation; the program is taken as an abstract syntax tree (AST), and code optimization applies a unique local code optimization module on each node of the AST. The class $C_4 \subset C_2$ takes the same assumption as C_2 plus an additional constraint that is the presence of a cost model: if the cost model is a discrete increasing function, and if the cost of the code optimization is bounded, then C_4 is a class of decidable phase ordering problem.

Section 1.5 investigates another essential question in optimizing compilation, which is parameter space exploration.

1.5. Compiler optimization parameter space exploration

Many compiler optimization methods are parameterized. For instance, loop unrolling requires an unrolling degree and loop blocking requires a blocking degree.

The complexity of phase ordering problem does not allow us to explore the best sequence of the compilation steps and the best combination of module parameters jointly. Usually, the community tries to find the *best* parameter combination when the compilation sequence is fixed. This section is devoted to studying the decidability of such problems.

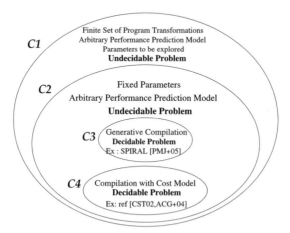

Figure 1.1. *Classes of phase-ordering problems*

1.5.1. *Toward a theoretical model*

First, we suppose that we have $s \in \mathcal{M}^*$ a given sequence of optimizing modules belonging to a finite set $\mathcal{M}$. We assume that s is composed of n compilation sequences.

We associate for each optimization module $m_i \in \mathcal{M}$ a unique integer parameter $k_i \in \mathbb{N}$. The set of all parameters is grouped inside a vector $\overrightarrow{k} \in \mathbb{N}^n$, such that the ith component of $\overrightarrow{k}$ is the parameter k_i of the m_i, the ith module inside the considered sequence s. If the sequence s contains multiple instances of the same optimization module m, the parameter of each instance may have a distinct value from those of the other instances.

For a given program $\mathcal{P}$, applying a program transformation module $m \in \mathcal{M}$ requires a parameter value. Then, we write the transformed program as $\mathcal{P}' = m(\mathcal{P}, \overrightarrow{k})$.

As in the previous sections devoted to the phase ordering problem, we assume here the existence of a performance evaluation function t that predicts (or evaluates) the execution time of a program $\mathcal{P}$ having I as input data. We denote by $t(\mathcal{P}, I)$ the predicted execution time. The formal problem of computing the best parameter values of a given set of program transformations in order to achieve the best performance can be written as follows.

PROBLEM 1.6.– Best-parameters.– Let t be a function that predicts the execution time of any program $\mathcal{P}$ given input data I. Let $\mathcal{M}$ be a finite set of program transformations and s be a particular optimization sequence. Does there exist an algorithm $\mathcal{A}_{t,s}$ that solves the following problem? $\forall T \in \mathbb{N}$ an execution time, $\forall \mathcal{P}$ a program and $\forall I$ input data, $\mathcal{A}_{t,s}(\mathcal{P}, I, T) = \overrightarrow{k}$ such that $t(s(\mathcal{P}, \overrightarrow{k}), I) < T$.

This general problem cannot be addressed as it is, since the answer depends on the shape of the function t. In this chapter, we assume that the performance prediction function is built by an algorithm a, taking s and $\mathcal{P}$ as parameters. Moreover, we assume the performance function $t = \text{a}(\mathcal{P}, s)$ built by a takes $\overrightarrow{k}$ and I as parameters and is a polynomial function. Therefore, the performance of a program $\mathcal{P}$ with input I and optimization parameters $\overrightarrow{k}$ is $\text{a}(\mathcal{P}, s)(I, \overrightarrow{k})$. We discuss the choice of a polynomial model after the statement of the problem. We want to decide whether there are some parameters for the optimization modules that make the desired performance bound reachable:

PROBLEM 1.7.– Modified best-parameters.– Let $\mathcal{M}$ be a finite set of program transformations and s be a particular optimization sequence of $\mathcal{M}^*$. Let a be an algorithm that builds a polynomial performance prediction function, according to a program and an optimization sequence. For all programs $\mathcal{P}$, for all inputs I and performance bound T, we define the set of parameters as:

$$P_{s,t}(\mathcal{P}, I, T) = \{ \overrightarrow{k} \,|\, \text{a}(\mathcal{P}, s)(\overrightarrow{k}, I) < T \}.$$

Is $P_{s,t}(\mathcal{P}, I, T)$ empty?

As noted earlier, choosing an appropriate performance model is a key decision in defining whether problem 1.6 is decidable or not. For instance, problem 1.7 considers polynomial functions, which are a family of usual performance models (arbitrary linear regression models, for instance). Even a simple static model of complexity counting assignments evaluates usual algorithms with polynomials (n^3 for a straightforward implementation of square matrix-matrix multiply for instance). With such a simple model, any polynomial can be generated. It is assumed that a realistic performance evaluation function would be as least as difficult as a polynomial function. Unfortunately, the following lemma shows that if t is an arbitrary polynomial function, then problem 1.7 is undecidable.

The following lemma states that problem 1.7 is undecidable if there are at least nine integer optimization parameters. In our context, this requires nine optimizations in the optimizing sequence. Note that this number is constant when considering the best parameters, and is not a parameter itself. This number is fairly low compared to the number of optimizations found in state-of-the-art compilers (such as *gcc* or *icc*). Now, if t is a polynomial and there are less than parameters (the user has switched off most optimizations, for instance): if there is only one parameter left, then the problem is decidable. For a number of parameters between 2 and 8, the problem is still open [MAT 04] and Matiyasevich conjectured it as undecidable.

LEMMA 1.3.– [TOU 06] The modified best-parameters problem is undecidable if the performance prediction function $t = a(\mathcal{P}, s)$ is an arbitrary polynomial and if there are at least nine integer optimization parameters.

1.5.2. *Examples of simplified decidable cases*

Our formal problem best-parameters is the formal writing of library optimizations. Indeed, in such areas of program optimizations, the applications are given with a training data set. Then, people try to find the best parameter values of optimizing modules (inside a compiler usually with a given compilation sequence) that holds in the best performance. In this section, we show that some simplified instances of best-parameters problem become easily decidable. We here give two examples of this problem: the first is the OCEAN project [AAR 97] and the second is the ATLAS framework [WHA 01].

The OCEAN project [AAR 97] optimizes a given program for a given data set by exploring all combinations of parameter values. Potentially, such value space is infinite. However, OCEAN restricts the exploration to finite set of parameter intervals. Consequently, the number of parameter combinations becomes finite, allowing a trivial exhaustive search of the best parameter values: each optimized program resulting from a particular value of the optimization parameters is generated and evaluated. The one performing best is chosen. Of course, if we use such an exhaustive search, the optimizing compilation time becomes very high. So, we can provide efficient heuristics for exploring the bounded space of the parameters [TRI 05]. Currently, this is outside our scope.

ATLAS [WHA 01] is another simplified case of the best-parameter problem. In the case of ATLAS, the optimization sequence is known, the programs to be optimized are known (BLAS variants) and it is assumed that the performance does not depend on the value of the input (independence with respect to the matrix and vector values). Moreover, there is a performance model for the cache hierarchy (basically, the size of the cache) that, combined with the dynamic performance evaluation, limits the number of program executions (i.e. performance evaluation) to do. For one level of cache and for matrix–matrix multiplication, there are three levels of blocking controlled by three parameters, bounded by the cache size and a small number of loop interchanges possible (for locality). Exhaustive enumeration inside admissible values enables us to find the best parameter value.

Figure 1.2 shows a complete view of the different classes of the investigated problems with their decidability results. The largest class of the best-parameters exploration problem that we consider, denoted by C_1, assumes a finite set of optimization parameters with unbounded values (infinite space); the compiler optimization sequence is assumed to be fixed. If the performance prediction function is arbitrary, then this problem is undecidable. The second class of the best-parameters exploration problem, denoted by $C_2 \subset C_1$, has the same hypothesis as C_1 except that the performance model is assumed as an arbitrary polynomial function. The problem is undecidable too. However, a trivial identified decidable class is the case of bounded (finite) parameters space. This is the case of the tools ATLAS (class C_3) and OCEAN (class C_4).

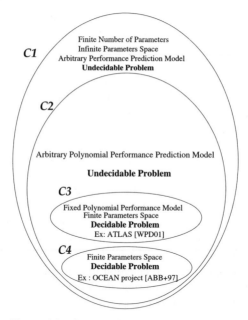

Figure 1.2. *Classes of best-parameters problems*

1.6. Conclusion on phase ordering in optimizing compilation

In this chapter, we presented a first formalization of two known problems: the phase ordering in optimizing compilation and the compiler optimization parameters space exploration. We set down the formal definition of the phase ordering problem in many compilation schemes such as static compilation, iterative compilation and library generation. Given an input data set for the considered program, the defined phase ordering problem is to find a sequence of code transformations (taken from a finite set of code optimizations) that increases the performance up to a fixed objective. Alternatively, we can also consider parametric code optimization modules, and then we can define the formal problem of best parameters space exploration. However, in this case, the compilation sequence is fixed, and the searching process looks for the best code optimization parameters that increase the program performance up to a fixed objective.

We showed that the decidability of both these problems is strongly correlated to the function used to predict or to evaluate the program performance. If such a function is an arbitrary polynomial function, or if it requires executing a Turing machine (by simulation or by real execution on the considered underlying hardware), then both these problems are undecidable. This means that we can never have automatic solutions for them. We provided some simplified cases that make these problems decidable: for instance, we showed that if we include a compilation cost in the model (compilation time, number of generated programs, number of compilation sequences, etc.), then the phase ordering becomes obviously decidable. This is what all actual *ad hoc* iterative compilation techniques really do. Also, we showed that if the parameter space is explicitly considered as bounded, then the best compiler parameter space exploration problem becomes trivially decidable too.

Our result proved then that the requirement of executing or simulating a program is a major fundamental drawback for iterative compilation and for library generation in general. Indeed, they try to solve a problem that can never have an automatic solution. Consequently, it is impossible to bring a formal method that makes it possible to accurately compare between the actual *ad hoc* or practical methods of iterative compilation or for library generation [COO 02, ALM 04, ZHA 05, TRI 05]. The experiments that can be made to highlight the efficiency of a method can never guarantee that such an iterative method would be efficient for other benchmarks. As a corollary, we can safely state that, since it is impossible to mathematically compare between iterative compilation methods (or between library generation tools), we can consider that any proposed method is sufficiently *good* for only its set of experimented benchmarks and cannot be generalized as a concept or as a method.

Our result also proved that using iterative or dynamic methods for compilation is not fundamentally helpful for solving the general problem of code optimization. Such dynamic and iterative methods define distinct optimization problems that are unfortunately as undecidable as static code optimizations, even with fixed input data.

However, our result does not yet give information about the decidability of phase ordering or parameter space exploration if the performance prediction function does not require program execution. The answer simply depends on the nature of such functions. If such a function is too simple, then it is highly probable that the phase ordering becomes decidable but the experimental results would be weak (since the performance prediction model would be inaccurate). The problem of performance modeling then becomes the essential question. As far as we know, we did not find any model in the literature that has been formally validated by rigorous statistical fitting checks.

Finally, our negative decidability results on iterative compilation and library generation do not mean that this active branch of research is a wrong way to tackle optimizing compilation. We simply say that these technical solutions are fundamentally as difficult as static compilation, and their accurate measurement of program performances based on real executions does not simplify the problem. Consequently, static code optimization using static performance models remains a key strategy in compilation.

PART 2

Instruction Scheduling

2

Instruction Scheduling
Problems and Overview

Instruction scheduling is a critical performance optimization that takes place when compiling applications for instruction-level parallel processors such as very long instruction word (VLIW) processors. An instruction scheduling problem is defined by a set of operations[1] to schedule, a set of dependences between these operations and a target processor micro-architecture. The objective of instruction scheduling is to build an operation sequence of minimum length (block instruction scheduling) or maximum throughput (software pipeline instruction scheduling) on the target processor.

2.1. VLIW instruction scheduling problems

2.1.1. *Instruction scheduling and register allocation in a code generator*

In a compiler, instruction scheduling is applied to the last stages of optimizations before assembly language output, inside the so-called *code generator*. The code generator has four major tasks: code selection, control optimizations, register allocation and instruction scheduling [DIN 00]. Code selection translates the computations from the upper stage of the compiler into efficient target processor operation sequences. Control optimizations reduce the runtime penalty of branches by predicating code [MAH 95] and by reordering the basic blocks [PET 90]. The register allocator maps the operation operands to the processor registers or memory locations. The instruction scheduler reorders the operations to reduce the runtime processor stalls. In modern compilers such as SGI's Open64 [OSG 13], the code generator is also in charge of several loop transformations and scalar optimizations that are applied before code selection.

---

1 An operation is an instance of an instruction in a program text.

The major component of the program representation in a code generator is the *code stream*, which contains a list of *basic blocks*. Each basic block itself is a list of target processor operations. A basic block can only be entered at the first operation and contains no control-flow operations (branch or call) except possibly for the last operation. The most important property of a basic block is that all its operations are executed when the program reaches its first operation. The program execution flow is itself represented by a *control flow graph*, whose nodes are the basic blocks and whose arcs materialize the possible control flow transfers between the basic blocks.

In the compiler code generator, instruction scheduling problems are of several types. A first parameter is the shape of the program regions that compose each instruction scheduling problem, or *scheduling regions*. While the simplest scheduling regions are the basic blocks, the *super blocks* are preferred [HAN 93], because they enlarge the instruction scheduling problem scope. A super block is a string of basic blocks where each basic block has a single predecessor, except possibly for the first basic block. The second parameter of instruction scheduling is whether the scheduling region is a whole inner loop body or not. If so, *cyclic scheduling* may be applied instead of the *acyclic scheduling* discussed so far. The third parameter of instruction scheduling is whether it runs before register allocation (*prepass scheduling*) or after (*prepass scheduling*).

In the code generator, the operations exchange values through *virtual registers*. Register allocation is the process of mapping the virtual registers in use at any program point either to the architectural registers or to memory locations. When a virtual register is mapped to a memory location, it needs to be *reloaded* before use. When space is exhausted in the register file, one or more virtual registers must be *spilled* to memory locations. In some cases, it is cheaper to recompute a virtual register value from the available register operands than reload it, an action called *rematerialization*. The register allocation may also *coalesce* some register live ranges to eliminate copy operations and, conversely, may have to *split* a register live range by inserting a copy operation in order to relax the register assignment constraints.

The *local register allocation* operates one program region at a time and deals with the virtual registers that are referenced in or live through that region. In practice, the program regions managed by the local register allocation are the basic blocks. Conversely, the *global register allocation* deals with the virtual registers that are live across the local register allocation regions. With state of the art compiler technology such as SGI's Open64 [OSG 13], global register allocation between the basic blocks is performed first, followed by local register allocation.

Most results and techniques for minimizing the penalty of register allocation assume a given operation order and insert extra operations order to spill, reload, rematerialize, or split the register live ranges. In this report, our focus is to minimize the penalty of register allocation by extending the prepass instruction scheduling problems with specific constraints or objectives.

In early compilers, the operation order used by register allocation was given to the code generator and instruction scheduling was only performed after register allocation. However, on RISC-like architectures with large-register files, the register dependences created by the reuse of the architectural registers significantly restrict the instruction-level parallelism [GOO 88a, CHA 95]. The practice in modern production compilers is thus to run a prepass instruction scheduler, the register allocation, then a postpass instructions scheduler, to obtain the final code.

Although an improvement over earlier solutions, instruction scheduling twice does not solve the phase-ordering problem between instruction scheduling and register allocation. In particular, when the prepass instruction scheduling creates high-register pressure, the register allocator may insert so much spill code that the resulting performance is degraded, compared to a less aggressive or even no prepass instruction scheduling. The strategies to address this issue are:

– The *lifetime-sensitive instruction scheduling problems* (LSISP) seek to minimize the register lifetimes during the prepass instruction scheduling. A *register lifetime* is a time interval in the instruction schedule that starts at the schedule date of the first operation that defines the register and stops at the schedule date of the last operation that uses the register.

– The *register pressure instruction scheduling problems* (RPISP) seek to minimize the maximum register pressure during the prepass instruction scheduling. The *register pressure* is defined for a given date as the number of register lifetimes that contain this date. The maximum register pressure is taken over all the dates spanned by the instruction schedule.

– The *register-constrained instruction scheduling problems* (RCISP) ensure that a given maximum register pressure is never exceeded during the prepass instruction scheduling. When it does not fail, this ensures that the local register allocation has minimal or no impact on the schedule.

– The *register allocation instruction scheduling problems* (RAISP) combine the register spilling, reloading, rematerialization and splitting with the instruction scheduling.

2.1.2. *The block and pipeline VLIW instruction scheduling problems*

We will illustrate instruction scheduling problems with the ST220 processor, a single-cluster implementation of the Lx core [FAR 00] produced by STMicroelectronics. This processor executes up to four operations per cycle with a maximum of one control operation (goto, jump, call and return), one memory operation (load, store and prefetch) and two multiply operations per cycle. All arithmetic instructions operate on integer values with operands belonging either to the general register file (64 × 32-bit), or to the branch register file (8 × 1-bit). In order to eliminate some conditional branches, the ST200 architecture also provides conditional selection. The processing time of any operation is a single cycle, while the latencies between operations range from zero to three cycles.

The resource constraints of the ST220 processor are accurately modeled with cumulative resources. In Figure 2.1, *Width* represents the issue width, *IMX* represents the extended immediate value generator, *MUL* represents the multiply operators, *MEM* represents the memory access unit and *CTL* represents the control unit. The artificial resource *ODD* represents the operation alignment constraints. For instruction scheduling purposes, the resource requirements of the operations are abstracted by *resource classes*, which in case of the ST220 processor are {*ALU, ALUX, MUL, MULX, MEM, MEMX, CTL*}. The resource classes *ALU, MUL, MEM* and *CTL* correspond, respectively, to the single-cycle, multiply, memory and control operations. Similarly, the resource classes *ALUX, MULX* and *MEMX* abstract the operations with an extended immediate operand.

Resource	Width	IMX	MUL	MEM	CTL	ODD
Availability	4	2	2	1	1	2
Resource Class Requirements	Width	IMX	MUL	MEM	CTL	ODD
ALU	1					
ALUX	2	1				1
MUL	1		1			1
MULX	2	1	1			1
MEM	1			1		
MEMX	2	1		1		1
CTL	1				1	1

Figure 2.1. *The ST220 cumulative resource availabilities and resource class requirements*

We define a *VLIW instruction scheduling problem* as a RCPSP with dependence constraints, where the dependence latencies θ_i^j are non-negative integers. Most of the VLIW instruction scheduling problems also have unit execution time (UET) operations. Indeed, in modern processors, all the functional units are pipelined, meaning there is an apparent processing time p_i of one cycle and a fixed non-negative latency θ_i^j, after which the result of an operation is available in a destination register. In addition to these so-called read-after-write (RAW) register dependences, the dependences of instruction scheduling problems include write-after-read (WAR), write-after-write (WAW), register dependences, memory dependences and control dependences.

We define a *block instruction scheduling problem* (BISP) as an acyclic instruction scheduling problem whose objective is the minimization of L_{max}, or C_{max} when there are no deadlines on the operations. In a BISP, release dates and deadline dates arise because of the interactions between the different scheduling regions [ABR 98]. A BISP may apply to a basic block, a super block or other acyclic scheduling region and can be either prepass or postpass. Conversely, we define a (software) *pipeline instruction scheduling problem* (PISP) as a cyclic instruction scheduling problem whose objective is the minimization of the average time between the execution of two successive loop iterations, also called the loop *initiation interval* [RAU 81].

These two specializations of instruction scheduling problems are illustrated on the sample C source code in Figure 2.2, which also displays the translation of the inner loop body in ST220 operations. When considering this inner loop body as a BISP, the ST200 LAO instruction scheduler (see section 4.1.4) generates an instruction schedule of seven cycles, shown in Figure 2.3, which starts at cycle [0] and stops at cycle [6]. In the right part of Figure 2.3, we display the *resource table*, the data structure of the instruction scheduler that tracks the resource uses of each scheduled operation (in the resource table, each operation is represented by its resource class).

When considering the inner loop of Figure 2.2 as a PISP, the result is a eight-cycle *local schedule*, shown in Figure 2.4. However, this local schedule allows the execution of the loop operations to be overlapped, or *software pipelined*, with a constant period of two cycles, as illustrated by the resource table in Figure 2.4. The software pipelining technique used by the ST200 LAO instruction scheduler to solve the PISP is *insertion scheduling* (section 4.1.4), a variant of *modulo scheduling* (section 2.2.2).

```
int                                  L?__0_8:
prod(int n, short a[], short b) {      LDH_1     g96 = 0, G92
  int s = 0, i;                        MULL_2    g97 = G91, g96
  for (i = 0; i < n ; i++) {           ADD_3     G94 = G94, g97
    s += a[i]*b;                       ADD_4     G93 = G93, 1
  }                                    ADD_5     G92 = G92, 2
  return s;                            CMPNE_6   b100 = G83, G93
}                                      BR_7      b100, L?__0_8
```

Figure 2.2. *Source code and the inner loop body code generator representation*

2.2. Software pipelining

2.2.1. *Cyclic, periodic and pipeline scheduling problems*

A *cyclic machine scheduling problem* [HAN 94] is given by a set of generic operations $\{O_i\}_{1 \le i \le n}$ with generic dependences between them. This set of operations needs to be executed repeatedly in a given machine environment and all the instances $\{O_i^k\}^{k>0}$ of a given generic operation O_i have the same resource requirements. In a feasible cyclic schedule[2] $\{\sigma_i^k\}^{k>0}_{0\leq i\leq n+1}$, the total resource requirement of the operation instances executing at any time is not greater than the resource availabilities and the dependences between the operation instances are respected. The common model of generic dependences in cyclic scheduling problems is the *uniform dependence* model [HAN 94]

$$O_i \xrightarrow{\theta_i^j,\omega_i^j} O_j \Longrightarrow \sigma_i^k + \theta_i^j \leq \sigma_j^{k+\omega_i^j} \quad \forall k > 0$$

[0] LDH_1	g96 = 0, G92	[0] ALU_5	MEM_1
[0] ADD_5	G92 = G92, 2	[1]	
[2] ADD_4	G93 = G93, 1	[2] ALU_4	
[3] MULL_2	g97 = G91, g96	[3] ALU_6	MUL_2
[3] CMPNE_6	b100 = G83, G93	[4]	
[6] ADD_3	G94 = G94, g97	[5]	
[6] BR_7	b100, L?__0_8	[6] ALU_3	CTL_7

Figure 2.3. *The block scheduled loop body and the block schedule resource table*

		[0] ALU_5.1 MEM_1.1
		[1]
[0] LDH_1	g96 = 0, G92	[2] ALU_4.1 ALU_5.2 MEM_1.2
[0] ADD_5	G92 = G92, 2	[3] ALU_6.1 MUL_2.1
[2] ADD_4	G93 = G93, 1	[4] ALU_4.2 ALU_5.2 MEM_1.3
[3] MULL_2	g97 = G91, g96	[5] ALU_6.2 MUL_2.2
[3] CMPNE_6	b100 = G83, G93	[6] ALU_3.1 ALU_4.3 ALU_5.3 MEM_1.4
[6] ADD_3	G94 = G94, g97	[7] ALU_6.3 MUL_2.3 CTL_7.1
[7] BRF_7	b100, .LA0001	[8] ALU_3.2 ALU_4.4 ALU_5.4 MEM_1.5
		[9] ALU_6.4 MUL_2.4 CTL_7.2

Figure 2.4. *The software pipeline local schedule and the software pipeline resource table*

The quality of a cyclic schedule is measured by its asymptotic throughput $R_\infty \overset{\text{def}}{=} \lim_{k\to\infty} \frac{k}{\sigma_{n+1}^k}$.

Periodic schedules are cyclic schedules defined by the property that the execution of the successive instances of a particular operation O_i is separated by a constant period $\lambda \in \mathbb{Q}$

$$\forall i \in [0, n+1], \forall k > 0 : \sigma_i^k = \sigma_i^0 + k\lambda$$

---

2 We assume dummy operations O_0^k and O_{n+1}^k such that $\sigma_0^k \overset{\text{def}}{=} \min_{1\leq i\leq n} \sigma_i^k$ and $\sigma_{n+1}^k \overset{\text{def}}{=} \max_{1\leq i\leq n} \sigma_i^k$.

Periodic schedules are a particular case of the K-periodic schedules, defined by $\sigma_i^k + K\lambda = \sigma_i^{k+K}$:

$$\forall i \in [0, n+1], \forall k > 0 : \sigma_i^k = \sigma_i^{k \bmod K} + K\lambda \left\lfloor \frac{k}{K} \right\rfloor$$

Given a cyclic machine scheduling problem with uniform dependences, there is always a K such that the K-periodic schedules contain an optimal solution [HAN 95], but this K is not guaranteed to equal one. The asymptotic throughput of a periodic schedule equals λ, so the *periodic scheduling problem* is the construction of a K-periodic schedule of minimum λ for a cyclic scheduling problem.

The lower bounds on λ for a K-periodic schedule are obtained using two types of relaxations. In the first class of relaxations, the *free schedule* ignores all the resource constraints. A refinement of this relaxation is the basic cyclic scheduling problem (BCSP) introduced by Hanen and Munier [HAN 94], where in addition to the original uniform dependences, the operations are constrained to be non-reentrant ($\sigma_i^k + p_i \leq \sigma_i^{k+1}$) through additional uniform dependences. In both cases [HAN 95]:

$$\lambda \geq \lambda_{rec} \overset{\mathrm{def}}{=} \max_C \frac{\sum_C \theta_i^j}{\sum_C \omega_i^j} : \quad C \text{ circuit of the dependence graph}$$

The maximum ratio λ_{rec} is reached in particular on simple circuits, the *critical cycles*. The discovery of the maximum ratio λ_{rec} and the identification of a critical cycle is called the optimum cost to time ratio problem, for which a number of efficient algorithms exist [DAS 99]. Solving the BCSP for any $\lambda \geq \lambda_{rec}$ then reduces to a simple longest path computation [GAS 94].

In the second class of relaxations, all the dependences are ignored and the operations are scheduled for a minimum length λ_{res}, which provides another lower bound on λ. In case of parallel machine environment, UET generic operations and acyclic dependence graph, the solution of this relaxation can always be converted into an optimal periodic schedule with $\lambda = \lambda_{res}$ [RAU 81]. This technique was generalized by Eisenbeis and Windheiser to non-UET generic operations [EIS 93].

In the pipeline scheduling techniques, a local schedule $\{\sigma_i^1\}_{1 \leq i \leq n}$ is created first; then, K copies of this schedule are overlapped in a way to achieve the maximum average throughput, thus creating a K-periodic schedule of constrained structure. These *pipeline scheduling problems* originated from hardware pipeline optimization [KOG 81] and were later adapted to the software pipelining of loops. Trying to adapt the local schedule so as to maximize the software pipeline throughput led to the discovery of the more effective modulo scheduling techniques discussed in section 2.2.2.

One heuristic technique to solve the K-periodic instruction scheduling problems is to schedule successive instances of the set of generic operations in an acyclic context, until a repeating pattern of K successive instances appears in the schedule [BOD 90, AIK 95]. To converge, this method requires that the span of any local schedule be bounded, a condition that is enforced by adding a span-limiting dependence from O_{n+1} to O_0. Although these techniques may suffer from slow convergence (large values of K) or from the sequential effect of the span-limiting dependence, they do not require the loop body to be a single basic block or super block.

The techniques that optimally solve the K-periodic instruction problems originated in the work by Feautrier [FEA 94], where the D-periodic schedules are defined by numbers $A, \{B_i\}_{1 \leq i \leq n}, D \in \mathbb{Z}$ and

$$\forall i \in [0, n+1], \forall k > 0 : \sigma_i^k = \left\lfloor \frac{Ak + B_i}{D} \right\rfloor$$

with A and D relatively prime and $\lambda \stackrel{\text{def}}{=} \frac{A}{D}$.

Unlike the K-periodic schedules discussed earlier, this definition ensures that the σ_i^k are integral, yet it does not prevent them from reaching optimal solutions of the cyclic scheduling problems.

For uniform dependences and exclusive resources (unit availability), Feautrier shows [FEA 94]:

$$O_i \xrightarrow{\theta_i^j, \omega_i^j} O_j \implies B_i + D\theta_i^j - A\omega_i^j \leq B_j \qquad [2.1]$$

O_i and O_j share a resource $\implies A(qij + 1) - Bj + Bi \geq Dpj \wedge Bj - Bi$

$$-Aqij \geq Dpi \qquad [2.2]$$

Here q_i^j is an integer variable. By guessing the value of D from the structure of the dependence circuits and by fixing the value of A in each step of an enumerative search for the minimum, these equations can be optimally solved by integer linear programming to compute $\{B_i\}_{1 \leq i \leq n}$.

In a series of contributions, Fimmel and Müller refine this work, first to manage register constraints [FIM 00], and then to find the optimal values of A and D without having to enumerate them [FIM 02].

2.2.2. *Modulo instruction scheduling problems and techniques*

Modulo scheduling is a framework for building 1-periodic schedules, where only the generic operations and the generic dependences are considered. The original modulo scheduling technique was introduced by Rau and Glaeser in 1981 [RAU 81], improved with *modulo expansion* by Lam in 1988 [LAM 88a] and later refined by Rau in 1992 under the name *iterative modulo scheduling* [RAU 96].

In applications to cyclic instruction scheduling, the restriction to 1-periodic schedules with integer λ is not a problem, as loop unrolling is applied before instruction scheduling in order to enable further optimizations [DAV 95]. Indeed, the K-periodic scheduling techniques mentioned so far only perform *loop unwinding*, that is, replicating K complete copies of the original loop body. With loop unrolling, code is factored across the K copies of the original loop body, critical paths can be reduced [LAV 95] and further memory access bandwidth optimizations are enabled [DIN 99].

To describe modulo scheduling problems, we extend the $\alpha|\beta|\gamma$ notation with the β field $\pi_i = \lambda$, which requires that all the operations cyclically execute with the same processing period λ [DIN 04b]. Formally, the modulo scheduling problem is defined as follows:

– Uniform dependence constraints $O_i \xrightarrow{\theta_i^j, \omega_i^j} O_j$: for each such dependence, a valid modulo schedule satisfies $\sigma_i + \theta_i^j - \lambda\omega_i^j \leq \sigma_j$. The *latency* θ_i^j and the *distance* ω_i^j of the dependences are non-negative integers. The *carried* dependences are such that $\omega_i^j > 0$. In addition, the dependence graph without the carried dependences is a directed acyclic graph (DAG).

– Cumulative modulo resource constraints: each operation O_i requires $\vec{b}_i \geq \vec{0}$ resources for all the time intervals $[\sigma_i + k\lambda, \sigma_i + k\lambda + p_i - 1], k \in \mathbb{N}$ and the total resource use at any time must not exceed $\vec{B}$. The positive integer value p_i is the processing time of operation O_i.

We define a *modulo instruction scheduling problem* (MISP) as an instruction scheduling problem with modulo resource constraints and uniform dependences whose latencies θ_i^j and distances ω_i^j are non-negative. Compared to the BISP, the main difficulties of the MISP are the possibly negative dependence latencies $\theta_i^j - \lambda\omega_i^j$, the modulo resource constraints and the fact that these constraints are parametric with λ. The MISP objective is to minimize the λ and then C_{max}.

In the classic modulo scheduling framework [RAU 81, LAM 88a, RAU 96], a dichotomy search for the minimum λ that yields a feasible schedule is performed, starting from $\lambda = \max(\lambda_{rec}, \lambda_{res})$. At each search step, heuristic scheduling is attempted, using a list scheduling algorithm extended to handling the modulo resource constraints. Because of the dependences with negative latencies, heuristic scheduling may fail even if the modulo scheduling problem is feasible at the current λ. To address this issue, limited backtracking is implemented with satisfactory results [HUF 93a, RAU 96, RUT 96b, ZAL 01]. When failure persists, the dichotomy search attempts heuristic scheduling at a higher λ.

A different heuristic approach for modulo scheduling was pioneered by Gasperoni and Schwiegelshohn [GAS 94]. The principle of *decomposed software pipelining* [WAN 94a] is to decompose the modulo schedule dates into a quotient and remainder by λ, that is $\forall i \in [0, n+1] : \sigma_i = \lambda \phi_i + \tau_i, 0 \leq \tau_i < \lambda$. Given an operation, O_i, ϕ_i is its *column number* or *stage number* and τ_i is its *row number*. The modulo scheduling problem is then approximately solved as follows [GAS 94]:

- build a resource-free schedule $\{\sigma_i^*\}_{1 \leq i \leq n}$ with $\lambda^* \stackrel{\text{def}}{=} \lambda_{rec}$;

- compute the column numbers of the operations as $\phi_i \stackrel{\text{def}}{=} \left\lfloor \frac{\sigma_i^*}{\lambda^*} \right\rfloor$;

- delete the dependences that appear to be violated with the row numbers $\{\tau_i^* \stackrel{\text{def}}{=} \sigma_i^* \bmod \lambda^*\}_{1 \leq i \leq n}$, that is, when $\tau_i^* + \theta_i^j > \tau_j^*$, yielding an acyclic modified dependence graph;

- schedule the operations with this modified acyclic dependence graph, this time taking into account the resource constraints;

- the resulting schedule dates are the final row numbers $\{\tau_i\}_{1 \leq i \leq n}$ and the resulting initiation interval λ is the length τ_{n+1} of this schedule.

The main idea is that fixing the column numbers reduces the modulo scheduling problem with UET operations to a minimum length scheduling problem involving only the row numbers $\{\tau_i\}_{1 \leq i \leq n}$ and ordinary resource constraints. This works because an apparent dependence violation on the row numbers implies that the difference between the column numbers is large enough: $\sigma_i + \theta_i^j - \lambda \omega_i^j \leq \sigma_j \wedge \tau_i + \theta_i^j > \tau_j \Rightarrow \phi_i < \omega_i^j + \phi_j$ (see corollary 4.1 in section 4.1.3). Ignoring these dependences while recomputing the row numbers at a higher λ is safe in a variety of cases.

The idea of decomposing the modulo scheduling problem has been generalized by Wang and Eisenbeis to compute either the column numbers first, or the row numbers first [WAN 94a]. In particular, given the row numbers, they proved that dependence-preserving column numbers exist iff [WAN 94a]:

$$\sum_{(O_i, O_j) \in C} \left\lceil \frac{\theta_i^j + \tau_i - \tau_j}{\lambda} \right\rceil - \omega_i^j \leq 0 \quad \forall C \text{ circuit of the dependence graph.}$$

Another generalization that still computes the column numbers first in resource-free context, then the row numbers with acyclic scheduling, is the loop shifting and compaction of Darte and Huard [DAR 00]. We also developed the idea of rescheduling while keeping the column numbers invariant in insertion scheduling [DIN 95], a modulo scheduling technique that neither assumes UET operations, nor requires a decomposition of the modulo scheduling problem (see section 4.1.3 and section 4.1.4).

2.3. Instruction scheduling and register allocation

2.3.1. *Register instruction scheduling problem solving approaches*

The simplest attempt to solve an LSISP is to perform prepass instruction scheduling backward. This works because many DAG expressions look like in-trees, while the instruction scheduling heuristics based on the list scheduling algorithms (LSA) are greedy. As a result, backward instruction scheduling keeps the operations that define registers close to their use on average, resulting in shorter register lifetimes, thus indirectly contributing to lower register pressure.

However, minimizing the register lifetimes sometimes requires that some operations be scheduled as early as possible, in particular with modulo scheduling for some of the register lifetimes that carry values from one iteration to the other. These observations led to the formulation of lifetime-sensitive instruction scheduling [HUF 93a], hyper-node reduction modulo scheduling [LLO 95], minimum cumulative register lifetime modulo scheduling [DIN 94] and swing modulo scheduling [LLO 96]. The general idea of these techniques is to schedule operations with scheduling slack near their early or late start dates, depending on the anticipated effects on the register lifetimes.

The RPISP are motivated by the fact that the amount of spill code generated by the register allocation is primarily dependent on the maximum register pressure *MaxLive* achieved in the instruction schedule; hence, *MaxLive* minimization should be part of the objective besides the schedule length or the modulo scheduling period λ. Unlike the register lifetimes, *MaxLive* is not linear with the schedule dates: therefore, its minimization is difficult to integrate even in resource-free instruction scheduling problems.

For the block RPISP, an integrated technique was proposed by Goodman and Hsu in 1988 [GOO 88a], where the instruction scheduling objective switches between the minimum length and the minimum register usage, whenever a threshold of register pressure is crossed. The block RPISP is now optimally solved with the effective enumeration procedure of Kessler [KES 98]. For the modulo RPISP, several heuristic approaches have been proposed, based on the *stage scheduling* of Eichenberger and Davidson [EIC 95a]. In stage scheduling, once a modulo schedule is computed, the stage (column) numbers of the operations are further adjusted to reduce the maximum register pressure.

The most advanced techniques for solving the RPISP are based on integer linear programming. Using the minimum buffer equations defined by Ning and Gao [NIN 93b] for the resource-free modulo scheduling problems, Govindarajan *et al.* [GOV 94] introduced a time-indexed formulation for the resource-constrained modulo scheduling problems that minimizes the number of buffers, a coarse approximation of *MaxLive*. The modern formulation of the modulo RPISP, discussed in section 3.3.2, was given in 1995 by Eichenberger, Davidson and Abraham [EIC 95b].

The RCISP are related to the RPISP, with the main difference that *MaxLive* is now constrained by a hard bound. This has two advantages: first, this allows instruction scheduling to focus on the single objective of minimizing the schedule length (of the local schedule in case of modulo scheduling) and this objective is achieved by the schedule as far as the hard bound on *MaxLive* is not reached; second, by setting the hard bound value lower than the number of allocatable registers, the register allocation is guaranteed to succeed without spilling any register.

Specifically, in case of acyclic scheduling of scheduling regions without control-flow merge points (such as basic blocks, super blocks and trees of blocks), register assignment is reduced to the problem of minimum node coloring the interference graph of the register live ranges, which is a chordal graph, since it is an intersection graph of tree paths. This problem is polynomial-time solvable and the number of registers needed is exactly *MaxLive*, the maximum clique size of this graph.

In the case of cyclic scheduling with basic block or super block regions, the interference graph of the register live ranges is a cyclic interval graph [HEN 93], whose minimum node coloring problem is NP-hard. As observed by Hendren *et al.* [HEN 93], splitting some of the register live ranges (by inserting copy operations) yields an interval graph that is colorable with *MaxLive* registers as in the acyclic case. Alternatively, by heuristically coloring the original interference graph, it is observed that most loops can be register assigned with *MaxLive*+1 registers [RAU 92a].

A heuristic for the block RCISP was proposed by Natarajan and Schlansker in 1995 [NAT 95]. Their approach was to schedule the operations for the minimum length and in case the maximum register pressure exceeds its hard bound, the dependence graph (which is a DAG) is split into two and each part is rescheduled with the same technique. The main contribution is how to split the DAG to decrease the maximum register pressure reached in the sub-DAG in a resource-free schedule.

For the periodic RCISP, Fimmel *et al.* [FIM 00] introduced time-indexed variables (binary decomposition), with register pressure equations that are similar to those proposed by Eichenberger *et al.* [EIC 95b]. For solving the modulo RCISP, we propose a new time-indexed formulation in section 4.1.6, which, unlike those approaches, does not require the λ-decomposition of the schedule dates. This modulo RCISP formulation also applies to the block RCISP by assuming a large enough λ.

In the RAISP, a hard bound on *MaxLive* lower than the number of allocatable registers is assumed as in the RCISP, but, in case the original scheduling problem is not feasible under such constraint or its solution is not satisfactory, operations that spill, restore or split the register live ranges are inserted into the schedule. The main objective is to perform the local register allocation of the scheduling region while scheduling. Solving the RAISP is a motivating area of research for compiler code generator design [ZAL 01]. In the case of the software pipelined loops, an effective heuristic is implemented in the MIPS-PRO production compiler [RUT 96b]. For the acyclic scheduling regions, an effective heuristic technique is implemented in the Multiflow Trace Scheduling compiler [LOW 93].

3

Applications of Machine Scheduling to Instruction Scheduling

Although instruction scheduling is a mature discipline, its relationship with the field of machine scheduling is often overlooked. This can be explained because the classic results of machine scheduling apply to problems that are too limited to be of practical use in instruction scheduling. For example, these results assume simple precedence constraints on the order of operations in a schedule, instead of precedences with time-lags like those in pipelined processors, and focus on machine models where each operation uses one of m identical processors for its execution.

3.1. Advances in machine scheduling

3.1.1. *Parallel machine scheduling problems*

In parallel machine scheduling problems, an operation set $\{O_i\}_{1 \leq i \leq n}$ is processed on m identical processors. To be processed, each operation O_i requires the exclusive use of one of the m processors during p_i time units, starting at its *schedule date* σ_i. This processing environment is called *non-preemptive*. In the *preemptive* case, the processing of any operation can be stopped to be resumed later, possibly on another processor. In parallel machine scheduling, the *resource constraints* are the limit m on the maximum number of operations that are being processed at any time.

Parallel machine scheduling problems also involve *temporal constraints* on the schedule dates. In case of *release dates* r_i, the schedule date of operation O_i is constrained by $\sigma_i \geq r_i$. In case of *due dates* d_i, there is a penalty whenever $C_i > d_i$, with C_i the *completion date* of O_i defined as $C_i \stackrel{\text{def}}{=} \sigma_i + p_i$. For problems where $C_i \leq d_i$ is mandatory, the d_i are called *deadlines*. Temporal constraints may also include *precedence constraints*, given by a partial order between the operations. A precedence constraint $O_i \prec O_j$ requires O_i to complete before O_j starts, that is

$\sigma_i + p_i \leq \sigma_j$. In case of *time-lags* or *precedence delays* l_i^j, the precedence constraint becomes $\sigma_i + p_i + l_i^j \leq \sigma_j$.

A *feasible schedule* is a mapping from operations to schedule dates $\{\sigma_i\}_{1 \leq i \leq n}$, such that both the resource constraints and the temporal constraints of the scheduling problem are satisfied.

Machine scheduling problems are denoted by a triplet notation $\alpha|\beta|\gamma$ [FIN 02], where α describes the processing environment, β specifies the operation properties and γ defines the optimality criterion. For the parallel machine scheduling problems, the common values of α, β, γ are:

α: 1 for a single processor, P for parallel processors, Pm for the given m parallel processors;

β: r_i for release dates, d_i for deadlines (if $\gamma = \bullet$) or due dates. Additional β fields include:

$prec(l_i^j)$: precedences that have time-lags l_i^j;

$prec(l_i^j = l)$: all the l_i^j have the same value l (applies to pipelined processing);

$inTree$ the precedence graph is an in-tree (each operation has one successor);

$outTree$ the precedence graph is an out-tree (each operation has one predecessor);

$chains$ the precedence graph is made of independent chains;

$intOrder(mono; l_i^j)$: the dependence graph is a monotone interval order (see section 3.2.2);

$p_i = 1$ all the processing times are 1 (*unit execution time* (UET) operations);

$p_i = p$ all the processing times have the same value p.

γ: $\bullet$ for the scheduling problem feasibility, C_{max} or L_{max} for the minimization of these objectives. $C_{max} \overset{def}{=} \max_i C_i$ is the *makespan* and $L_{max} \overset{def}{=} \max_i L_i : L_i \overset{def}{=} C_i - d_i$ is the *maximum lateness*.

A $\gamma = L_{max}$ scheduling problem is more general than a $\gamma = C_{max}$ scheduling problem, as $d_i \overset{def}{=} 0$ reduces L_{max} to C_{max}. A $\gamma = L_{max}$ scheduling problem without release dates is also equivalent to a $\gamma = C_{max}$ scheduling problem with release dates r_i, by inverting the precedence graph and by taking $r_i \overset{def}{=} \max_j d_j - d_i$. Finally, solving a $\gamma = \bullet$ scheduling problem with deadlines solves the corresponding $\gamma = L_{max}$ scheduling problem with due dates d_i, by dichotomy search of the smallest L_{max} such that the $\gamma = \bullet$ scheduling problem with deadlines $d_i + L_{max}$ is feasible.

Some significant complexity results of parallel machine scheduling are summarized in Table 3.1 for the polynomial-time solvable (PTS) problems and in Table 3.2 for the NP-hard problems. These tables illustrate the advances achieved in parallel machine scheduling, especially the recent discovery of several PTS machine scheduling problems. Although these new PTS parallel machine scheduling problems include precedence constraints, they are restricted to either constant processing time $(p_i = p)$ or UET $(p_i = 1)$.

Problem	Result	Source
$1\|\|L_{max}$	Jackson 1955	[ECK 03]
$1\|prec; r_i\|C_{max}$	Lawler 1973	[FIN 02]
$1\|prec\|L_{max}$	Lawler 1973	[FIN 02]
$1\|r_i; p_i = 1\|L_{max}$	Baker et al. 1974	[ECK 03]
$1\|prec; r_i; p_i = p\|L_{max}$	Simons 1978	[FIN 02]
$1\|prec(l_i^j = 1); r_i; p_i = 1\|L_{max}$	Bruno et al. 1980	[LEU 01]
$1\|prec(l_i^j = 1)\|C_{max}$	Finta and Liu 1996	[LEU 01]
$1\|prec(l_i^j \in \{0,1\})\|C_{max}$	Leung et al. 2001	[LEU 01]
$1\|prec(l_i^j \in \{0,1\}); r_i; p_i = 1\|L_{max}$	Leung et al. 2001	[LEU 01]
$P2\|prec; p_i = 1\|C_{max}$	Coffman and Graham 1972	[ECK 03]
$P2\|prec; p_i = 1\|L_{max}$	Garey and Johnson 1976	[ECK 03]
$P2\|prec; r_i; p_i = 1\|L_{max}$	Garey and Johnson 1977	[ECK 03]
$P2\|prec(l_i^j \in \{-1,0\}); r_i; p_i = 1\|L_{max}$	Leung et al. 2001	[LEU 01]
$P\|tree; p_i = p\|C_{max}$	Hu 1961	[ECK 03]
$P\|r_i; p_i = 1\|L_{max}$	Blazewicz 1977	[ECK 03]
$P\|outTree; r_i; p_i = p\|C_{max}$	Brucker et al. 1977	[ECK 03]
$P\|inTree; p_i = p\|L_{max}$	Brucker et al. 1977	[ECK 03]
$P\|inTree(l_i^j = l); p_i = 1\|L_{max}$	Bruno et al. 1980	[LEU 01]
$P\|outTree(l_i^j = l); r_i; p_i = 1\|C_{max}$	Bruno et al. 1980	[LEU 01]
$P\|intOrder(mono\ l_i^j); p_i = 1\|L_{max}$	Palem and Simons 1993	[LEU 01]
$P\|intOrder(mono\ l_i^j); r_i; p_i = 1\|L_{max}$	Leung et al. 2001	[LEU 01]

Table 3.1. *Polynomial-time solvable parallel machine scheduling problems*

3.1.2. *Parallel machine scheduling extensions and relaxations*

A first class of extensions of parallel machine scheduling problems is the replacement of the precedence graph with time lags by a *dependence graph*. Unlike the precedence graph, which represents a partial order, a dependence graph may include circuits. Each dependence arc represents the temporal constraint $\sigma_i + \theta_i^j \leq \sigma_j$, with the *dependence latency* θ_i^j unrelated to p_i or p_j and of arbitrary sign. In dependence graphs, it is often convenient to introduce the dummy start and stop operations O_0 and O_{n+1}. In particular, the release dates r_i can be expressed as dependences between O_0 and O_i with the latencies $\theta_0^i \overset{\text{def}}{=} r_i$. The deadlines d_i can also be expressed as dependences between O_i and O_0 by using the (negative) latencies $\theta_i^0 \overset{\text{def}}{=} p_i - d_i$. The dummy stop operation O_{n+1} is used for C_{max} minimization by using dependences between O_i and O_{n+1} of latency $\theta_i^{n+1} \overset{\text{def}}{=} p_i$.

Problem	Result	Source
$1\|r_i\|L_{max}$	Lenstra *et al.* 1977	[ECK 03]
$1\|prec(l_i^j); p_i = 1\|C_{max}$	Hennessy and Gross 1983	[LEU 01]
$1\|inTree(l_i^j = l); r_i; p_i = 1\|C_{max}$	Brucker and Knust 1998	[ECK 03]
$1\|outTree(l_i^j = l); p_i = 1\|L_{max}$	Brucker and Knust 1998	[ECK 03]
$P2\|\|C_{max}$	Karp 1972	[ECK 03]
$P2\|prec; p_i \in \{1,2\}\|C_{max}$	Ullman 1975	[LEU 01]
$P2\|chains\|C_{max}$	Du *et al.* 1991	
$P\|prec; p_i = 1\|C_{max}$	Ullman 1975	[ECK 03]
$P\|inTree; r_i; p_i = 1\|C_{max}$	Brucker *et al.* 1977	[ECK 03]
$P\|outTree; p_i = 1\|L_{max}$	Brucker *et al.* 1977	[ECK 03]
$P\|\|C_{max}$	Garey and Johnson 1978	[ECK 03]

Table 3.2. *NP-hard parallel machine scheduling problems*

A second class of extensions of parallel machine scheduling problems is to consider *multiprocessor tasks*. In this extension, denoted by $size_i$ in the β field, an operation O_i requires $size_i$ processors for p_i time units to execute. Multiprocessor scheduling is NP-hard even for the basic UET problem $P\|p_i = 1; size_i\|C_{max}$ [BRU 04]. Two-processor multiprocessor scheduling is more tractable, as $P2\|prec; p_i = p; size_i\|C_{max}$ and $P2\|r_i; p_i = 1; size_i\|L_{max}$ are polynomial-time solvable [BRU 04].

The multiprocessor scheduling model is further generalized in the *resource-constrained project scheduling problems* (RCPSPs) [BRU 99], where the m processors are replaced by a set of *renewable resources* or *cumulative resources*, whose availabilities are given by an integral vector $\vec{B}$. Each operation O_i is also associated with an integral vector $\vec{b_i}$ of resource requirements and the resource constraints become: $\forall t, \sum_{i \in I_t} \vec{b_i} \leq \vec{B}$, with $I_t \overset{\text{def}}{=} \{i \in [1,n] : \sigma_i \leq t < \sigma_i + p_i\}$. That is, the cumulative use of the resources by all the operations executing at any given time must not be greater than $\vec{B}$.

A *relaxation* is a simplified version of a given scheduling problem such that if the relaxation is infeasible, then the original problem is also infeasible. Relaxations are obtained by allowing preemption, by assuming a particular structure of the precedence constraints, by ignoring some or all resource constraints, or by removing the integrity constraints in problem formulations based on integer linear programming (see section 3.3.1). Relaxations are mainly used to prune the search space of schedule construction procedures, by detecting infeasible problems early and by providing bounds on the objective value and the schedule dates of the feasible problems.

A widely used relaxation of machine scheduling problems is to ignore the resource constraints, yielding a so-called *central scheduling problem* that is completely specified by the dependence graph of the original problem. Optimal scheduling of a central scheduling problem for C_{max} or L_{max} takes $O(ne)$ time where e is the number of dependences [AHU 93], as it reduces to a single-source longest path computation from operation O_0. The schedule dates computed this way are the *earliest start* dates of the operations. By assuming an upper bound D on the schedule length and computing the backward longest paths from operation O_{n+1}, we similarly obtain the *latest start* dates.

3.2. List scheduling algorithms

3.2.1. *List scheduling algorithms and list scheduling priorities*

The *list scheduling algorithms* (LSAs) are the workhorses of machine scheduling [KOL 99], as they are able to construct feasible schedules with low computational effort for the RCPSP with general temporal constraints, as long as the dependence graph has no circuits[1]. More precisely, an LSA is a greedy scheduling heuristic where the operations are ranked by priority order in a list. Greedy scheduling means that the processors or resources are kept busy as long as there are operations available to schedule. Two variants of list scheduling must be distinguished [MUN 98]:

– *Graham list scheduling* (parallel schedule generation scheme [KOL 99]) Scheduling is performed by scanning the time slots in increasing order. For each time slot, if a processor is idle, schedule the highest priority operation available at this time.

– *Job-Based list scheduling* (serial schedule generation scheme [KOL 99]) Scheduling is performed by scanning the priority list in decreasing order. For each operation of the list, schedule it at the earliest time slot available. This requires that the priority list order be compatible with the operation precedences.

In general, the Graham list scheduling algorithms (GLSAs) and the job-based list scheduling algorithms are incomparable with respect to the quality of the schedules they build [KOL 96]:

– The job-based LSA generates *active schedules*, where none of the operations can be started earlier without delaying some other operation.

---

1 In the case of dependence graphs with circuits, feasibility of the scheduling problem with resources is NP-complete.

– The Graham LSA constructs *non-delay schedules*, where, even though operation preemption is allowed, none of the operations can be started earlier without delaying some other operation.

– The set of non-delay schedules is a subset of the set of active schedules. It has the drawback that it might not contain an optimal schedule with a regular performance measure[2].

In the important case of UET operations, the set of active schedules equals the set of non-delay schedules. Moreover, given the same priorities, the two LSAs construct the same schedule.

The main results available on list scheduling are the performance guarantees of the GLSA for the C_{max} or L_{max} objectives [MUN 98], that is the ratio between the worst-case values of C_{max} or L_{max} and their optimal value. The performance guarantees of the GLSA, irrespective of the choice of the priority function, are given in Table 3.3. It is interesting to note that the performance guarantee of Graham 1966 does not apply to instruction scheduling problems, as these problems have non-zero time-lags l_i^j (see section 2.1.2). Rather, the bound of Munier *et al.* [MUN 98] should be considered and it is valid only in the cases of a GLSA applied to a parallel machine scheduling problem (not to an RCPSP).

Problem	Result	Performance ratio
$P\|prec\|C_{max}$	Graham 1966	$2 - \frac{1}{m}$
$P\|prec(l_i^j \in [0,l]); p_i = 1\|C_{max}$	Palem and Simons 1993	$2 - \frac{1}{m(l+1)}$
$1\|prec(l_i^j)\|C_{max}$	Munier *et al.* 1998	$\min(2 - \frac{1}{1+\rho}, 1 + \frac{\rho}{2})$
$P\|prec(l_i^j)\|C_{max}$	Munier *et al.* 1998	$2 - \frac{1}{m(1+\rho)}$

With $\rho \stackrel{\text{def}}{=} \frac{\max l_j^k}{\min p_i}$.

Table 3.3. *Performance guarantees of the GLSA with arbitrary priority*

The performance guarantees of the GLSA for a specific priority function are given in Table 3.4. We observe that all the priority functions that ensure optimal scheduling by the GLSA are either the earliest deadlines first, also known as *Jackson's rule*, or the earlier modified deadlines d_i' first. A modified deadline for operation O_i is a date d_i' such that for any feasible schedule $\sigma_i + p_i \leq d_i'$. For example, in the case of Hu's algorithm, since the precedences are an in-tree and given the UET operations, the highest in-tree level first is also a modified deadlines priority.

---

2 An optimality criterion γ such that $\gamma(C_1, \ldots, C_{n+1}) < \gamma(C_1', \ldots, C_{n+1}') \Rightarrow \exists j : C_j < C_j'$ (like C_{max} or L_{max}).

Problem	Result	Performance ratio	Priority
$1\|\|L_{max}$	Jackson 1955	1 (optimal)	earliest d_i first
$P\|inTree; p_i = 1\|C_{max}$	Hu 1961	1 (optimal)	highest levels first
$P\|\|C_{max}$	Graham 1969	$\frac{4}{3} - \frac{1}{3m}$	non-increasing p_i
$1\|r_i; p_i = 1\|L_{max}$	Baker et al. 1974	1 (optimal)	earliest d_i first
$P\|\|C_{max}$	1976*	$1 + \frac{1}{k} - \frac{1}{km}$	non-increasing p_i
$P2\|prec; p_i = 1\|L_{max}$	Garey et al. 1976	1 (optimal)	earliest d_i' first
$1\|prec; p_i = 1\|L_{max}$	Garey et al. 1981	1 (optimal)	earliest d_i' first
$P\|r_i; p_i = 1\|L_{max}$	Blazewicz 1977	1 (optimal)	earliest d_i first
$1\|prec(l_i^j \in \{0,1\}); r_i; p_i = 1\|L_{max}$	Leung et al. 2001	1 (optimal)	earliest d_i' first
$P2\|prec(l_i^j \in \{-1,0\}); r_i; p_i = 1\|L_{max}$	Leung et al. 2001	1 (optimal)	earliest d_i' first
$P\|intOrder(mono\ l_i^j); r_i; p_i = 1\|L_{max}$	Leung et al. 2001	1 (optimal)	earliest d_i' first
$P\|inTree(l_i^j = l); p_i = 1\|L_{max}$	Leung et al. 2001	1 (optimal)	earliest d_i' first

*With k the number of operations executed on the last active processor in the schedule.

Table 3.4. *Performance guarantees of the GLSA with a specific priority*

3.2.2. *The scheduling algorithm of Leung, Palem and Pnueli*

Leung et al. proposed in 2001 the following algorithm for scheduling UET operations on a parallel machine [LEU 01]:

1) For each operation O_i, compute an upper bound d_i', called *modified deadline'*, such that for any feasible schedule $\sigma_i < d_i' \leq d_i$.

2) Schedule with the GLSA using the earliest d_i' first as priorities, then check that the resulting schedule does not miss any deadlines.

3) In the case of minimizing L_{max}, binary search to find the minimum scheduling horizon such that the scheduling problem is feasible.

Steps 1 and 2 of this algorithm solve the problems of Table 3.5 in $O(n^2 \log n\alpha(n) + ne)$ time.

$1\|prec(l_i^j \in \{0,1\}); r_i; d_i; p_i = 1\|\bullet$	$P2\|prec(l_i^j \in \{-1,0\}); r_i; d_i; p_i = 1\|\bullet$
$P\|intOrder(mono\ l_i^j); r_i; d_i; p_i = 1\|\bullet$	$P\|inTree(l_i^j = l); d_i; p_i = 1\|\bullet$

Table 3.5. *Problems solved by the algorithm of Leung,*
Palem and Pnueli [LEU 01] steps 1 and 2

As introduced by Papadimitriou and Yannakakis [PAP 79], an *interval-order* is defined by an incomparability graph that is chordal. An interval-order is also the complement of an interval graph [PAP 79]. Thus, in an interval-order graph, each node can be associated with a closed interval on the real line and there is an arc between two nodes only if the two intervals do not intersect.

A *monotone interval-order* graph is an interval-order graph (V, E) with a weight function w on the arcs such that, given any $(v_i, v_j), (v_i, v_k) \in E : w(v_i, v_j) \leq w(v_i, v_k)$ whenever the predecessors of vertex v_j are included in the predecessors of vertex v_k.

In order to compute the modified deadlines in step 1, Leung *et al.* applied a technique of *optimal backward scheduling* [PAL 93], where a series of relaxations were optimally solved by the GLSA in order to find, for each operation, its latest schedule date such that the relaxations are feasible. More precisely, the implementation of optimal backward scheduling is as follows:

– Iterate in backward topological order on the operation set to build a series of scheduling subproblems $S_i \stackrel{\text{def}}{=} \{O_i, succ_i \cup indep_i, \{r'_j\}, \{d'_j\}\}$. Here $succ_i$ is the set of successors of O_i, $indep_i$ is the set of operations that are independent from O_i, $\{r'_j\}$ are the dependence-consistent release dates and $\{d'_j\}$ are the current modified deadlines.

– For each scheduling subproblem S_i, search for the latest schedule date p of O_i such that the constrained sub-problem $(r'_i = p) \wedge S_i$ is feasible. If there is a solution for such p, define the modified deadline of O_i as $d'_i \stackrel{\text{def}}{=} p + 1$. Else the original scheduling problem is infeasible.

– To find whether a constrained subproblem $(r'_i = p) \wedge S_i$ is feasible, convert the transitive dependence latencies from O_i to all the other O_j of S_i into release dates; then, forget the dependences. This yields a relaxation, which is the simpler scheduling problem $P|r_i; d_i; p_i = 1|\bullet$.

– Optimally solve this $P|r_i; d_i; p_i = 1|\bullet$ relaxation using the GLSA with the earliest d_i first priority (Jackson's rule). This gives the feasibility status of the relaxation.

Due to a fast list scheduling implementation based on union-find data-structures, solving a $P|r_i; d_i; p_i = 1|\bullet$ relaxation takes $O(n\alpha(n))$ time. Here, $\alpha(n)$ is the inverse Ackermann function and e is the number of dependence arcs. Leung *et al.* applied two binary searches to solve each subproblem S_i. These searches introduce a $\log n$ factor and there are n scheduling subproblems S_i to consider, each one implying a $O(n+e)$ transitive latency computation. Thus, the total time complexity of backward scheduling is $O(n^2 \log n\alpha(n) + ne)$. Because the final GLSA has a time complexity of $O(n^2)$, the full algorithm takes $O(n^2 \log n\alpha(n) + ne)$ time either to build a schedule or to report that the original scheduling problem is infeasible.

The main theoretical contributions of this work are the proofs that the feasible schedules computed this way are in fact optimal for all the cases listed in Table 3.5 and also the unification of many earlier modified deadlines techniques under a single framework [LEU 01]. On the implementation side, besides using the technique of fast list scheduling in $O(n\alpha(n))$ time for solving the $P|r_i; d_i; p_i = 1|\bullet$ relaxations, they prove that iterating once over the operations in backward topological order of the dependence graph yields the same set of modified deadlines as the brute-force approach of iterating the deadline modification process until a fixed point is reached.

3.3. Time-indexed scheduling problem formulations

3.3.1. *The non-preemptive time-indexed RCPSP formulation*

Due to its ability to describe the RCPSP with general temporal constraints and other extensions, the *non-preemptive time-indexed formulation* introduced by Pritsker *et al.* in 1969 [PRI 69] provides the basis for many RCPSP solution strategies. In this formulation, T denotes the time horizon and $\{0, 1\}$ variables $\{x_i^t\}$ are introduced such that $x_i^t \stackrel{\text{def}}{=} 1$ if $\sigma_i = t$, else $x_i^t \stackrel{\text{def}}{=} 0$. In particular, $\sigma_i = \sum_{t=1}^{T-1} t x_i^t$. The following formulation minimizes the schedule length C_{max} by minimizing the completion time of the dummy operation O_{n+1} (E_{dep} denotes the set of data dependences):

$$\text{minimize} \sum_{t=1}^{T-1} t\, x_{n+1}^t \quad : \tag{3.1}$$

$$\sum_{t=0}^{T-1} x_i^t = 1 \; \forall i \in [1, n+1] \tag{3.2}$$

$$\sum_{s=t}^{T-1} x_i^s + \sum_{s=0}^{t+\theta_i^j-1} x_j^s \leq 1 \; \forall t \in [0, T-1], \forall (i,j) \in E_{dep} \tag{3.3}$$

$$\sum_{i=1}^{n} \sum_{s=t-p_i+1}^{t} x_i^s \, \vec{b}_i \leq \vec{B} \; \forall t \in [0, T-1] \tag{3.4}$$

$$x_i^t \geq 0 \; \forall i \in [1, n+1], \forall t \in [0, T-1] \tag{3.5}$$

$$x_i^t \in \mathbb{Z} \; \forall i \in [1, n+1], \forall t \in [0, T-1] \tag{3.6}$$

Equations [3.2] ensure that any operation is scheduled once. The inequalities [3.3] describe the dependence constraints with T inequalities per dependence, as proposed by Christofides *et al.* [CHR 87]. While the original formulation [PRI 69] introduced only one inequality per dependence $\sum_{t=0}^{T-1} t(x_j^t - x_i^t) \geq \theta_i^j \Leftrightarrow \sigma_j - \sigma_i \geq \theta_i^j$, it was reported to be more difficult to solve in practice. The explanation of the dependence inequalities [3.3] is given in Figure 3.1: ensuring the sum of the terms $\sum_{s=t}^{T-1} x_i^s$ and $\sum_{s=0}^{t+\theta_i^j-1} x_j^s$ is not greater than 1 implies $\sigma_i + 1 \leq \sigma_j - \theta_i^j + 1$.

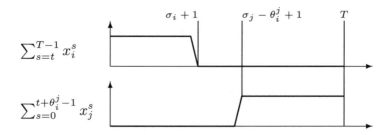

Figure 3.1. *The time-indexed dependence inequalities of Christofides et al. [CHR 87]*

Finally, inequalities [3.4] enforce the cumulative resource constraints for $p_i \geq 1$. The extensions of the RCPSP with time-dependent resource availabilities $\vec{B}(t)$ and resource requirements $\vec{b}_i(t)$ are described in this formulation by generalizing [3.4] into [3.7]:

$$\sum_{i=1}^{n}\sum_{s=0}^{t} x_i^s \, \vec{b}_i(t-s) \quad \leq \vec{B}(t) \; \forall t \in [0, T-1] \tag{3.7}$$

Although fully descriptive and extensible, the main problem with the time-indexed RCPSP formulations is the large size of the resulting integer programs. Indeed, Savelsbergh *et al.* [SAV 98] observed that such formulations could not be solved for problem instances involving more than about 100 jobs (operations), even with the column-generation techniques of Akker *et al.* [AKK 98].

3.3.2. *Time-indexed formulation for the modulo RPISP*

The modern formulation of the modulo RPISP is from Eichenberger *et al.* [EIC 95b, EIC 97]. This formulation takes a λ-decomposed view of the modulo scheduling problem, that is the time horizon is $[0, \lambda - 1]$ and the time-indexed variables represent the row numbers: $\{\tau_i \overset{\text{def}}{=} \sum_{t=0}^{\lambda-1} t x_i^t\}_{1 \leq i \leq n}$. However, the column numbers $\{\phi_i\}_{1 \leq i \leq n}$ are directly used in the formulation. The objective is to minimize the register pressure integer variable P (E_{dep} denotes the set of data dependences):

$$\text{minimize } P : \tag{3.8}$$

$$\sum_{t=0}^{\lambda-1} x_i^t = 1 \forall i \in [1,n] \tag{3.9}$$

$$\sum_{s=t}^{\lambda-1} x_i^s + \sum_{s=0}^{(t+\theta_i^j-1) \bmod \lambda} x_j^s + \phi_i - \phi_j \leq \omega_i^j - \left\lfloor \frac{t+\theta_i^j-1}{\lambda} \right\rfloor$$

$$+1 \forall t \in [0, \lambda-1], \forall (i,j) \in E_{dep} \tag{3.10}$$

$$\sum_{i=1}^{n} \sum_{r=0}^{p_i-1} x_i^{(t-r) \bmod \lambda} \vec{b}_i \leq \vec{B} \forall t \in [0, \lambda-1] \tag{3.11}$$

$$\sum_{s=0}^{t} x_i^s - \sum_{s=0}^{t-1} x_j^s + \phi_j - \phi_i - v_i^t \leq -\omega_i^j \forall t \in [0, \lambda-1], \forall (i,j) \in E_{reg} \tag{3.12}$$

$$\sum_{i=1}^{n} v_i^t - P \leq 0 \forall t \in [0, \lambda-1] \tag{3.13}$$

$$x_i^t \in \{0,1\} \forall i \in [1,n], \forall t \in [0, \lambda-1] \tag{3.14}$$

$$v_i^t \in \mathbb{N} \forall i \in [1,n], \forall t \in [0, \lambda-1] \tag{3.15}$$

$$\phi_i \in \mathbb{N} \forall i \in [1,n] \tag{3.16}$$

Although this formulation was elaborated without apparent knowledge of the time-indexed RCPSP formulation of Pritsker *et al.* [PRI 69], it is quite similar. Comparison with the formulation in section 3.3.1, equations [3.9]–[3.11] extend to modulo scheduling equations [3.2]–[3.4]. Besides the extension of the RCPSP formulation to the λ-decomposed view of modulo scheduling problems, the other major contribution of Eichenberger *et al.* [EIC 95b, EIC 97] is the development of the inequalities [3.12] that compute the contributions v_i^t to the register pressure at date t.

As explained in [EIC 95b], these equations derive from the observation that the function $D_i(t) \overset{\text{def}}{=} \sum_{s=0}^{t} x_i^s$ transitions from 0 to 1 for $t = \tau_i$. Similarly, the function $U_j(t) \overset{\text{def}}{=} \sum_{s=0}^{t-1} x_j^s$ transitions from 0 to 1 for $t = \tau_j + 1$. Assuming that $\tau_i \leq \tau_j$, then $D_i(t) - U_j(t) = 1$ exactly for the dates $t \in [\tau_i, \tau_j]$; else it is 0. Similarly, if $\tau_i > \tau_j$, then $D_i(t) - U_j(t) + 1 = 1$ exactly for the dates $t \in [0, \sigma_j] \cup [\sigma_i, \lambda-1]$; else it is 0. These expressions define the so-called *fractional lifetimes* of a register defined by

O_i and used by O_j. When considering the additional register lifetime created by the column numbers, an *integral lifetime* of either $\phi_j - \phi_i + \omega_i^j$ or $\phi_j - \phi_i + \omega_i^j - 1$ must be accounted for. This yields the inequalities [3.12] that define the v_i^t and the maximum register pressure P is computed by [3.13].

Like the other classic modulo scheduling techniques [LAM 88a, RAU 96, RUT 96b], this time-indexed formulation takes λ as a constant given in the scheduling problem description. Thus, the construction and the resolution of this formulation is only a step in the general modulo scheduling process that searches for the minimum value of λ that allows a feasible modulo schedule.

Instruction Scheduling Before Register Allocation

Since controlling the register pressure during instruction scheduling is a difficult problem, *lifetime-sensitive* modulo schedulers have been proposed [HUF 93a], which aim at minimizing the cumulative register lifetimes. In this chapter, we show that in the case of resource-free modulo scheduling problems, the modulo schedule that minimizes the cumulative register lifetimes is easily computed by solving a network flow problem on the dependence graph suitably augmented with nodes and arcs.

4.1. Instruction scheduling for an ILP processor: case of a VLIW architecture

As a case of interest, this section presents instruction scheduling for the ST200 architecture.

4.1.1. *Minimum cumulative register lifetime modulo scheduling*

The minimization of the cumulative register lifetimes on the sample dependence graph is illustrated in Figure 4.1. This dependence graph has been simplified by removing the memory access operations after converting the uniform dependences into register transfers [CAL 90]. We assume that the target architecture is such that the lifetime of a register starts at the time when the operation that produces it is issued. When this is not the case, the only difference is a constant contribution to the cumulative register lifetimes that does not impact the minimization.

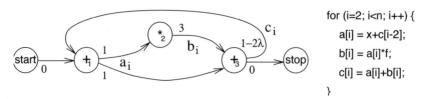

Figure 4.1. *Original dependence graph*

Taking the dependence graph in Figure 4.1, let $\vec{\sigma}$ be the schedule dates of the respective operations $+_1, *_2, +_3$ and let $\vec{l}$ be the lifetimes of the register defined by these operations [DIN 94]. Then we get the following system of inequalities:

$$\left(\begin{array}{c} dependence \\ inequalities \end{array}\right) \begin{cases} \sigma_2 - \sigma_1 \geq 1 \\ \sigma_3 - \sigma_1 \geq 1 \\ \sigma_3 - \sigma_2 \geq 3 \\ \sigma_1 - \sigma_3 \geq 1 - 2\lambda \end{cases} \qquad \left(\begin{array}{c} lifetime \\ inequalities \end{array}\right) \begin{cases} l_1 \geq \sigma_2 - \sigma_1 \\ l_1 \geq \sigma_3 - \sigma_1 \\ l_2 \geq \sigma_3 - \sigma_2 \\ l_3 \geq \sigma_1 + 2\lambda - \sigma_3 \end{cases}$$

This illustrates the equations we introduced in [DIN 94] and the minimum cumulative register lifetimes (MCRL) problem is defined with the objective to minimize $\sum_i l_i$. In [DIN 96], we introduced a transformation of the MCRL problem that makes it solvable in a simple and efficient way. The first step is to introduce the variables $\vec{r}$ such that $r_i \stackrel{\text{def}}{=} l_i + \sigma_i$ and to eliminate the variables $\vec{l}$:

$$\left(\begin{array}{c} dependence \\ inequalities \end{array}\right) \begin{cases} \sigma_2 - \sigma_1 \geq 1 \\ \sigma_3 - \sigma_1 \geq 1 \\ \sigma_3 - \sigma_2 \geq 3 \\ \sigma_1 - \sigma_3 \geq 1 - 2\lambda \end{cases} \qquad \left(\begin{array}{c} reduced \\ lifetime \\ inequalities \end{array}\right) \begin{cases} r_1 - \sigma_2 \geq 0 \\ r_1 - \sigma_3 \geq 0 \\ r_2 - \sigma_3 \geq 0 \\ r_3 - \sigma_1 \geq 2\lambda \end{cases}$$

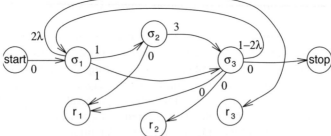

Figure 4.2. *Augmented dependence graph*

This new system of inequalities defines an *augmented dependence graph*, which is derived from the dependence graph as follows: any register lifetime *producer node* is paired with a *lifetime node* and for any lifetime arc between the producer node and a *consumer node*, we add an arc from the consumer node to the lifetime node. This transformation is illustrated in Figure 4.2 for the dependence graph in Figure 4.1. Since $l_i + \sigma_i \stackrel{\text{def}}{=} r_i \ \forall i$, the objective to minimize $\sum_i l_i$ becomes $\sum_i r_i - \sigma_i$.

It is interesting to compare these equations to those of the minimum buffers problem, as defined by Ning and Gao [NIN 93b]. In the minimum buffers problem, the so-called buffer variables $\vec{b}$ are defined and the objective is to minimize $\sum_i b_i$:

$$
\left(\begin{array}{c} dependence \\ inequalities \end{array} \right) \begin{cases} \sigma_2 - \sigma_1 \geq 1 \\ \sigma_3 - \sigma_1 \geq 1 \\ \sigma_3 - \sigma_2 \geq 3 \\ \sigma_1 - \sigma_3 \geq 1 - 2\lambda \end{cases} \qquad \left(\begin{array}{c} buffer \\ inequalities \end{array} \right) \begin{cases} \lambda b_1 \geq \sigma_2 - \sigma_1 \\ \lambda b_1 \geq \sigma_3 - \sigma_1 \\ \lambda b_2 \geq \sigma_3 - \sigma_2 \\ \lambda b_3 \geq \sigma_1 - \sigma_3 + 3\lambda - 1 \end{cases}
$$

Obviously, the dependence equations are the same, while the buffer and the lifetime equations are different, although related. To make the minimum buffers problem easier to solve, Ning and Gao [NIN 93b] make the change of variables $\lambda b_i \stackrel{\text{def}}{=} b_i'$; so the left-hand side of the buffer inequalities become identical to the left-hand side of the lifetime inequalities.

The MCRL problem is efficiently solved on the augmented dependence graph [DIN 96]. To see how, let us first assume that all the arcs of the original dependence graph carry a lifetime. Then, if U denotes the arc-node incidence matrix of the original dependence graph, the primal-dual relationships of linear programming can be written as:

$$
\left. \begin{array}{c} \min \left(\begin{array}{c} -\vec{1} \\ \vec{1} \end{array} \right)^{\mathrm{T}} \left(\begin{array}{c} \vec{\sigma} \\ \vec{r} \end{array} \right) \\ \left[\begin{array}{cc} U & 0 \\ 0 & -U \end{array} \right] \left(\begin{array}{c} \vec{\sigma} \\ \vec{r} \end{array} \right) \geq \left(\begin{array}{c} \vec{\theta} - \lambda\vec{\omega} \\ \lambda\vec{\omega} \end{array} \right) \\ \vec{\sigma}, \ \vec{r} \ \text{unrestricted in sign} \end{array} \right\} \rightleftharpoons \left\{ \begin{array}{c} \max \left(\begin{array}{c} \vec{\theta} - \lambda\vec{\omega} \\ \lambda\vec{\omega} \end{array} \right)^{\mathrm{T}} \left(\begin{array}{c} \vec{x} \\ \vec{y} \end{array} \right) \\ \left[\begin{array}{cc} U^{\mathrm{T}} & 0 \\ 0 & -U^{\mathrm{T}} \end{array} \right] \left(\begin{array}{c} \vec{x} \\ \vec{y} \end{array} \right) = \left(\begin{array}{c} -\vec{1} \\ \vec{1} \end{array} \right) \\ \vec{x} \geq \vec{0}, \ \vec{y} \geq \vec{0} \end{array} \right.
$$

Here, the linear program associated with the MCRL problem appears on the left and its dual on the right. Negating both sides of the equal sign in the dual linear program yields a maximum-cost network flow problem on the dependence graph augmented with the lifetime nodes, where each producer node supplies unit flow and where each lifetime node demands unit flow. In practice, only the nodes of the dependence graph that define a register are paired with a lifetime node.

Beyond the MCRL problems, the generalization of a resource-free scheduling problem, which is solved as a single-source longest path over the dependence graph, into a maximum cost network flow problem over the augmented dependence graph allows the introduction of "soft constraints" in instruction scheduling problems. In the STMicroelectronics ST100 linear assembly optimizer (LAO) code generator [DIN 00], increasing some of the flow requirements addressed the non-standard instruction scheduling features of the ST120 decoupled implementation. The augmented dependence graph is also used for the time-indexed integer linear programming formulations of the register pressure instruction scheduling problems (see section 4.1.6).

4.1.2. *Resource modeling in instruction scheduling problems*

The resource constraints for instruction scheduling on a very long instruction word (VLIW) processor are described in a micro-architecture manual by a set of admissible *bundles*, that is, combinations of operations that may issue without resource conflicts[1]. More precisely, a bundle is a sequence of resource classes, where each resource class is an abstraction for the resource requirements of the operations in the instruction scheduling problem. Going from the bundle specifications of a processor to an accurate model with cumulative resources is not guaranteed to succeed. Techniques to build the cumulative resource model, given a processor description, are described in [RAJ 00, RAJ 01]. Their idea is to introduce artificial resources where required, based on the identification of critical sets of resource classes.

Even with the introduction of artificial resources like ODD for the ST220 in Figure 2.1, a processor cumulative resource model can still be an approximation because the cumulative constraints can only represent convex regions of resource classes. To illustrate this point, consider a processor with two resource classes A, B and an issue width of 4. Then, no cumulative resource constraints may allow the combinations $\{A, A, A, B\}$ and $\{A, B, B, B\}$ while disallowing the combinations $\{A, A, B, B\}$. Indeed, this yields the contradiction $3a + b \leq c \wedge a + 3b \leq c \wedge 2a + 2b > c$, assuming that a and b are the resource requirements of A and B and that c is the resource availability.

Another limitation of the cumulative resources model is that all the resources involved in the execution of an operation O_i are assumed busy for its whole processing time p_i. Thus, when two operations O_i and O_j need to share an exclusive resource, either $\sigma_i + p_i \leq \sigma_j$ or $\sigma_j + p_j \leq \sigma_i$. To increase the precision of resource modeling, we need to express the fact that given an exclusive resource, either $\sigma_i + \rho_i^j$ or $\sigma_j + \rho_j^i \leq \sigma_i$, where ρ_i^j and ρ_j^i both depend on O_i and O_j. The interpretation of ρ_i^j is the minimum number of cycles between σ_i and σ_j that ensures there are no resource conflicts between O_i and O_j, assuming O_i is scheduled before O_j. Such resource constraints can be modeled with *regular reservation tables*.

---

1 Although this term seems to imply EPIC architectures, J. Fisher in particular uses it for VLIW architectures.

	0	1	2	3	4
bus1					
bus2	1				
abox		1			
cond			1	1	1
bbox					
ebox					
imul					
iwrt					
fbox					
fdiv					
fwrt					

	0	1	2
bus1			
bus2	1		
abox	1		
cond	1	1	1
bbox			
ebox			
imul			
iwrt			
fbox			
fdiv			
fwrt			

bus1	0
bus2	1
abox	1
cond	3
bbox	0
ebox	0
imul	0
iwrt	0
fbox	0
fdiv	0
fwrt	0

Figure 4.3. *A reservation table, a regular reservation table and a reservation vector*

A *regular reservation table* is the traditional Boolean pipeline reservation table of an operation [KOG 81, RAU 96], with the added restrictions that the ones in each row start at column zero and are all adjacent. In the case of exclusive resources, the regular reservation tables are also equivalent to *reservation vectors*. Figure 4.3 illustrates the representation of conditional store operation of the DEC Alpha 21064 using a reservation table, a regular reservation table and a reservation vector. The regular reservation tables are accurate enough to cover many pipelined processors. For example, when describing the DEC Alpha 21064 processor, we found [DIN 95] that the regular reservation tables were slightly inaccurate only for the integer multiplications and the floating-point divisions.

A main advantage of regular reservation tables is that expressing the modulo resource constraints yields inequalities that are similar to the dependence constraints. Let us assume a resource-feasible modulo scheduling problem at period λ and two operations O_i and O_j that conflict on an exclusive resource. Then, $1 \leq \rho_i^j, \rho_j^i \leq \lambda$ and the dates when operation O_i uses the exclusive resource belong to $\Upsilon_i^j(\lambda) \stackrel{\text{def}}{=} \cup_{k \in \mathbb{Z}}[\sigma_i + k\lambda, \sigma_i + k\lambda + \rho_i^j - 1]$. In the modulo scheduling problem, O_i and O_j do not conflict iff $\Upsilon_i^j(\lambda) \cap \Upsilon_j^i(\lambda) = \emptyset$, that is:

$$\forall k, k' \in \mathbb{Z}, \forall m \in [0, \rho_i^j - 1], \forall m' \in [0, \rho_j^i - 1] : \sigma_i + k\lambda + m \neq \sigma_j + k'\lambda + m'$$

$$\Longrightarrow \forall m \in [0, \rho_i^j - 1], \forall m' \in [0, \rho_j^i - 1] : (\sigma_i - \sigma_j) \bmod \lambda \neq (m' - m) \bmod \lambda$$

$$\Longrightarrow \max_{m' \in [0, \rho_j^i - 1]} m' < (\sigma_i - \sigma_j) \bmod \lambda < \min_{m \in [0, \rho_i^j - 1]} (\lambda - m)$$

$$\Longrightarrow \rho_j^i - 1 < \sigma_i - \sigma_j - \lfloor \frac{\sigma_i - \sigma_j}{\lambda} \rfloor \lambda < \lambda - \rho_i^j + 1$$

$$\Longrightarrow \sigma_i - \sigma_j \geq \rho_j^i + k_i^j \lambda \wedge \sigma_j - \sigma_i \geq \rho_i^j - (k_i^j + 1)\lambda \quad \text{with} \quad k_i^j \stackrel{\text{def}}{=} \lfloor \frac{\sigma_i - \sigma_j}{\lambda} \rfloor$$

This result is similar to inequalities [2.2] given by Feautrier [FEA 94] for the exclusive constraints of D-periodic scheduling, with the refinement that we express the value of k_i^j given σ_i and σ_j.

4.1.3. *The modulo insertion scheduling theorems*

Insertion scheduling [DIN 95] is a modulo scheduling heuristic that builds a series of partial modulo schedules by starting from a resource-free modulo schedule and by adding dependences or increasing λ to resolve the modulo resource conflicts until a complete modulo schedule is obtained. A *partial modulo schedule* is a modulo schedule where all the dependences are satisfied, while some of the resource conflicts are ignored. Insertion scheduling relies on conditions for transforming a partial modulo schedule $\{\sigma_i\}_{1 \leq i \leq n}$ at period λ into another partial modulo schedule $\{\sigma_i'\}_{1 \leq i \leq n}$ at period λ'. To present these conditions, we first define $\{\phi_i, \tau_i, \phi_i', \tau_i', \delta_i\}_{1 \leq i \leq n}$ such that:

$$\forall i \in [0, n+1] : \begin{cases} \sigma_i = \phi_i \lambda + \tau_i \wedge 0 \leq \tau_i < \lambda \\ \sigma_i' = \phi_i' \lambda' + \tau_i' \wedge 0 \leq \tau_i' < \lambda' \\ \delta_i = \tau_i' - \tau_i \end{cases} \quad [4.1]$$

We are interested in modulo schedule transformations where $\forall i \in [1, n] : \phi_i' = \phi_i$, $\tau_i' = \tau_i + \delta_i$ and $\delta_i \leq \Delta$ with $\Delta \overset{\text{def}}{=} \lambda' - \lambda$. Let $O_i \leadsto O_j$ denote the fact that O_i precedes O_j in the transitive closure of the loop-independent dependences ($\omega_i^j = 0$) of the dependence graph[2]. The following result states the conditions that must be met by the δ_i in order to preserve all the dependence constraints:

THEOREM 4.1.– Let $\{\sigma_i\}_{1 \leq i \leq n}$ be a dependence-feasible modulo schedule of a modulo scheduling problem P at period λ. Let $\{\sigma_i'\}_{1 \leq i \leq n}$ be n integers such that:

$$\forall i, j \in [0, n+1] : \begin{cases} \phi_i = \phi_i' \\ 0 \leq \delta_i \leq \Delta \\ \tau_i < \tau_j \implies \delta_i \leq \delta_j \\ \tau_i = \tau_j \wedge \phi_i > \phi_j \implies \delta_i \leq \delta_j \\ \tau_i = \tau_j \wedge \phi_i = \phi_j \wedge O_i \leadsto O_j \implies \delta_i \leq \delta_j \end{cases} \quad [4.2]$$

Then $\{\sigma_i'\}_{1 \leq i \leq n}$ is a dependence-feasible modulo schedule of P at period $\lambda + \Delta$.

PROOF.– Let $O_i \overset{\theta_i^j, \omega_i^j}{\longrightarrow} O_j$ be a dependence of P. From the definition of a dependence constraint, $\sigma_j - \sigma_i \geq \theta_i^j - \omega_i^j \lambda$, or equivalently $\phi_j \lambda + \tau_j - \phi_i \lambda - \tau_i \geq \theta_i^j - \omega_i^j \lambda$.

---

2 This relation can be safely approximated by taking the lexical order of the operations in the program text.

Given the hypothesis [4.2], let us show this dependence holds for $\{\sigma_i'\}_{1\le i\le n}$, that is, $\phi_j\lambda' + \tau_j' - \phi_i\lambda' - \tau_i' \ge \theta_i^j - \omega_i^j\lambda'$.

Dividing the dependence inequality by λ and taking the floor yields $\phi_j - \phi_i + \lfloor\frac{\tau_j-\tau_i}{\lambda}\rfloor \ge -\omega_i^j$, since all θ_i^j values are non-negative. We have $0 \le \tau_i < \lambda$, $0 \le \tau_j < \lambda$; hence, $0 \le |\tau_j - \tau_i| < \lambda$ and the value of $\lfloor\frac{\tau_j-\tau_i}{\lambda}\rfloor$ is -1 or 0. Therefore, $\phi_j - \phi_i \ge -\omega_i^j$ and we consider its subcases:

$\phi_j - \phi_i = -\omega_i^j$: Let us show that $\tau_j' - \tau_i' \ge \theta_i^j$.

Since $\theta_i^j \ge 0$, we have $\tau_j \ge \tau_i$. Several subcases need to be distinguished:

$\tau_i < \tau_j$: From [4.2], we have $\delta_j \ge \delta_i \Leftrightarrow \tau_j' - \tau_j \ge \tau_i' - \tau_i \Leftrightarrow \tau_j' - \tau_i' \ge \tau_j - \tau_i \ge \theta_i^j$.

$\tau_i = \tau_j \wedge \phi_i \ne \phi_j$: Either $\phi_i > \phi_j$ or $\phi_i < \phi_j$. The latter is impossible, for $\omega_i^j = \phi_i - \phi_j$ and since all ω_i^j are non-negative. From [4.2], $\tau_i = \tau_j \wedge \phi_i > \phi_j$ yields $\delta_j \ge \delta_i$; therefore, the conclusion is the same as above.

$\tau_i = \tau_j \wedge \phi_i = \phi_j$: Since $\omega_i^j = \phi_i - \phi_j = 0$, there are no dependence constraints unless $O_i \rightsquigarrow O_j$. In this case, taking $\delta_j \ge \delta_i$ works like in the cases above.

$\phi_j - \phi_i > -\omega_i^j$: Let us show that $(\phi_j - \phi_i + \omega_i^j)\lambda' + \tau_j' - \tau_i' - \theta_i^j \ge 0$.

We have $\phi_j - \phi_i + \omega_i^j \ge 1$, so $(\phi_j - \phi_i + \omega_i^j)\lambda' \ge (\phi_j - \phi_i + \omega_i^j)\lambda + \Delta$. From [4.2], we also have $\tau_i \le \tau_i' \le \tau_i + \Delta$ and $\tau_j \le \tau_j' \le \tau_j + \Delta$, so $\tau_j' - \tau_i' \ge \tau_j - \tau_i - \Delta$. Hence, $(\phi_j - \phi_i + \omega_i^j)\lambda' + \tau_j' - \tau_i' - \theta_i^j \ge (\phi_j - \phi_i + \omega_i^j)\lambda + \Delta + \tau_j - \tau_i - \Delta - \theta_i^j = (\phi_j - \phi_i + \omega_i^j)\lambda + \tau_j - \tau_i - \theta_i^j \ge 0$. $\square$

COROLLARY 4.1.– In a dependence-feasible modulo schedule $\{\sigma_i\}_{1\le i\le n}$, for any dependence $O_i \xrightarrow{\theta_i^j, \omega_i^j} O_j$, then:

$$\phi_i = \phi_j + \omega_i^j \implies \tau_i + \theta_i^j \le \tau_j \quad \text{and} \quad \tau_i + \theta_i^j > \tau_j \implies \phi_i < \phi_j + \omega_i^j$$

A result similar to theorem 4.1 holds for the modulo resource constraints of a modulo schedule, assuming these constraints only involve regular reservation tables and exclusive resources.

THEOREM 4.2.– Let $\{\sigma_i\}_{1\le i\le n}$ be schedule dates satisfying the modulo resource constraints at period λ, assuming regular reservation tables and exclusive resources. Let $\{\sigma_i'\}_{1\le i\le n}$ be such that:

$$\forall i, j \in [1, n] : \begin{cases} \phi_i = \phi_i' \\ 0 \le \delta_i \le \Delta \\ \tau_i < \tau_j \implies \delta_i \le \delta_j \end{cases} \qquad [4.3]$$

Then $\{\sigma_i'\}_{1\leq i \leq n}$ also satisfies the modulo resource constraints at period $\lambda + \Delta$.

PROOF.– With the regular reservation tables, the modulo resource constraints at λ for the schedule dates σ_i, σ_j of two operations O_i, O_j that need the exclusive resource are equivalent to (see section 4.1.2):

$$\sigma_i - \sigma_j \geq \rho_j^i + k_i^j \lambda \wedge \sigma_j - \sigma_i \geq \rho_i^j - (k_i^j + 1)\lambda \quad \text{with} \quad k_i^j \stackrel{\text{def}}{=} \lfloor \frac{\sigma_i - \sigma_j}{\lambda} \rfloor \qquad [4.4]$$

These constraints look exactly like ordinary dependence constraints, save the fact that the ω values are now of arbitrary sign. Since the sign of the ω values is only used in the proof of theorem 4.1 for the cases where $\tau_i = \tau_j$, which need not be considered here because they imply no resource conflicts between σ_i and σ_j, we deduce from the proof of theorem 4.1 that $\{\sigma_k'\}_{1\leq k \leq n}$ satisfies the modulo resource constraints at period λ'. □

THEOREM 4.3.– Let $\{\sigma_i\}_{1\leq i \leq n}$ be schedule dates satisfying the modulo resource constraints at period λ, assuming cumulative resources. Then, under the conditions [4.3], $\{\sigma_i'\}_{1\leq i \leq n}$ also satisfies the modulo resource constraints at period $\lambda' \stackrel{\text{def}}{=} \lambda + \Delta$.

PROOF.– In the proof of theorem 4.2, whenever [4.4] holds for $\{\sigma_i\}_{1\leq i \leq n}$, it holds under the conditions [4.3] for $\{\sigma_i'\}_{1\leq i \leq n}$, for any assumed values of ρ_i^j and ρ_j^i. This ensures that the simultaneous use of the cumulative resources does not increase in $\{\sigma_i'\}_{1\leq i \leq n}$. □

By theorem 4.1 and corollary 4.3, any transformation of a partial modulo schedule $\{\sigma_i\}_{1\leq i \leq n}$ at period λ into $\{\sigma_i'\}_{1\leq i \leq n}$ at period $\lambda' \stackrel{\text{def}}{=} \lambda + \Delta$, under the conditions [4.2], yields a partial modulo schedule.

4.1.4. Insertion scheduling in a backend compiler

Insertion scheduling [DIN 95] is a modulo instruction scheduling heuristic that *issues* the operations in a given priority order, where the issuing of an operation is materialized in the dependence graphs by adding dependence arcs to constrain the feasible schedule dates of this operation to be exactly its issue date. In addition, insertion scheduling applies the insertion theorems of section 4.1.3 to resolve the resource conflicts between the previously issued operations and the current operation to issue by increasing the period λ to make room for this operation. Under its simplest form, insertion scheduling relies on single-source longest path computations like most scheduling heuristics.

The ST200 LAO instruction scheduler implementation, however, uses MCRL minimization to achieve lifetime-sensitive instruction scheduling (section 4.1.1). To solve the MCRL problems, this implementation relies on a network simplex algorithm to optimize the maximum cost flow problems [AHU 93] and on a network simplex longest path algorithm to find the initial solutions [GOL 91]. Besides being efficient in practice [DIN 96], the network simplex algorithms maintain the explicit values of the primal (edge flows) and the dual (node potentials) variables. The latter are precisely the schedule dates of the operations. The ST200 LAO implementation of insertion scheduling is as follows:

Step 0 The resource-free MCRL modulo scheduling problem, called P_0, is built and solved. This problem is represented MCRL by the forward dependence graph, the backward dependence graph and the MCRL augmented graph. We solve P_0 with a network simplex longest path algorithm, followed by a dual network simplex algorithm. The network simplex longest path algorithm starts with λ the period set to the lower bound λ_{res} and solves the optimum cost to time ratio problem by increasing the period to λ_{rec} if necessary for P_0 feasibility.

Step j This step transforms the modulo scheduling problem P_{j-1} into P_j. Let $\{S_{i_k}^{j-1}\}$ denote the issue dates assigned to the operations $\{O_{i_k}\}_{1\leq k\leq j-1}$ in the previous steps, that is $P_{j-1} \stackrel{def}{=} P_0 \wedge \{\sigma_{i_1} = S_{i_1}^{j-1}\} \wedge \ldots \wedge \{\sigma_{i_{j-1}} = S_{i_{j-1}}^{j-1}\}$. The not yet issued operations are ranked in priority order and the operation with the highest priority, denoted by O_{i_j}, is issued as follows:

1) Run a primal network simplex algorithm on three dependence graphs to compute the early start date e_{i_j}, the late start date l_{i_j} and the MCRL date m_{i_j}, of O_{i_j} in P_{j-1}. Then, compute $a_{i_j} \stackrel{def}{=} \min(l_{i_j} - m_{i_j}, \lambda - 1)$ and $b_{i_j} \stackrel{def}{=} \min(m_{i_j} - e_{i_j}, \lambda - 1 - a_{i_j})$. The possible issue dates are scanned first in $[m_{i_j}, m_{i_j} + a_{i_j}]$ in increasing order and second in $[m_{i_j} - b_{i_j}, m_{i_j} - 1]$ in decreasing order. This ensures that no more than λ feasible dates are scanned and the issue dates next to the MCRL date m_{i_j} are scanned first.

2) Select $S_{i_j}^{j-1}$ as the first scanned date with the lowest modulo resource conflicts between O_{i_j} and $\{O_{i_k}\}_{1\leq k\leq j-1}$. This is measured by the minimum number of cycles Δ; the period λ_{j-1} needs to increase to remove the modulo resource conflicts at period $\lambda_j \stackrel{def}{=} \lambda_{j-1} + \Delta$. If there are no conflicts between O_{i_j} and $\{O_{i_k}\}_{1\leq k\leq j-1}$ for $\sigma_{i_j} = S_{i_j}^{j-1}$, then $\Delta = 0$.

3) Let $\{S_{i_k}^{j-1}\}_{1\leq k\leq j}$ be the issue dates in P_{j-1}, and $\{S_{i_k}^{j}\}_{1\leq k\leq j}$ be the issue dates in P_j. The issue dates in P_j are computed from the issue dates in P_{j-1} by applying theorem 4.1, with $\{\delta_{i_k}\}_{1\leq k\leq j}$ chosen to eliminate the modulo resource constraints between O_{i_j} and $\{O_{i_k}\}_{1\leq k\leq j-1}$. See [DIN 95] for the details of the δ_{i_k} computations.

4) Build the modulo scheduling problem $P_j \stackrel{def}{=} P_0 \wedge \{\sigma_{i_1} = S_{i_1}^{j}\} \wedge \ldots \wedge \{\sigma_{i_j} = S_{i_j}^{j}\}$ from $P_{j-1} \wedge \{\sigma_{i_j} = S_{i_j}^{j-1}\}$ and the $\{\delta_{i_k}\}_{1\leq k\leq j}$ and update the modulo resource table.

At the end of step j, all the dependence constraints are satisfied, as are the modulo resource constraints for the operations $\{O_{i_k}\}_{1 \leq k \leq j}$. At the end of step n, a modulo schedule is available.

In the ST200 LAO instruction scheduler, insertion scheduling operates both in prepass and postpass instruction scheduling and the instruction scheduling regions are super blocks. During prepass scheduling, the lifetime-sensitive scheduling is enabled and the inner loops are either modulo scheduled or loop scheduled. In postpass scheduling, the lifetime-sensitive scheduling is disabled and all inner loops, including the software pipelines created during prepass scheduling, are loop scheduled. Loop scheduling is a restricted form of modulo scheduling, where the period is exactly the same as the local schedule length. This is achieved by adding a dependence $O_{n+1} \rightarrow O_0$ with latency 1 and distance 1 to the P_0 problem. As a result, loop scheduling accounts for the effects of the loop-carried dependences, while preventing code motion between the loop iterations.

4.1.5. *Example of an industrial production compiler from STMicroelectronics*

The STMicroelectronics ST200 production compiler st200cc is based on the GCC compiler frontend components, the Open64 compiler technology [OSG 13], the ST200 LAO global instruction scheduler adapted from the ST100 LAO code generator [DIN 00], an instruction cache optimizer [BID 04] and the GNU backend tools. The Open64 compiler has been retargeted from the Intel IA64 to the STMicroelectronics ST200 architecture, except for the instruction predication, the global code motion (GCM) instruction scheduler and the software pipeliner (SWP). Indeed, these components appeared to be too dependent on the IA64 architecture predicated execution model and on its support of modulo scheduling through rotating register files.

In the st200cc compiler, the Open64 GCM and SWP components are replaced by the ST200 LAO instruction scheduler, which is enabled at optimization level -O3. At compiler optimization level -O2 and below, only the Open64 basic block instruction scheduler is active. The ST200 LAO instruction scheduling and software pipelining relies on the following techniques:

– A transactional interface between the Open64 code generator intermediate representation (CGIR) and the LAO intermediate representation (LIR).

– Parsing of the control flow graph into a loop nesting forest and super block formation. The super block formation does not include tail duplication [HAN 93], as this is performed in the Open64 code generator by the ST200-specific instruction predication.

– Prior to prepass and postpass scheduling, the algorithm of Leung *et al.* [LEU 01] is iterated over each resource of the ST220 model (Figure 2.1), starting with the more heavily used resources. This iteration starts with the period set to the minimum value λ_{res} such that the renewable resources $\vec{B}$ are not oversubscribed; then, the period is increased until the relaxation is feasible.

– Prepass instruction scheduling based on insertion scheduling, which performs lifetime-sensitive superblock scheduling, loop scheduling and modulo scheduling. The scheduling order is the lower MCRL dates first and the scheduling priorities are the modified deadlines computed by the scheduling algorithm of Leung *et al.* [LEU 01].

– Postpass instruction scheduling based on insertion scheduling, which performs block scheduling and loop scheduling. The scheduling order is the lower consistent release dates first and the scheduling priorities are the modified deadlines computed by the scheduling algorithm of Leung *et al.* [LEU 01].

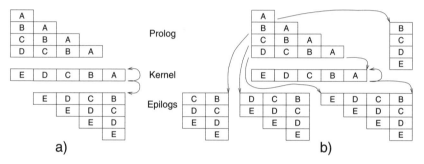

Figure 4.4. *Counted loop software pipeline construction with and without preconditioning*

Once a modulo schedule is available, it must be transformed into a software pipeline. In Figure 4.4, we illustrate the classic software pipeline construction for the local schedule of a counted loop that spans five stages named A, B, C, D and E. In the basic case (a), loop preconditioning [RAU 92b] is required to ensure that the software pipeline will execute enough iterations to run the prologue and the epilogues. Without preconditioning, case (b) software pipeline construction is required. In the embedded computing setting, these classic software pipeline construction schemes are not effective because they only apply to counted loops and involve significant code size expansion.

For the ST200 modulo scheduling, we construct all software pipelines like while-loops, as illustrated in Figure 4.5(a). This while-loop construction scheme speculatively starts executing the next iterations before knowing if the current iteration is the last iteration and relies on the dismissible loads of the ST200 architecture. Another refinement implemented in the ST200 LAO is induction variable relaxation [DIN 97a] and the restriction of modulo expansion to variables that are not live on loop exit. As a result, epilogues are unnecessary for virtually all the software pipelines.

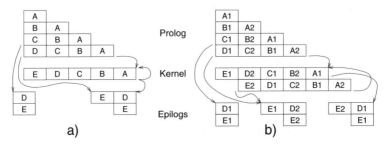

Figure 4.5. *While-loop software pipeline construction without and with modulo expansion*

Modulo expansion is a technique introduced by Lam [LAM 88a], where the non-RAW register dependences on variables are omitted from the dependence graph. This exposes more parallelism to the modulo scheduler, but when the software pipeline is constructed, each such variable may require more than one register for allocation. Modulo renaming is supported by architectures like the IA64 through *rotating registers* [RAU 92a]. On architectures without rotating registers like the ST200, modulo expansion is implemented by *kernel unrolling* [LAM 88a, DIN 97a, LLO 02], as illustrated in case (b) of Figure 4.5.

To compare the effects of the instruction scheduling techniques available for the ST220 processor, we use the benchmark suite collected by the Hewlett Packard (HP) Laboratories for embedded computing and we also include the performances of the HP/Lx multiflow-based compiler. This compiler implements trace scheduling [LOW 93] and targets the ST200 architecture including the ST220 processor. In Figure 4.6, we compare the performance in cycles and without the cache miss effects of the multiflow-based compiler at optimization level -O3 (MF), the st200cc compiler at -O3 with software pipelining disabled (O3-nopipe), and the st200cc at -O3 that enables software pipelining by default (O3). All the performances in Figure 4.6 are normalized by those of st200cc compiler at -O3 with the ST200 LAO disabled, where basic block scheduling is done in prepass and postpass by the Open64.

When enabling the ST200 LAO block scheduling and loop scheduling on super blocks, the geometric mean improvement is 5.5%, compared to the reference. When enabling the ST200 LAO software pipelining, the geometric mean improvement is 9.5%. This progression illustrates the benefits of the LAO super block scheduling over the Open64 basic block scheduling and the significant performance benefits brought by software pipelining. Due to the while-loop software pipeline construction scheme and due to the elimination of software pipeline epilogues, there are no significant performance degradations related to software pipelining. This explains why software pipelining is activated by default in the st200cc compiler at optimization level -O3.

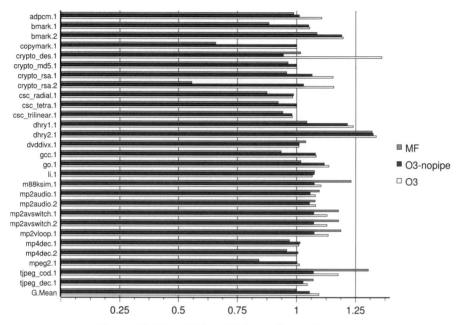

Figure 4.6. *The* st200cc *R3.2 compiler performances on the HP benchmarks*

With the ST200 LAO disabled, the performances of the st200cc compiler at -O3 and those of the multiflow-based compiler at -O3 are equivalent, as the geometric mean entry for MF is almost 1 (last bars in Figure 4.6). However, on benchmarks like the tjpeg_coder, the multiflow-based compiler significantly outperforms the st200cc compiler, even with software pipelining. Investigations revealed that virtually all such st200cc performance problems are triggered by high register pressure on large basic blocks, where the prepass scheduling/register allocation/postpass scheduling approach of Open64 is unable to compete with the integrated register allocation and instruction scheduling of the multiflow-based compiler [LOW 93].

When accounting for the cache miss effects, the R3.2 st200cc compiler at optimization level -O3 outperforms the multiflow-based compiler at optimization level -O3 by 15% in cycles in geometric mean on the HP benchmarks, with the best case having an 18% higher performance and the worst case having a 5% lower performance. This is explained by the 12% geometric mean code size reduction of the st200cc compiler and its effective instruction cache optimizations [BID 04].

4.1.6. *Time-indexed formulation of the modulo RCISP*

Based on the time-indexed formulation of the resource-constrained project scheduling problem (RCPSP) of Pritsker *et al.* [PRI 69] in section 3.3.1, the register-pressure equations of the modulo RPISP formulation of Eichenberger *et al.* [EIC 95b, EIC 97] in section 4.4.2 and the definition of the augmented dependence graph in section 4.1.1, we introduce a new time-indexed formulation for the modulo RCISP. This formulation is implemented in the ST200 LAO instruction scheduler as an experimental feature, as it requires linking with the commercial CPLEX package in order to solve the resulting integer linear programs.

The first extension of the RCPSP formulation needed for the modulo RCISP formulation is to account for the modulo resource constraints. In a modulo schedule, an operation O_i requires $\vec{b}_i$ resources for the dates in $[\sigma_i + k\lambda, \sigma_i + k\lambda + p_i - 1]$, $\forall k \in \mathbb{Z}$ (section 2.2.2). The resource requirement function $\vec{b}_i(t)$ of O_i is written $\sum_{k \in \mathbb{Z}} (t \in [k\lambda, k\lambda + p_i - 1]) \vec{b}_i$, so the inequalities [4.19] become:

$$\sum_{i=1}^{n} \sum_{k \in \mathbb{Z}} \sum_{s=0}^{t} x_i^s (t - s \in [k\lambda, k\lambda + p_i - 1]) \vec{b}_i \leq \vec{B} \quad \forall t \in [0, T-1]$$

$$\implies \sum_{i=1}^{n} \sum_{k \in \mathbb{Z}} \sum_{s=0}^{t} x_i^s (s \in [t + k\lambda - p_i + 1, t + k\lambda]) \vec{b}_i \leq \vec{B} \quad \forall t \in [0, T-1]$$

$$\implies \sum_{i=1}^{n} \sum_{k \in \mathbb{Z}} \sum_{s=t+k\lambda-p_i+1}^{t+k\lambda} x_i^s \vec{b}_i \leq \vec{B} \quad \forall t \in [0, T-1]$$

$$\implies \sum_{i=1}^{n} \sum_{k=0}^{\lfloor \frac{T-1}{\lambda} \rfloor} \sum_{s=t+k\lambda-p_i+1}^{t+k\lambda} x_i^s \vec{b}_i \leq \vec{B} \quad \forall t \in [0, \lambda - 1]$$

For the register pressure constraints, we consider the dependence graph augmented with the register lifetime nodes as defined in section 4.1.1. Let E_{life} denote the (i, j) pairs such that O_i is a producer node and O_j is its lifetime node. Let us also take advantage of the fact that most processors (in particular in the ST200 series) enable us to use and redefine a register at the same cycle and have a non-zero minimum register read after write (RAW) dependence latency. In such cases, it is correct to assume that a register lifetime extends from its definition date to its last use date minus one.

In the case $\omega_i^j = 0$, the contribution v_i^t to the register pressure at date t of the register produced by O_i and consumed by O_j is exactly the difference of two terms as illustrated in Figure 4.7. When $\omega_i^j > 0$, the contribution to register pressure extends from date σ_i to date $\sigma_j + \lambda \omega_i^j$. This yields the definition of v_i^t by equalities [4.5]. In

[4.6], we express the constraint that the register pressure at any date in the modulo schedule is not greater than the register availability R.

$$\sum_{s=0}^{t} x_i^s - \sum_{s=0}^{t} x_j^{s-\lambda\omega_i^j} = v_i^t \quad \forall t \in [0, T-1], \forall(i,j) \in E_{life} \qquad [4.5]$$

$$\sum_{i=1}^{n} \sum_{k=0}^{\lfloor \frac{T-1}{\lambda} \rfloor} v_i^{t+k\lambda} \leq R \quad \forall t \in [0, \lambda - 1] \qquad [4.6]$$

$$v_i^t \in \{0,1\} \; \forall i \in [1,n], \forall t \in [0, T-1] \qquad [4.7]$$

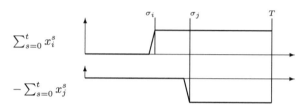

Figure 4.7. *Definition of the contributions v_i^t to the register pressure*

To complete the modulo RCISP formulation, we minimize the schedule date of operation O_{n+1}, adapt the dependence inequalities [3.3] to the dependence latencies of $\theta_i^j - \lambda\omega_i^j$ and eliminate the register pressure variables v_i^t from [4.6], due to the equalities [4.5]. This yields:

$$\text{minimize} \sum_{t=1}^{T-1} t \, x_{n+1}^t \quad : \qquad [4.8]$$

$$\sum_{t=0}^{T-1} x_i^t = 1 \; \forall i \in [1, n+1] \qquad [4.9]$$

$$\sum_{s=t}^{T-1} x_i^s + \sum_{s=0}^{t+\theta_i^j - \lambda\omega_i^j - 1} x_j^s \leq 1 \; \forall t \in [0, T-1], \forall(i,j) \in E_{dep} \qquad [4.10]$$

$$\sum_{i=1}^{n} \sum_{k=0}^{\lfloor \frac{T-1}{\lambda} \rfloor} \sum_{s=t+k\lambda-p_i+1}^{t+k\lambda} x_i^s \, \vec{b}_i \leq \vec{B} \; \forall t \in [0, \lambda-1] \qquad [4.11]$$

$$\sum_{(i,j)\in E_{life}} \sum_{k=0}^{\lfloor\frac{T-1}{\lambda}\rfloor} \left(\sum_{s=0}^{t+k\lambda} x_i^s - \sum_{s=0}^{t+k\lambda-\lambda\omega_i^j} x_j^s \right) \leq R \quad \forall t \in [0, \lambda-1] \qquad [4.12]$$

$$x_i^t \in \{0,1\} \ \forall i \in [1, n+1], \forall t \in [0, T-1] \qquad [4.13]$$

Here, we present some contributions to the field of instruction scheduling, in particular modulo scheduling:

– the equations that enable cumulative register lifetimes minimization and an efficient way of solving them as a maximum-cost network flow problem;

– some of the resource modeling issues that arise when defining instruction scheduling problems for a particular processor.;

– the modulo insertion scheduling theorems, which allow for the transformation of a partial modulo schedule by increasing its period without violating the dependence constraints or the modulo resource constraints of the already scheduled operations;

– the application of these results to the LAO instruction scheduler/software pipeliner we developed for the Cray T3E computers, improved for the STMicroelectronics ST100 [DIN 00] and which is now in use in the STMicroelectronics ST200 production compiler;

– a new time-indexed formulation for the modulo register-constrained instruction scheduling problem. The motivation for this formulation is to enable the application of the modern machine scheduling techniques for the resolution of the large-scale RCPSP [DEM 01].

To conclude, we anticipate that the techniques of machine scheduling will become increasingly relevant to VLIW instruction scheduling, in particular for the embedded computing applications. In such applications, high performances of the compiled applications enable the reduction of the system costs, whereas the compilation time is not really constrained. Embedded computing also yields instruction scheduling problems of significant size, especially for media processing.

Embedded computing thus motivates the development of advanced instruction scheduling techniques that deliver results close to optimality, rather than accepting the observed limitation of the traditional list-based instruction scheduling [COO 98, WIL 00]. An equally promising area of improvement of VLIW instruction scheduling is its full integration with the register allocation. In this area, the multiflow trace scheduling technology [LOW 93] is unchallenged.

Fortunately, modern embedded media processors, in particular VLIW processors such as the STMicroelectronics ST200 family, present a micro-architecture that allows for an accurate description using resources like in cumulative scheduling problems. This situation is all the more promising in cases of processors with clean pipelines like the ST200 family, as the resulting instruction scheduling problems only involve UET operations. Scheduling problems with cumulative resources and UET operations benefit from stronger machine scheduling relaxations, easier resource management in modulo scheduling and simpler time-indexed formulations.

With regards to the already compiler-friendly STMicroelectronics ST220 processor, the VLIW instruction scheduling problems it involves could be better solved if all its operation requirements on the cumulative resources were 0 or 1. This is mostly the case, except for the operations with immediate extensions, which require two issue slots (see Figure 2.1). Besides increasing the peak performances, removing this restriction enables the relaxation of the VLIW instruction scheduling problems into parallel machine scheduling problems with UET, problems which are optimally solved in polynomial time in several cases by the algorithm of *Leung et al.* [LEU 01].

4.2. *Large neighborhood search for the resource-constrained modulo scheduling problem*

The resource-constrained modulo scheduling problem (RCMSP) is motivated by the 1-periodic cyclic instruction scheduling problems that are solved by compilers when optimizing inner loops for instruction-level parallel processors. In production compilers, modulo schedules are computed by heuristics because even the most efficient integer programming formulation of resource-constrained modulo scheduling by Eichenberger and Davidson appears too expensive to solve relevant problems.

We present a new time-indexed integer programming formulation for the RCMSP and we propose a large neighborhood search heuristic to make it tractable. Based on experimental data from a production compiler, we show that this combination enables us to solve near-optimally RCMSPs of significant size. We also show that our large neighborhood search benefits to a lesser extent the resource-constrained modulo scheduling integer programming formulation of Eichenberger and Davidson.

Modulo scheduling is the cyclic instruction scheduling framework used by highly optimizing compilers to schedule instructions of innermost program loops [ALL 95]. Modulo scheduling is an effective optimization for instruction-level parallel processors [RAU 93a], especially the VLIW processors that are used for media processing in embedded devices such as set-top boxes, mobile phones, and DVD players. An example of a modern VLIW architecture is the Lx [FAR 00], which provides the basis of the successful STMicroelectronics ST200 VLIW processor family.

The modulo scheduling framework is distinguished by its focus on 1-periodic cyclic schedules with integral period, which leads to simplifications compared to the classic formulation of cyclic scheduling [HAN 95]. In the modulo scheduling framework, the period is called *initiation interval* and is the main indicator of the schedule quality. A RCMSP is a modulo scheduling problem where the resource constraints are adapted from the renewable resources of the RCPSP [BRU 99].

Optimal solutions to the RCMSP can be obtained by solving the classic integer programming formulations of Eichenberger and Davidson [EIC 97]. However, solving such a formulation is only tractable for modulo scheduling problems that comprise less than several tenth of operations[3]. While developing the ST200 production compiler at STMicroelectronics [DIN 04a], we found that modulo scheduling heuristics appeared to loosen effectiveness beyond such problem sizes, according to the lower bounds on the period obtained by relaxations.

To build high-quality modulo schedules for instruction scheduling problems of significant size, the contributions here are as follows: we show that for any assumed period λ, the RCMSP appears as a RCPSP with maximum time lags (RCPSP/max) and modulo resource constraints (section 4.3); we present a new time-indexed integer programming formulation for the RCMSP by adapting the time-indexed integer programming of Pritsker *et al.* [PRI 69] for the RCPSP/max (section 4.4); we propose a large neighborhood search (LNS) heuristic for the RCMSP, based on the adaptive reduction of margins and the resolution of the resulting time-indexed integer programming formulations by implicit enumeration (section 4.5).

4.3. Resource-constrained modulo scheduling problem

4.3.1. *Resource-constrained cyclic scheduling problems*

A *basic cyclic scheduling problem* [HAN 95] considers a set of generic operations $\{O_i\}_{1 \leq i \leq n}$ to be executed repeatedly, thus defining a set of operation instances $\{O_i^k\}_{1 \leq i \leq n}^{k > 0}, k \in \mathbb{N}$. We call *iteration* k the set of operation instances $\{O_i^k\}_{1 \leq i \leq n}$. For any $i \in [1, n]$ and $k > 0 \in \mathbb{N}$, let σ_i^k denote the schedule date of the operation instance O_i^k. Basic cyclic scheduling problems are constrained by *uniform dependences,* denoted as $O_i \xrightarrow{\theta_i^j, \omega_i^j} O_j$, where the *latency* θ_i^j and the *distance* ω_i^j are non-negative integers:

$$O_i \xrightarrow{\theta_i^j, \omega_i^j} O_j \implies \sigma_i^k + \theta_i^j \leq \sigma_j^{k+\omega_i^j} \quad \forall k > 0$$

---

3 An operation is an instance of an instruction in a program text. An instruction is a member of the processor instruction set architecture (ISA).

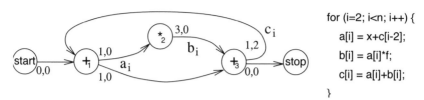

```
for (i=2; i<n; i++) {
    a[i] = x+c[i-2];
    b[i] = a[i]*f;
    c[i] = a[i]+b[i];
}
```

Figure 4.8. *Sample cyclic instruction scheduling problem*

In this section, we are focusing on *resource-constrained cyclic scheduling problems*, whose resource constraints are adapted from the RCPSPs [BRU 99]. Precisely, we assume a set of *renewable resources*, also known as *cumulative resources*, whose availabilities are given by an integral vector $\vec{B}$. Each generic operation O_i requires $\vec{b}_i$ resources for p_i consecutive units of time and this defines the resource requirements of all the operation instances $\{O_i^k\}^{k>0}$. For the cyclic scheduling problems we consider, the cumulative use of the resources by the operation instances executing at any given time must not exceed $\vec{B}$.

To illustrate the resource-constrained cyclic scheduling problems that arise from instruction scheduling, consider the inner loop source code and its dependence graph shown in Figure 4.8. To simplify the presentation, we did not include the memory access operations. Operation O_3 (c[i]=a[i]+b[i]) of iteration i must execute before operation O_1 (a[i]=x+c[i-2]) of iteration i+2 and this creates the uniform dependence with distance 2 between O_3 and O_1 (arc c_i in Figure 4.8). The dummy operations here labeled **start** and **stop** are introduced as source and sink of the dependence graph but have no resource requirements.

Assume that this code is compiled for a microprocessor whose resources are an adder and a multiplier. The adder and the multiplier may start a new operation every unit of time. However, due to pipelined implementation, the multiplier result is only available after three time units. This resource-constrained cyclic scheduling problem is defined by $p_1 = p_2 = p_3 = 1$, $\vec{B} = (1,1)^t$, $\vec{b}_1 = \vec{b}_3 = (0,1)^t$, $\vec{b}_2 = (1,0)^t$. The dependences are $O_1 \overset{1,0}{\prec} O_2, O_1 \overset{1,0}{\prec} O_3, O_2 \overset{3,0}{\prec} O_3, O_3 \overset{1,2}{\prec} O_1$.

4.3.2. *Resource-constrained modulo scheduling problem statement*

A *modulo scheduling problem* is a cyclic scheduling problem where all operations have the same processing period $\lambda \in \mathbb{N}$, also called the *initiation interval*. Compared to cyclic scheduling problems, a main simplification is that modulo scheduling problems only need to consider the set of generic operations $\{O_i\}_{1 \leq i \leq n}$. Precisely, by introducing the *modulo schedule dates* $\{\sigma_i\}_{1 \leq i \leq n}$ such that

$\forall i \in [1, n], \forall k > 0 : \sigma_i^k = \sigma_i + (k-1)\lambda$, the uniform dependence constraints become:

$$O_i \xrightarrow{\theta_i^j, \omega_i^j} O_j \implies \sigma_i^k + \theta_i^j \leq \sigma_j^{k+\omega_i^j} \implies \sigma_i + \theta_i^j - \lambda\omega_i^j \leq \sigma_j$$

Let $\{\sigma_i\}_{1 \leq i \leq n}$ denote the modulo schedule dates of a set of generic operations $\{O_i\}_{1 \leq i \leq n}$. An RCMSP is defined by [DIN 04a]:

– Uniform dependence constraints: for each such dependence $O_i \xrightarrow{\theta_i^j, \omega_i^j} O_j$, a valid modulo schedule satisfies $\sigma_i + \theta_i^j - \lambda\omega_i^j \leq \sigma_j$. The dependence graph without the dependences whose $\omega_i^j > 0$ is a directed acyclic graph (DAG);

– Modulo resource constraints: each operation O_i requires $\vec{b}_i \geq \vec{0}$ resources for all the time intervals $[\sigma_i + k\lambda, \sigma_i + k\lambda + p_i - 1]$, $k \in \mathbb{Z}$ and the total resource use at any time cannot exceed a given availability $\vec{B}$. The integer value p_i is the processing time of O_i.

The primary objective of RCMSPs is to minimize the period λ. The secondary objective is usually to minimize the iteration makespan. In the contexts where the number of processor registers is a significant constraint, secondary objectives such as minimizing the cumulative register lifetimes [DIN 94] or the maximum register pressure [EIC 95b] are considered. This is not the case for the ST200 VLIW processors, so we will focus on makespan minimization.

4.3.3. *Solving resource-constrained modulo scheduling problems*

Most modulo scheduling problems cannot be solved by classic machine scheduling techniques, as the modulo resource constraints introduce operation resource requirements of unbounded extent. Also, the uniform dependence graph may include circuits (directed cycles), unlike machine scheduling precedence graphs that are acyclic. Even without the circuits, some modulo dependence latencies $\theta_i^j - \lambda\omega_i^j$ may also be negative. Thus, the RCMSP appears as a resource-constrained project scheduling problem with maximum time-lags (RCPSP/max) and modulo resource requirements.

In practice, building modulo schedules with heuristics is much easier than building RCPSP/max schedules. This is because the maximum time-lags of RCMSPs always include a term that is a negative factor of the period λ. Such constraints can always be made redundant by sufficiently increasing the period λ. A similar observation holds for the modulo resource constraints.

In the classic modulo scheduling framework [RAU 81, LAM 88a, RAU 96], a dichotomy search for the minimum λ that yields a feasible modulo schedule is performed, starting from $\lambda_{\min} \stackrel{\text{def}}{=} \max(\lambda_{\text{rec}}, \lambda_{\text{res}})$ with:

$$\lambda_{\text{rec}} \stackrel{\text{def}}{=} \max_C \left\lceil \frac{\sum_C \theta_i^j}{\sum_C \omega_i^j} \right\rceil : \quad C\, \text{dependence circuit}$$

$$\lambda_{\text{res}} \stackrel{\text{def}}{=} \max_{1 \leq r \leq R} \left\lceil \frac{\sum_{i=1}^n p_i b_i^r}{B^r} \right\rceil : \quad R = \dim(\vec{B})$$

That is λ_{rec} is the minimum λ such that there are no positive length circuits in the dependence graph and λ_{res} is the minimum λ such that the renewable resources $\vec{B}$ are not oversubscribed.

4.4. Time-indexed integer programming formulations

4.4.1. *The non-preemptive time-indexed RCPSP formulation*

We use the formulation previously defined in section 3.3.1:

$$\sum_{t=1}^{T-1} t\, x_{n+1}^t : \qquad \text{minimize} \qquad\qquad [4.14]$$

$$\sum_{t=0}^{T-1} x_i^t = 1 \quad \forall i \in [1, n+1] \qquad\qquad [4.15]$$

$$\sum_{s=t}^{T-1} x_i^s + \sum_{s=0}^{t+\theta_i^j-1} x_j^s \leq 1 \quad \forall t \in [0, T-1], \forall (i,j) \in E_{dep} \qquad [4.16]$$

$$\sum_{i=1}^n \sum_{s=t-p_i+1}^t x_i^s\, \vec{b}_i \leq \vec{B} \quad \forall t \in [0, T-1] \qquad\qquad [4.17]$$

$$x_i^t \in \{0, 1\}\ \forall i \in [1, n+1], \forall t \in [0, T-1] \qquad [4.18]$$

Equation [4.15] ensures that any operation is scheduled once. The inequalities [4.16] describe the dependence constraints, as proposed by Christofides *et al.* [CHR 87]. Given [4.15], inequalities [4.16] for any dependence $(i,j) \in E_{dep}$ are equivalent to: $\sum_{s=t}^{T-1} x_i^s \leq \sum_{s=t+\theta_i^j}^{T-1} x_j^s\ \forall t \in [0, T-1]$ and this implies $\sigma_i \leq \sigma_j - \theta_i^j$. Finally, the inequalities [4.17] enforce the cumulative resource constraints for $p_i \geq 1$. The extensions of the RCPSP with time-dependent resource availabilities $\vec{B}(t)$ and resource requirements $\vec{b}_i(t)$ are described in this formulation by generalizing [4.17] into [4.19]:

$$\sum_{i=1}^{n}\sum_{s=0}^{t} x_i^s \, \vec{b}_i(t-s) \quad \leq \vec{B}(t) \; \forall t \in [0, T-1] \qquad [4.19]$$

4.4.2. *The classic modulo scheduling integer programming formulation*

The classic integer programming formulation of the RCMSP is from Eichenberger and Davidson [EIC 97]. This formulation is based on a λ-decomposition of the modulo schedule dates, that is, $\forall i \in [0, n+1] : \sigma_i = \lambda\phi_i + \tau_i, 0 \leq \tau_i < \lambda$. Given an operation O_i, ϕ_i is its *column number* and τ_i is its *row number*. The formulation of Eichenberger and Davidson introduces the time-indexed variables $\{y_i^\tau\}_{1\leq i\leq n}^{0\leq\tau\leq\lambda-1}$ for the row numbers, where $y_i^t \stackrel{\text{def}}{=} 1$ if $\tau_i = t$, otherwise $y_i^t \stackrel{\text{def}}{=} 0$. In particular, $\tau_i = \sum_{\tau=0}^{\lambda-1} \tau y_i^\tau \; \forall i \in [1, n]$. The column numbers $\{\phi_i\}_{1\leq i\leq n}$ are directly used in this formulation:

$$\sum_{\tau=0}^{\lambda-1} \tau y_{n+1}^\tau + \lambda\phi_{n+1} : \quad \text{minimize} \qquad [4.20]$$

$$\sum_{\tau=0}^{\lambda-1} y_i^\tau = 1 \forall i \in [1, n] \qquad [4.21]$$

$$\sum_{s=\tau}^{\lambda-1} y_i^s + \sum_{s=0}^{(\tau+\theta_i^j-1) \bmod \lambda} y_j^s + \phi_i - \phi_j \leq \omega_i^j - \lfloor \frac{\tau + \theta_i^j - 1}{\lambda} \rfloor + 1$$

$$\forall\tau \in [0, \lambda-1], \forall(i,j) \in E_{dep} \qquad [4.22]$$

$$\sum_{i=1}^{n}\sum_{r=0}^{p_i-1} y_i^{(\tau-r) \bmod \lambda} \vec{b}_i \leq \vec{B} \; \forall\tau \in [0, \lambda-1] \qquad [4.23]$$

$$y_i^\tau \in \{0,1\} \forall i \in [1, n], \forall\tau \in [0, \lambda-1] \qquad [4.24]$$

$$\phi_i \in \mathbb{N} \; \forall i \in [1, n] \qquad [4.25]$$

In this formulation, λ is assumed constant. Like in classic modulo scheduling, it is solved as the inner step of a dichotomy search for the minimum value of λ that allows a feasible modulo schedule.

4.4.3. *A new time-indexed formulation for modulo scheduling*

We propose a new time-indexed formulation for RCMSP, based on the time-indexed formulation of RCPSP/max of Pritsker *et al.* [PRI 69]. First, consider the modulo resource constraints. Each operation O_i requires $\vec{b}_i$ resources for the dates in $[\sigma_i + k\lambda, \sigma_i + k\lambda + p_i - 1], \forall k \in \mathbb{Z}$ (section 4.3.2). The resource requirement function $\vec{b}_i(t)$ of O_i is written as $\sum_{k \in \mathbb{Z}} (t \in [k\lambda, k\lambda + p_i - 1]) \vec{b}_{i,}$; so [4.19] becomes:

$$\sum_{i=1}^{n} \sum_{k \in \mathbb{Z}} \sum_{s=0}^{t} x_i^s (t - s \in [k\lambda, k\lambda + p_i - 1]) \vec{b}_i \leq \vec{B} \quad \forall t \in [0, T-1]$$

$$\Longrightarrow \sum_{i=1}^{n} \sum_{k \in \mathbb{Z}} \sum_{s=0}^{t} x_i^s (s \in [t + k\lambda - p_i + 1, t + k\lambda]) \vec{b}_i \leq \vec{B} \quad \forall t \in [0, T-1]$$

$$\Longrightarrow \sum_{i=1}^{n} \sum_{k \in \mathbb{Z}} \sum_{s=t+k\lambda-p_i+1}^{t+k\lambda} x_i^s \vec{b}_i \leq \vec{B} \quad \forall t \in [0, T-1]$$

$$\Longrightarrow \sum_{i=1}^{n} \sum_{k=0}^{\lfloor \frac{T-1}{\lambda} \rfloor} \sum_{s=t+k\lambda-p_i+1}^{t+k\lambda} x_i^s \vec{b}_i \leq \vec{B} \quad \forall t \in [0, \lambda-1]$$

To complete this new RCMSP formulation, we minimize the schedule date of operation O_{n+1} and adapt the inequalities [4.16] to the modulo dependence latencies of $\theta_i^j - \lambda \omega_i^j$. This yields:

$$\sum_{t=1}^{T-1} t\, x_{n+1}^t : \qquad \text{minimize} \qquad \qquad [4.26]$$

$$\sum_{t=0}^{T-1} x_i^t \quad = \quad 1 \quad \forall i \in [1, n+1] \qquad [4.27]$$

$$\sum_{s=t}^{T-1} x_i^s + \sum_{s=0}^{t+\theta_i^j-\lambda\omega_i^j-1} x_j^s \quad \leq \quad 1 \quad \forall t \in [0, T-1], \forall (i,j) \in E_{dep} \quad [4.28]$$

$$\sum_{i=1}^{n} \sum_{k=0}^{\lfloor \frac{T-1}{\lambda} \rfloor} \sum_{s=t+k\lambda-p_i+1}^{t+k\lambda} x_i^s \vec{b}_i \quad \leq \quad \vec{B} \quad \forall t \in [0, \lambda-1] \qquad [4.29]$$

$$x_i^t \quad \in \{0,1\} \; \forall i \in [1, n+1], \forall t \in [0, T-1] \; [4.30]$$

4.5. Large neighborhood search heuristic

4.5.1. *Variables and constraints in time-indexed formulations*

The time-indexed formulations for the RCMSP (and the RCPSP/max) involve variables and constraints in numbers that are directly related to any assumed earliest $\{e_i\}_{1 \leq i \leq n}$ and latest $\{l_i\}_{1 \leq i \leq n}$ schedule dates. Indeed, the number of variables is $\sum_{i=1}^{n} l_i - e_i + 1$. Most of the constraints are the dependence inequalities [4.28], and $e \overset{\text{def}}{=} |E_{dep}|$ non-transitively redundant dependences appear to generate eT inequalities with $T \overset{\text{def}}{=} \max_{1 \leq i \leq n} l_i + p_i$. However, the first sum of [4.28] is 0 if $t > l_i$. Likewise, the second sum of [4.28] is 0 if $t + \theta_i^j - \lambda\omega_i^j - 1 < e_j$. So [4.28] is actually equivalent to:

$$\sum_{s=t}^{T-1} x_i^s + \sum_{s=0}^{t+\theta_i^j - \lambda\omega_i^j - 1} x_j^s \leq 1 \; \forall t \in [e_j - \theta_i^j + \lambda\omega_i^j + 1, l_i], \forall(i,j) \in E_{dep} \quad [4.31]$$

So [4.31] is redundant whenever $e_j - \theta_i^j + \lambda\omega_i^j \geq l_i$ ($e_j - \theta_i^j \geq l_i$ in the case of the RCPSP/max).

The time-indexed formulation for the RCMSP (and the RCPSP/max) is therefore likely to become more tractable after reducing the possible schedule date ranges $\sigma_i \in [e_i, l_i]$. The basic technique is to initialize $e_i = r_i$ and $l_i = d_i - p_i$, with $\{r_i\}_{1 \leq i \leq n}$ and $\{d_i\}_{1 \leq i \leq n}$ being the release dates and the due dates, and then propagate the dependence constraints using a label-correcting algorithm. More elaborate techniques have been proposed for the RCPSP [DEM 05]. Ultimately, all these margins reduction techniques rely on some effective upper bounding of the due dates $\{d_i\}_{1 \leq i \leq n}$.

4.5.2. *A large neighborhood search heuristic for modulo scheduling*

In the case of the RCMSP, the primary objective is the period minimization. Heuristics build modulo schedules at some period λ that is often greater than the lower bound $\lambda_{\min} \overset{\text{def}}{=} \max(\lambda_{\text{rec}}, \lambda_{\text{res}})$. When this happens, the feasibility of modulo scheduling at period $\lambda - 1$ is open. Moreover, it is not known how to bound the makespan at period $\lambda - 1$ given a makespan at period λ. This means that the effective upper bounding of the due dates in RCMSP instances is not available either.

To compensate for the lack of upper bounding, we propose an LNS for the RCMSP, based on adaptive margins reduction and implicit enumeration of the resulting time-indexed integer programs (using an mixed integer programming (MIP) solver). The LNS [SHA 98] is a metaheuristic where a large number of solutions in the neighborhood of an incumbent solution are searched by means of branch and bound, constraint programming or integer programming. The large neighborhood is obtained by fixing some variables of the incumbent solution while releasing others.

In the setting of time-indexed formulations, we consider as the neighborhood of an incumbent solution $\{\sigma_i\}_{1\leq i\leq n}$ some schedule date ranges or *margins* $\{e_i, l_i : \sigma_i \in [e_i, l_i]\}_{1\leq i\leq n}$, which are made consistent under dependence constraint propagation. For each $x_i^{\sigma_i} = 1$, we fix variables $x_i^{r_i} \ldots x_i^{e_i-1}$, $x_i^{l_i+1} \ldots x_i^{d_i-p_i}$ to zero and release variables $x_i^{e_i} \ldots x_i^{l_i}$. The fixed variables and the dependence constraints [4.31] found redundant given the margins are removed from the integer program.

We adapt the generic LNS algorithm of [PAL 04] by using margins to define the neighborhoods and by starting from a heuristic modulo schedule. The period λ is kept constant while this algorithm searches increasingly wider margins under a time budget in order to minimize the makespan. The key change is to replace the diversification operator of [PAL 04] by a decrement of the period to $\lambda - 1$ while keeping the schedule dates. This yields a pseudo-solution that may no longer be feasible due to the period change. Computational experience shows that a new solution at period $\lambda - 1$ can often be found in the neighborhood of this pseudo-solution, whenever the problem instance is feasible at period $\lambda - 1$. In case a solution at period $\lambda - 1$ is found, go back to minimize the makespan.

4.5.3. *Experimental results with a production compiler*

We implemented the two time-indexed formulations of RCMSP described in section 4.4 in the production compiler for the STMicroelectronics ST200 VLIW processor family [DIN 04a], along with the proposed LNS heuristic, then used the CPLEX 9.0 Callable Library to solve the resulting MIPs.

The table below reports experimental data for the largest loops that could not be solved with these formulations, assuming a timeout of 300 s and a time horizon of $4\lambda_{min}$. Column *#O,#D* gives the number of operations and of non-redundant dependences. Column *Heuristic λ, M* displays the period and makespan computed by the ST200 production compiler insertion scheduling heuristic [DIN 04a]. The column groups *Formulation 300*, *Formulation 30* and *Eichenberger 300* correspond to the proposed LNS using our formulation and Eichenberger and Davidson's formulation for timeout values of 300 s, 30 s and 300 s. In each group, column *#V,#C* gives the number or variables and constraints of the integer program sent to CPLEX 9.0. In all these cases, the *Formulation* LNS reached the λ_{min}.

		Heuristic	Formulation 300		Formulation 30		Eichenberger 300	
Loop	#O,#D	λ, M	λ, M	#V,#C	λ, M	#V,#C	λ, M	#V,#C
q_plsf_5.0_215	231,313	81,97	75,77	1114,1236	75,78	1873,2042	*,*	18942,25989
q_plsf_5.0_227	121,163	42,92	39,46	982,1228	39,46	1378,1685	39,47	4840,6673
q_plsf_5.0_201	124,168	42,92	40,47	1086,1340	40,65	1197,1421	41,50	5208,7217
q_plsf_5.2_11	233,317	82,100	75,78	1113,1216	75,79	1897,2045	*,*	19339,26637
subbands.0_196	130,234	44,65	35,49	718,906	35,48	1008,1248	*,*	5850,10778
transfo.IMDCT_L	232,370	71,109	58,58	1133,1075	58,58	1985,1961	70,74	16472,26482

4.6. Summary and conclusions

The RCMSP is a resource-constrained cyclic scheduling problem whose solutions must be 1-periodic of integral period λ. The primary minimization objective of the RCMSP is the period and the secondary objective is the makespan. Given any period λ, the RCMSP appears as a RCPSP/max and so-called modulo resource constraints.

Based on the RCPSP/max integer programming formulation of Pritsker et al. [PRI 69] and the strong dependence equations of Christofides et al. [CHR 87], we presented a new time-indexed integer programming formulation for the RCMSP. This formulation differs from the classic time-indexed integer programming formulation of the RCMSP by Eichenberger and Davidson [EIC 97].

Both formulations of the RCMSP are impractical to solve problems that comprise over several tenths of operations; so we propose a large LNS heuristic based on solving those integer programming formulations by implicit enumeration after adapting the operation margins. Experiments showed that this LNS heuristic is quite effective to find a solution at period $\lambda - 1$ given an incumbent solution at period λ, even for RCMSP instances that comprise hundreds of operations. To our knowledge, this is the first application of LNS to cyclic scheduling.

5

Instruction Scheduling After Register Allocation

This chapter presents a postpass instruction scheduling technique suitable for just-in-time (JIT) compilers targeted to VLIW processors. Its key features are reduced compilation time and memory requirements, satisfaction of scheduling constraints along all program paths and the ability to preserve existing prepass schedules, including software pipelines. This is achieved by combining two ideas: instruction scheduling similar to the dynamic scheduler of an out-of-order superscalar processor and the satisfaction of inter-block scheduling constraints by propagating them across the control-flow graph until a fixed point. We implemented this technique in a Common Language Infrastructure JIT compiler for the ST200 VLIW processors and the ARM processors.

5.1. Introduction

Just-in-time (JIT) compilation of programs distributed as Java or .NET Common Language Infrastructure (CLI) byte-codes is becoming increasingly relevant for consumer electronics applications. A typical case is a game installed and played by the end user on a Java-enabled mobile phone. In this case, the JIT compilation produces native code for the host processor of the system-on-chip.

However, systems-on-chip for consumer electronics also contain powerful media processors that could execute software installed by the end user. Media processing software is usually developed in C or C++ and it exposes instruction-level parallelism. Such media processing software can be compiled to CLI byte-codes due to the Microsoft Visual Studio .NET compilers or the gcc/st/cli compiler branch contributed by STMicroelectronics [COR 08]. This motivates JIT compilation for embedded processors like the Texas Instruments C6000 VLIW-DSP family and the STMicroelectronics ST200 VLIW-media family[1].

In the setting of JIT compilation of Java programs, instruction scheduling is already expensive. For instance, the IBM Testarossa JIT team reported that combined prepass and postpass instruction scheduling costs up to 30% of the compilation time [TAN 06] for the IBM zSeries 990 and the POWER4 processors. To lower these costs, the IBM Testarossa JIT compiler relies on profiling to identify the program regions where instruction scheduling is enabled. In addition, the register allocator tracks its changes to the prepass instruction schedules in order to decide where postpass instruction scheduling might be useful.

In the case of JIT compilation of media processing applications for very long instruction word (VLIW) processors, more ambitious instruction scheduling techniques are required. First, software pipelining may be applied in spite of higher compilation costs, as these applications spend most of their time in inner loops where instruction-level parallelism is available. However, software pipelines implement cyclic schedules that may be destroyed when the code is postpass scheduled using an acyclic scheduler. Second, JIT instruction scheduling techniques should accommodate VLIW processors without interlocking hardware [MUC 04, ABR 98], such as the TI C6000 VLIW-DSP family or the STMicroelectronics ST210 / Lx [FAR 00]. This means that JIT compilation must ensure that no execution path presents scheduling hazards.

To address these issues specific to JIT compilation on VLIW processors, we propose a new postpass instruction scheduling whose main features are:

– efficiency (code quality) and speed (compilation time): this is possible due to *Scoreboard Scheduling*, that is instruction scheduling by emulating the hardware scheduler of an out-of-order superscalar processor;

– satisfaction of resource and dependence constraints along all program paths, as required by processors without interlocking hardware. We formulate and solve this *Inter-Block Scheduling* problem by propagating constraints until reaching a fixed point, in a way reminiscent of forward data-flow analysis.

In addition, we prove that our technique preserves the instruction schedules created by prepass scheduling and software pipelining, provided that register allocation and basic block alignment only introduced redundant scheduling constraints.

The presentation is as follows. In section 5.2, we review local instruction scheduling heuristics and propose Scoreboard Scheduling. We then describe an

1 The ST200 VLIW architecture is based on the Lx technology [FAR 00] jointly developed by Hewlett-Packard Laboratories and STMicroelectronics.

optimized implementation of this technique. In section 5.3, we discuss inter-region instruction scheduling and introduce inter-block scoreboard scheduling. This technique relies on iterative scheduling constraint propagation and we characterize its fixed points. In section 5.4, we provide an experimental evaluation of our contributions, which are implemented in the STMicroelectronics CLI-JIT compiler that targets the ST200 VLIW and the ARM processors.

5.2. Local instruction scheduling

5.2.1. *Acyclic instruction scheduling*

Acyclic instruction scheduling is the problem of ordering the execution of a set of *operations* on a target processor micro-architecture, so as to minimize the latest completion time. Executions of operations are partially ordered to ensure correct results. Precisely, effects on registers must be ordered in the following cases: read after write (RAW), write after read (WAR), and write after write (WAW). Other dependences arise from the partial ordering of memory accesses and from control-flow effects. We assume that the resource requirements of each operation are represented by a *reservation table* [RAU 96], where rows correspond to scheduled resources and columns correspond to time steps relative to the operation start date.

Classic instruction scheduling heuristics fall into two main categories [BAL 95]:

Cycle scheduling: scan time slots in non-decreasing order. For each time slot, order the dependence-ready operations in non-increasing priority and try to schedule each operation in turn, subject to resource availability. Dependence-ready means that execution of the operation predecessors has completed early enough to satisfy the dependences. This is Graham list scheduling.

Operation scheduling: consider each operation in non-increasing priority order. Schedule each operation at the earliest time slot where it is dependence-ready and its required resources are available. In order to prevent deadlock, the priority list order must be a topological type of the dependence graph.

Cycle Scheduling is a time-tested instruction scheduling heuristic that produces high-quality code on simple instruction pipelines, given a suitable priority of operations [MUC 04]. One such priority is the "critical path" length from any operation to the dependence graph sink node. A refinement is the "backward scheduling" priority that ensures optimal schedules on homogeneous pipelines [LEU 01] and on typed pipelines [DIN 07] for special classes of dependence graphs.

For the proofs of section 5.2.2, we assume *monotonic reservation tables*, that is reservation tables whose entries in any row are monotonically non-increasing.

Single-column reservation tables, which are virtually always found on modern VLIW processors, are obviously monotonic. Monotonicity enables leverage of classic results from resource-constrained project scheduling problems (RCPSP) [SPR 95]:

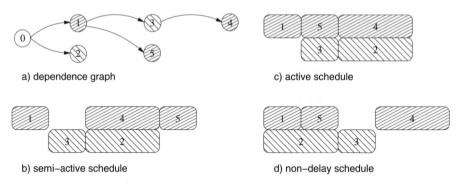

a) dependence graph   c) active schedule

b) semi–active schedule   d) non–delay schedule

Figure 5.1. *Sample schedules for a two-resource scheduling problem (horizontal time)*

Semi-active schedule: as in Figure 5.1(b). No operation can be completed earlier without changing some execution sequence. Equivalently, in a semi-active schedule, any operation has at least one dependence or resource constraint that is tight, preventing the operation from being locally left-shifted.

Active schedule: as in Figure 5.1(c). No operation can be completed earlier without delaying another operation. The schedule of Figure 5.1(b) is not active because operation 5 can be globally left-shifted to time slot 1, without delaying other operations. Operation scheduling generates active schedules.

Non-delay schedule: as in Figure 5.1(d). No execution resources are left idle if there is an operation that could start executing. The schedule of Figure 5.1(c) is not non-delay because operation 2 could start executing at time slot 0. Cycle Scheduling generates non-delay schedules.

The non-delay schedules are a subset of the active schedules, which are a subset of the semi-active schedules [SPR 95]. Active schedules and non-delay schedules are the same in the case of operations that require resources for a single time unit.

5.2.2. *Scoreboard Scheduling principles*

The main drawback of the classic scheduling heuristics is their computational cost. In the case of Cycle Scheduling, the time complexity contributions are:

1) constructing the dependence graph is $O(n^2)$ with n the number of operations, but can be lowered to $O(n)$ with conservative memory dependences [VER 02];

2) computing the operation priorities is $O(n+e)$ with e the number of dependences for the critical path, and it is as high as $O(n^2 \log n + ne)$ in [LEU 01, DIN 07];

3) issuing the operations in priority order is $O(n^2)$ according to [MUC 04], as each time step has a complexity proportional to m (where m is the number of dependence-ready operations), and m can be $O(n)$.

The complexity of operation issuing results from sorting the dependence-ready operations in priority order, and matching the resource availabilities of the current cycle with the resource requirements of the dependence-ready operations. The latter motivates the finite-state automata approach of Proebsting and Fraser [PRO 94], which was later generalized to Operation Scheduling by Bala and Rubin [BAL 95].

To reduce instruction scheduling costs, we rely on the following principles:

– Verbrugge [VER 02] replaces the dependence graph by an ADL), with one list per *dependence record* (see section 5.2.3). We show how Operation Scheduling can avoid the explicit construction of such lists.

– In the setting of JIT postpass scheduling, either basic blocks are prepass scheduled because their performance impact is significant, or their operations are in original program order. In either case, the order operations are presented to the postpass scheduler encodes a priority that is suitable for Operation Scheduling, since it is a topological ordering of the dependences. So (re)computing the operation priorities is not necessary.

– We limit the number of resource availability checks by restricting the number of time slots considered for issuing the current operation.

More precisely, we define *Scoreboard Scheduling* to be a scheduling algorithm that operates like Operation Scheduling, with the following additional restrictions:

– Any operation is scheduled within a time window of constant *window_size*.

– The *window_start* cannot decrease and is lazily increased while scheduling.

That is, given an operation to schedule, the earliest date considered is *window_start*. Moreover, if the earliest feasible schedule date *issue_date* of operation is greater than *window_start* + *window_size*, then the Scoreboard Scheduling *window_start* value is adjusted to *issue_date* − *window_size*.

THEOREM 5.1.– Scoreboard Scheduling an active schedule yields the same schedule.

PROOF.– By contradiction. Scheduling proceeds in non-decreasing time, as the priority list is a schedule. If the current operation can be scheduled earlier than it was, this is a global left shift so the priority list is not an active schedule.   □

COROLLARY 5.1.– Schedules produced by Operation Scheduling or Cycle Scheduling are invariant under Scoreboard Scheduling and Operation Scheduling.

5.2.3. Scoreboard Scheduling implementation

A *dependence record* is the atomic unit of state that needs to be considered for accurate register dependence tracking. Usually these are whole registers, except in cases of register aliasing. If so, registers are partitioned into subregisters, some of which are shared between registers, and there is one dependence record per subregister. Three technical records named *Volatile*, *Memory* and *Control* are also included in order to track the corresponding dependences.

Let *read_stage*[][] and *write_stage*[][] be processor-specific arrays indexed by operation and dependence record that tabulate the operand access pipeline stages. Let *RAW*[], *WAR*[] and *WAW*[] be latency tuning parameters indexed by dependence record. For any dependence record r and operations i and j, we generalize the formula of [WAH 03] and specify any dependence $latency_{i \rightarrow j}$ on r as follows:

RAW Dependence	$latency_{i \rightarrow j} \geq write\_stage[i][r] - read\_stage[j][r] + RAW[r]$	(a)
	$latency_{i \rightarrow j} \geq RAW[r]$	(b)
WAW Dependence	$latency_{i \rightarrow j} \geq write\_stage[i][r] - write\_stage[j][r] + WAW[r]$	(c)
	$latency_{i \rightarrow j} \geq WAW[r]$	(d)
WAR Dependence	$latency_{i \rightarrow j} \geq read\_stage[i][r] - write\_stage[j][r] + WAR[r]$	(e)
	$latency_{i \rightarrow j} \geq WAR[r]$	(f)

Assuming that $write\_stage[i][r] \geq read\_stage[j][r]$ $\forall i, j, r$, that is operand write is no earlier than operand read in the instruction pipeline for any given r, the dependence inequalities (b) and (e) are redundant. This enables dependence latencies to be tracked by maintaining only two entries per dependence record r: the latest access date and the latest write date. We call *access_actions* and *write_actions* the arrays with those entries indexed by dependence record.

The state of scheduled resources is tracked by a *resource_table*, which serves as the scheduler reservation table. This table has one row per resource and *window_size* + *columns_max* columns, where *columns_max* is the maximum number of columns across the reservation tables of all operations. The first column of the *resource_table* corresponds to the *window_start*. This is just enough state for checking resource conflicts in [*window_start, window_start* + *window_size*].

Scoreboard scheduling is performed by picking each operation i according to the priority order and by calling $add\_schedule(i, try\_schedule(i))$, defined by:

emphtry_schedule: Given an operation i, return the earliest dependence- and resource-feasible *issue_date* such that *issue_date* $\geq$ *window_start*. For each dependence record r, collect the following constraints on *issue_date*:

Effect	Constraints
Read[r]	$issue\_date \geq write\_actions[r] - read\_stage[i][r] + RAW[r]$
Write[r]	$issue\_date \geq write\_actions[r] - write\_stage[i][r] + WAW[r]$
	$issue\_date \geq access\_actions[r]$

The resulting *issue_date* is then incremented while there exists scheduled resource conflicts with the current contents of the *resource_table*.

emphadd_schedule: Schedule an operation i at a dependence- and resource-feasible *issue_date* previously returned by *try_schedule*. For each dependence record r, update the action arrays as follows:

Effect	Updates
Read[r]	$access\_actions[r] \leftarrow \max(access\_actions[r], issue\_date + WAR[r])$
Write[r]	$access\_actions[r] \leftarrow \max(access\_actions[r], issue\_date + WAW[r])$
	$write\_actions[r] \leftarrow issue\_date + write\_stage[i][r]$

In case *issue_date* > *window_start* + *window_size*, the *window_start* is set to *issue_date* − *window_size* and the *resource_table* is shifted accordingly. The operation reservation table is then added into the *resource_table*.

In Figure 5.2, we illustrate scoreboard scheduling of two ST200 VLIW operations, starting from an empty scoreboard. There are three scheduled resources: ISSUE, 4 units; MEM, one unit; and CTL, one unit. The *window_start* is zero and the two operations are scheduled at *issue_date* zero. We display *access_actions*[r] and *write_actions*[r] as strings of a and w from *window_start* to *actions*[r]. In Figure 5.3, many other operations have been scheduled since Figure 5.2, the latest being shl $r24 at *issue_date* 4. Then operation add $r15 is scheduled at *issue_date* 5, due to the RAW dependence on $r24. Because *window_size* is 4, the *window_start* is set to 1 and the *resource_table* rows ISSUE, MEM, CTL are shifted.

THEOREM 5.2.– Scoreboard Scheduling correctly enforces the dependence latencies.

PROOF.– Calling $add\_schedule(i, issue\_date_i)$ followed by $try\_schedule$ $(j, issue\_date_i + latency_{i \to j})$ implies that $latency_{i \to j}$ satisfies the inequalities $(a), (c), (d), (f)$. □

```
issue=0      ldb $r23 = 9[$r16]              issue=0      add $r18 = $r18, -12
start=0   | +0 +1 +2 +3 +4 +5 +6 +7          start=0   | +0 +1 +2 +3 +4 +5 +6 +7
----------|------------------------          ----------|------------------------
ISSUE     | 1                                ISSUE     | 2
MEM       | 1                                MEM       | 1
CTL       |                                  CTL       |
----------|------------------------          ----------|------------------------
Control   | a                                Control   | a
$r16      | a                                $r16      | a
          |                                  $r18      | aw aw  w  w
$r23      | aw aw  w  w  w  w                 $r23      | aw aw  w  w  w  w
Memory    | a  a                             Memory    | a  a
```

Figure 5.2. *Scoreboard Scheduling within the time window (window_size = 4)*

```
issue=4      shl $r24 = $r24, 24             issue=5      add $r15 = $r15, $r24
start=0   | +0 +1 +2 +3 +4 +5 +6 +7          start=1   | +0 +1 +2 +3 +4 +5 +6 +7
----------|------------------------          ----------|------------------------
ISSUE     | 3  2  1  3  1                     ISSUE     | 2  1  3  1  1
MEM       | 1  1  1  1                        MEM       | 1  1  1
CTL       |                                   CTL       |
----------|------------------------          ----------|------------------------
Control   | a  a  a  a  a                     Control   | a  a  a  a  a
          |                                   $r15      | aw aw aw aw aw aw  w  w
$r16      | aw aw aw aw aw  w  w              $r16      | aw aw aw aw  w  w
$r18      | aw aw  w  w                       $r18      | aw  w  w
$r23      | aw aw aw aw aw  w  w              $r23      | aw aw aw aw  w  w
$r24      | aw aw aw aw aw aw  w  w           $r24      | aw aw aw aw aw  w  w
Memory    | a  a                             Memory    | a
```

Figure 5.3. *Scoreboard Scheduling and moving the time window (window_size = 4)*

5.3. Global instruction scheduling

5.3.1. *Postpass inter-region scheduling*

We define the *inter-region scheduling problem* as scheduling the operations of each scheduling region such that the resource and dependence constraints inherited from the scheduling regions (transitive) predecessors, possibly including self, are satisfied. When the scheduling regions are reduced to basic blocks, we call this problem the *inter-block scheduling problem*. Only inter-region scheduling is allowed to move operations between basic blocks (of the same region).

The basic technique for solving the inter-region scheduling problem is to schedule each region in isolation, then correct the resource and latency constraint violations that may occur along control-flow transfers from one scheduling region to the other by inserting no-operation (NOP) operations. Such *NOP padding* may occur after region entries, before region exits, or both, and this technique is applied after postpass scheduling on state-of-the-art compilers such as the Open64.

Meld Scheduling is a prepass inter-region scheduling technique proposed by Abraham *et al.* [ABR 98] that minimizes the amount of NOP padding required after scheduling. This technique is demonstrated using superblocks, which are scheduled from the most frequently executed to the least frequently executed, however it applies to any program partition into acyclic regions.

Consider a dependence whose source operation is inside a scheduling region and whose target operation is outside the scheduling region. Its *latency dangle* is the minimum number of time units required between the exit from the scheduling region and the execution of the target operation to satisfy the dependence. For a dependence whose source operation is outside the scheduling region and whose target operation is inside, its latency dangle is defined in a symmetric way [ABR 98].

Meld Scheduling only considers dependence latency dangles, however, resource dangles can be similarly defined. Latency dangle constraints originate from predecessor regions or from successor regions, depending on the order the regions are scheduled. Difficulties arise with cycles in the control-flow graph, and also with latency dangles that pass through scheduling regions. These are addressed with conservative assumptions on the dangles.

Meld Scheduling is a prepass technique, so register allocation or basic block alignment may introduce extra code or non-redundant WAR and RAW register dependences. Also with JIT compilation, prepass scheduling is likely to be omitted on cold code regions. On processors without interlocking hardware, compilers must ensure that no execution path presents hazards. In the Open64 compiler, hazards are detected and corrected by a dedicated "instruction bundler".

When focusing on postpass scheduling, the latency and resource dangles of Meld Scheduling are implied by the scoreboard scheduler states at region boundaries. Moreover, we assume that the performance benefits of global code motion are not significant during the postpass scheduling of prepass scheduled regions, so we focus on inter-block scheduling. Finally, we would like to avoid duplicate work between an "instruction bundler" and postpass scheduling.

Based on these observations, we propose the *inter-block scoreboard scheduling* technique to iteratively propagate the dependence and resource constraints of local scheduling across the control-flow graph until the fixed point. As we will prove, it is possible to ensure that this technique converges quickly and preserves prepass schedules, including software pipelines, that are still valid.

5.3.2. *Inter-block Scoreboard Scheduling*

We propagate the scoreboard scheduler states at the start and the end of each basic block for all program basic blocks by using a worklist algorithm, like in forward dataflow analysis [NIE 99]. This state comprises *window_start*, the action array entries and the *resource_table*. Each basic block extracted from the worklist is processed by Scoreboard Scheduling its operations in non-decreasing order of their previous *issue_date*s (in program order the first time). This updates the operation *issue_date*s and the state at the end of the basic block.

Following this basic block update, the start scoreboard scheduler states of its successor basic blocks are combined through a meet function (described below) with the end scoreboard scheduler state just obtained. If any start scoreboard scheduler state is changed by the meet function, this means new inter-block scheduling constraints need to be propagated so the corresponding basic block is put on the worklist. Initially, all basic blocks are in the worklist and the constraint propagation is iterated until the worklist is empty.

In order to achieve quick convergence of this constraint propagation, we enforce a *non-decrease rule*: *the operation issue_dates do not decrease when rescheduling a basic block*. That is, when scheduling an operation, its release date is the *issue_date* computed the last time the basic block was scheduled. This is implemented in *try_schedule*(i) by initializing the search for a feasible $issue\_date_i$ to the maximum of the previous $issue\_date_i$ and the *window_start*.

The meet function propagates the scheduling constraints between two basic blocks connected in the control-flow graph. Each control-flow edge is annotated with a *delay* that accounts for the time elapsed along that edge. Delay is zero for fall-through edges and is the minimum branch latency for other edges. Then:

– advance the scoreboard scheduler state at the end of the origin basic block by elapsing time so *window_start* reaches the *issue_date* of the last operation plus one (zero if the basic block is empty), plus the *delay* of the connecting control-flow edge (zero if fall-through edge, else the taken branch latency);

– translate the time of this scoreboard scheduler state so that *window_start* becomes zero. With our implementation, this amounts to subtracting *window_start* from the action array entries and moving the *resource_table*;

– merge the two scoreboard scheduler states by taking the maximum of the entries of the *resource_table* and of the action arrays.

THEOREM 5.3.– Inter-block scoreboard scheduling converges in bounded time.

PROOF.– The latest *issue_date* of a basic block never exceeds the number of operations plus one times the maximum dependence latency or the maximum span of a reservation table (whichever is larger). The *issue_date*s are also non-decreasing by the non-decrease rule, so they reach a fixed point in bounded time. The fixed point of the scoreboard scheduler states follows.   □

5.3.3. *Characterization of fixed points*

THEOREM 5.4.– Any locally scheduled program that satisfies the inter-block scheduling constraints is a fixed point of inter-block scoreboard scheduling.

PROOF.– By hypothesis, all operations have valid *issue_date*s with respect to basic block instruction scheduling. Also, the inter-block scheduling constraints are satisfied. By the non-decrease rule, each operation previous *issue_date* is the first date tried by Scoreboard Scheduling, and this succeeds.   □

A first consequence is that for any prepass region schedule which satisfies the inter-block scheduling constraints at its boundary, basic blocks will be unchanged by inter-block scoreboard scheduling, provided that no non-redundant instruction scheduling constraints are inserted into the region by later compilation steps. Interestingly, this holds for any prepass region scheduling algorithm: superblock scheduling, trace scheduling, wavefront scheduling and software pipelining.

A second consequence is that inter-block scoreboard scheduling of a program with enough NOP padding to satisfy the inter-block scheduling constraints will converge with only one Scoreboard Scheduling pass on each basic block. In practice, such explicit NOP padding should be reserved for situations where a high-frequency execution path may suffer from the effects of latency and resource dangles at a control-flow merge with a low-frequency execution path, such as entry to an inner loop header from a loop preheader.

5.4. Experimental results

In the setting of the STMicroelectronics CLI-JIT compiler, we implemented Scoreboard Scheduling as described in section 5.2.3 and also a Cycle Scheduling algorithm that closely follows the description of Abraham [ABR 00], including reference counting for detecting operations whose predecessors have all been scheduled.

We further optimized this cycle scheduling implementation for compilation speed. In particular, we replaced the dependence graph by a variant of the ADL of Verbrugge [VER 02] to ensure a $O(n)$ time complexity of the dependence graph construction. This implies conservative memory dependences, however we assume such a restriction is acceptable for postpass scheduling.

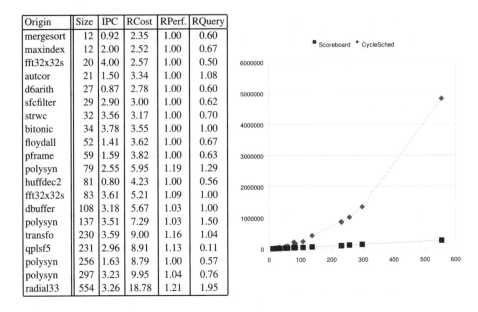

Origin	Size	IPC	RCost	RPerf.	RQuery
mergesort	12	0.92	2.35	1.00	0.60
maxindex	12	2.00	2.52	1.00	0.67
fft32x32s	20	4.00	2.57	1.00	0.50
autcor	21	1.50	3.34	1.00	1.08
d6arith	27	0.87	2.78	1.00	0.60
sfcfilter	29	2.90	3.00	1.00	0.62
strwc	32	3.56	3.17	1.00	0.70
bitonic	34	3.78	3.55	1.00	1.00
floydall	52	1.41	3.62	1.00	0.67
pframe	59	1.59	3.82	1.00	0.63
polysyn	79	2.55	5.95	1.19	1.29
huffdec2	81	0.80	4.23	1.00	0.56
fft32x32s	83	3.61	5.21	1.09	1.00
dbuffer	108	3.18	5.67	1.03	1.00
polysyn	137	3.51	7.29	1.03	1.50
transfo	230	3.59	9.00	1.16	1.04
qplsf5	231	2.96	8.91	1.13	0.11
polysyn	256	1.63	8.79	1.00	0.57
polysyn	297	3.23	9.95	1.04	0.76
radial33	554	3.26	18.78	1.21	1.95

Figure 5.4. *Benchmark basic blocks and instruction scheduling results*

We selected a series of basic blocks from STMicroelectronics media processing application codes and performance kernels compiled at the highest optimization level by the Open64-based production compiler for the ST200 VLIW family [DIN 04a]. The proposed CLI-JIT postpass scheduler was connected to this compiler.

These benchmarks are listed in the left side of Figure 5.4. Columns *Size* and *IPC*, respectively, give the number of instructions and of instructions per cycle after Cycle Scheduling. Column *RCost* is the ratio of compilation time between the cycle scheduler and the scoreboard scheduler at *window_size* $= 15$. Column *RPerf* is the relative performance of the two schedulers, as measured by inverse of schedule length. Column *RQuery* is the ratio of compilation time for resource checking between the cycle scheduler and the scoreboard scheduler. On the right side of Figure 5.4, we show the compilation time as a function of basic block size. Unlike the Cycle Scheduling, Scoreboard Scheduling clearly operates in linear time.

To understand how compilation time is spent, we show in Figure 5.5 the stacked contributions of the different scheduling phases normalized by the total instruction scheduling time; so their sum is 1. We also single out the cumulative time spent in resource checking, yielding the bars above one. For Cycle Scheduling (left side), the cost of computing the dependences *ADL* becomes relatively smaller, as it is linear with basic block size. The *Priority* computing phase is of comparable time complexity yet smaller than the operation *Issuing* phase. For Scoreboard Scheduling (right side), the *Try* schedule phase is consistently slightly more expensive than the *Add* schedule phase.

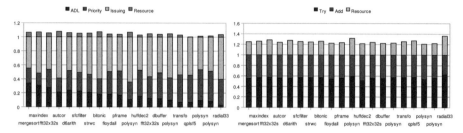

Figure 5.5. *Time breakdown for cycle scheduling and scoreboard scheduling*

It also appears from Figure 5.5 that using finite state automata as proposed by Bala and Rubin [BAL 95] for speeding up resource checking is not always justified, in particular for processors whose reservation tables are single cycle. For more complex processors, it would be straightforward to replace the *resource_table* of a Scoreboard Scheduling implementation by such finite state automata.

5.5. Conclusions

In this chapter, we proposed a postpass instruction scheduling technique motivated by JIT compilation for VLIW processors. This technique combines two ideas: Scoreboard Scheduling, a restriction of classic Operation Scheduling that considers only the time slots inside a window that moves forward in time; and Inter-Block Scheduling, an iterative propagation of the scheduling constraints across the control-flow graph, subject to the non-decrease of the schedule dates. This inter-block scoreboard scheduling technique has three advantages:

– reducing the instruction scheduling compilation time, compared to classic Cycle Scheduling and Operation Scheduling;

– ensuring that all program paths do not present scheduling hazards, as required by processors without interlocking hardware;

– preserving prepass region schedules that are still valid when postpass scheduling runs, in particular software pipelines without spill code.

Experiments with the STMicroelectronics ST200 VLIW production compiler and the STMicroelectronics CLI-JIT compiler confirm the significance of our approach.

Our results further indicated that compiler instruction schedules produced by Cycle Scheduling and Operation Scheduling are essentially unchanged by the hardware operation scheduler of out-of-order superscalar processors. Indeed, active schedules are invariant under Scoreboard Scheduling. Finally, the proposed non-decrease rule provides a simple way of protecting cyclic schedules, such as software pipelines, from the effects of rescheduling with an acyclic scheduler.

6

Dealing in Practice with Memory Hierarchy Effects and Instruction Level Parallelism

In the first section, we study memory disambiguation mechanisms in some high-performance processors. Such mechanisms, coupled with load/store queues in out-of-order processors, are crucial to improving the exploitation of instruction-level parallelism (ILP), especially for memory-bound scientific codes. Designing ideal memory disambiguation mechanisms is too complex in hardware because it would require precise address bit comparators; thus, microprocessors implement simplified and imprecise ones that perform only partial address comparisons. We study the impact of such simplifications on the sustained performance of some real high-performance processors. Despite all the advanced micro-architecture features of these processors, we demonstrate that memory address disambiguation mechanisms can cause deep program performance loss. We show that, even if data are located in low cache levels and enough ILP exist, the performance degradation may reach a factor of x21 slower if care is not taken on the generated streams of accessed addresses. We propose a possible software (compilation) technique based on the classical (and robust) load/store vectorization.

In the second section, we study cache effects optimization at instruction level for embedded very long instruction word (VLIW) processors. The introduction of caches inside processors provides micro-architectural ways to reduce the memory gap by tolerating long memory access delays. Usual cache optimization techniques for high-performance computing are difficult to apply in embedded VLIW applications. First, embedded applications are not always well structured, and few regular loop nests exist. Real-world applications in embedded computing contain hot loops with pointers, indirect arrays accesses, function calls, indirect function calls, non-constant stride accesses, etc. Consequently, loop nest transformations for reducing cache misses are impossible to apply by compilers, especially at the backend level. Second, the strides of memory accesses do not appear to be constant at the source code level because of indirect accesses. Hence, usual software prefetching techniques are not applicable by compilers. Third, embedded VLIW processors are cheap products, and they have limited hardware dynamic mechanisms compared to high-performance processors: no out-of-order executions, reduced memory hierarchy, small direct mapped caches, lower clock frequencies, etc. Consequently, the code optimization methods must be simple and take care of code size. This chapter presents a backend code optimization for tolerating non-blocking cache effects at the instruction level (not at the loop level). Our method is based on a combination of memory preloading with data prefetching, allowing us to optimize both regular and irregular applications at the assembly level.

6.1. The problem of hardware memory disambiguation at runtime

6.1.1. *Introduction*

Memory system performance is essential for today's processors. Therefore, computer architects have made, and are still making, great efforts in inventing sophisticated mechanisms to improve data access rate in terms of latency and bandwidth: multilevel and non-blocking caches, load/store queues for out-of-order execution, prefetch mechanisms to tolerate/hide memory latencies, memory banking and interleaving to increase the bandwidth, etc.

One key micro-architectural mechanism to tolerate/hide memory latency is the out-of-order processing of memory requests. With the advent of superscalar processors, the concept of load/store queues has become a micro-architectural standard. The basic principle is simple: consecutive issued memory requests are stored in a hardware queue and simultaneously processed. This allows the memory requests with shorter processing time (in the case of cache hits) to bypass requests with a longer processing time (in the case of cache misses, for example). Unfortunately, data dependences may exist between memory requests: for example, a load followed by a store (or vice versa) both addressing exactly the same memory location have to be executed strictly in order to preserve program semantics. This is done on-the-fly by specific hardware mechanisms whose task is, first, to detect memory request dependences and, second, to satisfy such dependences (if necessary). These mechanisms are under high pressure in memory-bound programs because numerous in-flight memory requests have to be treated.

In order to satisfy this high request rate, hardware memory dependence detection mechanisms are simplified at the expense of accuracy and performance [JOH 91]. To be accurate, the memory dependence detection mechanism must compare between all the bits of in flight accessed memory addresses: such precise address comparison is an expensive hardware design in the micro-architecture. In practice, the comparison between two accessed memory locations is carried out on a small portion of the addresses: usually, few low order bits are compared to detect data dependence or not. If these low-order bits match, the hardware takes a conservative action, i.e. it considers that the whole addresses match and triggers the procedure for a collision case (serialization of the memory requests).

In this chapter, we show how to study in detail the dynamic behavior of memory request processing. We provide examples on three superscalar processors (Alpha 21264, Power 4 and Itanium 2). Because of the high complexity of such analysis, our study is focused on the different memory hierarchy levels (L1, L2 and L3), excluding the main memory. Our micro-benchmarking codes are simple floating-point vector loops (memory-bound) that account for a large fraction of execution time in scientific computing. In addition, the structure of their address streams is regular, making possible a detailed performance analysis of the interaction between these address streams with the dependence detection mechanisms and bank conflicts. Our aim is not to analyze or optimize a whole program behavior, but only small fractions that consist of simple scientific computing loops. One of the reasons is that the load/store queue conflicts that we are interested in deal with *local* phenomena because, first, they strictly involve in-flight instructions (present in a limited instructions window). Second, they are not influenced by the context of a whole application as other events such as caches activities. So, it is useless to experiment complete complex applications to isolate these local events that we can highlight with micro-benchmarking. Finally, the number of side effects and pollution of the cache performance in whole complex applications (such as SPEC codes) makes the potential benefits smoothened out. We show that our micro-benchmarks are a good diagnostic tool. We can precisely quantify the effects of load/store vectorization on poor memory disambiguation. It allows us to experimentally reveal the limitations of dynamic hardware memory dependences check that may lead to severe performance loss and make the code performance very dependent on the order of access in the address streams.

This section is organized as follows. Section 6.1.2 presents some related work about the problem of improving load/store queues and memory disambiguation mechanisms. Section 6.1.3 gives a description of our experimental environment. Then, section 6.1.5 shows the most important results of our experiments that highlight some problems in modern cache systems, such as memory dependence detection mechanisms and bank conflicts. We propose in section 6.1.6 an optimization method that groups the memory requests in a vectorized way. We demonstrate by our experiments that this method is effective; then we conclude.

6.1.2. *Related work*

Improving load/store queues and memory disambiguation mechanisms is an issue of active research for micro-architects. Chrysos and Emer in [CHR 98] proposed store sets as a hardware solution for increasing the accuracy of memory dependence prediction. Their experiments were conclusive, demonstrating that they can nearly achieve the peak performance with the context of large instruction windows. Park *et al.* [PAR 03] proposed an improved design of load/store queues that scale better, i.e. they have improved the design complexity of memory disambiguation. A speculative technique for memory dependence prediction has been proposed by Yoaz *et al.* [YOA 99]: the hardware tries to predict colliding loads, relying on the fact that such loads tend to repeat their delinquent behavior. Another speculative technique devoted to superscalar processors was presented by Onder [OND 02]. The author presented a hardware mechanism that classifies the loads and stores to an appropriate speculative level for memory dependence prediction.

All the above sophisticated techniques are hardware solutions. In the domain of scientific computing, the codes are often regular, making it possible to achieve effective compile time optimizations. Thus, we do not require such dynamic techniques. In this section, we show that a simple load/store vectorization is useful (in the context of scientific loops) for solving the same problems tackled in [CHR 98, PAR 03, YOA 99, OND 02]. Coupling our costless software optimization technique with the actual imprecise memory disambiguation mechanisms is less expensive than pure hardware methods, nonetheless giving good performance improvement.

6.1.3. *Experimental environment*

In order to analyze the interaction between the processors (typically the cache systems) with the applications, we have designed a set of micro-benchmarks. Our set of micro-benchmarks consists of simple vector loops (memory-bound) that consume large fractions of execution times in scientific numerical applications. Besides their representativity, these vector loops present two key advantages: first, they are simple and, second, they can be easily transformed since they are fully parallel loops. We divide our micro-benchmarks into two families:

1) *Memory stress micro-benchmarks* are artificial loops that aim to only send consecutive bursts of independent loads and stores in order to study the impact of memory address streams on the peak performance.[1] Such loops do not contain any data dependences:

   i) the first micro-benchmark, called LxLy, corresponds to a loop in which two arrays X and Y are regularly accessed with only loads: Load X(0), Load Y(0), Load X(1), Load Y(1), Load X(2), Load Y(2), etc.;

   ii) the second micro-benchmark, called LxSy corresponds to a loop in which one array X is accessed with loads, while the Y array is accessed with stores: Load X(0), Store Y(0), Load X(1), Store Y(1), Load X(2), Store Y(2), etc.

2) *BLAS 1 micro-benchmarks* are simple vector loops that contain flow dependences. In this chapter, we use three simple FOR i loops:

   − *copy: Y(i) ← X(i);

   − vsum: Z(i) ← X(i) + Y(i);

   − daxpy: Y(i) ← Y(i) + a × X(i).

Despite the fact that we have experimented other BLAS 1 codes with various number of arrays, we chose these simple ones as illustrative examples, since they clearly exhibit the pathological behavior that we are interested in.

---

1 In this context, the peak performances refer to the ideal ones, that is the maximal theoretical performances as defined by the hardware specification.

6.1.4. *Experimentation methodology*

The performance of our micro-benchmarks is sensitive to several parameters that we explore. In this study, we focus on two major parameters:

1) *Memory array offsets*: the impact of each exact starting virtual memory address of each array[2] is analyzed. This is because varying such offsets changes the accessed addresses of the vector elements, and thus it has an impact on load/store queues behavior. This is because we know that the memory address of the double floating point (FP) element X(i) is $Offset(X) + i \times sizeof(typeX)$, where $typeX$ is floating point (FP) in our case (8 bytes per element in our experiments).

2) *Data location*: since we are interested in exploring the cache performance (L1, L2 and L3), we parameterize our micro-benchmarks in order to lock all our arrays in the desired memory hierarchy level. By choosing adequate vector lengths, and by using dummy loops that flush the data from the non-desired cache levels, we guarantee that our array elements are located exactly in the experimented cache level (checked by hardware performance counters).

Some other parameters, such as prefetch distances and modes, have also been carefully analyzed (see [JAL 06]). However, in order to be synthetic, we restrict ourselves in this chapter to the two parameters described above. Prefetch distances and modes are fixed to those that produce the best performances. Note that in all our experiments, the number of TLB misses is extremely negligible.

After presenting the experimental environment, the next section studies the performance of the cache systems in some target processors.

6.1.5. *Precise experimental study of memory hierarchy performance*

This section presents a summary of our experimental results on three micro-processors given as examples: Alpha 21264, Power 4 and Itanium 2. Alpha 21264 and Power 4 are two representative out-of-order superscalar processors, while Itanium 2 represents an in-order processor (an interesting combination between superscalar and VLIW).

In all our experiments, we focused on the performance of our micro-benchmarks expressed in terms of number of clock cycles (execution time), reported by the hardware performance counters available in each processor. Our measurements are normalized as follows:

---

2 It is the address of the first array element that we simply call the array offset. The address zero is the beginning of a memory page.

– in the case of memory stress micro-benchmarks, we report the minimal number of clock cycles needed to perform two memory accesses: depending on the micro-benchmark, it might be a pair of loads (LxLy micro-benchmark), or a load and a store (LxSy micro-benchmark);

– in the case of BLAS 1 micro-benchmarks, we report the minimal number of clock cycles needed to compute one vector element. For instance, the performance of the vsum micro-benchmark is the minimal time needed to perform one instruction Z(i)←X(i)+Y(i). Since all our micro-benchmarks are memory-bound, the performance is not sensitive to FP computations.

One of the major points of focus is the impact of array offsets on the performance. Since most of our micro-benchmarks access only two arrays (except vsum that accesses three arrays), we explore the combination of two dimensions of offsets (offset X versus offset Y). Therefore, 2D plots (ISO-surface) are used. A *geographical* color code is used: light colors correspond to the best performance (lowest number of cycles) while dark colors correspond to the worst performance.

In the following sections, we detail the most important and representative experiments that allow us to make a clear analysis of each hardware platform.

6.1.5.1. *Example with Alpha 21264 processor (superscalar)*

Figure 6.1(a) plots the performance of the LxSy micro-benchmark. As it can be seen, depending on the array offsets, the performance may be dramatically degraded (the worst case is 28 cycles instead of 1.3). Two clear diagonal zones appear. The main diagonal corresponds to the effects of the interactions between a stream of a load followed by a store, both accessing two distinct memory locations (Load X[i] followed by Store Y[i]). However, the hardware assumes that these memory operations are dependent because they have the same k address lower-bits (the hardware does not carry out a complete address comparison). This diagonal is periodic (not reported in this figure) and arises when the offset of X (respectively Y) is a multiple of 32 KB, which means that $k = 15$ bits. The magnitude of performance degradation depends on the frequency of the false memory collisions, and the distance between them: the nearer the issue time of two false colliding memory addresses, the higher the penalty. The second diagonal (upper-left) of Figure 6.1(a) corresponds to the effects of interactions between the prefetch instructions of X elements and the stores of Y elements. The periodicity of this diagonal is also 32 KB.

These performance penalties occur for all BLAS 1 micro-benchmarks. This is due to the compiler optimization strategy. Indeed, the Compaq compiler (version 6.3) generates a well-optimized code (loop unrolling with fine-grain acyclic scheduling) but keeps the same order of memory access as described by the C program (Load X[i] followed by Store Y[i]). This code generation allowed to reach peak performances only with ideal combination of array offsets, which is not controlled by the compiler.

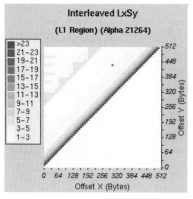 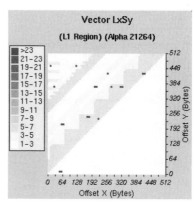

a) Cache behavior of Alpha 21264 Processor   b) Vectorization on Alpha 21264

Figure 6.1. *Example of Alpha 21264 processor*

6.1.5.2. *Example with Power 4 processor (superscalar)*

For this processor, we show the performance of some BLAS 1 micro-benchmarks because the other micro-benchmarks showed similar behaviors. The IBM compiler (version 5.02) also generates a well-optimized code. The loops were unrolled and optimized at the fine-grain level, but they perform the same order of the memory accesses as described by the source program (Load X[i] followed by Store Y[i] for copy micro-benchmark, and Load X[i], Load Y[i] followed by Store Z[i] for vsum). Prefetch instructions are not inserted by the compiler, since data prefetching is automatically done by hardware.

Figure 6.2(a) shows the performance of vsum code when the operands are located in L3. This figure is more complex:

– Along the main diagonal, a stripe is visible with a moderate performance loss (around 20%). This is due to the interaction between the two load address streams (load of X and Y elements).

– A clear vertical stripe can be observed where the execution times are larger (above 13 clock cycles). This is due to the interaction between the loads of X elements from one side with the stores of Z elements on the other side.

– Another clear horizontal stripe can be observed where the execution times are larger (above 13 clock cycles). This is due to the interaction between the loads of Y elements from one side with the stores of Z elements on the other side.

In all cases, the *bad* vertical and diagonal zones appear periodically every 4 KB offset. It confirms that the processor performs partial address comparison on 12 low-order bits.

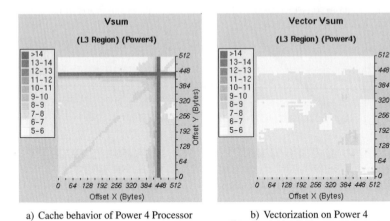

a) Cache behavior of Power 4 Processor   b) Vectorization on Power 4

Figure 6.2. *Example of Power 4 processor*

6.1.5.3. *Example with Itanium 2 processor (EPIC/IA64)*

Contrary to the two previous processors, Itanium 2 is in-order. The ILP is expressed by the program using instruction groups and bundles. Thus, analyzing the behavior of the memory operations is little easier. In this section, we show that the banking architecture of the distinct cache levels and the memory disambiguation mechanisms may cause deep performance degradation.

While the memory stress micro-benchmarks are coded at assembly level, we used the Intel compiler (version 7.0) to generate optimized codes for our BLAS 1 loops. Software pipelining, loop unrolling and data prefetching are used to enhance the fine-grain parallelism. The experiments are performed when data are located in L2 and L3, since on Itanium 2, L1 cannot contain FP operands (this is a design choice of the Itanium family architecture).

First, let us examine the impact of L2 banking architecture. Figure 6.3(a) plots the performance of the LxLy micro-benchmark (two streams of independent loads). The best execution time is 0.6 clock cycle, which is the optimal one. However, some regions exhibit performance loss, depending on the array offsets. Basically, two types of phenomena can be observed:

1) three diagonals separated by 256 bytes in which the performance is 1.2 cycle instead of 0.6 cycle;

2) a grid pattern (crossed by the three diagonal stripes). Inside this grid, the execution times in some points are 0.6 cycle, but 1 cycle in others.

Both phenomena can be easily attributed to bank conflicts resulting from the interactions between the L2 interleaving scheme and the address streams.

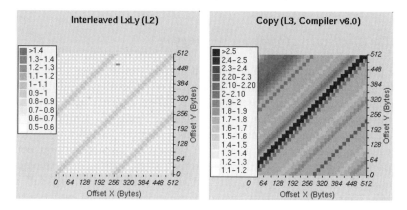

Figure 6.3. *Cache behavior of Itanium 2 processor*

All the performance bugs observed in L2 still exist in L3 level. Figure 6.3(b) shows the performance of the copy micro-benchmark. The memory disambiguation problem is more visible (wider diagonal stripes) because of the interaction between independent loads and stores. Another problem is highlighted by the upper-left diagonal zone, which is in fact due to the interferences between prefetch instructions (that behave as loads) and the store instructions.

6.1.5.4. *Summary of the experiments on cache behavior*

This section presented the behavior of the cache systems in Alpha 21264, Power 4 and Itanium 2 processors. We showed that the effectiveness of an enhanced instruction scheduling is not sufficient to sustain the best performance even in very simple codes, when we expect a maximal ILP extraction. We demonstrated that memory disambiguation mechanisms cause deep performance loss depending on array offsets. Bank conflicts in Itanium 2 are also an important source of performance troubles. Table 6.1 recapitulates the performance degradation factors caused by these micro-architectural restrictions, counted as the ratio between the best and worst performances.

We can use many code optimization techniques to reduce the performance penalties previously exposed (for instance, array padding, array copying and code vectorization). In the next section, we investigate the impact of load/store vectorization.

Processor	L1	L2	L3
Alpha 21264	21.54	12	-
Power 4	2.11	3.64	2.57
Itanium 2	-	2.17	1.5

Table 6.1. *Examples of measured performance degradation factors*

6.1.6. *The effectiveness of load/store vectorization*

The performance degradation depicted in the last section arises when a program performs parallel memory accesses to distinct arrays. Theoretically, if the processor has enough functional units (FUs), and if the different caches have enough ports, such memory operations can be executed in parallel. Unfortunately, for micro-architectural implementation reasons (design complexity), memory disambiguation mechanisms in actual ILP processors do not perform complete comparisons on address bits. Furthermore, some caches, such as those implemented on Itanium 2, contain several banks and do not allow sustaining full access bandwidth. Thus, parallel memory operations are serialized during execution, even if enough FUs and ILP exist, and even if data are located in low cache levels.

Let us think about ways to avoid the dynamic conflicts between memory operations. One of the ways to reduce these troubles is load/store vectorization. This is not a novel technique indeed, and we do not aim to bring a new one; we only want to show that the classical vectorization is a simple and yet robust solution to a difficult problem. Our load/store vectorization schedules memory access operations not only according to data dependences and resources constraints, but we must also take into account the accessed address streams (even if independent). Since we do not know the exact array offsets at compile time, we cannot precisely determine all memory locations (virtual memory addresses) that are accessed by the source code. However, we can rely on their relative address locations as defined by the arrays. For instance, we can determine at compile time the relative address between X(i) and X(i+1), but not between X(i) and Y(i) since array offsets are determined at linking time in the case of static arrays, or at execute time in the case of dynamically allocated arrays. Thus, we are sure at compile time that the different addresses of the elements X(i), X(i+1),..., X(i+k) do not share the same lower-order bits. This fact makes us group memory operations accessing the same vector since we know their relative addresses. Such memory access grouping is similar to vectorization, except that only loads and stores are vectorized. The other operations, such as the FP ones, are not vectorized, and hence they are kept free to be scheduled at the fine-grain level to enhance the performance.

Vectorization may be a complex code transformation, and many studies have been performed on this scope. In our framework, the problem is simplified since we tackle fully parallel innermost loops. We only seek a convenient vectorization degree.

Ideally, the higher this degree, the higher the performance, but the higher the register pressure too. Thus, we are constrained by the number of available registers. We showed in [JAL 06] how we can modify the register allocation step by combining load/store vectorization at the data dependence graph (DDG) level without hurting ILP extraction. This previous study [JAL 06] shows how we can seek a convenient vectorization degree which satisfies register file constraints and ILP extraction. To simplify the explanation, if a non-vectorized loop consumes r registers, then the vectorized version with degree k requires at most $k \times r$ registers. Thus, if the processor has $\mathcal{R}$ available registers, a trivial valid vectorization degree is $k = \left\lfloor \frac{\mathcal{R}}{r} \right\rfloor$. The following sections explore the effectiveness of load/store vectorization.

6.1.6.1. *Example with Alpha 21264 processor*

Figure 6.1(b) shows the impact of vectorization on the LxSy micro-benchmark (compare it to Figure 6.1(a)). Even if all the performance troubles do not disappear, the worst execution times in this case are less than 7 cycles instead of 28 cycles previously.

The best performance remains the same for the two versions, that is 1.3 cycles. This improvement is confirmed for all BLAS 1 micro-benchmarks and in all cache levels. Table 6.2 presents the gain of the worst performance resulted from vectorization. It is counted as the gain between the worst performance of the vectorized codes and the worst performance of the original codes. The best performance of all the micro-benchmarks is not altered by vectorization.

Cache	LxLy	LxSy	copy	vsum	daxpy
L1	0%	53.57%	45.83%	80%	29.17%
L2	26.32%	75%	48.15%	80%	30.77%

Table 6.2. *Worst-case performance gain on Alpha 21264*

6.1.6.2. *Example with Power 4 processor*

Figure 6.2(b) shows the performance of vectorized vsum micro-benchmark when the operands are located in L3 cache level (compare it to Figure 6.2(a)). As can be seen, all the stripes of bad performance disappear. Vectorizing memory operations improves the worst performance of all our micro-benchmarks in all cache levels by reducing the number of conflicts between the memory operations. The best performance of all the micro-benchmarks is not degraded by vectorization.

6.1.6.3. *Example with Itanium 2 processor*

The case of the Itanium 2 processor needs more efforts since there are bank conflicts in addition to imprecise memory disambiguation. Thus, the load/store vectorization is not as naive as for out-of-order superscalar processors. In order to eliminate bank conflicts, memory access operations are packed into instruction groups that access even or odd vector elements. For instance Load X(i), Load X(i+2), Load X(i+4),... and Load X(i+1), Load X(i+3), Load X(i+5), etc. Thus, each instruction group accesses a distinct cache bank. Since each bank can contain 16 bytes of consecutive data, two consecutive double FP elements may be assigned to the same bank. This fact prohibits accessing both elements at the same clock cycle (bank conflict). This is why we grouped the accesses in an odd/even way.

Figure 6.4(a) shows the performance of the vectorized LxLy micro-benchmark (compare it to Figure 6.3(a)). As can be seen, all bank conflicts and memory disambiguation problems disappear. The sustained performance is the peak one (optimal) for any vector offsets. When stores are performed, Figure 6.4(b) shows the L3 behavior for the vectorized copy micro-benchmark (compare it to Figure 6.3(b)). The original grid patterns are smoothed.

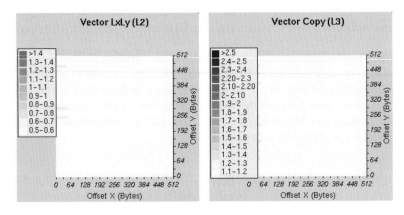

Figure 6.4. *Vectorization on Itanium 2*

This improvement occurs for all our micro-benchmarks and in all cache levels. Table 6.3 shows the performance gain resulted from vectorization, counted as the gain between the worst performance of the vectorized codes and the worst performance of the original codes. Again, load/store vectorization does not alter the peak performance in all cases.

Cache	LxLy	LxSy	Copy	Daxpy
L2	45.45%	18.18%	47.62%	40.91%
L3	28.57%	18.75%	54.55%	33.33%

Table 6.3. *Worst-case performance gain on Itanium 2*

6.1.7. *Conclusion on hardware memory disambiguation mechanisms*

Memory-bound programs rely on advanced compilation techniques that try to keep data in the cache levels, hoping to fully utilize a maximal amount of ILP on the underlying hardware functional units. Even in ideal cases when data operands are located in cache, and when compilers generate codes that can statically be considered as *good*, our study demonstrates that this is not sufficient for sustaining the peak performance at execution time.

First, the memory disambiguation mechanisms in ILP processors do not perform comparisons on whole address bits. If two memory operations access two distinct memory locations but have the same lower-order bits in their addresses, the hardware detects a false dependence and triggers a serialization mechanism. Consequently, load/store queues cannot be fully utilized to reorder the independent memory operations.

Second, the banking structure of some caches prevent from sustaining entire access bandwidth. If two elements are mapped to the same cache bank, independent loads are restricted to be executed sequentially, even if enough FUs are idle. This fact is a well-known source of troubles, but backend compilers still do not take it into account, and the generated codes can be much slower than expected.

The experimental study of this section demonstrates that a simple existing compilation technique can help us to generate faster codes that can reduce the load/store queue conflicts. Consecutive accesses to the same array are grouped together since their relative addresses are known at compile time. Coupling a simple vectorization technique with other classical ILP scheduling methods is demonstrated to be effective to sustain the peak performance. Even if we do not avoid all situations of bad relative array offsets in all hardware platforms, and thus few memory disambiguation penalties persist, we showed that we still get high-performance gains in all experimented processors. Slightly modifying the code of an application is a simple software solution that deals well with an imprecise memory disambiguation mechanism. It would be less expensive than proposing a precise memory disambiguation hardware mechanism.

Load/store vectorization is not the only way that we may solve the performance bugs highlighted in this section. Array padding for instance can change the memory layout in order to produce better array offset combinations. However, array padding may require us to analyze the whole source code application. In the case of scientific libraries on which we are focusing, we cannot apply this technique since the arrays are declared outside the functions (not available at the compilation time of the library).

In the next section, we will study another aspect of memory hierarchy, which is cache misses penalties.

6.2. How to deal in practice with memory latency by software data preloading and prefetching

6.2.1. *Introduction*

Program transformations for reducing cache penalties are well-established techniques in high-performance computing and desktop applications. Nowadays high-performance processors offer many hardware mechanisms helping either to hide or to tolerate memory latencies: multiple cache levels, higher cache sizes and degrees of associativity, memory banking and interleaving, non-blocking caches and out-of-order execution, etc. All these hardware mechanisms combined with program transformations at the loop nest level produce speedups in general.

In addition to a better harmony between hardware and software, cache optimization has been also introduced at the operating system (OS) level. Due to multitasking combined with multi-core architectures, we can now envisage methods where an independent parallel thread or OS service can prefetch application data. The OS can also detect some situations when dynamic recompilation during execution is necessary to generate better codes regarding cache miss penalties.

Consequently, nowadays cache optimization strategies for high-performance and desktop applications require increasingly conjunction between multiple complex techniques at various levels: application (loop nest, regions or control-flow graphs), OS and hardware (processor and memory).

The case of embedded applications is quite different. First, an embedded VLIW processor is at least hundred times cheaper than a high-performance processor: few hardware mechanisms for cache optimization exist (if any); the computation power is also reduced, there is little margin for tolerating code optimization based on aggressive speculation. Second, some embedded systems execute with a light OS, or even at bare mode (without any OS): no dynamic services or tasks can be used in parallel to improve cache effects. Third, embedded applications are rarely statically controlled programs with regular control or regular data accesses: such applications cannot meet the model requirements for loop transformations [ALL 02] and for usual software prefetching with regular strides. Finally, code size growth is an additional constraint to deal with.

In this section, we present a method to reduce processor stalls due to cache misses in presence of non-blocking cache architectures. We implement our method at the backend level where loop structures disappear. Our principal aim is not to reduce cache misses (as usually done with loop transformations) but to reduce the processor stalls due to them. It is a combination of software data prefetching (inserting special prefetch instructions) and preloading (increasing static load latencies). As we will explain later, it is especially designed for VLIW in-order processor that would include non-blocking caches instead of blocking caches.

6.2.2. Related work

Improving the cache effects at instruction level is an already a studied topic. We can classify related work following two directions: a theoretical direction, where some studies were done on instruction-level scheduling taking into account the cache constraints. The second direction is more practical. As a theoretical work, we quote the contribution published in [TOU 01]. It is the first intLP model that included the impact of the compulsory misses in an optimal acyclic scheduling problem in a single basic block. We model the exact scheduling problem by including the constraint of data dependences, functional units, registers and compulsory misses. Our current section will present a practical study, we try to cover all kinds of cache misses (compulsory, capacity and conflict). Also, we do not restrict ourselves to a single directed acyclic graph (DAG) (basic block) only, we are interested in optimizing a function as a whole.

Here, we are interested in practical ways that handle reducing cache miss penalties with two techniques: prefetch and instruction scheduling techniques. Using the prefetch solution, Al-Sukhni *et al.* [ALS 06] classified the load operations as *intrinsic* and *extrinsic* streams and developed a prefetch algorithm based on automaton taking into account the density and the affinity of these streams. The experiments were done on a simulator of a superscalar out-of-order processor: out-of-order execution helps us to hide cache miss penalties at execution time, in opposition to our case that is an in-order VLIW processor. Abraham *et al.* [ABR 93] proposed a prefetch technique. They described their technique by automaton: the first step of this automaton is profiling of load instructions, and the second step is the selection phase of loads that miss the cache. The final state is the prefetching of these delinquent loads. Another prefetch solution is dynamic prefetching as proposed by Beyler *et al.* [BEY 07]. They studied a dynamic prefetch mechanism using the load latency variation to classify the loads. The framework is based on finite state machine. They obtained positive results on the Itanium processor where the Intel compiler (icc) automatically generates prefetch instructions. Regarding dynamic prefetching, we always quote Lu *et al.* [LU 03] who developed a framework called ADORE. The authors proceed through three steps: tracking delinquent loads, selecting the data references and finally prefetching these loads. This solution is based on hardware monitor of the Itanium processor. The two previous works [BEY 07] and [LU 03] were done on Itanium architecture, which is used for high-performance computing. This section will present a technique done on a *light* embedded VLIW processor which generally executes a single task; so, the dynamic prefetch mechanism is an inappropriate solution for a target VLIW architecture.

We target two cache architectures: a blocking cache architecture and a non-blocking cache architecture. In the case of blocking cache architectures, only the prefetch method will be used (preloading is useless in this case). If non-blocking cache is present, prefetching is combined with preloading (as will be explained later).

This latter case is more interesting because some VLIW processors include non-blocking caches. Blocking cache architecture and optimizations have been covered in many studies. Tien *et al.* [CHE 92] studied the effects of pipelined loads and prefetch in MIPS3000 single issue processor, and tried some compiler optimizations such as changing static load latencies to exploit the pipelined execution of loads. In our case, we study the cache effects for a VLIW (multiple issue) processor.

For a non-blocking cache architecture, Oner *et al.* [ÖNE 93] made a study of kernel scheduling on an MIPS processor. The authors increased the load-use dependency distance in loop kernel using loop pipelining. In addition to loop kernels, our method is applied to basics blocks, functions and whole applications. In other words, we have no code granularity restrictions.

Ding *et al.* [DIN 97d] based their work on data reuse information, i.e. they made a first step static analysis to collect load statistics of selected kernels. Then, they used the collected statistics to combine data prefetching and instruction scheduling techniques to hide cache effects. Contrary to the work of Ding *et al.*, we do not restrict ourselves to loops and we do not use a virtual superscalar machine. Our target architecture is a real VLIW processor in the market (used in many real-world embedded systems).

The authors in [FAR 94] did a performance evaluation to study the hardware complexity of non-blocking cache architecture using SPEC92 benchmarks. They showed that a simple hit-under-miss non-blocking cache implementation (i.e. only two overlapped loads at the same time) is a good trade-off between hardware cost and performance. However, the work done by Ammenouche *et al.* [AMM 08] showed that non-blocking caches do not provide any performance improvement in the case of embedded VLIW processors because execution is in order and no dynamic instruction scheduling is done to hide cache miss penalties as in the case of superscalar processors. However, Ammenouche *et al.* showed [AMM 08] on two applications that non-blocking caches may provide good performance improvement if low-level code optimization based on preloading is used. Our current study extends the previous work by adding a prefetch method and making a more complete experimental study using MEDIABENCH and SPEC2000 benchmarks.

To clearly explain the position of the technique presented in this section, we say that our study aims to improve (at the software level) the efficiency of the non-blocking cache architecture on VLIW processors. We combine data prefetching and preloading in conjunction with a global instruction scheduler that handles an entire function. Such a global instruction scheduler does not necessarily target regular codes, such as loop nests. As we will explain later, our technical framework is based on profiling and trace analysis. The next section starts by explaining the problem of cache effects at the instruction level.

6.2.3. *Problems of optimizing cache effects at the instruction level*

Nowadays, cache memory is widely used in high-performance computing. It is generally organized in a hierarchical way making a trade-off between hardware cost and code performance. The drawback of this memory architecture is the unpredictability of the data location. Indeed, at any time during the program execution, we are uncertain about the data location: data may be located in any cache level, or in the main memory or in other buffers. This situation can be acceptable in high-performance architectures, but cannot be appreciated in embedded *soft* real-time systems because data access latencies are unpredictable. We focus our attention on embedded systems, especially those using VLIW processors. In this case, instruction scheduling is one of the most important sources of improving code performance. A static instruction scheduling method considering a cache model would be ideal for hiding/tolerating the unpredictability of execution times. Nowadays, general purpose compilers like gcc, icc and the st200cc do not manage cache effects: memory access latencies are considered fixed during compilation because the latencies of the load instructions are unknown at compile time. Many instruction scheduling techniques are developed and have been commented upon in the literature, but they always suppose well-defined latencies for all kinds of instructions. The fact is that the proposed models are simplified because of our lack of knowledge about data location and thus about load latencies.

Loop scheduling is a good example to assert our idea: software pipelining is a well-matured scheduling technique for innermost loops. Its aim is usually to minimize the Initiation Interval (II) and the prologue/epilogue length. The compiler assumes that the total execution time of the pipelined loop is the sum of the prologue and epilogue length and the kernel (II) multiplied by the number of iterations. Since almost all scheduling techniques assume fixed instructions latencies, the compiler has an artificial performance model for code optimization. Furthermore, the compilers quoted above schedule the load instructions with optimistic latencies, since they assume that all data reside in lower cache levels, and they schedule the consumer of the loaded data close to the load operation. Consequently, the instruction schedulers of compilers have optimistic view of the performance of their fine-grain scheduling. The case of the st200cc is relevant; this compiler schedules the consumers of a load only 3 cycles after the load (3 corresponds to the L1 cache hit latency, while a cache miss costs 143 clock cycles). If a load misses the L1 cache, the processor stalls for at least of 140 cycles, since a VLIW processor has no out-of-order mechanism. The icc compiler for Itanium also has the same behavior and schedules all loads with a fixed latency (7 cycles), a latency between the L2 (5 cycles) and L3 (13 cycles) levels of cache.

Another problem of instruction scheduling taking into account cache effects is the difficulty to precisely predict cache misses in the frontend of the compiler. While some cache optimization techniques are applied on some special loop constructs, it is hard for the compiler frontend to determine the cache influence on fine-grain scheduling and vice versa. Sometimes, this fact makes compiler designers implement cache optimization techniques in the backend, where the underlying target micro-architecture is precisely known (cache size, cache latencies, memory hierarchy, cache configuration and other available buffers). However, in the compiler backend, the high-level program is already transformed to a low-level intermediate representation and high-level constructs such as loops and arrays disappear. Consequently, loop nest transformations can no longer be applied to reduce the number of cache misses. Our question becomes how to hide the cache miss effects rather than how to avoid the cache misses.

Another important criterion for applying cache optimizations at different levels is the regularity of the program. At compilation, regularity can be seen on two orthogonal axes: regularity of control and regularity of data access (see Table 6.4, for example). Due to the orthogonality of these two axes, four scenarios are possible:

1) regular control with regular data access: data prefetch can be used in this case, for instance to prefetch regular array accesses;

2) regular control with irregular data access: depending on the shape of irregularity, data can sometimes be prefetched. Another possible solution is the preloading (this is explained later in section 6.2.5.2);

3) irregular control with regular data access: the data prefetching solution is possible, but inserting the prefetch code has to take care of multiple execution paths;

4) irregular control with irregular data access: also depending on the shape of irregularity data can sometimes be prefetched. The preloading is more suitable in this case.

Note that while data prefetching usually requires some regularity in data access, preloading can always be applied at the instruction level.

`while(i ≤ max)` `a+=T[i++];`	`while(i ≤ max)` `a+=T[V[i++]];`	`while(i ≤ max)` `if (cond)` `a+=T[i++];`	`while(i ≤ max)` `if (cond)` `a+=T[V[i++]];`
Regular control and data access	Regular control and irregular data access	Irregular control and regular data access	Irregular control and irregular data access

Table 6.4. *Examples of code and data regularity/irregularity*

The next section recalls the underlying architecture that we target in this study.

6.2.4. *Target processor description*

In the study used in this section, we use the ST231 core which is a VLIW processor from STmicroelectronics. These VLIW processors implement a single cluster derivative of the Lx architecture [FAR 00]. ST231 is an integer 32-bit VLIW processor with five stages in the pipeline. It contains four integer units, two multiplication units and one load/store unit. It has a 64 KB L1 cache. The latency of the L1 cache is 3 cycles. The data cache is a four-way associative. It operates with a write-back no-allocate policy. A 128-byte write buffer is associated with the Dcache. It also includes a separated 128-byte prefetch buffer that can store up to eight cache lines. As for many embedded processors, the power consumption should be low, hence limiting the amount of additional hardware mechanisms devoted to program acceleration. In addition, the price of this processor is very cheap compared to high-performance processors: a typical high-performance processor is more than one hundred times more expensive than the ST231.

Regarding the memory cache architecture, ST231 includes a blocking cache architecture. In [CHE 92], the non-blocking cache is presented as a possible solution for performance improvement in out-of-order (OoO) processors. So, several high-performance OoO processors use this cache architecture. The interesting aspect of this cache architectures is the ability to overlap the execution and the long memory data access (loads). Due to the non-blocking cache, when a cache miss occurs, the processor continues the execution of independent operations. This produces an overlap between bringing up the data from memory and the execution of independent instructions. However, the current embedded processors do not yet include this kind of memory cache because the ratio between its cost (in terms of energy consumption and price) and its benefit in terms of performance improvement was not demonstrated till our results published in [AMM 08]. Furthermore, in order to efficiently exploit the non-blocking cache mechanism, the main memory must be fully pipelined and multiported while these architectural enhancements are not necessary in case of blocking cache. Kroft [KRO 81] proposed a scheme with special registers called Miss Information Status Hold Registers (MSHRs), also called *pending load queue*. MSHRs are used to hold the information about the outstanding misses. He defines the notion of *primary* and *secondary* miss. The primary miss is the first pending miss requesting a cache line. All other pending loads requesting the same cache line are secondary misses – these can be seen as cache hits in a blocking cache architecture. The number of MSHR (pending load queue size) is the upper limit of the outstanding misses that can be overlapped in the pipeline. If a processor has n MSHRS, then the non-blocking cache can service n concurrent overlapped loads. When a cache miss occurs, the set of MSHRs is checked to detect whether there is a pending miss to the same cache line. If there is no pending miss to the same cache line, the current miss is set as a primary miss; if there is an available free MSHR, the targeted register is stored. If there is no available free MSHR, the processor stalls.

The next section shows a practical demonstration that optimizing cache effects at instruction level brings good performances.

6.2.5. *Our method of instruction-level code optimization*

Our method aims to hide the cache penalties (processor stalls) due to cache misses. We want to maximize the overlap between the stalls due to Dcache misses with the processor execution. For this purpose, we focus on delinquent loads, whether they occur in loops or in other parts of the code. We do not limit our method to a certain shape of code, we consider both regular and irregular control flow and data streams. We study two techniques, each of them corresponding to a certain case:

– for the case of irregular data memory accesses, we use the preloading technique;

– for the case of regular data memory accesses, we use the prefetch technique.

It is well known that combining many optimization techniques does not necessarily yield better performances. This may lead to a hard phase ordering problem. Our methodology shows how to solve this problem for the two combined optimizations. Since these two techniques are complementary, we can also combine them in the same compiler optimization pass. Let us explain in detail the usage of these two techniques, which are data prefetching and data preloading.

6.2.5.1. *Data prefetching method at instruction level*

The cache penalty is very expensive in terms of clock cycles (more than 140 cycles in the case of the ST231). The current hardware mechanisms fail to fully hide such long penalties. In the case of a superscalar processor, the OoO mechanism can partially hide the cache effects during few cycles (up to the size of a window of instructions in the pipeline). Rescheduling the instructions, with a software (compilation) method or hardware technique (execution), cannot totally hide a cache penalty.

The data prefetching technique is an efficient way to hide the cache penalty. However, the usual prefetching methods work well for regular data accesses that are analyzed at the source code level. In many embedded applications, data accesses do not appear to have regular strides when analyzed by the compiler because of indirect access, for instance. Furthermore, the memory accesses are not always performed inside a static control loop. Consequently, the usual prefetching techniques fail. In the method we are presenting, we analyze the regularity of a stride due to a precise instruction-level profiling.

Our data prefetching is based on predicting the addresses of the next memory access. If the prediction is correct the memory access will be costless. In the case of bad prediction, the penalty is low (ST231 includes a prefetch buffer, so the *bad* prefetched data does not pollute the cache). The only possible penalty consists of adding extra instructions in the code (code size growth) and executing them. However, in case of VLIW processors, we can take care of inserting these extra instructions inside free slots because not all the bundles contain memory operations. Consequently, no extra cost is added, neither in terms of code size nor in terms of executions. So, the most important aspect of this technique is the memory address predictor, or the generation of a code that computes the address of the next prefetched data.

Our method of prefetching requires us to perform three phases before generating an optimized code: profiling the code to generate a trace, then selecting some delinquents loads and finally inserting the prefetch instructions.

Phase 1: application profiling at instruction level – this step is the most expensive in terms of processing time, because we have to perform a precise instruction level profiling of the code by generating a trace. Classical profiling, as done with the gprof tool for instance, operates at medium coarse grain level (functions). In our case, we proceed in the finest profiling granularity, that is at the instruction level. To do this, we use a special software plug-in device, which can manage the execution events and statistics. This plug-in is an interface with the ST231 simulator, which is completely programmable. We use the plug-in to select all the loads which miss the cache, and for each load, collect its accessed addresses inside a trace. This trace highlights the delinquent loads. A load is said to be *delinquent* if it produces a large number of cache misses. In practice, we sort the loads according to the number of cache misses they produce, and we define the top ones as delinquents. The result of this profiling phase is a precise cartography of the accessed memory data addresses, tagged with the delinquent loads.

The next phase is to select the right loads to prefetch within the set of delinquent loads.

Phase 2: load selection – selecting which delinquent loads to prefetch depends on two parameters: the number of cache misses and the regularity of memory accesses. The most important criterion is the number of cache misses induced by a load. Indeed, in order to maximize the prefetch benefit, it is important to prefetch loads with a high frequency of cache misses. Choosing loads that produce many cache misses allows us to hide the cost of extra prefetch instructions, since prefetch instructions may introduce some additional bundles in the original code. Increasing the code size or changing the code shape may produce very undesirable effects and may slow down the performance because of the direct mapped structure of instruction cache. Consequently, for a given identified delinquent load, the higher the number of cache misses it produces, the better the performance can be achieved. We do not care about the ratio of hit/miss of the delinquent load; we only measure the frequency of cache misses and sort the loads according to this value.

Once a delinquent load is selected as a good candidate for prefetching, we should analyze the second parameter, which is the memory access regularity. Wu in [WU 02] classified the load with the next data stride patterns:

– strong single stride: it is a load with a near-constant stride i.e. the stride occurs with a very high probability;

– phased multistride: it is a load with many possible strides that occur frequently together;

– weak single stride: it is a load with only one of the non-zero stride values that occurs somewhat frequently.

On the basis of this simple classification, only strong single stride and some phased multistride are selected by our method. An example of strong single stride is shown in Figure 6.5(a). In this figure, we can observe a unique stride of a single delinquent load instruction from jpeg benchmark. In this figure, the x-axis corresponds to the numerous load instances of a unique selected delinquent load instruction (a load instance is a dynamic execution of a static load instruction), the y-axis is the stride between the addresses of consecutive data accesses. We recall that these regular strides do not appear when analyzing the source code at compilation time, but they appear with application profiling at the instruction level.

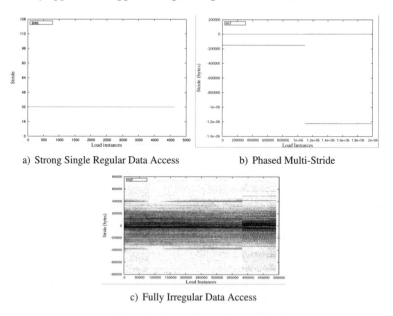

a) Strong Single Regular Data Access   b) Phased Multi-Stride

c) Fully Irregular Data Access

Figure 6.5. *Stride pattern classification*

Figure 6.5(b) corresponds to the phased multiple stride of delinquent load instruction from 181.mcf benchmark (SPEC2000 benchmark suite). Here we can clearly observe two regular strides.

In Figure 6.5(c), we observe fully irregular strides for a single load, this kind of load is not prefetched, but can be preloaded, as we will explain later.

Once we select delinquent loads with strong single stride or with phased multistride, we can proceed to the last step of prefetch instruction insertion.

Phase 3: prefetch instruction insertion – this step consists of adding a single or many prefetch instructions in the code. The syntax of a load instruction on the ST231 is: LD Rx= immediate[Ry]. The first argument of the instruction is Rx, the destination register, while the second argument is the memory address defined as the content of the index register Ry plus an immediate offset. The prefetch instruction has the same syntax pft immediate[Ry] except that it does not require a destination register. Executing a prefetch instruction brings data to the prefetch buffer (not to the cache) and does not induce any data dependence on a register. However, we should take care not to add an extra cost of the added prefetch instruction. In order to achieve this purpose, the prefetch instruction should be inserted inside a free issue slot inside a VLIW (each bundle may contain up to one memory access instruction). If no free slot is available, we could insert a new bundle but with the risk of increasing the code size and altering the execution time (making the critical path longer in a loop, disturb the instruction cache behavior, etc.).

Now, let us give more details on the inserted prefetch instruction. If the delinquent load has this form LD Rx= immediate[Ry] and has a single stride s, then we insert a prefetch instruction of the form pft s[Ry]. If the delinquent load has multiple strides $s_1, s_2, \ldots$, then we insert a prefetch instruction for each stride. However, our experiments indicate that it is not efficient to prefetch more than two distinct strides. The left column of Table 6.5 shows an example of prefetching with a data stride equal to 540 bytes. The bundle following the load includes the prefetch instruction: it prefetches the data for the next instance of the load.

Now, if the used index register Ry is altered/modified by the code after the delinquent load, this index register cannot be used as a base address for the prefetch instruction. We provide two solutions:

– Use Rz another free register (if available) used to insert a prefetch instruction. A copy operation Rz=Ry is inserted just before Ry modification. In almost all cases we found free slots to schedule such additional copy operations, but it is not always possible to find a free register.

– If no free register exists, then we insert a new VLIW bundle that contains the prefetch instruction. This new bundle is inserted between the delinquent load bundle and the bundle that modifies Ry.

The right column of Table 6.5 shows an example. Here, the base register $r27 is changed in the bundle after the load. The register $r27 is saved on a free register, say $r62. Then the prefetch instruction is inserted in a free VLIW slot.

L?_3_69:	L?_BB37_14:
ldw $r32 = 28[$r15] ; ; cmple $b5 = $r32, $r0 **pft 540[$r15]** ; ; brf $b5, L?_3_69:	**ldw $r28 = 16[$r27]** mov $r62 = $r27 ; ; sub $r27 = $r27, $r21 ldw $r4 = -4[$15] ; ; mul $r23 = $r4, $r17 **pft 32[$r62]** ; ; brf $b4, L?_BB37_14
Simple prefetch instruction with a stride of 540 bytes	Using $r62 register to save the memory address to prefetch

Table 6.5. *Examples of prefetch: simple case and using extra register case*

As mentioned before, the prefetch technique is an efficient low-level code optimization that reduces the frequency of cache misses. Its main weakness is the difficulty in making an efficient address predictor. It is especially hard to predict the right addresses to prefetch in irregular data accesses. For this case, the prefetch technique cannot be applied. Thus, we propose in the next section the preloading technique that can be applied for the case of irregular data access.

6.2.5.2. *Data preloading method*

The preloading technique is used if the processor includes a non-blocking cache. We have already published experiments in [AMM 08] to check the efficiency of non-blocking cache architectures on in-order processors (such as VLIW). Our results can be summarized in four points:

1) If the code is not transformed by the compiler (recompiled for considering the non-blocking cache architecture), replacing a blocking cache architecture by a non-blocking cache does not bring performance improvement.

2) No slowdown was noticed due to non-blocking cache.

3) If preloading is used (to be explained later), then a performance gain is observed.

4) A maximal performance gain was observed with 8 MSHRs.

In high-performance OoO processors, replacing a blocking cache with a non-blocking cache provides speedup even if the binary code is not optimized. In the case of VLIW in-order processors, the benefit of non-blocking caches is close to zero if the code is not modified. In order to understand this fact, we need to introduce the two following definitions:

– *Definition of static load-use distance:* static load-use distance is the distance in the assembly code (in terms of VLIW bundles) between a load instruction and the first consumer of the loaded data. This static distance is equivalent to a static measure of clock cycles between a load and its first consumption.

– *Definition of dynamic load-use distance:* dynamic load-use distance is the distance in terms of processor clock cycles between the execution time of a load instruction and the execution time of the first consumer of this loaded data.

In [AMM 08], we showed that the static load-use distance in the set of experimented benchmarks is short, about 3 bundles, i.e. the st200cc compiler has an optimistic compilation strategy regarding load latencies. It assumes that all data are in the L1 cache. The VLIW compiler schedules the consumer of data too close to its producer (load) in order to keep the register pressure low. In the case of an in-order processor with non-blocking cache architecture, it would be ideal if the compiler could generate codes with longer load-use distance. The problem is computing the right latency for each load i.e. considering the delinquent loads with higher latencies during instruction scheduling. This instruction scheduling method is called *preloading*. Of course, the purpose of preloading is not to increase the static load latencies of all load operations, otherwise this would increase the register pressure. Our preloading strategy selects a subset of delinquent loads as candidates. We proceed in two phases explained below.

The first phase of our preloading technique is the same used for the prefetching, i.e. we start with a precise profiling phase at instruction level. This profiling allows us to detect delinquent loads as well as the code fragment to which they belong (function or loop).

The second phase of our preloading technique defines the right load-use distance to each load. This is a major difficulty in practice: a compile time prediction of the probability of cache misses and hits is difficult (if not impossible) at the compiler backend level. This is why the first phase of fine-grain profiling provides useful information. Depending on ratio of hit/miss for each load, we compute a certain probability of dynamic load latencies that we set at compile time. For instance, if a load misses the cache 30% of the times (143 cycles of latency) and hits 70% of the time (3 cycles of latency), then its static latency is set to $0.3 \times 143 + 0.7 \times 3 = 45$. If the register pressure becomes very high because of this long static latency, the compiler cannot extract enough ILP to hide this latency, then we reduce the latency to avoid inserting spill code. Our preloading method iterates on different values of static load latencies until reaching a reasonable performance gain estimated at compile time. For the case of embedded systems, the compilation time is allowed to last during such iterative processes.

Due to the preloading technique, we can achieve a very good performance increase. However, we must be aware of the following points:

– Increasing static load latencies renders the compiler more aggressive regarding ILP extraction (deeper loop unrolling, global scheduling, superblock formation, etc.). Consequently, the code size may increase or the memory layout of the code can be modified. This can have negative effects on instruction cache misses. Furthermore, it is better to skip the preloading optimization for shorter trip count loop. It is especially the case of software pipelined loop with few iterations: increasing the static load latency increases the static II. If the number of loop iterations is not high enough, then the software pipelining would be too deep for reaching the steady state.

– For other kinds of code (i.e. non-loop code), if the increased load latencies are too long, the compiler may not find enough independent instructions to schedule between a delinquent load and its customer. To avoid that, many techniques can be applied in combination with preloading such as tail duplication, region scheduling, superblock instruction scheduling, trace scheduling, scheduling non-loop code with prologue/epilogue of loop blocks, etc. All these aggressive ILP extraction methods usually yield a code size increase.

– The last important point is that when increasing the load latency, the register pressure may increase. This fact can have bad effects if there are not enough free registers and oblige the compiler to introduce spill code to reduce the simultaneously-alive variables. If spill code cannot be avoided, preloading should not be applied.

The preloading technique is efficient and practical because it can be applied to irregular codes with or without irregular data strides. It can also be applied in combination with other high- or low-level code optimization techniques. An *ad hoc* algorithm in [AMM 09] details our whole methodology of data prefetching and preloading.

6.2.6. *Experimental results*

Appendix 6 summarizes our experimental results. Playing with the micro-architectural effects of caches at the instruction level is a complex task, especially for real applications such as FFMPEG, SPEC2000 and MEDIABENCH. Our method of data prefetching selects one or two delinquent loads per application that access a regular data stream that is not possible to analyze statically. Then, we insert one or two prefetch instructions into a VLIW bundle for bringing data before time to prefetch buffer or to cache. This simple method is efficient in the case of blocking and non-blocking caches, where we can get a whole application performance gain up to 9%. The code size does not increase in this situation.

Our method of preloading consists of increasing the static load distance inside a selected loop or a function. This method allows the instruction scheduler to extract more ILP in order to be exploited in the presence of a non-blocking cache. With preloading, we can get a minor code size growth (up to 3.9%) with an application performance gain up to 28.28% (FFMPEG). The advantage of preloading against prefetching is the fact that it is not restricted to regular data streams. When we combine data prefetching with preloading in the presence of a non-blocking cache, we get a better overall performance gain (up to 13% in jpeg) compared to optimized codes with -O3 compilation level. These performances are satisfactory in our case since they are evaluated on the whole application execution time and not on code fractions.

In order to demonstrate that preloading can also be combined with high-level loop nest restructuring methods improving data locality (tiling and blocking), we studied the case of a square matrix-matrix multiply (512×512 integer elements). We used a non-naive implementation, using loop tiling. We tuned the tile size manually to get the fastest code compiled with -O3 flag: we found that a block of 64×64 integer elements provides the best performance. When we combined preloading with this best code version, we obtained an additional speedup of 2.6.

6.2.7. Conclusion on prefetching and preloading at instruction level

We present an assembly-level code optimization method for reducing cache miss penalties. We target embedded VLIW codes executing on an embedded processor with non-blocking cache architecture. For experimental purpose, we used an embedded system based on a VLIW ST231 core. Contrary to high-performance or computationally intensive programs, the embedded applications that we target do not have regular data access or control flow, and the underlying hardware is cheap and simple. Our code optimization method is based on a combination of data prefetching and preloading.

The results of our study clearly show that the presence of non-blocking caches inside VLIW processors is a viable architectural improvement if the compiler applies some low-level code optimizations. Otherwise, introducing a non-blocking cache inside a VLIW does not produce performance improvement.

We have already defined a formal scheduling problem using integer linear programming that combines compulsory cache effects with fine-grain instruction scheduling [TOU 01]. However, we think that our theoretical model does not exactly define the practical problem because reducing the cost of compulsory cache misses would not be sufficient to observe performance gains. This section showed two techniques that produce real speedups but they are inherently *ad hoc*, because they need to be adapted to the micro-architecture. Our low-level study allows us to understand the phenomena that connect between ILP and cache misses. The performance improvement that we obtained makes us think that defining a good theoretical scheduling problem is possible in the future. We mean a scheduling problem that combines the classical instruction scheduling constraints (registers, functional units, VLIW bundling and data dependences) and cache effects (cache misses and memory disambiguation mechanisms).

PART 3

Register Optimization

7

The Register Need of a Fixed Instruction Schedule

This chapter defines our theoretical model for the quantities that we are willing to optimize (either to maximize, minimize or to bound). The register need, also called MAXLIVE, defines the minimal number of registers needed to hold the data produced by a code. We define a general processor model that considers most of the existing architectures with instruction-level parallelism (ILP), such as superscalar, very long instruction word (VLIW) and explicitly parallel instruction computing (EPIC) processors. We model the existence of multiple register types with delayed accesses to registers. We restrict our effort to basic blocks and superblocks devoted to acyclic instruction scheduling, and to innermost loops devoted to software pipelining (SWP).

The ancestor notion of the register need in the case of basic blocks (acyclic schedules) profits from plenty of studies, resulting in a rich theoretical literature. Unfortunately, the periodic (cyclic) problem somehow suffers from fewer fundamental results. Our fundamental results in this topic [TOU 07, TOU 02] enable a better understanding of the register constraints in periodic instruction scheduling, and hence help the community to provide better SWP heuristics and techniques. The first contribution in this chapter is a novel formula for computing the exact number of registers needed in a cyclic scheduled loop. This formula has two advantages: its computation can be made using a polynomial algorithm and it allows the generalization of a previous result [MAN 92]. Second, during SWP, we show that the minimal number of registers needed may increase when incrementing the initiation interval (II), contrary to intuition. We provide a sufficient condition for keeping the minimal number of registers from increasing when incrementing the II. Third, we prove an interesting property that enables us to optimally compute the minimal periodic register sufficiency of a loop for all its valid periodic schedules, irrespective of II. Fourth and last, we give a straightforward proof that the problem of optimal stage scheduling under register constraints is polynomially solvable for a subclass of data dependence graphs, while this problem is known to be NP-complete for arbitrary dependence graphs [HUA 01].

7.1. Data dependence graph and processor model for register optimization

A *data dependence graph* (DDG) is a directed multigraph $G = (V, E)$ where V is a set of vertices (also called instructions, statements, nodes and operations), E is a set of edges (data dependencies and serial constraints). Each statement $u \in V$ has a positive latency $lat(u) \in \mathbb{N}$. A DDG is a multigraph because it is possible to have multiple edges between two vertices.

The modeled processor may have several register types: we denote by $\mathcal{T}$ the set of available register *types*. For instance, $\mathcal{T} = \{BR, GR, FP\}$ for branch, general purpose and floating point registers, respectively. Register types are sometimes called register *classes*. The number of available registers of type t is denoted $\mathcal{R}^t$: $\mathcal{R}^t$ and may be the full set of architectural registers of type t, or may be a subset of it if some architectural registers are reserved for other purposes.

For a given register type $t \in \mathcal{T}$, we denote by $V^{R,t} \subseteq V$ the set of statements $u \in V$ that produce values to be stored inside registers of type t. We write u^t the value of type t created by the instruction $u \in V^{R,t}$. Our theoretical model assumes that a statement u can produce multiple values of distinct types; that is, we do not assume that a statement produces multiple values of the same type. Few architectures allow this feature, and we can model it by node duplication: a node creating multiple results of the same type is split into multiple nodes of distinct types.

Concerning the set of edges E, we distinguish between *flow* edges of type t – denoted $E^{R,t}$ – from the remaining edges. A flow edge $e = (u, v)$ of type t represents the producer–consumer relationship between the two statements u and v: u creates a value u^t read by the statement v. The set of *consumers* of a value $u \in V^{R,t}$ is defined as

$$Cons(u^t) = \{tgt(e) \mid e \in E^{R,t} \wedge src(e) = u\}$$

where $src(e)$ and $tgt(e)$ are the notations used for the source and target of the edge e.

When we consider a register type t, the set $E - E^{R,t}$ of non-flow edges are simply called *serial* edges.

If a value is not read inside the considered code scope ($Cons(u^t) = \emptyset$), it means that either u can be eliminated from the DDG as a dead code, or it can be kept by introducing a dummy node reading it.

7.1.1. *NUAL and UAL semantics*

Processor architectures can be decomposed into many families. One of the used classifications is related to the instruction set architecture (ISA) code semantics [SCH 94]:

– *UAL code semantic:* these processors have unit-assumed-latencies (UAL) at the architectural level. Sequential and superscalar processors belong to this family. In UAL, the assembly code has a sequential semantic, even if the micro-architectural implementation executes instructions of longer latencies, in parallel, out of order or with speculation. The compiler instruction scheduler can always generate a valid code if it considers that all operations have a unit latency (even if such a code may not be efficient).

– *NUAL code semantic:* these processors have non-unit-assumed-latencies (NUAL) at the architectural level. VLIW, EPIC and some Digital Signal Processing (DSP) processors belong to this family. In NUAL, the hardware pipeline steps (latencies, structural hazards and resource conflicts) may be visible at the architectural level. Consequently, the compiler has to know about the instructions latencies, and sometimes with the underlying micro-architecture. The compiler instruction scheduler has to take care of these latencies to generate a correct code that does not violate data dependences.

Our processor model considers both UAL and NUAL semantics. Given a register type $t \in \mathcal{T}$, we model possible delays when reading from or writing into registers of type t. We define two delay functions $\delta_{r,t} : V \mapsto \mathbb{N}$ and $\delta_{w,t} : V^{R,t} \mapsto \mathbb{N}$. These delay functions model NUAL semantics. Thus, the statement u reads from a register $\delta_{r,t}(u)$ clock cycles after the schedule date of u. Also, u writes into a register $\delta_{w,t}(u)$ clock cycles after the schedule date of u.

In UAL, these delays are not visible to the compiler, so we have $\delta_{w,t} = \delta_{r,t} = 0$.

The two next sections define both the acyclic register need (basic blocks and superblocks) and the cyclic register need one a schedule is fixed.

7.2. The acyclic register need

When we consider the code of a basic block or superblock, the DDG is a directed acyclic graph (DAG). Each edge of a DAG $G = (V, E)$ is labeled by latency $\delta(e) \in \mathbb{Z}$. The latency of an edge $\delta(e)$ and the latency of a statement $lat(u)$ are not necessarily in relationship.

An acyclic scheduling problem is to compute a scheduling function $\sigma : V \rightarrow \mathbb{Z}$ that satisfies at least the data dependence constraints: $\forall e = (u, v) \in E : \sigma(v) - \sigma(u) \geq \delta(e)$.

Once a schedule σ is fixed, we can define the *acyclic lifetime interval* of a value u^t as the date between the creation and the last consumption (called *killing* or *death* date):

$$\forall t \in \mathcal{T}, \forall u \in V^{R,t} : LT_\sigma(u^t) =]\sigma(u) + \delta_{w,t}(u), d_\sigma(u)]$$

Here, $d_\sigma(u) = \max_{v \in Cons(u^t)} (\sigma(v) + \delta_{r,t}(v))$ denotes the death (killing) date of u^t.

Figure 7.1 illustrates an example. Figure 7.1(b) is the DDG of the straight line code of Figure 7.1(a). If we consider floating point (FP) registers, we highlight values of FP type with bold circles in the DAG. Bold edges correspond to flow dependences of FP type. Once a schedule is fixed as illustrated in Figure 7.1(c), acyclic lifetime intervals are defined as shown in the figure: since we assume a NUAL semantic in this example, lifetime intervals are delayed from the schedule date of the instructions. Remark that the writing clock cycle of a value does not belong to the acylic lifetime interval (which is defined a left open interval), because data cannot be read before finishing the writing.

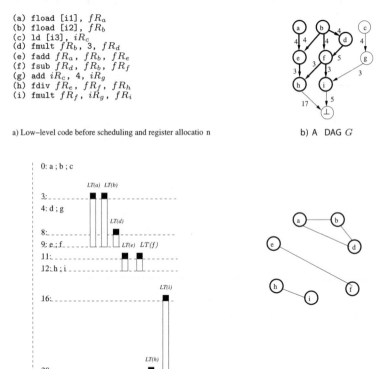

```
(a) fload [i1], fRₐ
(b) fload [i2], fR_b
(c) ld [i3], iR_c
(d) fmult fR_b, 3, fR_d
(e) fadd fRₐ, fR_b, fR_e
(f) fsub fR_d, fR_b, fR_f
(g) add iR_c, 4, iR_g
(h) fdiv fR_e, fR_f, fR_h
(i) fmult fR_f, iR_g, fR_i
```

a) Low–level code before scheduling and register allocatio n

b) A DAG G

c) $RN_\sigma^{FP}(G) = 3$

d) Interference Graph with Maximal Clique

Figure 7.1. *DAG example with acyclic register need*

Now, $RN_\sigma^t(G)$ the acyclic register need of type t for the DAG G with respect to (w.r.t.) the schedule σ is the maximal number of values simultaneously alive of type t. $RN_\sigma^t(G)$ is also called MAXLIVE. Figure 7.1(c) shows that we have at most three values simultaneously alive, which are $\{a, b, d\}$. Consequently, $RN_\sigma^{FP}(G) = 3$. The set of a maximal number of values simultaneously alive is called an *excessive set*, any value belonging to it is called an *excessive value*.

Computing $RN_\sigma^t(G)$ for a DAG is an easy problem, it is equal to the size of the stable set (maximal clique) in the indirected interference graph shown in Figure 7.1(d). In general, computing the stable set of a graph is NP-complete. But the special case of interval graphs allows us to compute it in $\mathcal{O}(\|V\| \times \log \|V\|)$ [GUP 79].

Once a schedule is fixed, the problem of register allocation is also easy. The number of required registers (chromatic number of the interference graph) of type t is exactly equal to $RN_\sigma^t(G)$, and can be solved due to the algorithm defined in [GUP 79].

As mentioned previously, the acyclic register need has gained a lot of attention in computer science, with good fundamental research results on register allocation with fixed schedules [BOU 06, BOU 07b, BOU 07a]. However, the cyclic problem suffers from a lack of attention from the computer science perspective. The next section defines the cyclic register need and explains our contribution to its formal characterization.

7.3. The periodic register need

When we consider an innermost loop, the DDG $G = (V, E)$ may be cyclic. Each edge $e \in E$ becomes labeled by a pair of values $(\delta(e), \lambda(e))$. $\delta : E \to \mathbb{Z}$ defines the latency of edges and $\lambda : E \to \mathbb{Z}$ defines the distance in terms of number of iterations. To exploit the parallelism between the instructions belonging to different loop iterations, we rely on periodic scheduling instead of acyclic scheduling. The following section recalls the notations and the notions of SWP.

7.3.1. *Software pipelining, periodic scheduling and cyclic scheduling*

An SWP is defined by a periodic schedule function $\sigma \colon V \to \mathbb{Z}$ and an II. The operation u of the ith loop iteration is denoted by $u(i)$, it is scheduled at time $\sigma(u) + i \times II$. Here, the schedule time $\sigma(u)$ represents the execution date of $u(0)$ (the first iteration).

The schedule function σ is valid *iff* it satisfies the periodic precedence constraints

$$\forall e = (u, v) \in E : \sigma(u) + \delta(e) \leq \sigma(v) + \lambda(e) \times II$$

Throughout this part of the book, devoted to register optimization, we also use the terms *cyclic* or *periodic* scheduling instead of SWP. If G is cyclic, a necessary condition for a valid SWP schedule to exist is that

$$II \geq \max_{\text{ca graph circuit}} \frac{\sum_{e \in c} \delta(e)}{\sum_{e \in c} \lambda(e)} = MII$$

where MII is the *minimum initiation interval* defined by data dependences. Any graph circuit C such that $\frac{\sum_{e \in c} \delta(e)}{\sum_{e \in c} \lambda(e)} = MII$ is called a *critical circuit*.

If G is acyclic, we define $MII = 1$ and not $MII = 0$. This is because code generation is impossible if $MII = 0$, because $MII = 0$ means infinite ILP.

Wang *et al.* [WAN 94a] modeled the kernel (steady state) of a software pipelined schedule as a two-dimensional matrix by defining a column number cn and a row number rn for each statement. This brings a new definition for SWP, which becomes a triple (rn, cn, II). The row number rn of a statement u is its issue date inside the kernel. The column number cn of a statement u inside the kernel, sometimes called *kernel cycle*, is its stage number. The last parameter II is the kernel length (initiation interval). This triple formally defines the SWP schedule σ as:

$$\forall u \in V, \ \forall i \in \mathbb{N}: \qquad \sigma\left(u(i)\right) = rn(u) + II \times \left(cn(u) + i\right)$$

where $cn(u) = \left\lfloor \frac{\sigma(u)}{II} \right\rfloor$ and $rn(u) = \sigma(u) \mod II$. In the rest of the chapter, we will write $\sigma = (rn, cn, II)$ to reflect the equivalence (equality) between the SWP scheduling function σ, defined from the set of statements to clock cycles, and the SWP scheduling function defined by the triple (rn, cn, II).

Let $\Sigma(G)$ be the set of all valid software pipelined $\Sigma(G)$ schedules of a loop G. We denote by $\Sigma_L(G)$ the set of all valid software pipelined schedules whose durations (total schedule time of one original iteration) do not exceed L:

$$\forall \sigma \in \Sigma_L(G), \ \forall u \in V: \qquad \sigma(u) \leq L$$

$\Sigma(G)$ is an infinite set of schedules, while $\Sigma_L(G) \subset \Sigma(G)$ is finite. Bounding the duration L in SWP scheduling allows us, for instance, to look for periodic schedules with finite prologue/epilogue codes, since the size of the prologue/epilogue codes is $L - II$ and $0 \leq II \leq L$.

7.3.2. *The circular lifetime intervals*

The value $u^t(i)$ of the ith loop iteration is written $u(i)$ at the absolute time $\sigma(u) + \delta_{w,t}(u) + i \times II$ (starting from the execution date of the whole loop) and killed at the absolute time $d_\sigma(u^t) + i \times II$. Thus, the endpoints of the lifetime intervals of the distinct operations of any statement u are all separated by a constant time equal to II. Given a fixed period II, we can model the periodic lifetime intervals during the steady state by considering the lifetime interval of only one instance $u(i)$ per statement (say $u(0)$) that we will simply abbreviate as u.

We recall that the acyclic lifetime interval of the value $u \in V^{R,t}$ is equal to $LT_\sigma(u^t) =]\sigma(u) + \delta_{w,t}(u), d_\sigma(u^t)]$. The *lifetime* of a value $u \in V^{R,t}$ is the total number of clock cycles during which this value is alive according to the schedule σ. It is the difference between the death and the birth date, and is given as:

$$\text{Lifetime}_\sigma(u^t) = d_\sigma(u^t) - (\sigma(u) + \delta_{w,t}(u))$$

For instance, the lifetimes of $v1$, $v2$ and $v3$ in Figure 7.2 are (respectively) 2, 3 and 6 clock cycles.

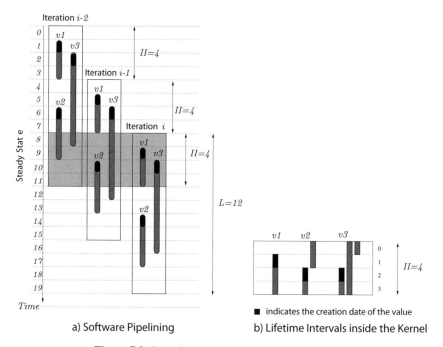

a) Software Pipelining   b) Lifetime Intervals inside the Kernel

Figure 7.2. *Periodic register need in software pipelining*

The periodic register need (MAXLIVE) is the maximal number of values that are simultaneously alive in the SWP kernel. In the case of a periodic schedule, some values may be alive during several consecutive kernel iterations and different instances of the same variable may interfere. Figure 7.2 illustrates an example: the value v_3 for instance interferes with itself.

Previous results [HEN 92, WER 99] show that the lifetime intervals during the steady state describe a circular lifetime interval graph around the kernel: we wrap (roll up) the acyclic lifetime intervals of the values around a circle of circumference II, and therefore the lifetime intervals become cyclic. We give here a formal definition of such circular intervals.

DEFINITION 7.1.– Circular lifetime interval.– *A circular lifetime interval produced by wrapping a circle of circumference II by an acyclic interval $I =]a, b]$ is defined by a triplet of integers (l, r, p), such that:*

- *$l = a \bmod II$ is called the **left** end of the cyclic interval;*

- *$r = b \bmod II$ is called the **right** end of the cyclic interval;*

- *$p = \left\lfloor \frac{b-a}{II} \right\rfloor$ is the number of complete **periods** (turns) around the circle.*

Let us consider the examples of the circular lifetime intervals of v_1, v_2 and v_3 in Figure 7.2(b). These intervals are drawn in a circular way inside the SWP kernel. Their corresponding acyclic intervals are drawn in Figure 7.2(a). The left ends of the cyclic intervals are simply the dates when the lifetime intervals begin inside the SWP kernel. So, the left ends of the intervals of v_1, v_2 and v_3 are 1, 2, 2, respectively (according to definition 7.1). The right ends of the cyclic intervals are simply the dates when the intervals finish inside the SWP kernel. So the corresponding right ends of v_1, v_2 and v_3 are 3, 1, 0, respectively. Concerning the number of periods of a circular lifetime interval, it is the number of complete kernels (II fractions) spanned by the considered interval. For instance, the intervals v_1 and v_2 do not cross any complete SWP kernel; their number of complete periods is then equal to zero. The interval v_3 crosses one complete SWP kernel, so its number of complete period is equal to one. Finally, the definition of a circular lifetime interval is that it groups its left end, right end and number of complete periods inside a triple. The circular interval of v_1, v_2 and v_3 are then denoted as $(1, 3, 0)$, $(2, 1, 0)$ and $(2, 0, 1)$, respectively.

The set of all the circular lifetime intervals around the kernel defines a circular interval graph which we denote by $\mathcal{CG}(G)$. As an abuse of language, we use the short term "circular interval" to indicate a circular lifetime interval and the term "circular graph" for indicating a circular lifetime intervals graph. Figure 7.3(a) gives an example of a circular graph. The maximal number of simultaneously alive values is the width of this circular graph, i.e. the maximal number of circular intervals that interfere at a certain point of the circle. For instance, the width of the circular graph of Figure 7.3(a) is 4. Figure 7.2(b) is another representation of the circular graph. We denote by $PRN_\sigma^t(G)$ the periodic register need of type $t \in \mathcal{T}$ for the DDG G according to the schedule σ, which is equal to the width of the circular graph.

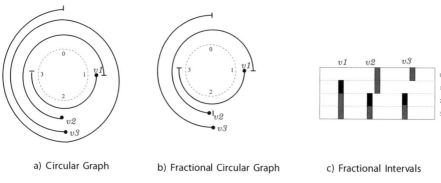

a) Circular Graph   b) Fractional Circular Graph   c) Fractional Intervals

Figure 7.3. *Circular lifetime intervals*

7.4. Computing the periodic register need

Computing the width of a circular graph (i.e. the periodic register need) is straightforward. We can compute the number of values simultaneously alive at each clock cycle in the SWP kernel. This method is commonly used in the literature [HUF 93b, JAN 01, NIN 93b, SAW 97, WAN 94b]. Unfortunately, it leads to a method whose complexity depends on the initiation interval II. This factor is pseudo-polynomial, because it does not strictly depend on the size of the input DDG, but rather depends on the specified latencies in the DDG, and on its structure (critical circuit). It is better to use a polynomial method for computing the width of a circular graph, as can be deduced from [HUA 01].

Here, we want to show a novel method for computing the periodic register need whose complexity depends polynomially on the size of the DDG, i.e. it depends only on $\|V\|$, the number of loop statements (number of DDG vertices). This new method will help us to prove other properties (which we will describe later). For this purpose, we find a relationship between the width of a circular interval graph and the size of a maximal clique in the interference graph [1].

In general, the width of a circular interval graph is not equal to the size of a maximal clique in the interference graph [TUC 75]. This is contrary to the case of

---

1 Remember that the interference graph is an undirected graph that models interference relations between lifetime intervals: two statements u and v are connected iff their (circular) lifetime intervals share a unit of time.

acyclic intervals graphs where the size of a maximal clique in the interference graph is equal to the width of the intervals graph. In order to effectively compute this width (which is equal to the register need), we decompose the circular graph $CG(G)$ into two parts:

1) The first part is the integral part. It corresponds to the number of complete turns around the circle, i.e. the total number of value instances simultaneously alive during the whole steady state of the SWP schedule: $\sum_{(l,r,p)}$ a circular interval p.

2) The second part is the fractional (residual) part. It is composed of the remainder of the lifetime intervals after removing all the complete turns (see Figures 7.3(b) and (c)). The size of each remaining interval is strictly less than II, the duration of the SWP kernel. Note that if the left end of a circular interval is equal to its right end ($l = r$), then the remaining interval after ignoring the complete turns around the circle is empty ($]l, r] =]l, l] = \emptyset$). These empty intervals are then ignored from this second part. Two classes of intervals that remain are as follows:

a) intervals that do not cross the kernel barrier, i.e. when the left end is less than the right end ($l < r$). In Figures 7.3(b) and (c), v_1 belongs to this class;

b) intervals that cross the kernel barrier, i.e. when the left end is greater than the right end ($l > r$). In Figures 7.3(b) and (c), v_2 and v_3 belong to this class. These intervals can be seen as two fractional intervals ($]l, II]$ and $]0, r]$) which represent the left and right parts of the lifetime intervals. If we merge these two acyclic fractional intervals of two successive SWP kernels, a new contiguous circular interval will be created.

These two classes of intervals define a new circular graph. We call it a *fractional circular graph* because the size of its lifetime intervals is less than II. This circular graph contains the circular intervals of the first class, and those of the second class after merging the left part of each interval with its right part (see Figure 7.3(b)).

DEFINITION 7.2.– Fractional circular graph.– *Let $CG(G)$ be a circular graph of a DDG $G = (V, E)$. The fractional circular graph, denoted by $\overline{CG}(G)$, is the circular graph after ignoring the complete turns around the circle:*

$$\overline{CG}(G) = \{(l, r) \mid \exists (l, r, p) \in CG(G) \land r \neq l\}$$

We call the circular interval (l, r) a *circular fractional interval*. The length of each fractional interval $(l, r) \in \overline{CG}(G)$ is less than II clock cycles. Therefore, the periodic register need of type t is equal to:

$$PRN_\sigma^t(G) = \left(\sum_{(l,r,p) \in CG(G)} p \right) + w\left(\overline{CG}(G)\right) \qquad [7.1]$$

where w denotes the width of the fractional circular graph (the maximal number of values simultaneously alive). Computing the first term of formula [7.1] (complete turns around the circle) is easy and can be computed in linear time (provided lifetime intervals) by iterating over the $\|V^{R,t}\|$ lifetime intervals and adding the integral part of $\left\lfloor \frac{\text{Lifetime}_\sigma(u)}{II} \right\rfloor$.

However, the second term of formula [7.1] is more difficult to compute in polynomial time. This is because, as stated before, the size of a maximal clique (in the case of an arbitrary circular graph) in the interference graph is not equal to the width of the circular interval graph [TUC 75]. In order to find an effective algorithmic solution, we use the fact that the fractional circular graph $\overline{CG}(G)$ has circular intervals that do not make complete turns around the circle. Then, if we unroll the kernel exactly once to consider the values produced during two successive kernel iterations, some circular interference patterns become visible inside the unrolled kernel. For instance, the circular graph of Figure 7.4(a) has a width equal to 2. Its interference graph in Figure 7.4(b) has a maximal clique of size 3. Since the size of these intervals does not exceed the period II, we unroll the circular graph once as shown in Figure 7.4(c). The interference graph of the circular intervals in Figure 7.4(d) has a size of a maximal clique equal to the width, which is 2: note that $v2$ does not interfere with $v3'$ because, as said before, we assume that all lifetime intervals are left open.

When unrolling the kernel once, each fractional interval $(l, r) \in CG(G)$ becomes associated with two acyclic intervals I and I' constructed by merging the left and the right parts of the fractional interval of two successive kernels. I and I' are then defined as follows:

- If $r \geq l$, then $I =]l, r]$ and $I' =]l + II, r + II]$.
- If $r < l$, then $I =]l, r + II]$ and $I' =]l + II, r + 2 \times II]$.

THEOREM 7.1.– [TOU 07, TOU 02] Let $\overline{CG}(G)$ be a circular fractional graph (no complete turns around the circle exists). For each circular fractional interval $(l, r) \in CG(G)$, we associate the two corresponding acyclic intervals I and I'. The cardinality of any maximal clique in the interference graph of all these acyclic intervals is equal to the width of $\overline{CG}(G)$.

The next section presents some of the mathematical results that we proved due to equation [7.1] and theorem 7.1.

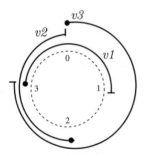

a) Initial Circular Graph

b) Initial Interference Graph

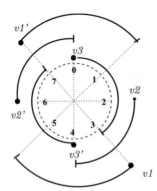

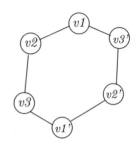

c) Circular Graph after Unrolling Once

d) Interferences after Unrolling Once

Figure 7.4. *Relationship between the maximal clique and the width of a circular graph*

7.5. Some theoretical results on the periodic register need

In this section, we show how to compute the minimal periodic register need of type t for any valid SWP independently of II. We call it *the periodic register sufficiency*. We define it as:

$$PRF^t(G) = \min_{\sigma \in \Sigma(G)} PRN^t_\sigma(G) \qquad [7.2]$$

where $\Sigma(G)$ is the set of all valid SWP schedules for G.

Computing the periodic register sufficiency allows us, for instance, to determine if spill code cannot be avoided for a given loop: if $\mathcal{R}^t$ is the number of available registers of type t, and if $PRF^t(G) > R^t$ then there are not enough registers to allocate to any loop schedule. Spill code has to be introduced necessarily, independently of II.

Let us start by characterizing a relationship between minimal periodic register need for a fixed II.

7.5.1. Minimal periodic register need versus initiation interval

The literature contains many SWP techniques about reducing the periodic register need for a fixed II. It is intuitive that, the lower the initiation interval II, the higher the register pressure, since more parallelism requires more memory. If we succeed in finding a software pipelined schedule σ which needs $R^t = PRN_\sigma^t(G)$ registers of type t, and without assuming any resource conflicts, then it is possible to get another software pipelined schedule that needs no more than R^t registers with a higher II. We prove here that increasing the maximal duration L is a sufficient condition, bringing the first formal relationship that links the periodic register need, the II and the duration. Note that the following theorem has been proved when $\delta_{w,t} = \delta_{r,t} = 0$ only (no delay to access registers).

THEOREM 7.2.– [TOU 07, TOU 02] Let $G = (V, E)$ be a loop DDG with zero delays in accessing registers ($\delta_{r,t} = \delta_{w,t} = 0$). If there exists an SWP $\sigma = (rn, cn, II)$ that needs R^t registers of type t having a duration at most L, then there exists an SWP $\sigma' = (rn', cn', II + 1)$ that needs R^t registers also having at most a duration $L' = L + 1 + \lfloor L/II \rfloor$. Formally:

$$\forall \sigma = (rn, cn, II) \in \Sigma_L(G), \exists \sigma' = (rn', cn', II + 1) \in \Sigma_{L+1+\lfloor L/II \rfloor}(G) :$$

$$PRN_{\sigma'}^t(G) = PRN_\sigma^t(G)$$

7.5.2. Computing the periodic register sufficiency

The periodic register sufficiency defined by equation [7.2] is *the absolute register sufficiency* because it is defined for all valid SWP schedules belonging to $\Sigma(G)$ (an infinite set). In this section, we show how to compute it for a finite subset $\Sigma_L(G) \subseteq \Sigma(G)$, i.e. for the set of SWP schedules such that the duration does not exceed L. This is because many practical SWP schedulers assume a bounded duration L in order to limit the code size. However, we can choose a sufficiently large value for L such that:

$$PRF^t(G) = \min_{\sigma \in \Sigma(G)} PRN_\sigma^t(G) = \min_{\sigma \in \Sigma_L(G)} PRN_\sigma^t(G)$$

Some existing solutions show how to determine the minimal register need given a fixed II [ALT 95, FIM 01, SAW 97, TOU 04]. If we use such methods to compute periodic register sufficiency, we have to solve many combinatorial problems, one for each II, starting from MII to a maximal duration L. Fortunately, the following corollary states that it is sufficient to compute the periodic register sufficiency by solving a *unique* optimization problem with $II = L$ if we increase the maximal duration (the new-maximal duration is denoted L' to distinguish it from L). Let us start by the following lemma, which is a direct consequence of theorem 7.2:

LEMMA 7.1.– [TOU 07, TOU 02] Let $G = (V, E)$ be a DDG with zero delays in accessing registers. The minimal register need (of type $t \in \mathcal{T}$) of all the software pipelined schedules with an initiation interval II assuming duration at most L is greater than or equal to the minimal register need of all the software pipelined schedules with an initiation interval $II' = II + 1$ assuming duration at most $L' = L + 1 + \lfloor L/II \rfloor$. Formally,

$$\min_{\sigma=(rn,cn,II)\in\Sigma_L(G)} PRN_\sigma^t(G) \geq \min_{\sigma'=(rn',cn',II+1)\in\Sigma_{L+1+\lfloor L/II\rfloor}(G)} PRN_{\sigma'}^t(G)$$

COROLLARY 7.1.– [TOU 07, TOU 02] Let $G = (V, E)$ be a DDG with zero delays in accessing registers. Then, the exact periodic register sufficiency of G (of type t) assuming duration at most L is greater than or equal to the minimal register need with $II = L$ assuming duration at most $L' \geq L$. L' is computed formally as follows:

$$\min_{\sigma=(rn,cn,II)\in\Sigma_L(G)} PRN_\sigma^t(G) \geq \min_{\sigma=(rn,cn,L)\in\Sigma_{L'}(G)} PRN_\sigma^t(G)$$

where L' is the $(L - MII)^{th}$ term of the following recurrent sequence ($L' = U_L$):

$$\begin{cases} U_{MII} = L \\ U_{II+1} = U_{II+1+\lfloor U_{II}/II \rfloor} \end{cases}$$

In other words, corollary 7.1 proves the following implication:

$$\begin{cases} \min PRN_\sigma^t(G) \\ II = L \\ \forall u \in V, \sigma(u) \leq L' \end{cases} \Longrightarrow \begin{cases} \min PRN_\sigma^t(G) \\ MII \leq II \leq L \\ \forall u \in V, \sigma(u) \leq L \end{cases}$$

where the value of L' is given by corollary 7.1.

7.5.3. *Stage scheduling under register constraints*

Stage scheduling, as studied in [EIC 96], is an approach that schedules loop operations given a fixed II and a fixed reservation table (i.e. after satisfying resource constraints). In other terms, the problem is to compute the minimal register need given a fixed II and fixed row numbers (rn), while column numbers (cn) are left free (i.e. variables to optimize). This problem has been proved NP-complete by Huard [HUA 01]. A careful study of his proof allows us to deduce that the complexity of this problem comes from the fact that the last readers (consumers) of the values are not known before scheduling the loop. Huard in [HUA 01] has already claimed that if the killer is fixed, then stage scheduling under register constrains is a polynomial problem. Mangione-Smith [MAN 92] proved that stage scheduling under register constraints has a polynomial time complexity in the case of data dependence trees and forest of trees. This section proves a more general case than [MAN 92] by showing that if every value has a unique killer (last consumer) known or fixed before instruction scheduling, as in the case of expression trees, then stage scheduling under register constraints is a polynomial problem. This claim was already known by few experts; here we provide a straightforward proof using the formula of periodic register need given in equation [7.1].

Before proving this general case, we first start by proving it for the case of trees (for clarity).

Let us begin by writing the formal problem of SWP with register need minimization. Note that the register type $t \in \mathcal{R}^t$ is fixed, performing a stage scheduling among all register types conjointly remains an open problem.

$$\begin{cases} \text{Minimize} \quad PRN_\sigma^t(G) \\ \\ \text{Subject to:} \\ \forall e = (u, v) \in E,\ \sigma(v) - \sigma(u) \geq \delta(e) - II \times \lambda(e) \end{cases} \qquad [7.3]$$

This standard problem has been proved NP-complete in [EIS 95a], even for trees and chains. Eichenberger *et al.* studied a modified problem by considering a fixed reservation table. By considering the row and column numbers ($\sigma(u) = rn(u) + II \times cn(u)$), fixing the reservation table amounts to fixing row numbers while letting column numbers as free integral variables. Thus, by considering the given row numbers as conditions, problem [7.3] becomes:

$$\begin{cases} \text{Minimize} \quad PRN_\sigma^t(G) \\ \\ \text{Subject to:} \\ \forall e = (u, v) \in E,\ II \times cn(v) - II \\ \qquad \times cn(u) \geq \delta(e) - II \times \lambda(e) - rn(v) + rn(u) \end{cases}$$

$$[7.4]$$

That is,

$$
\begin{cases}
\text{Minimize} \qquad PRN_\sigma^t(G) \\
\\
\text{Subject to:} \\
\forall e = (u, v) \in E, \;\; cn(v) - cn(u) \geq \frac{\delta(e) - II \times \lambda(e) - rn(v) + rn(u)}{II}
\end{cases}
\qquad [7.5]
$$

It is clear that the constraints matrix of problem [7.5] constitutes an incidence matrix of the graph G. If we succeed in proving that the objective function $PRN_\sigma^t(G)$ is a linear function of the cn variables, then problem [7.5] becomes an integer linear programming system with a totally unimodular constraints matrix, and consequently, it can be solved with polynomial time algorithms [SCH 87]. Since the problem of stage scheduling defined by problem [7.5] has been proved NP-complete, it is evident that $PRN_\sigma^t(G)$ cannot be expressed as a linear function of cn for an arbitrary DDG. In this section, we restrict ourselves to the case of DDGs where each value $u \in V^{R,t}$ has a unique possible killer k_{u^t}, such as the case of expression trees. In an expression tree, each value $u \in V^{R,t}$ has a unique killer k_{u^t} that belongs to the same original iteration, i.e. $\lambda((u, k_{u^t})) = 0$. With this latter assumption, we will prove in the remaining of this section that $PRN_\sigma^t(G)$ is a linear function of column numbers.

Let us begin by recalling the formula of $PRN_\sigma^t(G)$

$$
PRN_\sigma^t(G) = \left(\sum_{(l,r,p) \in C\mathcal{G}(G)} p \right) + w\left(\overline{C\mathcal{G}}(G)\right) \qquad [7.6]
$$

The first term of the equation corresponds to the total number of turns around the circle, while the second term corresponds to the maximal fractional intervals simultaneously alive (the width of the circular fractional graph). We set $P = \sum_{(l,r,p) \in C\mathcal{G}(G)} p$ and $W = w\left(\overline{C\mathcal{G}}(G)\right)$.

We know that $\forall (l, r, p) \in C\mathcal{G}(G)$ the circular interval of a value $u \in V^{R,t}$, its number of turns around the circle is $p = \left\lfloor \frac{\text{Lifetime}_\sigma(u^t)}{II} \right\rfloor = \left\lfloor \frac{d_\sigma(u^t) - \sigma(u) - \delta_{w,t}(u)}{II} \right\rfloor$.

Since each value u is assumed to have a unique possible killer k_{u^t} belonging to the same original iteration (case of expression trees),

$$
p = \left\lfloor \frac{\sigma(k_{u^t}) - \sigma(u) - \delta_{w,t}(u)}{II} \right\rfloor = cn(k_{u^t}) - cn(u)
$$

$$
+ \left\lfloor \frac{rn(k_{u^t}) + \delta_{r,t}(k_{u^t}) - rn(u) - \delta_{w,t}(u)}{II} \right\rfloor.
$$

Here, we succeed in writing $P = \sum p$ as a linear function of column numbers cn, since rn and II are constants in problem [7.5]. Now, let us explore W. The fractional graph contains the fractional intervals $\{(l, r) | (l, r, p) \in \mathcal{CG}(G)\}$. Each fractional interval (l, r) of a value $u \in V^{R,t}$ depends only on the row numbers and II as follows:

$$-l = (\sigma(u) + \delta_{w,t}(u)) \bmod II = (rn(u) + II \times cn(u) + \delta_{w,t}(u)) \bmod II = (rn(u) + \delta_{w,t}(u)) \bmod II.$$

$$-r = d_\sigma(u^t) \bmod II = (\sigma(k_{u^t}) + \delta_{r,t}(k_{u^t})) \bmod II = (rn(k_{u^t}) + II \times cn(k_{u^t}) + \delta_{r,t}(k_{u^t})) \bmod II = (rn(k_{u^t}) + \delta_{r,t}(k_{u^t})) \bmod II.$$

As can be seen, the fractional intervals depend only on row numbers and II, which are constants in problem [7.5]. Hence, W, the width of the circular fractional graph is a constant too. From all the previous formulas, we deduce that:

$$PRN_\sigma^t(G) = P + W =$$

$$\sum_{u \in V^{R,t}} cn(k_{u^t}) - cn(u) + \left\lceil \frac{rn(k_{u^t}) + \delta_{r,t}(k_{u^t}) - rn(u) - \delta_{w,t}(u)}{II} \right\rceil + W$$

yielding to:

$$PRN_\sigma^t(G) = \sum_{u \in V^{R,t}} cn(k_{u^t}) - cn(u) + constant \qquad [7.7]$$

Equation [7.7] rewrites problem [7.5] as the following integer linear programming system (by neglecting the constants in the objective function):

$$\begin{cases} \text{Minimize} & \sum_{u \in V^{R,t}} cn(k_{u^t}) - cn(u) \\ \text{Subject to:} & \qquad\qquad\qquad\qquad\qquad\qquad [7.8] \\ \forall e = (u, v) \in E, \; cn(v) - cn(u) \geq \left\lceil \frac{\delta(e) - II \times \lambda(e) - rn(v) + rn(u)}{II} \right\rceil \end{cases}$$

The constraints matrix of system [7.8] describes an incidence matrix; so it is totally unimodular. It can be solved with a polynomial time algorithm.

This section proves that stage scheduling of expression trees is a polynomial problem. Now, we can consider the larger case of the DDGs assigning a unique possible killer k_{u^t} for each value u^t of type t. Such a killer can belong to a different iteration $\lambda_k = \lambda((u, k_{u^t}))$. Then, the problem of stage scheduling in this class of loops remains also polynomial as follows:

1) If the DDG is acyclic, then we can apply a loop retiming [LEI 91] to bring all the killers to the same iteration. Thus, we come back to the case similar to expression trees studied in this section.

2) If the DDG contains circuits, it is not always possible to shift all the killers to the same iteration. Thus, by including the constants λ_k in the formula P becomes equal to:

$$P = \sum_{u \in V^{R,t}} cn(k_{u^t}) - cn(u) + \lambda_k + \left\lfloor \frac{rn(k_{u^t}) + \delta_{r,t}(k_{u^t}) - rn(u) - \delta_{w,t}(u)}{II} \right\rfloor$$

$$= \sum_{u \in V^{R,t}} cn(k_{u^t}) - cn(u) + constant$$

Since II and row numbers are constants, W remains a constant as proved by the following formulas of fractional intervals:

- $l = \sigma(u) + \delta_{w,t}(u) \bmod II = (rn(u) + II \times cn(u) + \delta_{w,t}(u)) \bmod II = (rn(u) + \delta_{w,t}(u)) \bmod II$;

- $r = d_\sigma(u^t) \bmod II = \sigma(k_{u^t}) + II \times \lambda_k + \delta_{r,t}(k_{u^t}) \bmod II = (rn(k_{u^t}) + II \times cn(k_{u^t}) + II \times \lambda_k + \delta_{r,t}(k_{u^t})) \bmod II = (rn(k_{u^t}) + \delta_{r,t}(k_{u^t})) \bmod II$.

Consequently, $PRN_\sigma^t(G)$ remains a linear function of column numbers, which means that system [7.8] can still be solved via polynomial time algorithms (usually with network flow algorithms).

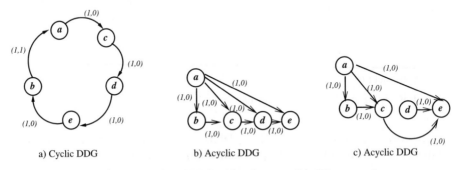

a) Cyclic DDG   b) Acyclic DDG   c) Acyclic DDG

Figure 7.5. *Examples of DDG with unique possible killer per value*

Our result in this section is more general than expression trees. We extend the previous result [MAN 92] in two ways. Figure 7.5 shows some examples, where all edges are flow dependences labeled by the pairs $(\delta(e), \lambda(e))$.

1) *Cyclic DDGs:* our result takes into account cyclic DDGs with a unique killer per value. As an example, Figure 7.5(a) is a cyclic DDG with a unique possible killer per value. Such DDG is not considered in [MAN 92], because it is cyclic while it is neither a tree nor an acyclic DDG.

2) *Acyclic DDG:* our result also takes into account acyclic DDGs with a unique possible killer per value, which are not necessarily trees or forest of trees. For instance, Figure 7.5(b) and Figure 7.5(c) are examples of acyclic DDG where every node has a unique possible killer (because of the transitive relationship between nodes). These DDGs are not trees. Analyzing such unique killer relationships in general acyclic DDGs can be done using the so-called *potential killing relation,* which has been formally defined in [TOU 05, TOU 02]. In Figure 7.5(b), we have the following unique killers: $k_{a^t} = e, k_{b^t} = c, k_{c^t} = d, k_{d^t} = e$. In Figure 7.5(c), we have the following unique killers: $k_{a^t} = e, k_{b^t} = c, k_{c^t} = e, k_{d^t} = e$.

7.6. Conclusion on the register requirement

The register requirement of a DAG in acyclic scheduling is a well-studied topic: when the schedule is fixed, the register requirement (MAXLIVE) is exactly equal to the number needed for register allocation. So nothing new is introduced here. The case of fixed schedules for arbitrary codes (with possible branches) is a distinct problem, since the notion of MAXLIVE is not precise statically when the compiler cannot guess the taken branch. Consequently, computing the minimal number of allocated registers needs sophisticated algorithms as proposed in [BOU 06, BOU 07b, BOU 07a].

The periodic register requirement in cyclic scheduling has got less fundamental results in the literature, compared to the acyclic case. The work presented in this chapter analyzes some of our results published in [TOU 07]. The first contribution brings a polynomial method for computing the exact register need $(PRN_\sigma^t(G))$ of an already scheduled loop. Given a register type $t \in \mathcal{T}$, the complexity to compute $PRN_\sigma^t(G)$ is $\mathcal{O}(\|V^{R,t}\| \log \|V^{R,t}\|)$, where $V^{R,t}$ is the number of loop statements writing a value of type t. The complexity of the cited methods depends on II, which is a pseudo-polynomial factor. Our new formula to compute $PRN_\sigma^t(G)$ in polynomial time does not really solve an open problem; it, however, allows us to deduce other formal results explained below.

A second contribution provides a sufficient condition so that the minimal register need under a fixed II does not increase when incrementing II. We gave in [TOU 07] an example to show that it is sometimes possible that the minimal register need increases when II is incremented. Such situations may occur when the maximal duration L is not relaxed (increased). This fact contradicts the general thought that incrementing II would require fewer registers (unless the constraint on L is loosened).

Guaranteeing that the register need is a non-increasing function versus II when relaxing the maximal duration allows us now to easily write the formal problem of scheduling under register constraints instead of scheduling with register minimization as usually done in the literature. Indeed, according to our results, we can finally apply a binary search on II. If we have $\mathcal{R}^t$, a fixed number of available registers of type t, and since we know how to increase L so as the curve of $PRN^t_\sigma(G)$ versus II becomes non-increasing, we can use successive binary search on II until reaching a $PRN^t_\sigma(G)$ below $\mathcal{R}^t$. The number of such binary search steps is at most $\lg_2(L)$.

A third contribution proves that computing the minimal register need with a fixed $II = L$ is exactly equal to the periodic register sufficiency if L sufficiently large, i.e. the minimal register need of all valid SWP schedules. Computing the periodic register sufficiency ($PRF^t(G)$) allows us to check for instance if introducing spill code is unavoidable when $PRF^t(G)$ is greater than the number of available registers.

While stage scheduling under registers constraints for arbitrary loops is an NP-complete problem, the fourth and final contribution gives a straightforward proof that stage scheduling with register minimization is a polynomial problem in the special case of expression trees, and generally in the case of DDGs providing a unique possible killer per value. This general result has already been claimed by few experts, but a simple proof of it is made possible due to our polynomial method of $PRN^t_\sigma(G)$ computation.

This chapter proposes new open problems. First, an interesting open question would be to provide a necessary condition so that the periodic register need would be a non-increasing function of II. Second, in the presence of architectures with non-zero delays in accessing registers, is theorem 7.2 still valid? In other words, can we provide any guarantee that minimal register need in such architectures does not increase when incrementing II? Third, we have shown that there exists a finite value of L such that the periodic register sufficiency assuming a maximal duration L is equal to the absolute periodic register sufficiency without assuming any bound on the duration. The open question is how to compute such appropriate value of maximal duration. Fourth and last, we require a DDG analysis algorithm to check whether each value has one and only one possible killer. We have already published such an algorithm for the case of DAG in [TOU 05], but the problem here is to extend it to loop DDG.

The next chapter (Chapter 8) studies the notion of register saturation, which is the maximal register requirement of a DDG, for all possible valid schedules.

The Register Saturation

The register constraints are usually taken into account during the scheduling pass of a data dependence graph (DDG): any schedule of the instructions inside a basic block, superblock or loop must bound the register requirement under a certain limit. In this chapter, we show how to handle the register pressure before the instruction scheduling of a DDG. We mathematically study an approach that consists of managing the exact upper bound of the register need for all the valid schedules of a considered DDG, independently of the functional unit constraints. We call this computed limit the *register saturation* of the DDG. Its aim is to detect possible obsolete register constraints, i.e. when the register saturation does not exceed the number of available registers. The register saturation concept aims to decouple register constraints from instruction scheduling without altering ILP extraction.

8.1. Motivations on the register saturation concept

The introduction of instruction-level parallelism (ILP) has rendered the classical techniques of register allocation for sequential code semantics inadequate. In [FRE 92], the authors showed that there is a phase ordering problem between classical register allocation techniques and ILP instruction scheduling. If a classical register allocation (by register minimization) is done early, the introduced false dependences inhibit instruction scheduling from extracting a schedule with a high amount of ILP. However, this conclusion does not prevent a compiler from effectively performing an early register allocation, with the condition that the allocator is sensitive to the scheduler. Register allocation sensitive to instruction scheduling has been studied either from the computer science or the computer engineering point of view in [AMB 94, GOO 88b, GOV 03, JAN 01, NOR 94, PIN 93, DAR 07].

Some other techniques on acyclic scheduling [BER 89, BRA 95, FRE 92, MEL 01, SIL 97] claim that it is better to combine instruction scheduling with register constraints in a single complex pass, arguing that applying each method separately has a negative influence on the efficiency of the other. This tendency has been followed by the cyclic scheduling techniques in [EIC 96, FIM 01, WAN 95].

We think that this phase ordering problem arises only if the applied first pass (ILP scheduler or register allocator) is *selfish*. Indeed, we can effectively decouple register constraints from instruction scheduling if enough care is taken. In this contribution, we show how we can treat register constraints before scheduling, and we explain why we think that our methods provide better techniques than the existing solutions.

Register saturation is a concept well adapted to situations where spilling is not a favored or possible solution for reducing register pressure compared to ILP scheduling: spill operations request memory data with a higher energy consumption. Also, spill code introduces unpredictable cache effects: it makes worst-case execution time (WCET) estimation less accurate and add difficulties to ILP scheduling (because spill operations latencies are unknown). Register saturation (RS) is concerned about register maximization not minimization, and has some proven mathematical characteristics [TOU 05]:

– As in the case of WCET research, the RS is an exact upper bound of the register requirement of all possible valid instruction schedules. This means that the register requirement is not overestimated. RS should not be overestimated, otherwise it would waste hardware registers for embedded VLIW designers, and would produce useless spilling strategies for compiler designers. Contrary to WCET where an exact estimation is hard to model, the RS computation and reduction are exactly modeled problems and can be optimally solved.

– The RS is a *reachable* exact upper bound of the register requirement for any functional units configuration. This means that, for any resource constraint of the underlying processor (even sequential ones), there is always an instruction schedule that requires RS registers: this is a mathematical fact proved by lemma 3 in [TOU 05]. This is contrary to the well-known register sufficiency, which is a minimal bound of register requirement. Such a minimal bound is *not* always reachable, since it is strongly correlated to the resource constraints. A practical demonstration is provided in Chapter 5 of [TOU 02] proving that the register sufficiency is not a reachable lower bound of register need, and hence cannot be used to decouple register constraints from functional units constraints.

There are practical motivations that convince us to carry on fundamental studies on RS:

– *High performance VLIW computing*: embedded systems in general cover a wide area of activities which differ in terms of stakes and objectives. In particular, embedded high performance very long instruction word (VLIW) computing requires cheap and fast VLIW processors to cover the computation budget of telecommunications, video and audio processing, with a tight energy consumption.

Such embedded VLIW processors are designed to execute a typical set of applications. Usually, the considered set of typical applications is rarely represented by the set of common benchmarks (mibench, spec, mediabench, BDTI, etc.), but is given by the industrial client. Then, the constructor of the embedded processor considers only such applications (which are not public) for the hardware design. Nowadays, some embedded VLIW processors (such as ST2xx family) have 32 or 64 registers, and the processor designers have no idea whether such number is adequate or not. Computing the RS of the considered embedded codes allows the hardware designers to precisely gauge with a static method the maximal amount of required registers without worrying about how many functional units they should put on the VLIW processor. RS provides the mathematical guarantee that this maximal register need limit is reachable for any VLIW configuration.

– *Circuit synthesis*: as studied in [SUC 06], optimal cyclic scheduling under resource constraints is currently used to design dynamic reconfigurable circuits with field-programmable gate array (FPGA). In that study, storage and registers are not considered because of practical resolution complexity. Due to the RS concept, register constraints can be satisfied prior to the cyclic scheduling problem, with a formal guarantee of providing enough registers for any cyclic schedule.

– *Embedded code optimization and verification*: As done in [TOU 05], computing RS allows us to guide instruction scheduling heuristics inside backend compilers. For instance, if RS is below $\mathcal{R}^t$ the number of available registers of type t, then we can guarantee that the instruction scheduling process can be carried on without considering register constraints. If RS is greater than $\mathcal{R}^t$, then register pressure reduction methods could be used (to be studied in next chapter).

– *High performance computing*: RS may be used to control high-level loop transformations, such as loop unrolling without causing low-level register spilling. In practice, this means that the unrolling degree is chosen so that RS remains below $\mathcal{R}^t$.

– *Just-in-time (JIT) compilation*: the compiler can generate a byte-code with a bounded RS. This means that the generated byte-code holds RS metrics as static annotations, providing information about the maximal register need for any underlying processor characteristics. At program execution, when the processor is known, the JIT can access such static annotations (present in the byte-code) and eventually schedule operations at runtime under only resource constraints without worrying about registers and spilling.

– *Compiler construction strategy*: another reason for handling register constraints prior to ILP scheduling is that register constraints are much more complex than resource constraints. Scheduling under resource constraints is a performance issue. Given a DDG, we are sure to find at least one valid schedule for any underlying hardware properties. However, scheduling a DDG with a limited number of registers is more complex. Unless we generate superscalar codes with sequential semantics, we cannot guarantee in the case of VLIW the existence of at least one schedule. In some cases, we must introduce spill code and hence we change the problem (the input DDG). Also, a combined pass of scheduling with register allocation presents an important drawback if not enough registers are available. During scheduling, we may need to insert load-store operations if not enough free registers exist. We cannot guarantee the existence of a valid issue time for these introduced memory accesses in already scheduled code. This fact forces an iterative process of scheduling followed by spilling until reaching a solution.

For all the above applications, we can have many solutions and strategies, and the literature is rich with articles about the topics. The RS concept is not the unique and main strategy. It is a concept that may be used in conjunction and complementary with other strategies. RS is helpful due to two characteristics:

1) The RS concept can give a *formal* guarantee of avoiding useless spilling in some codes. Avoiding useless spilling allows us to reduce the amount of memory requests and cache effects, which may save power and increase performance.

2) Since RS is a *static* metric, it does not require program execution or simulation. Usually, the results provided with existing methods are not formally guaranteed and always depend on input data, functional units configurations, the precision of the simulator and the presence or absence of a processor prototype, etc.

The next two sections formally define the register saturation in acyclic and cyclic scheduling, and provide efficient ways to compute it.

8.2. Computing the acyclic register saturation

We assume DAG $G = (V, E)$ constructed from an initial data dependence analysis. Consequently, its edges have positive latencies initially. However, we will see in later chapters (when bounding the register pressure) that we can insert new edges with non-positive latencies.

To simplify the writing of some mathematical formulas, we assume that the DAG has one source ($\top$) and one sink ($\bot$). If not, we introduce two fictitious nodes ($\top, \bot$) representing nops (evicted at the end of the RS analysis). We add a virtual serial edge $e_1 = (\top, s)$ to each source with $\delta(e_1) = 0$, and an edge $e_2 = (t, \bot)$ from each sink with the latency of the sink operation $\delta(e_2) = lat(t)$. The total schedule time of a schedule is then $\sigma(\bot)$. The null latency of an added edge e_1 is not inconsistent with our assumption that latencies must be strictly positive because the added virtual serial edges do not exist in the original DAG. Furthermore, we can avoid introducing these virtual nodes without any impact on our theoretical study, since their purpose is only to simplify some mathematical expressions.

Figure 8.1(b) gives the DAG that we use in this section constructed from the code of part (a). In this example, we focus on the floating point registers: the values and flow edges are illustrated by bold lines. We assume for instance that each read occurs exactly at the schedule time and each write at the final execution step ($\delta_{r,t}(u) = 0$, $\delta_{w,t}(u) = lat(u) - 1$). The nodes with non-bold lines are any other operations that do not write into registers (as stores), or write into registers of unconsidered types. The edges with non-bold lines represent the precedence constraints that are not flow dependences through registers, such as data dependences through memory, or through registers of unconsidered types, or any other serial constraints.

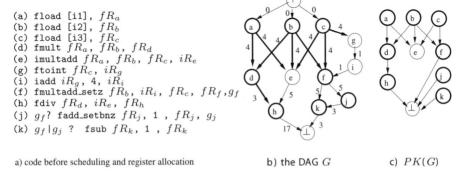

```
(a) fload [i1], fRa
(b) fload [i2], fRb
(c) fload [i3], fRc
(d) fmult fRa, fRb, fRd
(e) imultadd fRa, fRb, fRc, iRe
(g) ftoint fRc, iRg
(i) iadd iRg, 4, iRi
(f) fmultadd_setz fRb, iRi, fRc, fRf,gf
(h) fdiv fRd, iRe, fRh
(j) gf? fadd_setbnz fRj, 1 , fRj, gj
(k) gf|gj ? fsub fRk, 1 , fRk
```

a) code before scheduling and register allocation   b) the DAG G c) $PK(G)$

Figure 8.1. *DAG model*

The acyclic register saturation (RS) of a register type $t \in \mathcal{T}$ is the maximal register need of type t for all the valid schedules of the DAG:

$$RS^t(G) = \max_{\sigma \in \Sigma(G)} RN_\sigma^t(G)$$

We call σ a *saturating acylic schedule* iff $RN_\sigma^t(G) = RS^t(G)$. The values belonging to an excessive set (maximal values simultaneously alive) of σ are called *saturating values* of type t.

THEOREM 8.1.– [TOU 05, TOU 02] Let $G = (V, E)$ be a DAG and $t \in \mathcal{T}$ a register type. Computing $RS^t(G)$ is NP-complete.

The next section provides formal characterization of RS helping us to provide an efficient heuristics. We will see that computing RS comes down to answering the question: which operation must kill this value?

8.2.1. *Characterizing the register saturation*

When looking for saturating schedules, we do not worry about the total schedule time. Our aim is only to prove that the register need can reach the RS but cannot exceed it. Furthermore, we prove that, for the purpose of maximizing the register need, looking for only one suitable killer of a value is sufficient rather than looking for a group of killers: for any schedule that assigns more than one killer for a value u^t, we can build another schedule with at least the same register need such that this value u is killed by only one consumer. Therefore, the purpose of this section is to select a suitable killer for each value in order to saturate the register requirement.

Since we do not assume any schedule, the lifetime intervals are not defined yet, so we cannot know at which date a value is killed. However, we can deduce which consumers in $Cons(u^t)$ are impossible killers for the value u. If $v_1, v_2 \in Cons(u^t)$ and $\exists$ a path $(v_1 \cdots v_2)$, v_1 is always scheduled before v_2 by at least $lat(v_1)$ processor clock cycles. Then v_1 can never be the last reader of u (remember our assumption of positive latencies in the initial DAG). We can consequently deduce which consumers can *potentially* kill a value (possible killers). We denote by $pkill_G(u)$ the set of operations which can kill a value. $u \in V^{R,t}$:

$$pkill_G(u) = \{v \in Cons(u^t)|\, _\vee \cap Cons(u^t) = \{v\}\}$$

Here, $_\vee = \{w \mid v \vee \exists \text{ a path } v \rightsquigarrow w \in G\}$ denotes the set of all nodes reachable from v by a path the DAG G (including v itself).

A potential killing operation for a value u^t is simply a consumer of u that is neither a descendant nor an ascendant of another consumer of u. One can check that all operations in $pkill_G(u)$ are parallel in G. Any operation which does not belong to $pkill_G(u)$ can never kill the value u^t. The following lemma proves that for any value u^t and for any schedule σ, there exists a potential killer v that is a killer of u according to σ. Furthermore, for any potential killer v of a value u, there exists a schedule σ that makes v a killer of u.

LEMMA 8.1.– [TOU 05, TOU 02] Given a DAG $G = (V, E)$, then $\forall u \in V^{R,t}$

$$\forall \sigma \in \Sigma(G), \quad \exists v \in pkill_G(u): \quad \sigma(v) + \delta_{r,t}(v) = d_\sigma(u^t) \qquad [8.1]$$

$$\forall v \in pkill_G(u), \quad \exists \sigma \in \Sigma(G): \quad d_\sigma(u^t) = \sigma(v) + \delta_{r,t}(v) \qquad [8.2]$$

A *potential killing DAG* of G, noted $PK(G) = (V, E^{PK})$, is built to model the potential killing relations between the operations, (see Figure 8.1(c)), where:

$$E^{PK} = \{(u, v)|\, u \in V^{R,t} \wedge v \in pkill_G(u)\}$$

There may be more than one operation candidate for killing a value. Next, we prove that looking for a unique suitable killer for each value is sufficient for maximizing the register need: the next theorem proves that for any schedule that assigns more than one killer for a value, we can build another schedule with at least the same register need such that this value is killed by only one consumer. Consequently, our formal study will look for a unique killer for each value instead of looking for a group of killers.

THEOREM 8.2.– [TOU 05] Let $G = (V, E)$ be a DAG and a schedule $\sigma \in \Sigma(G)$. If there is at least one excessive value that has more than one killer according to σ, then there exists another schedule $\sigma' \in \Sigma(G)$ such that:

$$RN_{\sigma'}^t(G) \geq RN_{\sigma}^t(G)$$

and each excessive value is killed by a unique killer according to σ'.

COROLLARY 8.1.– [TOU 05, TOU 02] Given $G = (V, E)$ a DAG. There is always a saturating schedule for G with the property that each saturating value has a unique killer.

Let us begin by assuming a *killing function*, k_{u^t}, which guarantees that an operation $v \in pkill_G(u)$ is the killer of $u \in V^{R,t}$. If we assume that k_{u^t} is the unique killer of $u \in V^{R,t}$, we must always satisfy the following assertion:

$$\forall v \in (pkill_G(u) - \{k_{u^t}\}) : \quad \sigma(v) + \delta_{r,t}(v) < \sigma(k_{u^t}) + \delta_{r,t}(k_{u^t}) \qquad [8.3]$$

There is a family of schedules that ensures this assertion. In order to define them, we extend G by new serial edges that force all the potential killing operations of each value u to be scheduled before k_{u^t}. This leads us to define an extended DAG associated with k and denoted $G^{\to k} = G\backslash^{E^k}$ where:

$$E^k = \{e = (v, k_{u^t}) | u \in V^{R,t} \ v \in (pkill_G(u) - \{k_{u^t}\})$$
$$\text{with } \delta(e) = \delta_{r,t}(v) - \delta_{r,t}(k_{u^t}) + 1\}$$

Then, any schedule $\sigma \in \Sigma(G^{\to k})$ ensures property [8.3]. The necessary existence of such a schedule defines the condition for a *valid killing function*:

$$k \text{ is a valid killing function} \iff G^{\to k} \text{ is acyclic}$$

Figure 8.2 gives an example of a valid killing function k. This function is illustrated by bold edges in part (a), where each target of a bold edge kills its source. Part (b) is the DAG associated with k.

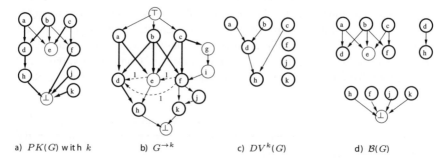

a) $PK(G)$ with k b) $G^{\rightarrow k}$ c) $DV^k(G)$ d) $\mathcal{B}(G)$

Figure 8.2. *Valid killing function and bipartite decomposition*

Provided a valid killing function k, we can deduce the values which can never be simultaneously alive for any $\sigma \in \Sigma(G^{\rightarrow k})$. Let $\downarrow_R (u) =_u \cap V^{R,t}$ be the set of the descendant nodes of $u \in V$ that are values of type t. We call them *descendant values*.

LEMMA 8.2.– [TOU 05, TOU 02] Given a DAG $G = (V, E)$ and a valid killing function k, then:

1) the descendant values of k_{u^t} cannot be simultaneously alive with u^t:

$$\forall u \in V^{R,t}, \ \forall \sigma \in \Sigma(G^{\rightarrow k}), \ \forall v \in \downarrow_R (k_{u^t}) : \quad LT_\sigma(u^t) \prec LT_\sigma(v^t) \qquad [8.4]$$

where $\prec$ is the usual symbol used for precedence relationship between intervals ($[a, b] \prec [a', b'] \Longleftrightarrow b \le a'$);

2) there exists a valid schedule which makes any values non-descendant of k_{u^t} simultaneously alive with u^t, i.e. $\forall u \in V^{R,t}, \ \exists \sigma \in \Sigma(G^{\rightarrow k})$:

$$\forall v \in \left(\bigcup_{v' \in pkill_G(u)} \downarrow_R (v') \right) - \downarrow_R (k_{u^t}) : \quad LT_\sigma(u^t) \cap LT_\sigma(v^t) \ne \phi \qquad [8.5]$$

We define a DAG which models the values that can never be simultaneously alive when assuming k_{u^t} as a killing function. The *disjoint value DAG* of G associated with k, and denoted by $DV^k(G) = (V^{R,t}, E^{DV})$, is defined by:

$$E^{DV} = \left\{ (u, v) | u, v \in V^{R,t} \wedge v \in \downarrow_R (k_{u^t}) \right\}$$

Any edge (u, v) in $DV^k(G)$ means that the lifetime interval of u^t is always before the lifetime interval of v^t according to any schedule of $G^{\rightarrow k}$ (see Figure 8.2(c)); this DAG is simplified by transitive reduction. This definition permits us to state theorem 8.3 as follows.

THEOREM 8.3.– [TOU 05, TOU 02] Given a DAG $G = (V, E)$ and a valid killing function k, let MA^k be a maximal antichain in the disjoint value DAG $DV^k(G)$. Then:

– the register need of any schedule of $G^{\to k}$ is always less than or equal to the size of a maximal antichain in $DV^k(G)$. Formally,

$$\forall \sigma \in \Sigma(G^{\to k}),\ RN_\sigma^t(G) \leq \|MA^k\|$$

– there is always a schedule which makes all the values in this maximal antichain simultaneously alive. Formally,

$$\exists \sigma \in \Sigma(G^{\to k}),\ RN_\sigma^t(G) = \|MA^k\|$$

Theorem 8.3 allows us to rewrite the RS formula as

$$RS^t(G) = \max_{k \text{ a valid killing function}} \|MA^k\|$$

where MA^k is the maximal antichain in $DV^k(G)$. We call each function k that maximizes $\|MA^k\|$ a *saturating killing function*, and MA^k a set of *saturating values*. A saturating killing function is a killing function that produces a saturated register need. The saturating values are the values that are simultaneously alive, and their number reaches the maximal possible register need. Unfortunately, computing a saturating killing function is NP-complete [TOU 02]. The next section presents an efficient heuristic.

8.2.2. Efficient algorithmic heuristic for register saturation computation

The heuristic GREEDY-K of [TOU 05, TOU 02] relies on theorem 8.3. It works by establishing greedily a valid killing function k which aims at maximizing the size of a maximal antichain in $DV^k(G)$.

The heuristic examines each *connected bipartite component* of $PK(G)$ one by one and constructs progressively a killing function.

A connected bipartite component of $PK(G)$ is a triple $cb = (S_{cb}, T_{cb}, E_{cb})$ such that:

– $E_{cb} \subseteq E_{PK}$; E_{PK} is the set of the edges in $PK(G)$.

– $S_{cb} \subseteq V^{R,t}$.

– $T_{cb} \subseteq V$ such that any operation $v \in T_{cb}$ is a potential killer of at least one value of S_{cb}.

A bipartite decomposition of $PK(G)$ is a set of connected bipartite component $\mathcal{B}(G)$ such that for any $e \in E_{PK}$, there exists $cb = (S_{cb}, T_{cb}, E_{cb}) \in \mathcal{B}(G)$ such that $e \in E_{cb}$. This decomposition is unique [TOU 02].

For further details on connected bipartite components and bipartite decomposition, we refer the interested readers to [TOU 02].

Algorithm 8.1. GREEDY-K heuristic

Require: A DAG $G = (V, E)$
Require: A register type $t \in \mathcal{T}$
Ensure: A valid killing function k with $\|MA^k\| \leq RS^t(G)$.
  for all $u \in V^{R,t}$ **do**
    $k_{u^t} \leftarrow \perp$
  end for
  Build $\mathcal{B}(G)$ the bipartite decomposition of $PK(G)$
  for all connected bipartite component $cb = (S_{cb}, T_{cb}, E_{cb}) \in \mathcal{B}(G)$ **do**
    $X \leftarrow S_{cb}$ {Values to kill}
    $Y \leftarrow \emptyset$
    while $X \neq \emptyset$ **do**
      Select $w \in T_{cb}$ which maximizes $\rho_{X,Y,cb}(w)$ {Chose a killer}
      for all $s \in \Gamma_{cb}^-(tw)$ **do** {Make it kill its yet unkilled parents}
        if $k_{s^t} = \perp$ **then**
          $k_{s^t} \leftarrow w$
        end if
      end for
      $X \leftarrow \left(X - \Gamma_{cb}^-(w)\right)$ {Remove killed values}
      $Y \leftarrow \left(Y \cup (\downarrow w \cap V^{R,t})\right)$ {Add descendant values}
    end while
  end for
  return k

The GREEDY-K heuristic is detailed in algorithm 8.1. It examines each $(S_{cb}, T_{cb}, E_{cb}) \in \mathcal{B}(G)$ one after the other and selects greedily a killer $w \in T_{cb}$ that maximizes the ratio $\rho_{X,Y,cb}(w)$ to kill values of S_{cb}. The ratio $\rho_{X,Y,cb}(w)$ was initially given by the following formula:

$$\rho_{X,Y,cb}(w) = \frac{\left\|X \cap \Gamma_{cb}^-(w)\right\|}{\max(1, \|Y \cup (\downarrow w \cap V^{R,t})\|)}$$

This ratio is a trade-off between the number of values killed by w, and the number of edges that will connect w to descendant values in $DV^k(G)$.

By always selecting a killer that maximizes this ratio, the GREEDY-K heuristic aims at minimizing the number of edges in $DV^k(G)$; the intuition being that the more edges there are in $DV^k(G)$, the less its width (the size of a maximal antichain) is.

However, the above cost function has been improved lately due to the contribution of Sebastien Briais [BRI 09a]. We find out that the following cost function provides better experimental results:

$$\rho'_{X,Y,cb}(w) = \frac{\|X \cap \Gamma_{cb}^-(w)\|}{1 + \|Y \cup (\downarrow w \cap V^{R,t})\|}$$

Thus, we have removed the max operator that acted as a threshold.

Given a DAG $G = (V, E)$ and a register type $t \in \mathcal{T}$, the estimation of the register saturation by the GREEDY-K heuristic is the size of a maximal antichain MA^k in $DV^k(G)$ where $k = \text{GREEDY-K}(G, t)$. Computing a maximal antichain of a DAG can be done in polynomial time due to Dilworth's decomposition.

Note that since the computed killing function is valid, the approximated RS computed by GREEDY-K is always lesser than or equal to the optimal $RS^t(G)$. Fortunately, we have some trivial cases for optimality.

COROLLARY 8.2.– [TOU 05, TOU 02] Let $G = (V, E)$ be a DAG. If $PK(G)$ is a tree, then Greedy-k computes an optimal RS.

The case when $PK(G)$ is a tree contains, for instance, expression trees (numerical, computer-intensive loops such as BLAS kernels). However, this does not exclude other classes of DAG since $PK(G)$ may be a tree even if the initial DAG is not.

Figure 8.3(a) shows a saturating killing function computed by GREEDY-K: bold edges mean that each source is killed by its sink. Each killer is labeled by its cost ρ. Figure 8.3(b) gives the disjoint value DAG associated with k. The approximate saturating values are $\{a, b, c, d, f, j, k\}$, so the approximate RS is 7.

8.2.3. Experimental efficiency of Greedy-k

RS computation (optimal and GREEDY-K) is released as a public code, named RSlib, under LGPL licence in [BRI 09a]. Full experimental data are also released and analyzed in [BRI 09a] with a summary in Appendix 2.

Experiments, led over a large set of public and industrial benchmarks (MEDIABENCH, FFMPEG, SPEC2000, SPEC2006), have shown that GREEDY-K is nearly optimal. Indeed, in most of the cases, register saturation is estimated correctly for any register type (FP, GR or BR). We have measured the mean error ratio to be under 4%. If we enlarge the codes by loop unrolling ($\times 4$, multiplying the size by a factor of 5), then the mean error ratio of register saturation estimation reaches 13%.

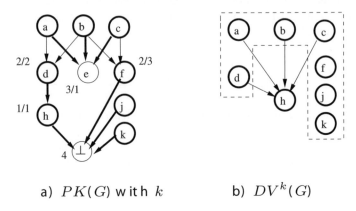

a) $PK(G)$ with k b) $DV^k(G)$

Figure 8.3. *Example of computing the acyclic register saturation*

The speed of the heuristic is satisfactory enough to be included inside an interactive compiler: the median of the execution times of GREEDY-K on a current linux workstation is less than 10 ms.

Another set of experimentations concerns the relationship between register saturation and shortest possible instruction schedules. We find that, experimentally, minimal instruction scheduling does not necessarily correlate with maximal register requirements, and vice versa. This relationship is not a surprise, since we already know that aggressive instruction scheduling strategies do not necessarily increase the register requirement.

Register saturation is indeed interesting information that can be exploited by optimizing compilers before enabling aggressive instruction scheduling algorithms. The fact that our heuristics do not compute optimal RS values is not problematic because we have shown that best instruction scheduling does not necessarily maximize the register requirement. Consequently, if an optimal RS is underevaluated by one of our heuristics, and if the compilation flow allows an aggressive instruction scheduling without worrying about register pressure, then it is highly improbable that the register requirement would be maximized. This may compensate the error made by the RS evaluation heuristic.

This section studied the register saturation inside a DAG devoted to acyclic instruction scheduling. Section 8.3 extends the notion to loops devoted to software pipelining (SWP).

8.3. Computing the periodic register saturation

Let $G = (V, E)$ be a loop DDG. The periodic register saturation (PRS) is the maximal register requirement of type $t \in \mathcal{T}$ for all valid software pipelined schedules:

$$PRS^t(G) = \max_{\sigma \in \Sigma(G)} PRN^t_\sigma(G)$$

where $PRN^t_\sigma(G)$ is the periodic register need for the SWP schedule σ. A software pipelined schedule which needs the maximum number of registers is called a *saturating SWP schedule*. Note that it may not be unique.

In this section, we show that our formula for computing $PRN^t_\sigma(G)$ (see equation [7.1]) is useful for writing an exact modeling of PRS computation. In the current case, we are faced with a difficulty: for computing the periodic register sufficiency as described in section 7.5.2, we are requested to minimize a *maximum* (minimize MAXLIVE), which is a common optimization problem in operational research; however, PRS computation requires us to *maximize* a maximum, namely to maximize MAXLIVE. Maximizing a maximum is a less conventional linear optimization problem. It requires the writing of an exact equation of the maximum, which has been defined by equation [7.1].

In practice, we need to consider loops with a bounded code size. That is, we should bound the duration L. This yields to computing the PRS by considering a subset of possible SWP schedules $\Sigma_L(G) \subseteq \Sigma(G)$: we compute the maximal register requirement in the set of all valid software pipelined schedules with the property that the duration does not exceed a fixed limit L and $MII \geq 1$. Bounding the schedule space has the consequence of bounding the values of the scheduling function as follows: $\forall u \in V, \sigma(u) \leq L$.

Computing the optimal register saturation is proved as an NP-complete problem in [TOU 05, TOU 02]. Now, let us study how we exactly compute the PRS using integer linear programming (intLP). Our intLP formulation expresses the logical operators ($\implies, \vee, \iff$) and the max operator ($\max(x, y)$) by introducing extra binary variables. However, expressing these additional operators requires that the domain of the integer variables should be bounded, as explained in details in [TOU 05, TOU 02].

Next, we present our intLP formulation that computes a saturating SWP schedule $\sigma \in \Sigma_L(G)$ considering a *fixed II*. Fixing a value for the initiation interval is necessary to have linear constraints in the intLP system. As far as we know, computing the exact periodic register need (MAXLIVE) of a SWP schedule with a non-fixed II is not a mathematically defined problem (because a SWP schedule is defined according to a fixed II).

8.3.1. *Basic integer linear variables*

1) For the lifetime intervals, we define:

– one schedule variable $\sigma_u \in \mathbb{N}$ for each $u \in V$;

– one variable which contains the killing date $k_{u^t} \in \mathbb{N}$ for each statement $u \in V^{R,t}$.

2) For the periodic register need, we define:

– $p_u \in \mathbb{N}$ the number of the instances of $u \in V^{R,t}$ simultaneously alive, which is the number of complete periods around the circle produced by the cyclic lifetime interval of $u \in V^{R,t}$;

– $l_u \in \mathbb{N}$ and $r_u \in \mathbb{N}$ the left and the right of the cyclic lifetime interval of $u \in V^{R,t}$;

– the two acyclic fractional intervals $I_u =]a_u, b_u]$ and $I'_u =]a'_u, b'_u]$ after unrolling the kernel once.

3) For a maximal clique in the interference graph of the fractional acyclic intervals, we define:

– interference binary variables $s_{I,J}$ for all the fractional acyclic intervals I, J: $s_{I,J} = 1$ iff I and J interfere with each other;

– a binary variable x_I for each fractional acyclic interval: $x_I = 1$ iff I belongs to a maximal clique.

8.3.2. *Integer linear constraints*

1) Periodic scheduling constraints: $\forall e = (u,v) \in E, \qquad \sigma_u - \sigma_v \leq +\lambda(e) \times II - \delta(e)$

2) The killing dates are computed by:

$$\forall u \in V^{R,t}, \qquad k_{u^t} = \max_{\substack{v \in Cons(u^t) \\ e=(u,v) \in E^{R,t}}} (\sigma_v + \delta_{r,t}(v) + \lambda(e) \times II)$$

We use the linear constraints of the *max* operator as defined in [TOU 05, TOU 02]. k_{u^t} is bounded by $\underline{k_{u^t}}$ and $\overline{k_{u^t}}$ where:

– $\underline{k_{u^t}} = \min_{v \in Cons(u^t)} \left(\delta_{r,t}(v) + \max_{e=(u,v) \in E^{R,t}} \lambda(e) \times II \right)$

– $\overline{k_{u^t}} = \max_{v \in Cons(u^t)} \left(L + \delta_{r,t}(v) + \max_{e=(u,v) \in E^{R,t}} \lambda(e) \times II \right)$

3) The number of interfering instances of a value (complete turns around the circle) is the integer division of its lifetime by II. We introduce an integer variable $\alpha_u \geq 0$ which holds the rest of the division:

$$\begin{cases} k_{u^t} - \sigma_u - \delta_{w,t}(u) = II \times p_u + \alpha_u \\ \alpha_u < II \\ \alpha_u \in \mathbb{N} \end{cases}$$

4) The lefts (section 7.3.2) of the circular intervals are the rest of the integer division of the birth date of the value by II. We introduce an integer variable $\beta_u \geq 0$ which holds the integral quotient of the division:

$$\begin{cases} \sigma_u + \delta_{w,t}(u) = II \times \beta_u + l_u \\ l_u < II \\ \beta_u \in \mathbb{N} \end{cases}$$

5) The rights (section 7.3.2) of the circular intervals are the rest of the integer division of the killing date by II. We introduce an integer variable $\gamma_u \geq 0$ which holds the integer quotient of the division:

$$\begin{cases} k_{u^t} = II \times \gamma_u + r_u \\ r_u < II \\ \gamma_u \in \mathbb{N} \end{cases}$$

6) The fractional acyclic intervals are computed by considering an unrolled kernel once (they are computed depending on whether the cyclic interval crosses the kernel barrier):

$$\begin{cases} a_u = l_u \\ r_u \geq l_u \implies b_u = r_u \\ \text{case when the cyclic interval crosses } II: \\ r_u < l_u \implies b_u = r_u + II \\ a'_u = a_u + II \\ b'_u = b_u + II \end{cases}$$

Since the variable domains are bounded, we can use the linear constraints of implication defined in [TOU 05, TOU 02]: we know that $0 \leq l_u < II$, so $0 \leq a_u < II$ and $II \leq a'_u < 2 \times II$. Also, $0 \leq l_u < II$ so $0 \leq b_u < 2 \times II$ and $II \leq b'_u < 3 \times II$.

7) For any pair of distinct fractional acyclic intervals I, J, the binary variable $s_{I,J} \in \{0, 1\}$ is set to 1 if the two intervals are non empty and interfere with each other. It is expressed in the intLP by adding the following constraints.

$\forall$ acyclic intervals I, J:

$$s_{I,J} = 1 \Longleftrightarrow \big[(length(I) > 0)$$
$$\wedge \, (length(J) > 0)$$
$$\wedge \, \neg(I \prec J \vee J \prec I)\big]$$

where $\prec$ denotes the usual relation *before* in the interval algebra. Assuming that $I = \,]a_I, b_I]$ and $J = \,]a_J, b_J]$, $I \prec J$ means that $b_I \leq a_J$, and the above constraints are written as follows. $\forall$ acyclic intervals I, J,

$$s_{I,J} = 1 \Longleftrightarrow \begin{cases} b_I - a_I > 0 & (\text{i.e., } length(I) > 0) \\ b_J - a_J > 0 & (\text{i.e., } length(J) > 0) \\ b_I > a_J & (\text{i.e., } \neg(I \prec J)) \\ b_J > a_I & (\text{i.e., } \neg(J \prec I)) \end{cases}$$

8) A maximal clique in the interference graph is an independent set in the complementary graph. Then, for two binary variables x_I and x_J, only one is set to 1 if the two acyclic intervals I and J do not interfere with each other:

$$\forall \text{ acyclic intervals } I, J : \qquad s_{I,J} = 0 \Longrightarrow x_I + x_J \leq 1$$

9) To guarantee that our objective function maximizes the interferences between the non-zero length acyclic intervals, we add the following constraint:

$$\forall \text{ acyclic intervals } I, \qquad length(I) = 0 \Longrightarrow x_I = 0$$

Since $length(I) = b_I - a_I$, it amounts to:

$$\forall \text{ acyclic intervals } I, \qquad b_I - a_I = 0 \Longrightarrow x_I = 0$$

8.3.3. *Linear objective function*

A saturating SWP schedule can be obtained by maximizing the value of:

$$\sum_{\text{acyclic fractional interval } I} x_I + \sum_{u \in V^{R,t}} p_u$$

Solving the above intLP model yields a solution $\bar{\sigma}$ for the scheduling variables, which define a saturating SWP, such that $PRS^t(G) = PRN^t_{\bar{\sigma}}(G)$. Once $\bar{\sigma}$ computed by intLP, then $PRN^t_{\bar{\sigma}}(G)$ is equal to the value of the objective function. Finally, $PRS^t(G) = \max_{MII \leq II \leq L} PRN^t_{\bar{\sigma}}(G)$.

The size of our intLP model is $\mathcal{O}(\|V^{R,t}\|^2)$ variables and $\mathcal{O}(\|\|E\| + \|V^{R,t}\|^2)$ constraints. The coefficients of the constraints matrix are all bounded by $\pm L \times \lambda_{max} \times$

II, where λ_{max} is the maximal dependence distance in the loop. To compute the PRS, we scan all the admissible values of II, i.e. we iterate II the initiation interval from MII to L and then we solve the intLP system for each value of II. The PRS is finally the maximal register need among of all the ones computed by all the intLP systems. It can be noted that the size of out intLP model is polynomial (quadratic) on the size of the input DDG.

Contrary to the acyclic RS, we do not have an efficient algorithmic heuristic for computing PRS. So computing PRS is not intended for interactive compilers, but for longer embedded compilation. What we can do is to use heuristics for intLP solving. For instance, the CPLEX solver has numerous parameters that can be used to approximate an optimal solution. An easy way, for instance, is to put a time-out for the solver. Appendix A2.2 shows to experimental results on this aspect.

8.4. Conclusion on the register saturation

In this chapter, we formally study the RS notion, which is the exact maximal register need of all the valid schedules of the DDG. Many practical applications may profit from RS computation: (1) for compiler technology, RS calculation provides new opportunities for avoiding and/or verifying useless spilling; (2) for JIT compilation, RS metrics may be embedded in the generated byte-code as static annotations, which may help the JIT to dynamically schedule instructions without worrying about register constraints; (3) for helping hardware designers, RS computation provides a static analysis of the exact maximal register requirement irrespective of other resource constraints.

We believe that register constraints must be taken into account before ILP scheduling, but by using the RS concept instead of the existing strategies that minimize the register need. Otherwise, the subsequent ILP scheduler is restricted even if enough registers exist.

The first case of our study is when the DDG represents a DAG of a basic block or a superblock. We give many fundamental results regarding the RS computation. First, we prove that choosing an appropriated unique killer is sufficient to saturate the register need. Second, we prove that fixing a unique killer per value allows us to optimally compute the RS with polynomial time algorithms. If a unique killer is not fixed per value, we prove that computing the RS of a DAG is NP-complete in the general case (except for expression trees, for instance). An exact formulation using integer programming and an efficient approximate algorithm are presented in [TOU 02, TOU 05]. Our formal mathematical modeling and theoretical study enable us to give a nearly optimal heuristic named GREEDY-K. Its computation time is fast enough to be included inside an interactive compiler.

The second case of our study is when the DDG represents a loop devoted to SWP. Contrary to the acyclic case, we do not provide an efficient algorithmic heuristic, the cyclic problem or register maximization being more complex. However, we provide an exact intLP model to compute the PRS, by using our formula of MAXLIVE (equation [7.1]). Currently, we rely on the heuristics present in intLP solvers to compute an approximate PRS in reasonable time. While our experiments show that this solution is possible, we do not think that it would be appropriate for interactive compilers. Indeed, it seems that computing an approximate PRS with intLP heuristics requires times which are more convenient to aggressive compilation for embedded systems.

Finally, if the computed RS exceeds the number of available registers, we can bring a method to reduce this maximal register need in a way sufficient enough to just bring it below the limit without minimizing it at the lowest possible level. RS reduction must take care to not increase the critical path of a DAG (or the MII of a loop). This problem is studied in Chapter 9.

9

Spill Code Reduction

Register allocation in a loop data dependence graph (DDG) is generally performed after or during the instruction scheduling process. This is because doing a conventional register allocation as a first step without assuming a schedule lacks the information of interferences between values' live ranges. Thus, the register allocator may introduce a large amount of false dependences that dramatically reduce the instruction-level parallelism (ILP). We present a theoretical framework for bounding the register requirements of all types conjointly before the instruction scheduling. This framework is called schedule independent register allocation (SIRA). SIRA tends to precondition the DDG in order to ensure that no register spill instructions are inserted by the register allocator into the scheduled loop. If spilling is not necessary for the input code, preconditioning techniques insert anti-dependence edges so that the maximum register pressure MAXLIVE achieved by any ILP schedule is below the number of available registers, without hurting the schedule if possible.

The inserted anti-dependences are modeled by *reuse* edges labeled with *reuse distances*. We prove that the maximal register need is determined by these reuse distances. Consequently, the determination of register and distance reuse are parameterized by the desired critical circuit (MII) as well as by the register pressure constraints. We give an optimal exact intLP model for SIRA, and an exact intLP model for a simplified problem in the case of buffers and rotating register files. SIRA being NP-complete, we present an efficient polynomial heuristic called SIRALINA.

9.1. Introduction to register constraints in software pipelining

Media processing and compute-intensive applications spend most of their runtime in inner loops. Software pipelining is a key instruction scheduling technique used to improve performances, by converting loop-level parallelism into ILP [LAM 88b, RAU 94]. However, on wide issue or deeply pipelined processors, the performance of software-pipelined loops is especially sensitive to the effects of register allocation [LAM 88b, EIS 95b, FIS 05], in particular the insertion of memory access instructions for spilling the live ranges.

Usually, loops are software pipelined assuming that no memory access miss the cache, and a significant amount of research has been devoted to heuristics that produce near-optimal schedules under this assumption [RAU 92d, RUT 96b]. The code produced by software pipelining is then processed by the register allocation phase. However, a cache miss triggered by a spill instruction introduced by the register allocator has the potential to reduce the dynamic ILP below the level of the non-software pipelined loop without the cache miss.

In addition to limiting the negative effects of cache misses on performances, reducing spill code has other advantages in embedded very long instruction word (VLIW) processors. For instance, energy consumption of the generated embedded VLIW code is reduced, because memory requests need more power than regular functional units instructions. Also, reducing the amount of spill code improves the accuracy of static program performance models: indeed, since memory operations have unknown static latencies (except if we use scratch-pad memories), the precision of worst-case execution time (WCET) analysis and static compilation performance models is altered. When performance prediction models are inaccurate, static compiler transformation engines may be guided to bad optimization decisions. Consequently, we believe that an important code quality criterion is to have a reduced amount of memory requests upon the condition of not altering the ILP scheduling.

9.2. Related work in periodic register allocation

Classic register allocation involves three topics: which live ranges to evict from registers (register spilling), which register-register copy instructions to eliminate (register coalescing) and what architectural register to use for any live range (register assignment). The dominant framework for classic register allocation is the graph coloring approach pioneered by Chaintin et al. [CHA 82] and refined by Briggs et al. [BRI 94]. This framework relies on the vertex coloring of an interference graph, where vertices correspond to live ranges and edges to interferences. Two live ranges interfere if one is live at the definition point of the other and they carry different values.

In the area of software pipelining, live ranges may span multiple iteration, so the classic register allocation techniques are not directly applicable because of the self-interference of such live ranges. One solution is to unroll the software pipelined loop until no live range self-interferes, then apply classic register allocation. A better solution is to rely on techniques that understand the self-interferences created by loop iterations, also known as *periodic register allocation techniques*.

Because of the restrictions on the inner loops that are candidates for software pipelining, the periodic register allocation techniques mostly focus on the issues related to register spilling and register coalescing. In particular, the register coalescing problem of a software pipeline can be solved by using modulo expansion and kernel unrolling [WER 99, HEN 92, LAM 88b, RAU 92c], or by exploiting hardware support known as rotating register files [RAU 92c]. Without these techniques, register-register copy instructions may remain in the software pipelined loop [NIC 92a]. For the register spilling problems, we can either try to minimize the impact of spill code in the software pipeline [NAG 07], or precondition the scheduling problem so that spilling is avoided [TOU 04].

The SIRA framework [TOU 04] is distinct from the the previous research on periodic register allocation [WER 99, HEN 92] since it considers unscheduled loops. The motivations for handling register constraints by preconditioning software pipelining are as follows:

1) *Separating register pressure control from instruction scheduling:* with the increase of loop code size of media processing applications, methods that formulate software pipelining under both register pressure and resource constraints as integer linear programming problems [EIC 97, NAG 07, RUT 96b] are not applicable in practice. Indeed, such exact methods are limited to loops with a few dozen instructions. In real media processing applications, it is not uncommon to schedule loops with hundreds of instructions. So, in order to reduce the difficulty of scheduling large loops, we satisfy the register constraints before the scheduled resource constraints (issue width, execution units)

2) *Handling registers constraints before scheduled resource constraints:* this is because register constraints are more complex: given a bounded number of available registers, increasing the loop initiation interval (II) to reduce the register pressure does not necessarily provide a solution, even with optimal scheduling. Sometimes, spilling is mandatory to reduce register pressure. Spilling modifies the DDG, bringing an iterative problem of spilling followed by scheduling. In contrast, resource constraints are always solvable by increasing the II. For any DDG, there always exists at least one schedule under resource constraints, whatever these resource constraints are.

3) *Avoiding spilling instead of scheduling spill code:* this is because spilling introduces memory instructions whose exact latencies are unknown. Consequently, when the code is executed, any cache miss may have dramatic effects on performance, especially for VLIW processors. In other words, even if we succeed to optimally schedule spill instructions as done in [NAG 07], actual performance will not necessarily follow the static schedule because spill instructions may not hit the cache as assumed by the compiler. Even if the data reside in the cache, some microarchitectural implementations of the memory hierarchy (memories disambiguation, banking, etc.) introduce additional nops that cannot be guessed at compile time [JAL 06, LEM 04].

Section 9.3 explains the SIRA theoretical framework and its application.

9.3. SIRA: schedule independant register allocation

9.3.1. *Reuse graphs*

A simple way to explain and recall the concept of SIRA is to provide an example. All the theory has already been presented in [TOU 04, TOU 02]. Figure 9.1(a) provides an initial DDG with two register types t_1 and t_2. Statements producing results of type t_1 are in dashed circles, and those of type t_2 are in bold circles. Statement u_1 writes two results of distinct types. Flow dependence through registers of type t_1 are in dashed edges, and those of type t_2 are in bold edges.

As an example, $Cons(u_2^{t_2}) = \{u_1, u_4\}$ and $Cons(u_3^{t_1}) = \{u_4\}$. Each edge e in the DDG is labeled with the pair of values $(\delta(e), \lambda(e))$. In this simple example, we assume that the delay of accessing registers is zero ($\delta_{w,t} = \delta_{r,t} = 0$). Now, the question is how to compute a periodic register allocation for the loop in Figure 9.1(a) without increasing the critical circuit if possible.

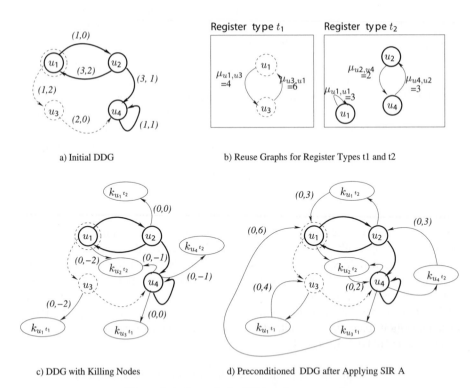

Figure 9.1. *Example for SIRA and reuse graphs*

As formally studied in [TOU 02, TOU 04], periodic register constraints are modeled due to *reuse graphs*. We associate a reuse graph $G^{\text{reuse},t}$ with each register type t, see Figure 9.1(b). The reuse graph has to be computed by the SIRA framework, Figure 9.1(b) is one of the examples that SIRA may produce. Note that the reuse graph is not unique, other valid reuse graphs may exist.

A reuse graph $G^{\text{reuse},t} = (V^{R,t}, E^{\text{reuse},t})$ contains $V^{R,t}$, i.e. only the nodes writing inside registers of type t. These nodes are connected by *reuse edges*. For instance, in G^{reuse,t_2} of Figure 9.1(b), the set of reuse edges is $E^{\text{reuse},t_2} = \{(u_2, u_4), (u_4, u_2), (u_1, u_1)\}$. Also, $E^{\text{reuse},t_1} = \{(u_1, u_3), (u_3, u_1)\}$. Each reuse edge $e_r = (u, v)$ is labeled by an integral distance $\mu^t(e_r)$, that we call *reuse distance*. The existence of a reuse edge $e_r = (u, v)$ of distance $\mu^t(e_r)$ means that the two operations $u(i)$ and $v(i + \mu^t(e_r))$ *share the same destination register* of type t. Hence, reuse graphs allows to completely define a periodic register allocation for a given loop. In the example of Figure 9.1(b), we have in G^{reuse,t_2} $\mu^{t_2}((u_2, u_4)) = 2$ and $\mu^{t_2}((u_4, u_2)) = 3$.

To be valid, reuse graphs should satisfy two main constraints [TOU 04]: (1) They must describe a bijection between the nodes, that is, they must be composed of elementary and disjoint circuits. (2) The *associated DDG* (to be defined later) must be schedulable, i.e. it should have at least one valid software pipelining (SWP).

Let C be a reuse circuit in the reuse graph $G^{\text{reuse},t}$. By abuse of notation, we write $\mu^t(C) = \sum_{e_r \in C} \mu^t(e_r)$. The following theorem states that the sum of the reuse distances of a valid reuse graph defines the number of allocated registers in the loop.

THEOREM 9.1.– [TOU 02, TOU 04] Let $G = (V, E)$ be a loop DDG and $G^{\text{reuse},t} = (V^{R,t}, E^{\text{reuse},t})$ be a valid reuse graph of type $t \in \mathcal{T}$. Then the reuse graph $G^{\text{reuse},t}$ defines a periodic register allocation for G with exactly $\sum_{e_r \in E^{\text{reuse},t}} \mu^t(e_r)$ registers of type t if we unroll the loop α_t times where:

$$\alpha_t = lcm(\mu^t(C_1), \cdots, \mu^t(C_n))$$

with $\{C_1, \cdots, C_n\}$ is the set of all reuse circuits, and lcm is the least common multiple.

As a corollary, we can build a periodic register allocation for all register types.

COROLLARY 9.1.– [TOU 02, TOU 04] Let $G = (V, E)$ be a loop DDG with a set of register types $\mathcal{T}$. To each register type $t \in \mathcal{T}$ is associated a valid reuse graph $G^{\text{reuse},t} = (V^{R,t}, E^{\text{reuse},t})$. The loop can be allocated with $\sum_{e_r \in E^{\text{reuse},t}} \mu^t(e_r)$ registers for each type t if we unroll it α times, where:

$$\alpha = lcm(\alpha_{t_1}, \cdots, \alpha_{t_n})$$

α_{t_i} is the unrolling degree of the reuse graph of type t_i as defined in theorem 9.1.

We should make an important remark regarding loop unrolling. Indeed, we can avoid loop unrolling before the SWP step in order not to increase the DDG size, and hence not to exhibit more statements to the scheduler. Since we allocate registers directly into the DDG by inserting loop carried anti-dependencies, the DDG can be scheduled without unrolling it (but the inserted anti-dependence edges restrict the scheduler). In other words, loop unrolling can be applied at the code generation step (after SWP) in order to apply the register allocation computed before scheduling.

After defining the reuse graphs, section 9.3.2 explains what are the implications on the initial DDG in terms of additional edges.

9.3.2. DDG associated with reuse graph

Now, let us describe what we mean by the DDG *associated with* a reuse graph. Once a reuse graph is fixed before SWP, say the reuse graphs of types t_1 and t_2 in Figure 9.1(b), the register constraints create new periodic scheduling constraints between loop statements. These scheduling constraints result from the anti-dependencies created by register reuse. Since each reuse edge (u, v) in the reuse graph $G^{\text{reuse},t}$ describes a register sharing between $u(i)$ and $v(i + \mu^t((u, v)))$, we must guarantee that $v(i + \mu^t((u, v))$ writes inside the same register after the execution of all the consumers of $u^t(i)$. That is, we should guarantee that $v(i + \mu^t((u, v)))$ writes its result after the killing date of $u^t(i)$. If the loop is already scheduled, the killing date is known. However, if the loop is not already scheduled, then the killing date is not known and hence we should be able to guarantee the validity of periodic register allocation for all possible SWP schedules.

Guaranteeing the precedence relationship between lifetime intervals for any subsequent SWP is done by creating *the associated DDG* with the reuse graph. This DDG is an extension of the initial one in two steps:

1) *Killing nodes:* first, we introduce dummy nodes representing the killing dates of all values [DIN 97b]. For each value $u \in V^{R,t}$, we introduce a node k_{u^t}, which represents the killing date of u^t. The killing node k_{u^t} must always be scheduled after all u^t's consumers, so we add edges of the form $e = (v, k_{u^t})$ where $v \in Cons^t(u)$. If a value u^t has no consumer (not read inside the loop), it means that the node can be killed just after the creation of its result. Figure 9.1(c) illustrates the DDG after adding all the killing nodes for all register types. For each added edge $e = (v, k_{u^t})$, we set its latency to $\delta(e) = \delta_{r,t}(v)$ and its distance to $-\lambda$, where λ is the distance of the flow dependence edge $(u, v) \in E^{R,t}$. As explained in [TOU 04], this negative distance is a mathematical convention, it simplifies our mathematical formula and does not influence the fundamental results of reuse graphs. Formally, if $u \in V^{R,t}$ is a node writing a value of type $t \in \mathcal{T}$, then we note k_{u^t} the killer node of type t of the value u^t. The set of killing nodes of type t is noted $V^{k,t}$. For each type $t \in \mathcal{T}$, we note $E^{k,t}$

the set of edges defining the precedence constraints between $V^{R,t}$ nodes and the killer nodes:

$$E^{k,t} = \{e = (v, k_{u^t}) \mid u \in V^{R,t} \land v \in Cons^t(u) \land \delta(e) = \delta_{r,t}(v)\}$$
$$\cup \{(u, k_{u^t}) \mid u \in V^{R,t} \land Cons^t(u) = \emptyset \land \delta(e) = 1\}$$

For instance, in Figure 9.1(b), we have $V^{k,t_2} = \{k_{u_1 t_2}, k_{u_2 t_2}, k_{u_4 t_2}\}$, and we have $E^{k,t_2} = \{(u_2, k_{u_1 t_2}), (u_1, k_{u_2 t_2}), (u_4, k_{u_2 t_2}), (u_4, k_{u_4 t_2})\}$.

If we note $K = \bigcup_{t \in \mathcal{T}} V^{k,t}$ and $E^k = \bigcup_{t \in \mathcal{T}} E^{k,t}$, then the DDG with killing nodes is defined by $(V \cup K, E \cup E^k)$.

2) *Anti-dependence edges:* second, we introduce new anti-dependence edges implied by periodic register constraints. For each reuse edge $e_r = (u, v)$ in $G^{\text{reuse},t}$, we add an edge $e'_r = (k_{u^t}, v)$ representing an *anti-dependence* in the associated DDG. We say that the anti-dependence $e'_r = (k_{u^t}, v)$ in the DDG G is associated with the reuse edge $e_r = (u, v)$ in $G^{\text{reuse},t}$. We write $\Phi(e_r) = e'_r$ and $\Phi^{-1}(e'_r) = e_r$.

The added anti-dependence edge $e'_r = (k_{u^t}, v)$ has a distance equal to the reuse distance $\lambda(e'_r) = \mu^t(e_r)$, and a latency equal to:

– $\delta(e'_r) = -\delta_{w,t}(v)$ if the processor has non-unit-assumed-latencies (NUAL) semantics.

– $\delta(e'_r) = 1$ if the processor has unit-assumed-latencies (UAL) semantics. Note that we can still assume a latency $\delta(e'_r) = \delta_{w,t} - \delta_{r,t} = 0$, since the instruction scheduler will generate a sequential code; so this zero edge imposes to schedule k_{u^t} before v.

Figure 9.1(d) illustrates the DDG associated with the two reuse graphs of Figure 9.1(b). Periodic register constraints with multiple register types are satisfied conjointly on the same DDG even if each register type has its own reuse graph. The reader may notice that the critical circuit of the DDG in Figure 9.1(a) and (c) are the same and equal to $MII = \frac{4}{2} = 2$ (a critical circuit is (u_1, u_2)). The set of added anti-dependence edges of type t is denoted by $E^{\mu,t}$

$$E^{\mu,t} = \{e = (k_{u^t}, v) \mid e_r = (u, v) \in E^{\text{reuse},t} \land \Phi(e_r) = e\}$$

In Figure 9.1(d), $E^{\mu,t_1} = \{(k_{u_1 t_1}, u_3), (k_{u_3 t_1}, u1)\}$ and $E^{\mu,t_2} = \{(k_{u_1 t_2}, u_1), (k_{u_2 t_2}, u_4), (k_{u_4 t_2}, u_2)\}$.

If we note $E^\mu = \bigcup_{t \in \mathcal{T}} E^{\mu,t}$, then the DDG G' (with killing nodes) associated with the reuse graphs $\left(V^{R,t}, E^{\text{reuse},t}\right)_{t \in \mathcal{T}}$ is defined by $G' = (\mathcal{V} = V \cup K, \mathcal{E} = E \cup E^k \cup E^\mu)$.

As can be seen, computing a reuse graph of a register type t implies the creation of new edges with μ^t distances. As proved by theorem 9.1, if a reuse graph $G^{\text{reuse},t}$ is valid, then it describes a periodic register allocation with exactly $\sum_{e_r \in E^{\text{reuse},t}} \mu^t(e_r)$ registers of type t. Consequently, the following corollary holds.

COROLLARY 9.2.– Let $G = (V, E)$ be a loop DDG with a set of register types $\mathcal{T}$. To each register type $t \in \mathcal{T}$ is associated a valid reuse graph $G^{\text{reuse},t} = (V^{R,t}, E^{\text{reuse},t})$. Let $G' = (\mathcal{V} = V \cup K, \mathcal{E} = E \cup E^k \cup E^\mu)$ be the extended DDG resulted from adding all the anti-dependences for all register types. Then,

$$\forall \sigma \in \Sigma(G'), \forall t \in \mathcal{T} : \quad PRN^t \leq \sum_{e_r \in E^{\text{reuse},t}} \mu^t(e_r)$$

That is, any SWP schedule cannot require more than $\sum_{e_r \in E^{\text{reuse},t}} \mu^t(e_r)$ registers of type t, and this upper bound is reachable.

Now the SIRA problem is to compute a valid reuse graph with minimal $\sum_{e_r \in E^{\text{reuse},t}} \mu^t(e_r)$, without increasing the critical circuit if possible. Or, instead of minimizing the register requirement, SIRA may simply look for a solution such that $\sum_{e_r \in E^{\text{reuse},t}} \mu^t(e_r) \leq \mathcal{R}^t$, where $\mathcal{R}^t$ is the number of available registers of type t. Unfortunately, such problem is proved NP-complete in [TOU 04, TOU 02]. The next section defines the exact problem using intLP.

9.3.3. *Exact SIRA with integer linear programming*

In this section, we give an intLP model for solving SIRA. It is built for a fixed initiation interval II. Note that II is not the initiation interval of the final schedule, since the loop is not already scheduled. II denotes the value of the new desired critical circuit MII.

Our SIRA exact model uses the linear formulation of the logical implication ($\Longrightarrow$) by introducing binary variables, as previously explained in [TOU 02]. The usage of $\Longrightarrow$ imposes that the variables of the intLP must be bounded.

9.3.3.1. *Basic integer variables*

– A schedule variable $\sigma_u \in \mathbb{N}$ for each operation $u \in V$, including one for each killing node k_{u^t}. We assume that these schedule variables are bounded by a maximal duration L. So, $\forall u \in V : \sigma_u \leq L$.

– A binary variable $\theta^t_{u,v}$ for each $(u, v) \in V^{R,t} \times V^{R,t}$, and for each register type $t \in \mathcal{T}$. It is set to 1 iff (u, v) is a reuse edge of type t.

– $\widehat{\mu}^t(u, v)$ for reuse distance for all pairs $(u, v) \in V^{R,t} \times V^{R,t}$, and for each register type $t \in \mathcal{T}$.

9.3.3.2. *Integer linear constraints*

– Data dependences (the existence of at least one valid software pipelining schedule):

$$\forall e = (u, v) \in E : \sigma_u + \delta(e) \leq \sigma_v + II \times \lambda(e)$$

– Schedule killing nodes for consumed values:

$$\forall u \in V^{R,t}, \forall v \in Cons(u^t) \mid e = (u, v) \in E^{R,t} : \sigma_{k_{u^t}} \geq \sigma_v$$
$$+\delta_{r,t}(v) + \lambda(e) \times II$$

if a value is not consumed, we can create a fictitious killer as follows:

$$\forall u \in V^{R,t} \mid Cons(u^t) = \emptyset : \sigma_{k_{u^t}} \geq \sigma_u + 1$$

– There is an anti-dependence between k_{u^t} and v if (u, v) is a reuse edge of type t:

$$\forall t \in \mathcal{T}, \forall (u, v) \in V^{R,t} \times V^{R,t} : \theta_{u,v}^t = 1 \Longrightarrow \sigma_{k_{u^t}} - \delta_{w,t}(v) \leq \sigma_v$$
$$+II \times \widehat{\mu}^t(u, v)$$

– If there is no register reuse between two statements, then $\theta_{u,v}^t = 0$. The reuse distance $\widehat{\mu}^t(u, v)$ must be set to 0 in order to not be accumulated in the objective function. $\forall t \in \mathcal{T}, \forall (u, v) \in V^{R,t} \times V^{R,t} : \theta_{u,v}^t = 0 \Longrightarrow \widehat{\mu}^t(u, v) = 0$

The reuse relation must be a bijection from $V^{R,t}$ to $V^{R,t}$:

– A register can be reused by one operation: $\forall t \in \mathcal{T}, \forall u \in V^{R,t}$: $\sum_{v \in V^{R,t}} \theta_{u,v}^t = 1$.

– A statement can reuse one released register: $\forall t \in \mathcal{T}, \forall u \in V^{R,t}$: $\sum_{v \in V^{R,t}} \theta_{v,u}^t = 1$.

9.3.3.3. *Objective function*

– We can, for instance, minimize the maximal register requirement. If we have a single register type t, we use the following objective function:

$$\text{Minimize} \quad \sum_{(u,v) \in V^{R,t} \times V^{R,t}} \widehat{\mu}^t(u, v)$$

If we want to minimize the register requirement of multiple register types conjointly, we are faced to a multiobjective problem. We can, for instance, write a linear objective function that defines a weighted sum as follows:

$$\text{Minimize} \sum_{t \in \mathcal{T}} \omega^t \sum_{(u,v) \in V^{R,t} \times V^{R,t}} \widehat{\mu}^t(u,v)$$

where $\omega^t \in \mathbb{R}$ is a weight attributed to the register type t in order to balance between the relative importance of the register types. For simplicity, we can assume a unit weight $\omega^t = 1$ for all types.

– If the number of available registers is fixed, register minimization is not always required, so we can simply avoid the creation of an objective function to minimize. This is done by just bounding the maximal register requirement by the additional constraints as follows:

$$\forall t \in \mathcal{T}, \sum_{(u,v) \in V^{R,t} \times V^{R,t}} \widehat{\mu}^t(u,v) \leq \mathcal{R}^t$$

where $\mathcal{R}^t$ is the number of available register of type t. If these constraints are used instead of a minimization objective function, a solution of the intLP may not necessarily exist.

The size of our intLP system defined above is bounded by $\mathcal{O}(\|V\|^2)$ variables and $\mathcal{O}(\|E\| + \|V\|^2)$ linear constraints.

The above intLP system defines a valid reuse graph for each register type $t \in \mathcal{T}$ as follows:

$$E^{\text{reuse},t} = \{e_r = (u,v) \mid \theta^t_{u,v} = 1 \wedge \mu^t(e_r) = \widehat{\mu}^t(u,v)\}$$

The DDG associated with this reuse graph has a critical circuit equal to II. If the above intLP system has no solution, we have to use a binary search over II by taking care of increasing L as explained in section 7.5 .

Section 9.3.4 studies a special case of SIRA, allowing us to model special register architectures such as buffers and rotating register files.

9.3.4. *SIRA with fixed reuse edges*

Some architectural constraints, such as buffers and rotating register files, impose a particular shape for the reuse graphs. For instance, buffers impose that each statement reuses the register freed by itself. Rotating register files impose that the reuse graph must be Hamiltonian. Consequently, restricting the shape of reuse graphs leads us to study a simplified problem as follows.

PROBLEM 9.1.– SIRA with fixed reuse edges.– Let $G = (V, E)$ be a loop DDG. Let $E^{\text{reuse},t}$ be a set of already fixed reuse edges of a register type t. Find a distance $\mu^t(e_r)$ for each reuse edge $e_r E^{\text{reuse},t}$ such that the reuse graph $G^{\text{reuse},t} = (V^{R,t}, E^{\text{reuse},t})$ is valid.

Fixing reuse edges simplifies the SIRA intLP constraints as follows:

$$\begin{aligned} \forall t \in \mathcal{T}, \forall e_r = (u, v) \in E^{\text{reuse},t}, \quad II \times \widehat{\mu}^t(e_r) + \sigma_v - \sigma_{k_u t} \geq -\delta_{w,t}(v) \\ \forall e = (u, v) \in E \cup E^k, \qquad \sigma_v - \sigma_u \geq \delta(e) - II \times \lambda(e) \end{aligned} \qquad [9.1]$$

The objective function remains the same as in the exact SIRA: we can either minimize the register requirement or bound it. The size of our intLP system defined above is bounded by $\mathcal{O}(\|V\|)$ variables and $\mathcal{O}(\|E\| + \|V\|)$ linear constraints. However, while the system is easier to solve than the exact SIRA, it is still not polynomial.

Fixing reuse edges is sometimes problematic. For instance, it is not always clear how to decide on a good reuse decision that leads to a satisfactory register requirement. We designed some heuristics for this purpose [TOU 09]. We find out that, for the purpose of reducing the register requirement, it is better to first compute reuse distances before fixing reuse edges. Section 9.4 presents an efficient polynomial heuristic tackling this problem [DES 08, TOU 11].

9.4. SIRALINA: an efficient polynomial heuristic for SIRA

Our resolution strategy is based on the analysis of the exact integer linear model of SIRA in section 9.3.3. As the problem involves scheduling constraints and assignment constraints, and the reuse distances are the link between these two sets of constraints, we attempt to decompose the problem into two sub-problems:

– *A periodic scheduling problem*: to find a scheduling for which the potential reuse distances are as small as possible. This step essentially minimizes the total sum of all lifetime intervals for all register types $t \in \mathcal{T}$, i.e. the total sum of the times between the killing nodes schedules $\sigma_{k_u t}$ and the nodes schedules σ_u. This first step is independent of the reuse graph. The second step creates a correct reuse graph based on the costs computed in this first step.

– *An assignment problem*: to select which pairs of statements will share the same register. Based on the schedule information of the first step, this second step builds reuse edges so that the reuse graph is valid.

For the case of a unique register type, a two-step heuristic has been presented in [DES 08, DES 11] and demonstrated as being effective on some toy benchmarks. Here, we provide a generalization of that heuristic in the case of multiple register types [TOU 11], with full industry-quality implementation and experimentation.

9.4.1. *Integer variables for the linear problem*

- An integral schedule variable $\sigma_u \in \mathbb{Z}$ for each statement $u \in V$.

- $\forall t \in \mathcal{T}, u \in V^{R,t}$ has a killing node k_{u^t}, thus a scheduling variable $\sigma_{k_{u^t}} \in \mathbb{Z}$.

- An integral reuse distance $\widehat{\mu}^t(u, v) \in \mathbb{Z}, \forall (u, v) \in V^{R,t} \times V^{R,t}, \forall t \in \mathcal{T}$.

- A binary variable $\theta_{u,v}^t$ for each $(u, v) \in V^{R,t} \times V^{R,t}, \forall t \in \mathcal{T}$. It is set to 1 iff (k_{u^t}, v) is an anti-dependence edge (i.e. iff (u, v) is a reuse edge of type t).

When we have multiple register types, we are faced to optimize multiple objectives. If we note $z^t = \sum_{(u,v) \in V^{R,t} \times V^{R,t}} \widehat{\mu}^t(u, v)$, we combine all these objective functions into a single linear objective function by introducing general weights between register types:

$$\text{Minimize} \sum_{t \in \mathcal{T}} \omega^t . z^t = \sum_{t \in \mathcal{T}} \omega^t \sum_{(u,v) \in V^{R,t} \times V^{R,t}} \widehat{\mu}^t(u, v)$$

where ω^t defines a weight associated with the register type t. For instance, the branch register type on a VLIW processor such as ST231 may be more critical than the general purpose register type: this is because there are few branch registers, and they are single bits so not easily spillable. Consequently, we may be asked to give higher weights for a register type against another if needed. In our context, a unit weight ($\omega^t = 1, \forall t \in \mathcal{T}$) is sufficient to have satisfactory results as will be shown later in the experiments. However, other contexts may require distinct weights that the user is free to fix depending on the priority between the registers types.

9.4.2. *Step 1: the scheduling problem*

This scheduling problem is built for a fixed II, which indeed describes the desired critical circuit of the DDG when SIRA is performed before SWP. We first solve a periodic scheduling problem for the DDG described in Figure 9.1(c), independently of a chosen reuse graph. That is, we handle the DDG with killing nodes only without any anti-dependences. The goal of this first step of SIRALINA is to compute the potential values of all $\widehat{\mu}^t(u, v)$ variables for all pairs $(u, v) \in V^{R,t} \times V^{R,t}$, independently of the reuse graph that will be constructed in the second step.

If $e = (k_{u^t}, v)$ is an anti-dependence edge associated with a reuse edge (u, v) (this will be decided in the second step of SIRALINA, i.e. to decide if $\theta_{u,v}^t = 1$), then its reuse distance must satisfy the following inequality (see section 9.3.3):

$$\forall (k_{u^t}, v) \in E^{\mu,t} : \widehat{\mu}^t(u, v) \geq \frac{1}{II}(\sigma_{k_{u^t}} - \delta_{w,t}(v) - \sigma_v) \qquad [9.2]$$

This inequality gives a lower bound for each reuse distance of anti-dependence arc; We recall that $E^{\mu,t}$ denotes the set of anti-dependence edges of type t.

If (k_{u^t}, v) is not an anti-dependence edge then $\theta_{u,v}^t = 0$. In this case, according to section 9.3.3, $\widehat{\mu}^t(u, v)$ is equal to zero:

$$\forall (k_{u^t}, v) \notin E^{\mu,t} : \widehat{\mu}^t(u, v) = 0 \qquad [9.3]$$

Now we can write:

$$z^t = \sum_{(u,v) \in V^{R,t} \times V^{R,t}} \widehat{\mu}^t(u, v) = \sum_{(k_{u^t}, v) \in E^{\mu,t}} \widehat{\mu}^t(u, v) + \sum_{(k_{u^t}, v) \notin E^{\mu,t}} \widehat{\mu}^t(u, v)$$

From equation [9.3] we know that $\sum_{(k_{u^t}, v) \notin E^{\mu,t}} \widehat{\mu}^t(u, v) = 0$. Consequently, by considering inequality [9.2]:

$$z^t \geq \frac{1}{II} \sum_{(k_{u^t}, v) \in E^{\mu,t}} \left(\sigma_{k_{u^t}} - \delta_{w,t}(v) - \sigma_v \right) \qquad [9.4]$$

As the reuse relation is a bijection from $V^{R,t}$ to $V^{R,t}$, then $E^{\mu,t}$ describes a bijection between $V^{k,t}$ the set of killing nodes of type t and $V^{R,t}$. This bijection implies that, in the right sum of inequality [9.4], we can have one and only one $\sigma_{k_{u^t}}$ term. Also, we can have one and only one σ_v term. inequality [9.4] can then be separated into two parts as follows:

$$\sum_{(k_{u^t}, v) \in E^{\mu,t}} \left(\sigma_{k_{u^t}} - \delta_{w,t}(v) - \sigma_v \right) = \sum_{u \in V^{R,t}} \sigma_{k_{u^t}} - \sum_{v \in V^{R,t}} \left(\delta_{w,t}(v) + \sigma_v \right)$$

$$= \sum_{u \in V^{R,t}} \sigma_{k_{u^t}} - \sum_{v \in V^{R,t}} \sigma_v - \sum_{v \in V^{R,t}} \delta_{w,t}(v)$$

$$\qquad [9.5]$$

We deduce from equality [9.5] a lower bound for the number of required registers of type t:

$$z^t \geq \frac{1}{II} \left(\sum_{u \in V^{R,t}} \sigma_{k_{u^t}} - \sum_{v \in V^{R,t}} \sigma_v - \sum_{v \in V^{R,t}} \delta_{w,t}(v) \right) \qquad [9.6]$$

In this context, it is useful to find an appropriate schedule in which the right-hand side of inequation [9.6] is minimal for all register types $t \in \mathcal{T}$. Since II and $\sum_{v \in V^{R,t}} \delta_{w,t}(v)$ are two constants, we can ignore them in the following linear optimization problem. We consider *the scheduling problem (P)*:

$$
\begin{cases}
\min \sum_{t\in\mathcal{T}} \omega^t \left(\sum_{u\in V^{R,t}} \sigma_{k_{u^t}} - \sum_{v\in V^{R,t}} \sigma_v \right) \\
\text{subject to:} \\
\forall e = (u,v) \in E: & \sigma_v - \sigma_u \geq \delta(e) - II \times \lambda(e) \\
\forall t \in \mathcal{T}, \forall u \in V^{R,t}, \ \forall v \in Cons(u^t): & \sigma_{k_{u^t}} - \sigma_v \geq \delta_{r,t}(v) + II \times \lambda(e)
\end{cases}
\quad [9.7]
$$

These constraints guarantee that the resulting reuse graph is valid, i.e. its associated DDG is schedulable with SWP. As can be seen, the constraints matrix of the integer linear program of system [9.7] is an incidence matrix of the graph $(\mathcal{V}, E \cup E^k)$; therefore, it is totally unimodular [SCH 87]. Consequently, we can use a polynomial algorithm to solve this problem. We can, for instance, use a linear solver instead of a mixed integer linear one. Also, we can use a minimum-cost network-flow algorithm to solve this scheduling problem in $O(\|V\|^3 \log \|V\|)$ [RAV 91].

The resolution of the scheduling problem (P) (by simplex method or by network-flow algorithm) provides optimal values σ_u^* for each $u \in V$ and optimal values $\sigma_{k_{u^t}}^*$ for each killing node k_{u^t}. The objective function of the scheduling problem described above tries to minimize the sum of the lifetime intervals of all register types considering them as weighted.

9.4.3. *Step 2: the linear assignment problem*

The goal of this second step is to decide about reuse edges (compute the values of $\theta_{u,v}^t$ variables) such that the resulting reuse graph is valid. Once the scheduling variables have been fixed in the same conjoint scheduling problem (P) for all register types, the minimal value of each potential reuse distance becomes equal to $\widehat{\mu^*}^t(u,v) = \left\lceil \frac{\sigma_{k_{u^t}}^* - \delta_{w,t}(v) - \sigma_v^*}{II} \right\rceil$ according to inequation [9.2]. Knowing the reuse distance values $\widehat{\mu^*}^t(u,v)$, the periodic register allocation becomes now a problem of deciding which instruction reuses which released register, i.e. compute the value of $\theta_{u,v}^t$ variables. This problem can be modeled as a linear assignment problem for each register type t. The constraint is that the produced reuse graph (modeled by an assignment relationship) should be a bijection between loop statements. We consider *the linear assignment problem (A^t) for the register type t* as:

$$
\begin{cases}
\min \quad \sum_{(u,v)\in V^{R,t}\times V^{R,t}} \widehat{\mu^*}^t(u,v)\theta_{u,v}^t \\
\text{Subject to} \\
\forall u \in V^{R,t}, & \sum_{v\in V^{R,t}} \theta_{u,v}^t = 1, \\
\forall v \in V^{R,t}, & \sum_{u\in V^{R,t}} \theta_{u,v}^t = 1 \\
\theta_{u,v}^t \in \{0,1\}
\end{cases}
\quad [9.8]
$$

where $\widehat{\mu^*}^t(u,v)$ is a fixed value for each arc $e = (u,v) \in V^{R,t} \times V^{R,t}$.

Each linear assignment problem A^t is optimally solved with the well-known Hungarian algorithm [KUH 55] in $O(\|V\|^3)$ complexity. The Hungarian algorithm computes for each register type t the optimal values $\theta_{u,v}^t{}^*$. Such an optimal bijection defines a set of reuse edges $E^{\text{reuse},t}$ as follows.

$$E^{\text{reuse},t} = \{e_r = (u, v) \mid u \in V^{R,t} \wedge \theta_{u,v}^t{}^* = 1 \wedge \mu^t(e_r) = \widehat{\mu^*}^t(u, v)\}$$

That is, if $\theta_{u,v}^t{}^* = 1$, then (k_{u^t}, v) is a anti-dependence edge and the reuse distance is equal to $\widehat{\mu^*}^t(u, v)$. Otherwise, (k_{u^t}, v) does not exist.

Our two-step heuristic has now computed all that we need for a valid periodic register allocation for all register types: the set of anti-dependence arcs of type t (represented by the set of $\theta_{u,v}^t{}^*$ variables equal to one), and the reuse distances (represented by the values $\widehat{\mu^*}^t(u, v)$).

Finally, provided a number $\mathcal{R}^t$ of available registers of type t, we should check that $\forall t \in \mathcal{T}, \sum_{e_r \in E^{\text{reuse},t}} \mu^t(e_r) \leq \mathcal{R}^t$. If not, this means that SIRALINA did not find a solution for the desired value of the critical circuit II. We thus increase II as explained in section 7.5. If we reach the upper limit for II without finding a solution, this means that the register pressure is too high and spilling becomes necessary: we can do spilling either before SWP (this is an open problem), or after SWP. The SIRA framework does not insert any spill, it is let for a subsequent pass of the compiler (the register allocator, for instance).

Note that SIRALINA applies a register minimization. If register minimization is not required, it is always possible to increment the values of the reuse distances $\mu^t(e_r)$: for instance, we can increment them to reach a maximal value $\sum_{e_r \in E^{\text{reuse},t}} \mu^t(e_r) = \mathcal{R}^t$.

9.5. Experimental results with SIRA

Nowadays, evaluating the performance of a new code optimization method must be designed carefully. The reason is that any new code optimization can behave differently inside a compiler, depending on its order in the optimization flow, on the target machine, the input benchmark, etc. The experimental methodology that we followed is based on a stand-alone evaluation and on an integrated evaluation. A stand-alone evaluation means that we evaluate the efficiency of SIRA without studying the implication on code quality generated by the previous and the following compilation passes. An integrated evaluation means that we evaluate the final assembly code quality generated by the compiler when we plug our code optimization method. We target an embedded VLIW architecture (ST231) because it represents the range of applications that are sensitive to spill code reduction.

We have many experimental results on SIRA: exact SIRA, SIRA with fixed reuse edges and SIRA with heuristics (see [TOU 04, DES 08, TOU 03, TOU 09, BRI 09b]). The most satisfactory results are brought by the SIRALINA method, shown in Appendix 3. This section provides experimental conclusions. Note that the source code of SIRALINA, named SIRAlib, is made public in [BRI 09b]. Our implementation includes three possible solvers that can be chosen when building the software: LP_SOLVE, GPLK and minimum-cost flow.

When considering the stand-alone DDG, the experiments demonstrate that SIRALINA succeeds in significantly reducing the register pressure of innermost loops (thus avoiding the generation of spill code). We have also observed that the increase of the MII remains null in most of the cases. For the cases where we observe an increase in the value of MII, we observe that it remains quite low in most of the cases (less than 3% in average for SPEC2000, SPEC2006 and MEDIABENCH), but cannot be neglected in the worst cases (up to 15% of MII increase in the worst case for FFMPEG). Finally, we have noted that it is usually better to optimize all register types conjointly instead of one by one: not only the obtained results in terms of register pressure minimization are better but SIRALINA execution times are also much faster.

We integrated SIRA inside the ST231 toolchain, and we compiled all MEDIABENCH, FFMPEG and SPEC2000 C applications. We tested the combination of SIRALINA with three possible SWP: SWP under resource constraints, exact SWP with integer linear programming (with time-out enabled for large loops), and lifetime sensitive SWP. Combining SIRA with the three SWP methods always reduce spill code significantly. Surprisingly enough, the insertion of additional edges by SIRA into the DDG before SWP improves the II. This is due to two factors: (1) spill code is reduced so that fewer operations have to be scheduled and (2) adding extra edges helps the heuristic schedulers to generate better codes.

Concerning the resulted execution times, everything depends on the chosen data input and on the interaction with other microarchitectural mechanisms. When considering the standard input of FFMPEG and MEDIABENCH, profiling information shows that the execution times spent in the SWP loops are marginal. Consequently, the possible overall speedup of the whole applications should be marginal too. After doing precise simulation, we found some impressive speedups (up to 2.45) and some slowdowns (up to 0.81). We did a careful performance characterization of the slowdown and speedup cases, and we found that they originate from Icache effects. Indeed, periodic register allocation alters the instruction scheduler, which in turn alters the memory layout. Since the Icache of the ST231 is direct mapped, modifying the memory layout of the code greatly impacts Icache conflicts. These phenomena show again that code optimization is complex, because optimizing one aspect of the code may hurt another uncontrolled aspect. However, we noticed the case of FFMPEG where Dcache stalls are significantly reduced when spill code is reduced too.

9.6. Conclusion on spill code reduction

This chapter showed how to satisfy the periodic register constraints before SWP. The case of acyclic scheduling for basic blocks and superblocks is a trivial extension, as studied in [BRI 09b].

The approach of SIRA is to guarantee the absence of spilling without hurting ILP extraction if possible. Our formal reasoning allows the building of a graph theoretical approach called SIRA. SIRA handles the register pressure of multiple types conjointly by adding extra edges to the DDG. We are able to guarantee that any subsequent SWP schedule would not require more registers than the available ones. SIRA is sensitive to ILP scheduling by taking care of not increasing the critical circuit if possible.

We have defined the exact intLP model of SIRA. Its application to the special cases of buffers and rotating register files simplifies the intLP system by fixing reuse edges before minimizing the reuse distances. Our experiments show that minimizing the register requirement is sensitive to the structure of the reuse graphs. That is, it is better to first minimize the reuse distances before fixing reuse edges.

This amounts to the creation of an efficient polynomial heuristic, called SIRALINA. SIRALINA has a complexity of $\mathcal{O}(\|V\|^3 \times \log \|V\|)$ and works in two steps. The first step solves a cyclic scheduling problem (either using a minimum-cost flow algorithm or a simplex solver). The second step consists of computing a linear assignment (bijection between loop statements) using the Hungarian algorithm.

SIRALINA has been implemented and the source code has been made public in [BRI 09b]. We did extensive experiments on FFMPEG, MEDIABENCH, SPEC2000 and SPEC2006 C applications. Its efficiency on stand-alone DDG is promising in terms of fast compilation time, register pressure reduction and critical circuit increase.

SIRALINA has been integrated inside a real-world compiler, namely st231cc for the VLIW ST231. We studied the interaction of SIRALINA with three types of SWP methods: heuristic SWP under resource constraints, optimal SWP using CPLEX solver and lifetime sensitive SWP. Our experiments on FFMPEG, MEDIABENCH and SPEC2000 showed a significant spill code reduction in all cases. Concerning the II, surprisingly enough, it turns out that SIRA results in a reduction of II. Consequently, as a compiler strategy, we advise to decouple register constraints from resource constraints by using the SIRA framework.

Concerning the execution times of the optimized applications, most of the speedup with the standard data input of FFMPEG and MEDIABENCH were close to 1. This can be easily explained by the fact that the execution times spent in the optimized SWP loops are very marginal. However, we noticed some overall impressive speedups, ranging from 1.1 to 2.45, as well as some slowdowns (down to 0.81). After a careful analysis, we found that these speedups and slowdowns result from a modification in the interaction with Icache effects.

Our experiments highlight the fact that nowadays it is very difficult to isolate the benefit of a code optimization method plugged inside a compilation framework. Observing the overall execution times are not sufficient because some speedups may result from hidden side effects: the complex interaction between compilation passes, the current micro-architecture and the chosen data input, all may help to obtain a speedup that has no direct relationship with the isolated code optimization under study. We thus open the debate about the significance of the speedups if no performance characterization is made to really demonstrate that the observed dynamic performance of the code is not a result of an uncontrolled side effect. This is why we preferred to rely on static metrics to evaluate the quality of a code optimization from a compilation strategy point of view.

In the context of processor architecture with NUAL semantics, an open problem arises when we optimize register pressure before instruction scheduling. Chapter 10 studies and solves this problem.

Exploiting the Register Access Delays
Before Instruction Scheduling

Usual periodic scheduling problems deal with precedence constraints having non-negative latencies. This seems a natural way for modeling scheduling problems, since task or instruction delays are generally non-negative quantities. However, in some cases, we need to consider edge latencies that not only model instruction latencies, but also model other precedence constraints. For instance, in register optimization problems devoted to optimizing compilation, a generic machine or processor model can allow considering access delays into/from registers. Edge latencies may be then non-positive, leading to a difficult scheduling problem in the presence of resource constraints.

This chapter is related to the problem of periodic scheduling with register requirement optimization; its aim is to solve the practical problem of register optimization in optimizing compilation. We show that preconditioning a data dependence graph (DDG) to satisfy register constraints before periodic scheduling under resources constraints may create circuits with non-positive distances, resulting from the acceptance of non-positive edge latencies. As a compiler construction strategy, it is forbidden to allow the creation of circuits with non-positive distances during the compilation flow because such DDG circuits do not guarantee the existence of a valid instruction schedule under resource constraints. We study two solutions to avoid the creation of these problematic circuits. The first solution is reactive; it tolerates the creation of non-positive circuits in a first step, and if detected in a further check step, makes a backtrack to eliminate them. The second solution is proactive; it prevents the creation of non-positive circuits in the DDG during the register optimization process. It is based on shortest path equations that define a necessary and sufficient condition to free any DDG from these problematic circuits. Then we deduce a linear program accordingly. We have implemented our solutions and we present successful experimental results.

10.1. Introduction

In an optimizing compilation process for instruction-level parallelism, we may be faced with the opportunity of bounding the register pressure before instruction scheduling. A typical problem, which we solve in this chapter, arises for all strategies handling registers before instruction scheduling. Indeed, when we have a target processor with architecturally visible delays to access registers (such as in very long instruction word (VLIW), Digital Signal Processing (DSP), explicitly parallel instruction computing (EPIC) and transport triggered architectures (TTA)), the model of register requirement offers more opportunities to reduce the register pressure than in a regular sequential/ superscalar processor. Such architectures are also called non-unit-assumed-latencies (NUAL).

Unfortunately, the opportunities offered by NUAL architectures are not fully or optimally exploited in existing register allocators. Two main reasons are as follows:

1) Periodic instruction scheduling uses a model based on DDG, that represents the periodic precedence constraints between the instructions of a loop. The exploitation of register access delay means the usage of non-positive edges latencies in a DDG. As far as we know, current instruction schedulers implemented inside compilers do not exploit these sort of edges yet, and consider them as positive edges latencies.

2) If the register constraints are handled before instruction scheduling, an open problem arises regarding the possible creation of circuits with non-positive distances.

This chapter studies the latter point, i.e. we show that minimizing the number of registers in a loop program may prohibit the compiler from generating a code. That is, in theory, if registers are optimized before instructions scheduling as done in some optimizing compilers, we may be faced with the problem of impossible instructions scheduling. This situation is not acceptable in optimizing compilation, because when a programer writes a correct code, the compiler must be able to generate a executable low-level code.

We follow a formal methodology to deal with the above problem. We use a graph theoretical framework to define the exact problem and to prove a necessary and sufficient condition for its existence. We provide solutions based on graphs and linear programming. This chapter demonstrates the following points:

– The DDG circuits with non-positive distances may prohibit periodic instruction scheduling under resource constraints from finding a solution, making the compilation process to fail.

– DDG circuits with non-positive distances are not rare in practice, so the problem is not marginal.

– We show how to avoid the creation of non-positive circuits with two strategies: a reactive strategy (tolerate the problem and then fix it if detected) and a proactive strategy (prevent the problem).

While the problem of non-positive circuits may arise in theory for any register optimization method performing before periodic scheduling, this chapter shows how to avoid the problem in the schedule independent register allocation (SIRA) framework [TOU 04]. As far as we know, the SIRA framework is the only existing formal method that handles register constraints before periodic instruction scheduling with multiple register types and delayed access to registers.

Before continuing, readers must be familiar with our notations on DDG and periodic instruction scheduling (SIRA) defined in previous chapters. This chapter is organized as follows. We start with describing the problem in section 10.2: we explain the problem resulted if we insert non-positive edges inside DDG (which in turn create non-positive circuits). Section 10.3 studies a sufficient and necessary condition that defines a DDG without non-positive circuits. This mathematical characteristic is used to propose a linear program in section 10.4, which is the core of our proactive method. Section 10.5 summarizes our experimental results and draws comparisons between the efficiency of the reactive and the proactive methods.

10.2. Problem description of DDG circuits with non-positive distances

A circuit C is said to be lexicographic-positive if $\lambda(C) > 0$, while $\lambda(C)$ is a notation for $\sum_{e \in C} \lambda(e)$. A DDG is said to be lexicographic-positive iff all its circuits are also lexicographic-positive. A DDG is said to be schedulable iff there exists a valid SWP, that is an SWP satisfying all its cyclic precedence constraints, not necessarily satisfying other constraints such as resources or registers. A DDG computed from a sequential program is always lexicographic-positive, it is an inherent characteristic of imperative sequential languages. When a DDG is lexicographic-positive, there is a guarantee that a schedule exists for it (at least the initial sequential schedule).

Since SIRA is applied before instruction scheduling (see section 9.3), it modifies the DDG under the condition that it remains schedulable. If the target architecture has unit-assumed-latencies (UAL) code semantics (sequential code), then the introduced edges by any SIRA method (such as SIRALINA) have unit-assumed latencies, and the DDG remains lexicographic-positive. If the target architecture has explicit architectural delays in accessing registers (NUAL code semantics), then the introduced edges by SIRA are of the form $e' = (k_{u^t}, v)$ with latencies $\delta(e') = -\delta_{w,t}(v)$. Such latencies are non-positive.

If an edge latency is non-positive, this does not create specific problems for cyclic scheduling in theory, unless the latency of a circuit is negative too. The following lemma proves that if $\delta(C) < 0$, then the DDG may not be lexicographic-positive.

LEMMA 10.1.– [BRI 10] Let G be a schedulable loop DDG with SWP. Let C be an arbitrary circuit in G. Then the following implications are true:

1) $\delta(C) \geq 0 \Longrightarrow \lambda(C) \geq 0$;

2) $\delta(C) \leq 0 \Longrightarrow \lambda(C)$ may be non-positive.

The previous lemma proves that inserting negative edges inside a DDG can generate circuits with $\lambda(C) \leq 0$. So, what is the problem with such circuits? Indeed, the answer comes from the cyclic scheduling theory. Given a cyclic DDG, let C^+ be the set of circuits with $\lambda(C) > 0$, let C^- be the set of circuits with $\lambda(C) < 0$ and let C^0 be the set of circuits with $\lambda(C) = 0$. Then the following inequality is true [KOR 11]:

$$\max_{C \in C^+} \frac{\delta(C)}{\lambda(C)} \leq II \leq \min_{C \in C^-} \frac{\delta(C)}{\lambda(C)}$$

In other words, the existence of circuits inside C^- imposes hard real-time constraints on the value of II. Such constraints can be satisfied with cyclic scheduling if we consider only precedence constraints [KOR 11]. However, if we add resource constraints (as will be carried out during the subsequent instruction scheduling pass), then the DDG may not be schedulable. Simply, it may be possible that the conflicts on the resources do not allow us to have an II lower than $\min_{C \in C^-} \frac{\delta(C)}{\lambda(C)}$.

When a circuit $C \in C^0$ exists, this means that there is a precedence relationship between the statements belonging to the same iteration: that is, the loop body is no longer an acyclic graph as in the initial DDG.

For the sake of brevity, we also say that a circuit in $C^0 \cup C^-$ is a *non-positive circuit*. Some concrete examples demonstrating the possible existence of non-positive circuits are drawn in [BRI 10]. According to our experiments in [BRI 10], inserting non-positive edges inside a large sample of representative DDG produce non-positive circuits in 30.77% of loops in SPEC2000 C applications (respectively, 28.16%, 41.90% and 92.21% for SPEC 2006, MEDIABENCH and FFMPEG loops). Note that this problem of non-positive circuits is not related exclusively to SIRA, but it is related to any pass of register optimization performing on the DDG level before SWP. As shown in [TOU 02, BRI 10], if register requirement is minimized or bounded (with any optimal method) before instruction scheduling, it may create a non-positive circuit.

As a compiler construction strategy, we must guarantee that the schedulable DDG produced after applying SIRA is always lexicographic-positive. Otherwise, there is no guarantee that the subsequent SWP pass would find a solution under resource constraints, and the code generation may fail. This problem is studied and solved in the next section.

10.3. Necessary and sufficient condition to avoid non-positive circuits

As mentioned previously, we need to ensure that the associated DDG computed by any SIRA method is lexicographic-positive. We have also noted that if the processor has UAL semantics then it is guaranteed that any associated DDG found by SIRA is lexicographic-positive. This is because the UAL semantic is used to model sequential processors; all inserted anti-dependence edges have latency equal to 1. Since all the edges in the associated DDG have positive latencies, and since the associated DDG is schedulable by SWP (guaranteed by SIRA), the DDG is necessarily lexicographic-positive.

Hence, a naive strategy is to always consider UAL semantics, which defines the first sufficient condition to eliminate non-positive circuits. That is, we do not exploit the access delays to registers. This solution works in practice but the register requirement model is not optimal, since it does not exploit NUAL code semantics. Consequently, the computed register requirement is not well optimized.

A more clever, yet naive, way to ensure that any associated DDG computed by SIRA is lexicographic-positive is to have a *reactive* strategy. It tolerates the problem as follows:

1) consider SIRA with NUAL semantics;

2) check whether the associated DDG is lexicographic-positive[1] and

   – if it is, then return the computed solution;

   – if it is not, then apply SIRA considering UAL semantics.

Considering a UAL semantic for SIRA on a processor that has a NUAL semantic cannot hurt: it just possibly implies a loss of optimality in either II or in the register requirement. The above method is optimistic (reactive) in the sense that it considers that non-lexicographic DDGs are rare in practice. This is not true in theory of course, but maybe the practice would highlight that the proportion of the problems producing DDG that must be *corrected* is low. In this case, it is better in practice not to try to restrict SIRA, but to correct the solution afterwards if we detect the problem.

Thus, the question that naturally arises is the following: is it possible to devise a better method to ensure *a priori* that the associated DDG computed by SIRA is lexicographic-positive while exploiting the benefit of NUAL semantics? That is, we are willing to study a *proactive* strategy that prevents the problem. The following simple lemmas, deduced from [COR 01], are a basis for a necessary and sufficient condition to eliminate non-positive circuits. Their proof is easy due to shortest path equations.

LEMMA 10.2.– [TOU 13a] Let $G = (V, E)$ be a directed graph and $w : E \to \mathbb{Z}$ be a cost function. Then G has a circuit C of non-positive cost with respect to cost

---

1 Due to Corollary 10.1, to be defined later.

w *if and only if* G has a circuit of negative cost with respect to cost w' defined by $w'(e) = \|V\| \cdot w(e) - 1$:

$$\sum_{e \in C} w(e) \leq 0 \iff \sum_{e \in C} w'(e) < 0$$

LEMMA 10.3.– [TOU 13a] Let $G = (V, E)$ be a directed graph and $w : E \to \mathbb{R}$ be a cost function.

Then G has a circuit C of negative cost (i.e. $\sum_{e \in C} w(e) < 0$) *if and only if* the constraints' system $\mathcal{S}_{G,w}$ defined below is infeasible.

$$(\mathcal{S}_{G,w}) \begin{cases} \forall e \in E, x_{tgt(e)} - x_{src(e)} \leq w(e) \\ \forall v \in V, x_v \in \mathbb{R} \end{cases}$$

From lemmas 10.2 and 10.3, we deduce the following corollary, which defines a necessary and sufficient condition to eliminate non-positive circuits.

COROLLARY 10.1.– Let $G = (V, E)$ be a directed graph and $w : E \to \mathbb{Z}$ be a cost function.

Then G has a circuit C of non-positive cost with respect to cost w (i.e. $\sum_{e \in C} w(e) \leq 0$) *if and only if* the system composed of the following constraints is infeasible.

$$\forall e \in E, x_{tgt(e)} - x_{src(e)} \leq \|V\| \cdot w(e) - 1$$

where $\forall v \in V, x_v \in \mathbb{R}$.

Now, any produced DDG by any register optimization method (hence, any SIRA method), must guarantee the above condition to eliminate non-positive circuits. In this chapter, we show how to combine the above condition with an efficient heuristic of SIRA that constructs a reuse graph (and hence the associated DDG accordingly), named SIRALINA. The next section studies this question.

10.4. Application to the SIRA framework

The problem that must be solved by SIRA is to construct a reuse graph. There are many heuristics and methods that may be used. SIRALINA [DES 11, TOU 11] is our most powerful method; we have already demonstrated that it is really an efficient heuristic for SIRA: it considers an initial DDG with multiple register types and produces an associated DDG to bound or to minimize the register requirement before SWP. SIRALINA is a two-step heuristic, with an algorithmic complexity equal to

$O(\|V\|^3 \log \|V\|)$, where $\|V\|$ is a notation for the cardinality of a set. It has been shown that SIRALINA, applied on a large set of benchmarks [DES 11, TOU 11], is fast and efficient in practice. So it has been connected to an industry quality compiler for embedded systems targeting VLIW ST231 processors. The next section briefly recalls SIRALINA; if the readers are familiar with our previous publication on the topic, they may skip the section. The following section shows how to eliminate non-positive circuits in the context of SIRALINA.

10.4.1. Recall on SIRALINA heuristic

Computing a valid reuse graph for a fixed-period II that minimizes $\sum_{e_r \in E^{\text{reuse},t}} \mu^t(e_r)$ is NP-complete [TOU 04]. SIRALINA heuristic [DES 11, TOU 11] computes an approximate solution to this problem for all register types conjointly. In order to balance between the importance of each involved register type, we assume to have a weight $\psi_t \in \mathbb{R}$ attributed to each type $t \in \mathcal{T}$. This weight may be set to 1 if all register types have the same importance.

SIRALINA is composed of two polynomial steps summarized as follows (here, the period II is fixed):

1) Step 1 (scheduling problem): determine minimal reuse distances for all pairs of values (i.e. compute, for each type t, a function $\widehat{\mu}^t : V^{R,t} \times V^{R,t} \to \mathbb{Z}$);

2) Step 2 (linear assignment problem): determine a bijection $E^{\text{reuse},t} : V^{R,t} \to V^{R,t}$ that minimizes $\sum_{(u,v) \in V^{R,t} \times V^{R,t}} \widehat{\mu}^t(u,v)$ for each t.

These two steps allow the construction of a reuse graph for a period II. Then $G' = (\mathcal{V}, \mathcal{E})$ the associated DDG is constructed as explained previously: $\mathcal{V} = V \cup K$ and $\mathcal{E} = E \cup E^k \cup E^\mu$. The two following sections detail each of the two above steps.

10.4.2. Step 1: the scheduling problem for a fixed II

The objective of the scheduling problem [DES 11, TOU 11] is to guarantee the existence of a SWP schedule for the associated DDG. The problem is formulated as an integer linear problem with a totally unimodular constraints matrix. In addition, it aims to determine minimal reuse distances for all pairs of values. The two next paragraphs define the integer linear program of the scheduling problem.

Integer variables of the linear problem

For any $u \in \mathcal{V}$, define a variable $\sigma_u \in \mathbb{Z}$ representing a scheduling date.

Linear program formulation

The scheduling problem is expressed as follows (section 9.4):

$$
\begin{cases}
\text{minimize} & \sum_{t\in\mathcal{T}} \psi_t \left(\sum_{u\in V^{R,t}} \sigma_{k_u t} - \sum_{u\in V^{R,t}} \sigma_u \right) \\
\text{subject to} & \\
& \forall e \in E \cup E^k, \sigma_{tgt(e)} - \sigma_{src(e)} \geq \delta(e) - II \times \lambda(e)
\end{cases}
$$

The constraints matrix of this integer linear program is an incidence matrix of the DDG G (with killing nodes); consequently, it is totally unimodular. Hence, it can be solved with a polynomial algorithm.

Let $\sigma_u{}^*$ and $\sigma_{k_u t}{}^*$ be the values of the variables of the optimal solution of the above scheduling problem. The minimal reuse distance function, denoted by $\widehat{\mu^*}^t$, is then defined as follows for all pairs of values (u, v):

$$
\widehat{\mu^*}^t(u, v) = \left\lceil \frac{\sigma_{k_u t}{}^* - \delta_{w,t}(v) - \sigma_v{}^*}{II} \right\rceil
$$

This minimal reuse distance constitutes the lower bound of the optimal values of the optimization problem solved by SIRALINA.

10.4.3. *Step 2: the linear assignment problem*

The objective of the linear assignment problem for a register type t is to find a bijection $\theta^t : V^{R,t} \rightarrow V^{R,t}$ such that $\sum_{u\in V^{R,t}} \widehat{\mu^*}^t(u, \theta^t(u))$ is minimal. It can be solved in polynomial time complexity with the so-called Hungarian algorithm [KUH 55]. Such an optimal bijection θ^t defines a set of reuse edges $E^{\text{reuse},t}$ as follows:

$$
E^{\text{reuse},t} = \{e_r = (u, \theta^t(u)) \mid u \in V^{R,t} \wedge \mu^t(e_r) = \widehat{\mu^*}^t(u, \theta^t(u))\}
$$

10.4.4. *Eliminating non-positive circuits in SIRALINA*

Thus, our idea is the following. Once an initial reuse graph has been computed by SIRALINA, the DDG associated with it may contain non-positive circuits. So, we have to eliminate these circuits. All the edge distances are fixed, except that we can increase the anti-dependence edge distances. That is, we can modify the values of $\widehat{\mu}^t$ to eliminate non-positive circuits. Modifying these reuse distances is a valid transformation as long as it does not violate the scheduling constraints. However, this transformation may require the use of more registers.

Indeed, observe that in the associated DDG, the added edges $e'_r = (k^t_u, v) \in E^{\mu,t}$, where $e_r = (u, v)$ is a reuse edge of type t, have a distance equal to $\lambda(e) = \widehat{\mu}^t(u, v)$, and that the distances of the other edges are entirely determined by the initial DDG and are not subject to changes. By modifying $\widehat{\mu}^t(u, v)$, the optimal solution to the linear assignment problem may be affected (step 2 of SIRALINA). In this case, we may choose to recompute the linear assignment. This defines an iterative process. We start by explaining this iterative process; then we describe how we modify the reuse distances.

Algorithm 10.1. The algorithm $IterativeSIRALINA$

Require: G a loop DDG
Require: n maximal number of iterations

$(\widehat{\mu}^t_{(0)})_{t\in\mathcal{T}} \leftarrow (\widehat{\mu^*}^t)_{t\in\mathcal{T}}$ {Compute initial distance functions by solving the scheduling problem}

for $t \in \mathcal{T}$ **do**

$\quad E^{\text{reuse},t}_{(0)} \leftarrow LinearAssignment(G, \widehat{\mu}^t_{(0)})$ {Compute initial reuse edges}

end for

$i \leftarrow 0$

repeat

$\quad i \leftarrow i + 1$

$\quad (\widehat{\mu}^t_{(i)})_{t\in\mathcal{T}} \leftarrow UpdateReuseDistances(G, (\widehat{\mu}^t_{(i-1)})_{t\in\mathcal{T}}, (E^{\text{reuse},t}_{(i-1)})_{t\in\mathcal{T}})$

$\quad$ **for** $t \in \mathcal{T}$ **do**

$\quad\quad E^{\text{reuse},t}_{(i)} \leftarrow LinearAssignment(G, \widehat{\mu}^t_{(i)})$

$\quad$ **end for**

$\quad$ **if** $E^{\text{reuse},t}_{(i)} = E^{\text{reuse},t}_{(i-1)}$ for every $t \in \mathcal{T}$ **then**

$\quad\quad$ **break** {A fixed point has been reached}

$\quad$ **end if**

until $i > n$

return $(\widehat{\mu}^t_{(i)})_{t\in\mathcal{T}}$ and $(E^{\text{reuse},t}_{(i)})_{t\in\mathcal{T}}$

Our iterative process is thus given by algorithm 10.1. At each iteration i of the algorithm, it computes new reuse distances $\widehat{\mu}^t_{(i)}$ and new reuse edges $E^{\text{reuse},t}_{(i)}$, based on the previous reuse distances $\widehat{\mu}^t_{(i-1)}$ and previous reuse edges $E^{\text{reuse},t}_{(i-1)}$. This algorithm is parameterized by two functions:

– $LinearAssignment(G, \widehat{\mu}^t)$ computes a bijection θ^t : $V^{R,t} \times V^{R,t}$ that minimizes $\sum_{(u,v)\in V^{R,t} \times V^{R,t}} \widehat{\mu}^t(u, v)$. In other words, it solves the linear assignment problem and is typically implemented by the Hungarian algorithm, as done in the second step of SIRALINA. The result of this function is a new set of reuse edges $E^{\text{reuse},t}_{(i)}$.

– $UpdateReuseDistances(G, (\widehat{\mu}^t_{(i-1)})_{t\in\mathcal{T}}, (E^{\text{reuse},t}_{(i-1)})_{t\in\mathcal{T}})$ uses corollary 10.1 to compute new distance functions $(\widehat{\mu}^t_{(i)})_{t\in\mathcal{T}}$ such that the associated DDG with respect to $(\widehat{\mu}^t_{(i)})_{t\in\mathcal{T}}$ and $(E^{\text{reuse},t}_{(i)})_{t\in\mathcal{T}}$ is lexicographic-positive.

Our process stops after a certain number of iterations according to the time budget allowed for this optimization process. The body of the repeat-until loop is executed with a finite number of iterations, denoted n. The loop may be interrupted before reaching n iterations when a fixed point is reached, that is when the set of reuse edges stabilizes from one iteration to another ($E^{\text{reuse},t}_{(i)} = E^{\text{reuse},t}_{(i-1)}$). Since the body of algorithm loop is executed at least once, it is guaranteed that the associated DDG will be lexicographic-positive.

The following section explains our implementation of the function $UpdateReuseDistances$.

10.4.5. *Updating reuse distances*

Our proactive method, named shortest path equations (SPE), is based on corollary 10.1. We deduce from it that the associated DDG is lexicographic-positive *if and only if* there exist $|\mathcal{V}|$ variables $x_v \in \mathbb{R}$ for $v \in \mathcal{V}$ such that

$$\forall e \in \mathcal{E} : x_{tgt(e)} - x_{src(e)} \leq \|\mathcal{V}\| \cdot \lambda(e) - 1$$

Recall that $\mathcal{V} = V \cup K$ where V is the set of vertices of the initial DDG and K is the set of all killing nodes. We are willing to modify each reuse distance by adding an integral increment γ^t to it. Our objective is still to minimize the register requirement, which means that we need to minimize the sum of γ^t. We thus define a linear problem as follows, which is our main contribution in this chapter.

For each vertex $v \in \mathcal{V}$, we define a *continuous* variable x_v. For each anti-dependence edge $e = (k^t_u, v)$ corresponding to the reuse edge $e_r = (u, v)$, we define a variable $\gamma^t(u, v)$, so that the distance of e is $\lambda(e) = \widehat{\mu}^t_{(i-1)}(u, v) + \gamma^t(u, v)$.

We seek to minimize the register requirement, which means minimizing $\sum_{t \in \mathcal{T}} \psi_t \sum_{(u,v) \in E^{\text{reuse},t}} \gamma^t(u, v)$, where ψ_t is a weight given to a register type, as defined in section 9.4. In order to guarantee that modifying the reuse distances is a valid transformation, we must ensure that the scheduling constraints are not violated. This means that the modified reuse distances must be greater than or equal to their minimal values: $\widehat{\mu}^t_{(i-1)}(u, v) + \gamma^t(u, v) \geq \widehat{\mu^*}^t(u, v)$ for any $(u, v) \in E^{\text{reuse},t}$, where $\widehat{\mu^*}^t(u, v)$ is the solution of the scheduling problem (step 1 of SIRALINA), which are indeed the minimal valid values for the reuse distances. Since γ^t denotes integral values, we should write a mixed integer linear program. But such a solution is computationally expensive. So we decided to write a relaxed linear program in Figure 10.1, where γ^t variables are declared as continuous. Afterwards, we safely ceil these variables to obtain integer values. The linear program of Figure 10.1 contains $O(|\mathcal{V}| + |\mathcal{E}|)$ variables and $O(|\mathcal{E}|)$ linear equations. Once a solution is found for the linear program of Figure 10.1, we set the new distance of $e = (k_{u^t}, v) \in E^{\mu,t}$ as equal to $\lambda(e) = \widehat{\mu}^t_{(i-1)}(u, v) + \lceil \gamma^t(u, v) \rceil$.

$$
\begin{cases}
\text{minimize} & \displaystyle\sum_{t \in \mathcal{T}} \psi_t \left(\sum_{(u,v) \in E^{\text{reuse},t}} \gamma^t(u, v) \right) \\
\text{Subject to:} & \\
\forall e \in E \cup E^k, & x_{tgt(e)} - x_{src(e)} \leq \|\mathcal{V}\| \cdot \lambda(e) - 1 \\
\forall t \in \mathcal{T}, \forall e = (k^t_u, v) \in E^{\mu,t}, & x_{tgt(e)} - x_{src(e)} - \|\mathcal{V}\| \cdot \gamma^t(u, v) \leq \|\mathcal{V}\| \cdot \widehat{\mu}^t_{(i-1)}(u, v) - 1 \\
\forall t \in \mathcal{T}, \forall (u, v) \in E^{\text{reuse},t}_{(i-1)}, & \gamma^t(u, v) \geq \widehat{\mu^*}^t(u, v) - \widehat{\mu}^t_{(i-1)}(u, v) \\
\forall u \in \mathcal{V}, & x_u \in \mathbb{R} \\
\forall t \in \mathcal{T}, \forall (u, v) \in E^{\text{reuse},t}_{(i-1)}, & \gamma^t(u, v) \in \mathbb{R} \\
\text{where:} & \\
\forall t \in \mathcal{T}, & E^{\mu,t} \overset{\text{def}}{=} \{\Phi(e_r) \mid e_r \in E^{\text{reuse},t}_{(i-1)}\}
\end{cases}
$$

Figure 10.1. *Linear program based on shortest paths equations (SPE)*

Hence, our implementation of $UpdateReuseDistances(G, (\widehat{\mu}^t)_{t \in \mathcal{T}}, (E^{\text{reuse},t})_{t \in \mathcal{T}})$ is given by Algorithm 10.2.

Algorithm 10.2. The function $UpdateReuseDistances$

Require: $(\widehat{\mu}^t_{(i-1)})_{t \in \mathcal{T}}$ previously computed reuse distances for all register types

Require: $(E^{\text{reuse},t}_{(i-1)})_{t \in \mathcal{T}}$ previously computed reuse edges for all register types

Solve the linear program of Figure 10.1 to compute $(\gamma^t(u, v))$

return $(\widehat{\mu}^t_{(i)})_{t \in \mathcal{T}}$ where $\widehat{\mu}^t_{(i)}(u, v) \overset{\text{def}}{=} \begin{cases} \widehat{\mu}^t_{(i-1)}(u, v) + \lceil \gamma^t(u, v) \rceil & \text{if } (u, v) \in E^{\text{reuse},t}_{(i-1)} \\ \widehat{\mu}^t_{(i-1)}(u, v) & \text{otherwise} \end{cases}$

10.5. Experimental results on eliminating non-positive circuits

Our SPE method is integrated inside SIRAlib, available as an open source in [BRI 10]. Full experiments and public data are also exposed. A summary is provided in Appendix 4.

Our experiments declare the following conclusions:

– Regarding the register requirement, considering a UAL code semantic for eliminating non-positive circuits is a working, inefficient solution. Indeed, if a UAL code semantic is used to model a processor with NUAL code semantic, the waste of registers is significant. However, the execution time of SIRALINA is faster with this method, since no extra processing is needed to eliminate non-positive circuits.

– The reactive strategy is a working efficient solution if the number of architectural registers is already fixed in the architecture. Indeed, tolerating the problem of non-positive circuits at the first step, and fixing it using a UAL model at the second step if the problem is detected, turns out to be a practical solution. The reason is that when the number of available registers is fixed, register minimization is not always necessary. Consequently, the waste of registers induced by a UAL semantic is hidden if enough registers are available. The execution time of SIRALINA stays fast enough with the reactive strategy.

– The proactive strategy using the SPE method gives the best results in terms of minimal register requirement, with a slight increase in the execution time of SIRALINA. Consequently, the proactive strategy is recommended for the situations where register minimization is necessary on NUAL processors. For instance, the context of circuit synthesis and reconfigurable architectures asks for minimizing the number of required registers. Also, in the case of architectures with frame registers (such as Itanium), minimal register reduces the cost of context saving for function calls;

– The practical satisfactory number of iterations required for the Iterative SIRALINA algorithm is five only. However, the convergence of the algorithm is not proved, and currently fixing a maximal number of iterations is required.

10.6. Conclusion on non-positive circuit elimination

Preconditioning a DDG before SWP is a beneficial approach for reducing spill code and improving the performance of loops. Until now, schedule-sensitive register optimization was studied only for sequential and superscalar codes, with UAL code semantics.

When considering NUAL code semantics, the access to registers may be architecturally delayed. These delay accesses provide interesting compilation opportunities to save registers. These opportunities are exploited by the insertion of edges with non-positive latencies inside DDG.

Inserting edges with non-positive latencies inside DDG highlights two open questions. First, existing SWP and periodic scheduling methods do not handle these non-positive latencies yet. Second, a preconditioning step that optimizes registers before SWP may create circuits with non-positive distances.

DDG with non-positive circuits have the drawback of not being lexicographic-positive. This means that, when resource constraints are considered, the existence of a valid SWP is no longer guaranteed. This may cause the failure of the compilation process (no code is generated while the program is correct). Our experiments show that, if care is not taken, 30.77% of loops in SPEC2000 applications induce non-lexicographic positive circuits (respectively, 28.16%, 41.90% and 92.21% for SPEC 2006, MEDIABENCH and FFMPEG loops).

In order to avoid the situation of creating non-lexicographic positive DDG, we studied two strategies. First, we studied a reactive strategy that tolerates the problem: we start by optimizing the register pressure at the DDG level without special care; if a non-positive circuit is detected, then backtrack and consider a UAL code semantic instead of NUAL; this means that we degrade the model of the processor architecture by not exploiting the opportunities offered by delayed accesses to registers. Second, we designed a proactive strategy that prevents the problem. The proactive strategy is based on a necessary and sufficient condition that we prove. It is implemented as an iterative process that increases the reuse distances until a fixed point is observed (or until we reach a limit in terms of iterations).

Concerning the efficiency of the methods presented in this chapter, the reactive strategy seems to perform well in practice in a regular compilation process: when the number of architectural registers is fixed, register minimization is not necessary (just be sure to be below the architectural capacity). In this context, it is advised not to try preventing the problem of non-positive circuits, but to tolerate it in order to save compilation time. In other contexts of compilation, the number of architectural registers is not fixed. This is the case of reconfigurable circuits where the number of registers needed may be decided after code optimization and generation. It is also the case of architectures with *frame* registers such as EPIC IA64, where a minimal register requirement reduces the cost of function calls. Also, this may be used to keep as many registers as possible free in order to be used for other code optimization methods. In such situations, our proactive strategy is efficient in practice: the iterative register minimization saves better registers than in the reactive strategy, while the compilation time stays reasonable (although greater than the reactive strategy).

The SIRA framework allows us to make a formal relationship between the register requirement, the initiation interval and the unrolling degree. This formal relationship proved in theorem 9.1 gives us the opportunity to define an interesting problem of minimal loop unrolling using the set of remaining registers, as shown in the next chapter.

Loop Unrolling Degree Minimization for Periodic Register Allocation

We address the problem of generating compact code for software pipelined loops. Although software pipelining is a powerful technique for extracting fine-grain parallelism, it generates lifetime intervals spanning multiple loop iterations. These intervals require periodic register allocation (also called variable expansion), which in turn yields a code generation challenge. We are looking for the minimal unrolling factor enabling the periodic register allocation of software pipelined kernels. This challenge is generally addressed through one of the following: (1) hardware support in the form of rotating register files, which solve the unrolling problem but are expensive in hardware; (2) register renaming by inserting register moves, which increase the number of operations in the loop, and may damage the schedule of the software pipeline and reduce throughput; (3) postpass loop unrolling that does not compromise throughput but often leads to impractical code growth. The latter approach relies on the proof that MAXLIVE registers are sufficient for periodic register allocation [HEN 92, WER 99, TOU 04, TOU 03]; yet the only heuristic to control the amount of postpass loop unrolling does not achieve this bound or leads to undesired register spills [WER 99, LAM 88b].

This chapter gathers our research results on the open problem of minimal loop unrolling allowing a software-only code generation that does not trade the optimality of the initiation interval (II) for the compactness of the generated code. Our novel idea is to use the remaining free registers after periodic register allocation to minimize the constraints on register reuse.

The problem of minimal loop unrolling arises either before or after software pipelining, either with a single or with multiple register types (classes). We provide a formal problem definition for each situation, and we propose and study a dedicated algorithm for each problem.

11.1. Introduction

When a loop is software pipelined, variable lifetimes may extend beyond a single iteration of the loop. Therefore, we cannot use regular register allocation algorithms because of self-interferences in the usual interference graph [WER 99, FIS 05, LAM 88b]. In compiler construction, when no hardware support is available, kernel loop unrolling is *the* method of code generation that does not alter the initiation interval after software pipelining. In fact, unrolling the loop allows us to avoid introducing unnecessary move and spill operations after a periodic register allocation.

In this chapter, we are interested in the minimal loop unrolling factor which allows a periodic register allocation for software pipelined loops (without inserting spill or move operations). Having a minimal unroll factor reduces code size, which is an important performance measure for embedded systems because they have a limited memory size. Regarding high-performance computing (desktop and supercomputers), loop code size may not be important for memory size, but may be so for Icache performance. In addition to minimal unroll factors, it is necessary that the code generation scheme for periodic register allocation does not generate additional spill; The number of required registers must not exceed MAXLIVE (the number of values simultaneously alive). Prohibiting spill code aims to maintain II and to save performance. Spill code can increase the initiation interval and, thus, reduce the performance in the following ways:

1) adding spill code may increase the length of data dependence chains, which may increase the achievable initiation interval;

2) spill code consumes execution resources which restrains the opportunity for achieving a high degree of instruction-level parallelism;

3) memory requests consume more power than accessing the same values in registers;

4) memory operations (except with scratch-pad local memories) have unknown static latencies. Compilers usually assume short latencies for memory operations, despite the fact that the memory access may miss the cache. Without good estimates of the performance of a piece of code, the compiler may be guided to bad optimization decisions.

When the schedule of a pipelined loop is known, there are a number of known methods for computing unroll factors and performing periodic register allocation, but none of them are fully satisfactory:

– Modulo variable expansion (MVE) [FIS 05, LAM 88b] computes a minimal unroll factor but may introduce spill code because it does not provide an upper bound on register usage.

– Hendren's heuristic [HEN 92] computes a sufficient unroll factor to avoid spilling, but with no guarantee in terms of minimal register usage or unrolling degree.

– The meeting graph framework [WER 99] which guarantees that the unroll factor will be sufficient to minimize register usage (reaching MAXLIVE), but not that the unroll factor will itself be minimal.

In addition, periodic register allocation can be performed before SWP or after SWP, depending on the compiler construction strategy, see Figure 11.1. We focus on the loop unrolling minimization problem in the context of these two phase orders. If periodic register allocation is done before SWP as in Figure 11.1(a), the instruction schedule is not fixed, and hence the cyclic lifetime intervals are not known by the compiler. We propose a method for minimal kernel unrolling when SWP is not carried out yet, by computing a minimal unroll factor that is valid for the family of all valid SWP schedules of the DDG. If the register allocation is done after SWP as in Figure 11.1(b), the instruction schedule is fixed and hence the cyclic lifetime intervals and MAXLIVE are known. In this situation, there are a number of known methods for computing unroll factors. These are (1) MVE [FIS 05, LAM 88b] which computes a minimal unroll factor but may introduce spill (since MVE may need more than MAXLIVE registers without proving an appropriate upper bound); (2) Hendren's heuristic [HEN 92] which computes a sufficient unroll factor without introducing spill, but with no guarantee in terms of minimal register usage or unrolling degree and (3) the meeting graph framework [WER 99] which is based on mathematical proofs that guarantee that the unroll degree will be sufficient to reach register minimality (i.e. MAXLIVE), but not that the unroll degree itself will be minimal. Our results improve the latter method by providing an algorithm for reducing the unroll factor within the meeting graph framework.

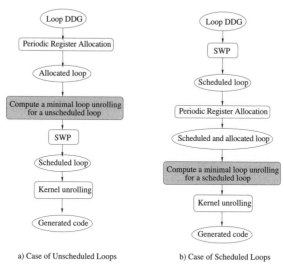

a) Case of Unscheduled Loops   b) Case of Scheduled Loops

Figure 11.1. *Minimal unroll factor computation depending on phase ordering*

As explained before, the existing work in the field of kernel unrolling deals with already-scheduled loops [WER 99, HEN 92, FIS 05, LAM 88b] and a single register type. We extend the model to handle not only unscheduled loops, but also processor architectures with multiple register types. In a target architecture with multiple register types (also known as (a.k.a.) classes), the state-of-the-art algorithms [WER 99, TOU 04, TOU 03] propose computing the *sufficient unrolling degree* that we should apply to the loop so that it is always possible to allocate the variables of each register type with a minimal number of registers (MAXLIVE [HUF 93b]). We demonstrate that minimizing the unroll factor on each register type separately does not define a global minimal unroll factor, and we provide an appropriate problem definition and an algorithmic solution in this context.

This chapter advances the state of the art in the following directions:

1) We improve the meeting graph method, achieving *significantly smaller unroll factors* while *preserving an optimal register usage* on already-scheduled loops. The key idea of our method is to exploit unused registers beyond the minimal number required for periodic register allocation (MAXLIVE [HUF 93b]).

2) The existing work in the field of kernel unrolling for periodic register allocation deals with already-scheduled loops [WER 99, HEN 92, FIS 05, LAM 88b]. As mentioned earlier, we also wish to handle not-yet-scheduled loops, on which the cyclic lifetime intervals are not known by the compiler. This chapter shows a method for minimal kernel unrolling when software pipelining (SWP) has not yet been carried out, by *computing a minimal unroll factor that is valid for the family of all valid cyclic schedules* of the data dependence graph (DDG). However, if register allocation is performed after SWP as in Figure 11.1(b), the instruction schedule is fixed and hence the cyclic lifetime intervals and MAXLIVE are known.

3) We also extend the model of periodic register allocation to handle processor architectures with multiple register types (a.k.a. classes). On such architectures, the state-of-the-art algorithms [EIS 95b, TOU 04] compute the *sufficient unrolling degree*, that is the unrolling degree that should be applied to a loop so that it is always possible to allocate the variables of each register type with a minimal number of registers. This chapter demonstrates that minimizing the unroll factor on each register type separately does not define a global minimal unroll factor, and we provide an appropriate problem definition and an algorithmic solution in this context.

4) We contribute to the enlightenment of a poorly understood dilemma in backend compiler construction. First, as mentioned earlier and as shown in Figure 11.1, we offer the compiler designer more choices to control the register pressure and the unroll factor for periodic register allocation at different epochs of the compilation flow. Second, we greatly simplify the phase ordering problem induced by the interplay of modulo scheduling, periodic register allocation, and postpass unrolling. We achieve this by providing strong guarantees, not only in terms of register usage (the absence of spills induced by insufficient unrolling), but also in terms of reduction of the unroll factor.

5) Our methods are implemented within an industrial-strength compiler for STMicroelectronics' ST2xx VLIW embedded processor family. Our experiments on

multiple benchmarks suites LAO, FFMPEG, MEDIABENCH, SPEC CPU2000, and SPEC CPU2006, are unprecedented in scale. They demonstrate the maturity of the techniques and contribute valuable empirical data never published in research papers on software pipelining and periodic register allocation. They also demonstrate the effectiveness of the proposed unroll degree minimization, both in terms of code size and in terms of initiation intervals (throughout), along with satisfactory compilation times. Furthermore, our techniques outperform the existing compiler for the ST2xx processor family that allocates registers after software pipelining and unrolls using MVE. Our techniques generate less spill codes, fewer move operations and yield a lower initiation interval on average, with a satisfactory code size (loops fitting within the instruction cache). These experiments are also informative in their more negative results. As expected, they show that achieving strong guarantees on spill-free periodic register allocation yields generally higher unroll factors than heuristics providing no such guarantees like MVE [FIS 05, LAM 88b]. It was more unexpected (and disappointing) to observe that the initiation intervals achieved with MVE remain generally excellent, despite the presence of spills and a higher number of move operations. This can be explained by the presence of numerous empty slots in the cyclic schedules, where spills and move operations can be inserted, and by the rare occurrence of these spurious operations on the critical path of the dependence graph.

The chapter is organized as follows. Section 11.2 describes existing research results that are necessary for understanding the rest of this chapter. Section 11.3 formalizes the problem of minimizing the loop unrolling degree in the presence of multiple register types when the loop is unscheduled. For clarity, we start the explanation of our loop-unrolling minimization algorithm in section 11.4 with the case of a single register type. Then, section 11.5 generalizes the solution to multiple register types. When the loop is already scheduled, an adapted algorithm is provided in section 11.6 based on the meeting graph framework. Section 11.7 presents detailed experimental results on standard benchmark suites. In section 11.8, we discuss related work on code generation for periodic register allocation, and we explain the contribution of this chapter compared to the previous work. Finally, we conclude with section 11.9.

11.2. Background

SWP allows instructions to be scheduled independently of the original loop iteration barriers. The maximal number of values of type t simultaneously alive, denoted MAXLIVE^t, defines the minimal number of registers required to allocate periodically the variables of the loop without introducing spill code. However, since some live ranges of variables span multiple iterations, special care must be taken when allocating registers and coloring an interference graph; this is the core focus of this chapter and will be detailed later.

Let RC^t be the number of registers of type t to be allocated for the kernel of the pipelined loop. If the register allocation is optimal, we must have $RC^t = \text{MAXLIVE}^t$ for all register types $t \in \mathcal{T}$. We will see that there are only two theoretical frameworks that guarantee this optimality for SWP code generation. Other frameworks have $RC^t \geq \text{MAXLIVE}^t$, with no guaranteed upper bound for RC^t.

11.2.1. *Loop unrolling after SWP with modulo variable expansion*

Code generation for SWP has to deal with many issues: prologue/epilogue codes, early exits from the loops, variables spanning multiple kernel iterations, etc. In this chapter, we focus on the last point: how can we generate a compact kernel for variables spanning multiples iterations when no hardware support exists in the underlying processor architecture? When no hardware support exists, and when prohibiting the insertion of additional move operations (i.e. no additional live range splitting), kernel loop unrolling is the only option. The resulting loop body itself is bigger but no extra operations are executed in comparison with the original code. Lam designed a general loop unrolling scheme called MVE [LAM 88b]. In fact, the major criterion of this method is to minimize the loop unrolling degree because the memory size of the i-WARP processor is low [LAM 88b]. The MVE method defines a minimal unrolling degree to enable code generation after a given periodic register allocation. This unrolling degree is obtained by dividing the length of the longest of all live ranges LT_v of variables v defined in the pipelined kernel by the initiation interval, i.e. $\left\lceil \frac{\max_v LT_v}{II} \right\rceil$.

MVE is easy to understand and implement, and it is practically effective in limiting code growth. This is why it has been adopted by several SWP frameworks [DIN 97c, HUF 93b], and included in commercial compilers. The problem with MVE is that it does not guarantee a register allocation with MAXLIVE^t registers of type t, and in general it may lead to unnecessary spills breaking the benefits of software pipelining. A concrete example of this limitation is illustrated in Figures 11.2 and 11.3; we will use it as a running example in this section. Figure 11.2 is an SWP example with two variables v_1 and v_2. For simplicity, we consider here a single register type t. New values of v_1 and v_2 are created in every iteration. For instance, the first value of v_1 is alive during the time interval $[0, 2]$, and the other values (v_1' and v_1'') are created every multiple of II. This figure shows a concrete example with a SWP kernel having two variables v_1 and v_2 spanning multiple kernel iterations. In the SWP kernel, we can see that $\text{MAXLIVE}^t = 3$.

To generate a code for this SWP kernel, MVE unrolls it with a factor of $\left\lceil \frac{\max(LT_{v_1}, LT_{v_2})}{II} \right\rceil = \left\lceil \frac{\max(3,3)}{2} \right\rceil = 2$. Figure 11.3 illustrates the considered unrolled SWP kernel. The values created inside the SWP kernel are v_1, v_2, v_1', and v_2'. Because of the periodic nature of the SWP kernel, the variables v_1' and v_2' are alive as entry and exit values (see the figure of the lifetime intervals in the SWP kernel). Now, the interference graph of the SWP kernel is drawn, and we can see that it cannot be colored with less than 4 colors (a maximal clique is $\{v_1, v_2, v_1', v_2'\}$). Consequently, it is impossible to generate a code with $RC^t = 3$ registers, except if we add extra copy operations in parallel. If inserting copy operations is not allowed or possible (no free slots and no explicit ILP), then we need $RC^t = 4$ registers to generate a correct code. This example gives a simple case where $RC^t > \text{MAXLIVE}^t$, and it is not known whether RC^t is bounded. As a result, it is possible that the computed SWP schedule has $\text{MAXLIVE}^t \leq \mathcal{R}^t$, but the code generation performed with MVE requires $RC^t > \mathcal{R}^t$. This means that spill code has to be inserted even if $\text{MAXLIVE}^t \leq \mathcal{R}^t$, which is unfortunate and unsatisfactory.

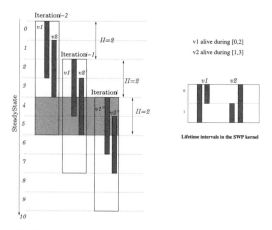

Figure 11.2. *Example to highlight the shortcomings of the MVE technique*

Fortunately, an algorithm exists that achieves an allocation with a minimal number of registers equal to $RC^t = \text{MAXLIVE}^t$ [WER 99, EIS 95b]. This algorithm exploits the meeting graph introduced in the next section.

11.2.2. *Meeting graphs (MG)*

The algorithm of Eisenbeis *et al.* [WER 99, EIS 95b] can generate a periodic register allocation using MAXLIVE^t registers if the kernel is unrolled, due to a dedicated graph representation called the *meeting graph* (MG). It is a more accurate graph than the usual interference graph, as it holds information on the number of clock cycles of each live range and on the succession of the live ranges along the loop iterations. It allows us to compute an unrolling degree that enables an allocation of the loops with $RC^t = \text{MAXLIVE}^t$ registers.

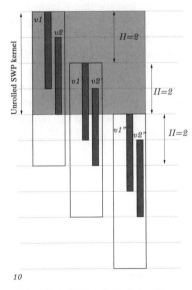

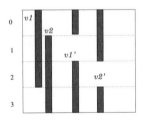

MVE unrolls the SWP kernel with a factor of 2

Lifetime intervals in the SWP kernel

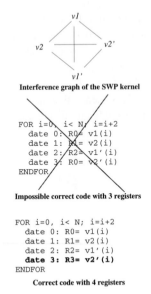

Interference graph of the SWP kernel

```
FOR i=0, i< N, i=i+2
    date 0: R0= v1(i)
    date 1: R1= v2(i)
    date 2: R2= v1'(i)
    date 3: R0= v2'(i)
ENDFOR
```

Impossible correct code with 3 registers

```
FOR i=0, i< N; i=i+2
    date 0: R0= v1(i)
    date 1: R1= v2(i)
    date 2: R2= v1'(i)
    date 3: R3= v2'(i)
ENDFOR
```

Correct code with 4 registers

```
FOR i=0, i< N; i=i+2
    date 0: R0= v1(i)    || R1 = R0
    date 1: R1= v2(i)    || R2 = R1
    date 2: R2= v1'(i)   || R0=R2
    date 3: R0= v2'(i)
ENDFOR
```

Correct code with 3 registers and parallel copy operations

Figure 11.3. *SWP kernel unrolled with MVE*

Intuitively, the MG is useful because it captures information about pairs of values where one value dies on the same clock cycle that another value becomes alive. If we try to allocate such values to the same register, then there is no dead time when the register contains a dead value. By identifying circuits in the MG, we find sets of live values that can be allocated to one or more registers with no dead time.

Let us consider again the running example in Figure 11.2. The MG that corresponds to that SWP is illustrated in Figure 11.4: a node is associated to every variable created in the SWP kernel. Hence, we have two nodes v_1 and v_2. A node u is labeled with a weight $\omega(u) \in \mathbb{N}$ corresponding to the length of its respective live range, here 3 clock cycles for variables v_1 and v_2. There is an edge connecting a source node to a sink node *if and only if* the lifetime interval of the first node ends when the sink one starts. By examining the SWP kernel in Figure 11.2, we see that the copies of v_1 end when those of v_2 start, and vice versa. Consequently, in the MG of Figure 11.4, we have an edge from v_1 to v_2 and vice versa to model an abstraction of the register reuse for this fixed SWP schedule.

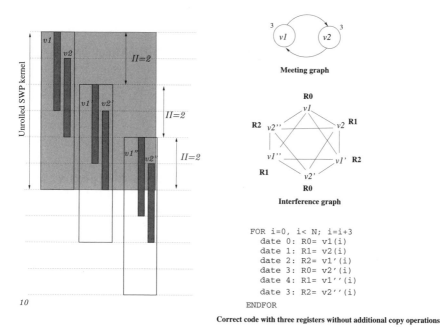

Figure 11.4. *Example to explain the optimality of the meeting graph technique*

Now, the question is: what is the benefit of such a graph structure? Using this graph structure we are able to compute a provably sufficient unrolling factor to apply in order to achieve an optimal register allocation, that is $RC^t = \text{MAXLIVE}^t$ [WER 99, EIS 95b].

Let us consider the set of strongly connected components (SCC) of the MG. In our simple example, there is a single SCC. The weight of every SCC numbered k is defined as $\mu_k = \frac{\sum_{v \in SCC_k} \omega(v)}{II}$. Note that one of the properties of the MG is that $\sum_{v \in SCC_k} \omega(v)$ is always a multiple of II, and $\frac{\sum_{\forall v} \omega(v)}{II} = \text{MAXLIVE}^t$. In our simple example with a single SCC, its weight is equal to $\mu_1 = \frac{3+3}{2} = 3$.

Then, the *sufficient* unrolling factor computed using the MG is equal to $\rho = lcm(\mu_1, ..., \mu_k)$, where lcm denotes the least common multiple [EIS 95b]. It has been proved that if the SWP kernel is unrolled ρ times, then we can generate code with $RC^t = \text{MAXLIVE}^t$ registers. In the example illustrated in Figure 11.4, we have a single SCC so $\rho = \mu_1 = 3$, which means that the kernel has to be unrolled with a factor equal to 3. The interference graph shows that three colors are sufficient, which allows us to generate correct code with only three registers, rather than the four required with modulo variable expansion (compared to Figure 11.3).

Without formally proving the correctness of the unrolling factor defined above (interested readers are referred to study [WER 99, EIS 95b]), the intuition behind the LCM formula comes from the following fact: if we successfully generate code for an SCC by unrolling the kernel μ_i times, then we can generate a correct code for the same SCC by unrolling the kernel with any multiple of μ_i. Hence, if we are faced with a set of SCCs, it is sufficient to consider the LCM of the μ_i's to have a correct unrolling factor for all the SCCs.

In addition to the previous unroll factor formula, the MG also allows us to guarantee that MAXLIVE^t or $\text{MAXLIVE}^t + 1$ are sufficient unrolling factors. In the example of Figure 11.4, we have the coincidence that $\rho = \text{MAXLIVE}^t$, but this is not always the case. Indeed, one of the purposes of MG is to have unrolling factors ρ lower than MAXLIVE^t. This objective is not always reachable if we want to have $RC^t = \text{MAXLIVE}^t$; Eisenbeis *et al.* [EIS 95b] try to reach it by decomposing the MG into a maximal number of elementary circuits. In practice, it turns out that ρ may be very high, reducing the practical benefit of register optimality $RC^t = \text{MAXLIVE}^t$.

The next section recalls a theoretical framework that applies periodic register allocation before SWP, while allowing the computation of a sufficient unrolling degree for a complete set of possible SWP schedules.

11.2.3. *SIRA, reuse graphs and loop unrolling*

As detailed in Chapter 9.3, *Reuse graphs* are a generalization of previous work by de Werra *et al.* and Hendren *et al.* [WER 99, HEN 92]. Unlike the previous approaches for periodic register allocation, reuse graphs are used before software pipelining to generate a move-free or a spill-free periodic register allocation in the presence of multiple register types. Reuse graphs provide a formalized approach to generating code which requires neither register spills nor move operations. Of course, it is not always possible to avoid spill code, some DDGs are complex enough to always require spilling, the SIRA framework is able to detect such situations before SWP.

A simple way to recall SIRA is to provide an example. All the theory has already been presented in [TOU 04], and we recently showed that optimizing the register requirement for multiple register types in one go is a better approach than optimizing for every register type separately [TOU 11]. Figure 11.5(a) provides an initial DDG with two register types t_1 and t_2. Statements producing results of type t_1 are in dashed circles, and those of type t_2 are in bold circles. Statement u_1 writes two results of distinct types. Flow dependence through registers of type t_1 have dashed edges, and those of type t_2 have bold edges.

Each edge e in the DDG is labeled with the pair of values $(\delta(e), \lambda(e))$. Now, the question is how to compute a periodic register allocation for the loop in Figure 11.5(a) without hurting the instruction level parallelism if possible.

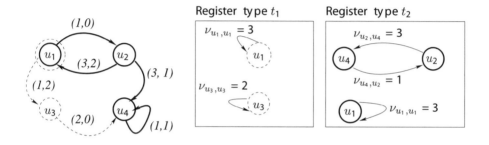

a) Initial DDG   b) Reuse Graphs for Register Types t1 and t2

Figure 11.5. *Example for SIRA and reuse graphs*

Periodic register constraints are modeled using *reuse graphs*. We associate a reuse graph $G^{\text{reuse},t}$ to each register type t, see Figure 11.5(b). The reuse graph is computed by the SIRA framework, Figure 11.5(b) is one of the examples that SIRA may produce. Note that the reuse graph is not unique, other valid reuse graphs may exist.

A reuse graph $G^{\text{reuse},t} = (V^{R,t}, E^{\text{reuse},t})$ contains $V^{R,t}$, i.e. only the nodes writing to registers of type t. These nodes are connected by *reuse edges*. For instance, in G^{reuse,t_2} of Figure 11.5(b), the set of reuse edges is $E^{\text{reuse},t_2} = \{(u_2, u_4), (u_4, u_2), (u_1, u_1)\}$. Also, $E^{\text{reuse},t_1} = \{(u_1, u_3), (u_3, u_1)\}$. Each reuse edge $e_r = (u, v)$ is labeled by an integral distance $\mu^t(e_r)$, that we call *reuse distance*. The existence of a reuse edge $e_r = (u, v)$ of distance $\mu^t(e_r)$ means that $u(i)$ (iteration i of u) and $u(i + \mu^t(e_r))$ (iteration $i + \mu^t(e_r)$ of v) *share the same destination register* of type t. Hence, reuse graphs allow us to completely define a periodic register allocation for a given loop. In the example of Figure 11.5(b) and for register type t_2, we have $\mu^{t_2}((u_2, u_4)) = 3$ and $\mu^{t_2}((u_4, u_2)) = 1$.

Let C be a circuit in the reuse graph $G^{\text{reuse},t}$ of type t; we call C a *reuse circuit*. We note $\mu^t(C) = \sum_{e_r \in C} \mu^t(e_r)$ the weight of the reuse circuit C. The following corollary provides a sufficient unrolling factor for all register types.

COROLLARY 11.1.– [TOU 04] Let $G = (V, E)$ be a loop DDG with a set of register types $\mathcal{T}$. Each register type $t \in \mathcal{T}$ is associated with a valid reuse graph $G^{\text{reuse},t} = (V^{R,t}, E^{\text{reuse},t})$. The loop can be allocated with $RC^t = \sum_{e_r \in E^{\text{reuse},t}} \mu^t(e_r)$ registers for each type t if we unroll it ρ times, where:

$$\rho = lcm(\rho_1^t, \cdots, \rho_n^t)$$

ρ^{t_i} is the unrolling degree of the reuse graph of type t_i, defined as

$$\rho^t = lcm(\mu^t(C_1), \cdots, \mu^t(C_n))$$

The above corollary seems to be close to the MG result. This is not exactly true, since here we are generalizing the MG result to unscheduled loops in the presence of multiple registers types. Unlike the MG, the above-defined unrolling factor is valid for a whole set of SWP schedules, not for a fixed one. In addition, the reuse graph allows us to guarantee that prior to software pipelining $RC^t = \sum_{e_r \in E^{\text{reuse},t}} \mu^t(e_r) \le \mathcal{R}^t$ for any register type, while maintaining instruction level parallelism if possible (by taking care not to increase the critical circuit of the loop, known as the MII_{dep}).

Note that when compilation time matters, we can avoid unrolling the loop before the SWP step. This avoids increasing the DDG size, which would result in significantly more work for the scheduler. Because we allocate registers directly on the DDG by inserting loop carried anti-dependencies, the DDG can be scheduled without unrolling it. In other words, loop unrolling can be applied at the code generation step (after SWP) in order to apply the register allocation computed before scheduling.

EXAMPLE 11.1.– Let consider as illustration the example of Figure 11.5. Here $\rho_{t_1} = lcm(3, 2) = 6$ and $\rho_{t_2} = lcm(3 + 1, 3) = 12$. That is, the register type t_1 requires that we unroll the loop six times if we want to consume $RC^{t_1} = 3 + 2 = 5$ registers of type t_1. At this compilation step, SWP has not been carried out but SIRA guarantees that the computed unroll factor and register count are valid for any subsequent SWP. As an illustration, a valid sequential trace for the for the register type t_1 is given in listing 11.1 (we do not show the trace for register type t_2 and we omit the prologue/epilogue of the trace).

The reader may check that we have used five registers of type t_1. According to the reuse graph, every pair of statements $(u_1(i), u_1(i + 3))$ uses exactly the same destination register, because there is a reuse edge (u_1, u_1) with a reuse distance $\mu^{t_1}(u_1, u_1) = 3$. Every pair of statements $(u_3(i), u_3(i + 2))$ uses the same destination register too, because there is a reuse edge (u_3, u_3) with a reuse distance $\mu^{t_1}(u_3, u_3) = 2$. We can check in the generated code that the reuse circuit (u_1, u_1), which contains a single reuse edge in this example, uses three registers (R_1, R_2 and R_3); The reuse circuit (u_3, u_3) uses two registers (R_4 and R_5).

```
FOR i=0,  i<N,  i=i+6
  u_1(i)    :  R1 =  ...
  u_2(i)    :
  u_3(i)    :  R4 = R2 ...
  u_4(i)    :  ... = R4 ...

  u_1(i+1):  R2 =  ...
  u_2(i+1):
  u_3(i+1):  R5 = R3 ...
  u_4(i+1):  ... = R5 ...

  u_1(i+2):  R3 =  ...
  u_2(i+2):
  u_3(i+2):  R4 = R1 ...
  u_4(i+2):  ... = R4 ...

  u_1(i+3):  R1 =  ...
  u_2(i+3):
  u_3(i+3):  R5 = R2 ...
  u_4(i+4):  ... = R5 ...

  u_1(i+4):  R2 =  ...
  u_2(i+4):
  u_3(i+4):  R4 = R3 ...
  u_4(i+4):  ... = R4 ...

  u_1(i+5):  R3 =  ...
  u_2(i+5):
  u_3(i+5):  R5 = R1 ...
  u_4(i+5):  ... = R5 ...
ENDFOR
```

Listing 11.1. *Example of a sequential kernel code generation for the register type t_1*

Regarding the register type t_2, it requires an unrolling factor equal to 12 if we want to consume $RC^{t_2} = 3 + 1 + 3 = 7$ registers of type t_2. Consequently, a common valid unroll factor for both the register types t_1 and t_2 is equal to $\rho = lcm(6, 12) = 12$. For reasons of space, we do not show the full code generation for the loop in Figure 11.5 with an unrolling factor of 12. However, later in section 11.5, we will show how we will minimize the unrolling degree to get a reasonable value equal to 4, it will be then possible to write a reasonably short code for the example.

The main advantage of the MG and reuse graph approaches over MVE is their ability to guarantee spill-free and move-free code generation, before or after SWP. However, they have an important drawback, which is that the unroll factor may be very large. The next section defines the problem of unroll degree minimization for unscheduled loops. Later, we will extend the problem to scheduled loops.

11.3. Problem description of unroll factor minimization for unscheduled loops

The reuse graph method, which guarantees a register allocation with exactly MAXLIVE registers, may result in a large unrolling factor. However, there may be additional unused registers: each register type t may have some remaining registers $R^t = \mathcal{R}^t - RC^t$ (where $\mathcal{R}^t$ is the number of available architectural registers of type t). We have developed a method for using any remaining registers to reduce the unrolling factor. This method is applied after the periodic register allocation step performed by the SIRA framework. This postpass minimization consists of adding zero or more unused registers to each reuse circuit in order to minimize the LCM of the size of the circuits (denoted ρ^*). This idea is described in the next problem.

PROBLEM 11.1.– Loop unroll minimization (LUM).– Let ρ be the initial loop unrolling degree and let $\mathcal{T} = \{t_1, \dots, t_n\}$ be the set of register types. For each register type $t_j \in \mathcal{T}$, let $R^{t_j} \in \mathbb{N}$ be the number of remaining registers after a periodic register allocation for this register type. Let k_j be the number of reuse circuits of type t_j. We note $\mu_{i,t_j} \in \mathbb{N}$ as the weight of the ith reuse circuit of the register type t_j. For each reuse circuit i and each register type t_j, we must compute the added registers r_{i,t_j} such that we find a new periodic register allocation with a minimal loop unrolling degree. This is described by the following constraints:

1) $\rho^* = lcm(lcm(\mu_{1,t_1} + r_{1,t_1}, \dots, \mu_{k_1,t_1} + r_{k_1,t_1}), \dots, lcm(\mu_{1,t_n} + r_{1,t_n}, \dots, \mu_{k_n,t_n} + r_{k_n,t_n}))$ is minimal (optimality constraint).

2) $\forall t_j \in \mathcal{T}, \sum_{i=1}^{k_j} r_{i,t_j} \leq R^{t_j}$ (validity constraints)

That is, this formal problem describes the idea of increasing the number of allocated registers without exceeding the number of available ones (to guarantee the absence of spilling), with the goal of minimizing the global unroll factor. Increasing the number of allocated registers is done by increasing the weights of the reuse circuit. If a reuse circuit consists of multiple edges, then increasing the weight of any edge inside this reuse circuit is a valid solution. The validity of this solution is proved in the next lemma. Intuitively, this lemma states that if we succeed in building a periodic register allocation with RC_1^t registers of type t, then we can build a periodic register allocation with RC_2^t registers of type t, where $RC_1^t \leq RC_2^t \leq \mathcal{R}^t$

LEMMA 11.1.– [BAC 13] Let $G = (V, E)$ be a loop DDG. Let $G^{\text{reuse},}$ be a valid reuse graph of each register type $t \in \mathcal{T}$ associated with the loop G. Let $\mathcal{R}$ be the number of available registers of type t. Let (u_i^t, u_j^t) a single arbitrary reuse arc in $G^{\text{reuse},t}$ with its associated reuse distance $\mu_{i,j}^t \in \mathbb{Z}$. Then: $\mu_{i,j}^t \leq \mathcal{R}^t \implies \forall x \in [0, \mathcal{R}^t - \mu_{i,j}^t], \mu_{i,j}^t + x$ is a valid reuse distance for the reuse arc (u_i^t, u_j^t)

For clarity, we first present a solution to problem 11.1 in the case of a single register type, and then generalize to multiple register types.

11.4. Algorithmic solution for unroll factor minimization: single register type

In this section, we solve the problem of minimal unroll degree in the case of a single register type, based on reuse graphs (unscheduled loops). When we consider a single register type, then we have a single reuse graph for the considered register type. The formula for computing the unrolling degree becomes equal to a single LCM of the weights of the reuse circuits of the implicit register type. By replacing the notations of $\mu_{i,t}$ ($r_{i,t}$ and R^t, respectively) by μ_i (r_i and R, respectively), problem 11.1 amounts to the following:

PROBLEM 11.2.– LCM-MIN.– Let $R \in \mathbb{N}$ be the number of remaining registers. Let $\mu_1, \ldots, \mu_k \in \mathbb{N}$ be the weights of the reuse circuits. Compute the added registers $r_1, \ldots, r_k \in \mathbb{N}$ such that:

1) $\sum_{i=1}^k r_i \leq R$ (validity constraints)

2) $lcm(\mu_1 + r_1, \ldots, \mu_k + r_k)$ is minimal (optimization objective).

To our knowledge, problem 11.2 has no simple, closed-form solution, and its algorithmic complexity is still an open problem. Indeed, a similar reduced problem exists in cryptography theory: given two natural numbers a, b, compute $x \leq R^t \in \mathbb{N}$ such that $gcd(a, b + x)$ is maximal (gcd denotes the greatest common divisor (GCD)). This GCD maximization problem is defined for two integers only, it is equivalent to minimizing the LCM of two integers because $lcm(a, b) = \frac{a \times b}{gcd(a,b)}$. The GCD maximization problem of two integers is known to be equivalent to the integer factorization problem: the decision problem of integer factorization has unknown complexity class till now. It is currently solved with approximate methods devoted to very large numbers [HOW 01]. Problem 11.2 is a generalization of the GCD maximization problem. The heuristic presented in [HOW 01] is not appropriate in our case because: (1) the problem tackled in [HOW 01] deals with two integers only, which we cannot generalize to minimize the LCM to multiple integers because $LCM(x_0, \cdots, x_k) \neq \frac{x_0 \times \cdots \times x_k}{gcd(x_0, \cdots, x_k)}$ for $k > 2$; (2) we deal with multiple small numbers (in practice, $R \leq 128$), allowing to design optimal methods efficient in practice instead of heuristics.

Before stating our solution for problem 11.2, we propose finding a solution for a subproblem that we call the *fixed loop unrolling problem*. The solution of this subproblem constitutes the basis of the solution of problem 11.2. The *fixed loop unrolling problem* proposes finding, for a fixed unrolling degree β, the number of registers that should be added to each circuit to ensure that the size of each circuit is a divisor of β. That is, we find the number of registers added to each circuit $r_1, ..., r_k$ such that $\sum_{i=1}^{k} r_i \leq R$ and β is a common multiple of the different updated weights $\mu_1 + r_1, ... + \mu_k + r_k$. A formal description is given in the next section.

11.4.1. *Fixed loop unrolling problem*

We formulate the *fixed loop unrolling problem* as follows:

PROBLEM 11.3.– Fixed loop unrolling problem.– Let $R \in \mathbb{N}$ be the number of remaining registers. Let $\mu_1, \ldots, \mu_k \in \mathbb{N}$ be the weights of the reuse circuits. Given a positive integer β, compute the different added registers $r_1, \ldots, r_k \in \mathbb{N}$ such that:

1) $\sum_{i=1}^{k} r_i \leq R$

2) β is the common multiple of the new circuit weights $\mu_1 + r_1, \ldots, \mu_k + r_k$

To improve readability, we use CM to denote *common multiple*.

Before describing our solution for problem 11.3, we state lemma 11.2 and lemma 11.3 that we need to use afterwards.

LEMMA 11.2.– [BAC 13] Let us note some properties of the *fixed loop unrolling problem*:

1) $\beta \geq \max_i \mu_i \implies \exists (r_1, \ldots, r_k) \in \mathbb{N}^k$ such that: $CM(\mu_1 + r_1, \ldots, \mu_k + r_k) = \beta$

2) Let $r_1, \ldots, r_k$ be the solution of problem 11.3 such that $\sum_{i=1}^{k} r_i$ is minimal. If $\sum_{i=1}^{k} r_i > R$ then the *fixed loop unrolling problem* cannot be solved.

LEMMA 11.3.– [BAC 13] Let β be a positive integer and D_β be the set of its divisors. Let $\mu_1, \ldots, \mu_k \in \mathbb{N}$ be the weights of the reuse circuits. If we find a list of the added registers $r_1, \ldots, r_k \in \mathbb{N}$ for problem 11.3, then we have the following results:

1) $\beta = CM(\mu_1 + r_1, \ldots, \mu_k + r_k) \Rightarrow \forall i = 1, k : \beta \geq \mu_i$

2) $\beta = CM(\mu_1 + r_1, \ldots, \mu_k + r_k) \Rightarrow \forall i = 1, k : \exists d_i, r_i = d_i - \mu_i$ with $d_i \in D_\beta \wedge d_i \geq \mu_i$.

After showing lemma 11.3 and by using lemma 11.2, we describe our solution for the *fixed loop unrolling problem* in the next section.

11.4.2. *Solution for the fixed loop unrolling problem*

PROPOSITION 11.1.– [BAC 13] Let β be a positive integer and D_β be the set of its divisors. Let R be the number of remaining registers. Let $\mu_1, \ldots, \mu_k \in \mathbb{N}$ be the weights of the reuse circuits. A minimal list of the added registers $(r_1, \ldots, r_k \in \mathbb{N}$ with $\sum_{i=1}^{k} r_i$ is minimal) can be found by adding to each reuse circuit μ_i a minimal value r_i, such as $r_i = d_i - \mu_i$ with $d_i = \min\{d \in D_\beta \mid d \geq \mu_i\}$. If we denote by CM the common multiple, then the two following implications are true:

1) $\beta = CM(\mu_1 + r_1, \ldots, \mu_k + r_k) \wedge \sum_{i=1}^{k} r_i \leq R \Rightarrow$ we find a solution for problem 11.3;

2) $\beta = CM(\mu_1 + r_1, \ldots, \mu_k + r_k) \wedge \sum_{i=1}^{k} r_i > R \Rightarrow$ problem 11.3 has no solution.

Figure 11.6 represents a graphical solution for the *fixed loop unrolling problem*. We assume that the different weights and the different divisors of β are sorted on the same axis in an ascending order.

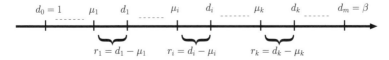

Figure 11.6. *Graphical solution for the fixed loop unrolling problem*

Algorithm 11.1 implements our solution for the *fixed loop unrolling problem*. This algorithm tries to divide the remaining registers R among the circuits to achieve a fixed CM of k integers (the different weights of reuse circuits μ_i). It checks whether β can become the new loop unrolling degree. For this purpose, algorithm 11.1 uses algorithm 11.2 that returns the smallest divisor just after an integer value. Algorithm 11.1 finds out the list of added registers among the remaining registers R

between the reuse circuits (the different values of $r_i \; \forall i = 1, k$), if such a list of added registers exists. It also returns a Boolean $success$ which takes the following values:

$$success = \begin{cases} \textbf{true if } \sum_{i=1}^{k} r_i \leq R \\ \textbf{false otherwise} \end{cases}$$

Algorithm 11.1. Fixed loop unrolling problem

Require: k: the number of reuse circuits; μ_i: the different weights of reuse circuits; $\mathcal{R}^t$: the number of architectural registers, and β: the loop unrolling degree

Ensure: the different added registers $r_1, \ldots, r_k$ with $\sum_{i=1}^{k} r_i \; minimal$ if it exists and a Boolean success

$R = \mathcal{R}^t - \sum_{1 \leq i \leq k} \mu_i$ {the remaining register}

sum $\leftarrow 0$

success $\leftarrow$ **true** {defines if we find a valid solution for the different added registers}

$i \leftarrow 1$ {represents the number of reuse circuits}

$D \leftarrow$ DIVISORS$(\beta, \mathcal{R}^t)$ {calculate the sorted list of divisors of β that are $\leq \mathcal{R}^t$ including β}

while $i \leq k \wedge success$ **do**

    $d_i \quad \leftarrow \quad$ DIV_NEAR(μ_i, D) {DIV_NEAR returns the smallest divisors of β greater or equal to μ_i}

    $r_i \leftarrow d_i - \mu_i$

    sum $\leftarrow$ sum $+ r_i$

    if sum $> R$ **then**

        success $\leftarrow$ **false**

    else

        $i \leftarrow i + 1$

    end if

end while

return $(r_1, \ldots, r_k)$, success

Algorithm 11.2. DIV_NEAR

Require: μ_i: the weight of the reuse circuits; $D = (d_1, \ldots, d_n)$: the n divisors of β sorted by ascending order

Ensure: d_i the smallest divisors of β greater or equal to μ_i

  $i \leftarrow 1$ {represents the index of the divisor of β}

  while $i \leq n$ **do**

    if $d_i \geq \mu_i$ **then**

      return (d_i)

    end if

    $i \leftarrow i + 1$

  end while

Algorithm 11.3. DIVISORS

Require: β: the loop unrolling degree; $\mathcal{R}^t$: the number of architectural registers
Ensure: D the list of the divisors of β that are $\leq \mathcal{R}^t$, including β
  bound $\leftarrow \min(\mathcal{R}^t, \beta/2)$
  $D \leftarrow \{1\}$
  for $d = 2$ to bound **do**
    if β mod $d = 0$ **then**
      $D \leftarrow D \cup \{d\}$ {Keep the list ordered in ascending order}
    end if
  end for
  $D = D \cup \{\beta\}$
  return (D)

11.4.2.1. *Analysis of the complexity of algorithm 11.1*

Below, we show that the maximal algorithmic complexity of algorithm 11.1 (*fixed loop unrolling problem*) is then dominated by the while loop, which is $\mathcal{O}((\mathcal{R}^t)^2)$.

– Regarding the DIVISORS algorithm:

  - the maximal number of iterations is bound $\leq \mathcal{R}^t$;

  - inserting an element inside the list costs at most $\log(\mathcal{R}^t)$;

  - the maximal complexity of DIVISORS algorithm is $O(\mathcal{R}^t \times \log(\mathcal{R}^t))$.

– Regarding the DIV_NEAR algorithm: $O(n) \leq O(\mathcal{R}^t)$.

– Regarding the fixed loop unrolling problem algorithm:

  - calling DIVISORS costs $O(\mathcal{R}^t \times \log(\mathcal{R}^t))$;

  - the while loop iterates at most $k \leq \mathcal{R}^t$ times;

  - at each iteration, calling DIV_NEAR costs $O(\mathcal{R}^t)$.

The solution of the *fixed loop unrolling problem* constitutes the basis of a solution for the *LCM-MIN problem* explained in the next section.

11.4.3. *Solution for LCM-MIN problem*

For the solution of the *LCM-MIN problem* (problem 11.2) we use the solution of the *fixed loop unrolling problem* and the result of lemma 11.3. According to lemma 11.3, the solution space S for ρ^* (the solution of the *LCM-MIN problem*) is bounded by ρ, the initial unroll factor.

$$\begin{cases} \forall i = 1, k : \rho^* \geq \mu_i \text{ (From Lemma 11.3)} \\ \rho^* \leq \rho \end{cases} \Rightarrow \max_{1 \leq i \leq k} \mu_i \leq \rho^* \leq \rho$$

In addition, ρ^* is a multiple of each $\mu_i + r_i$ with $0 \leq r_i \leq R$. If we assume that $\mu_k = \max_{1 \leq i \leq k} \mu_i$, then ρ^* is a multiple of $\mu_k + r_k$ with $0 \leq r_k \leq R$. Furthermore, the solution space S can be defined as follows:

$$S = \{\beta \in \mathbb{N} \mid \beta \text{ is multiple of } (\mu_k + r_k) \; \forall r_k = 0, R \; \wedge \; \mu_k \leq \beta \leq \rho\}$$

After describing the set S of all possible values of ρ^*, the minimal ρ^*, that is the solution for problem 11.2, is defined as follows:

$$\rho^* = \min\{\beta \in S \mid \exists (r_1, \ldots, r_k) \in \mathbb{N}^k \wedge lcm(\mu_1 + r_1, \ldots, \mu_k + r_k)$$

$$= \beta \wedge \sum_{i=1}^{k} r_i \leq R\}$$

Figure 11.7 portrays all values of the set S as a partial lattice. An arrow between two nodes means that the value in the first node is less than the value of the second node: $a \rightarrow b \implies a < b$. The value μ_k represents the value of the reuse circuit number k. Because we assumed that μ values are sorted in ascending order, μ_k is the highest weight of all reuse circuits. ρ is the initial loop unrolling value. Each node is a potential solution (β), which can be considered as the minimal loop unrolling degree. A dashed node cannot be a potential candidate because its value is greater than ρ. Let $\tau = \rho \; div \; \mu_k$ be the number of the lines of the lattice. Each line describes a set of multiples. For example, the line j describes a set of multiples $S_j = \{\beta \mid \exists r_k, 0 \leq r_k \leq R^t, \beta = j \times (\mu_k + r_k) \wedge \beta \leq \rho\}$.

In order to find ρ^*, the minimal unroll factor, our solution consists of checking if each node of S can be a solution for the *fixed loop unrolling problem*: finally, we are sure that the minimum of all these values is the minimal loop unrolling degree.

Despite traversing all the nodes of S, we describe in Figure 11.7 an efficient way to find the minimal ρ^*. We proceed line by line in the figure. In each line, we apply algorithm 11.1 to each node until the value of the predicate *success* returned by algorithm 11.1 is **true** or until we arrive at the last line when $\beta = \rho$. If the value β of the node i of the line j verifies the predicate (*success* = **true**), then we have two cases:

1) if the value of this node is less than the value of the first node of the next line, then we are sure that this value is optimal ($\rho^* = \beta$). This is because all the remaining nodes are greater than β (by construction of the lattice S);

2) else we have found a unroll factor less than the original ρ. We denote this new value by ρ' and we try once again to minimize it until we find the minimal (the first case). The search space shrinks: $S' = \{\beta \in \mathbb{N} \mid \forall r_k = 0..R : \beta \text{ is multiple of } (\mu_k + r_k) \wedge (j+1) \times \mu_k \leq \beta \leq \rho'\}$.

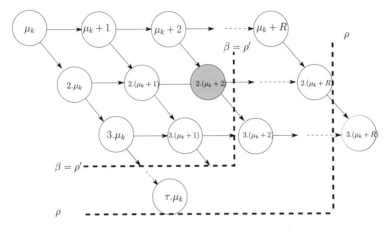

Figure 11.7. *How to traverse the lattice S*

Algorithm 11.4 implements our solution for the *LCM-MIN problem*. This algorithm minimizes the loop unrolling degree ρ, which is the LCM of k reuse circuits whose weights are $\mu_1, \ldots, \mu_k$. Our method is based on using the remaining registers R. This algorithm computes ρ^* the minimal value of loop unrolling degree and the minimal list $r_1, \ldots, r_k$ of the added registers to the different reuse circuits.

11.4.3.1. *Algorithmic complexity analysis of algorithm 11.4*

In the worst case, algorithm 11.1 is processed on all the nodes of the set S in Figure 11.7. The set S has $\frac{R \times \rho}{\mu_k}$ nodes ($\mu_k = \max \mu_i$ and $\rho = lcm(\mu_1, ..., \mu_k)$). We know that $1 \leq \mu_k \leq \mathcal{R}^t$. Consequently, the size of the set S is less than or equal to $\mathcal{R}^t \times \rho$. On each node, we process algorithm 11.1. Hence, the maximal algorithmic complexity of is $O(R \times \rho \times (\mathcal{R}^t)^2) = O(R \times (\mathcal{R}^t)^2 \times lcm(\mu_1, ..., \mu_k))$.

EXAMPLE 11.2.– Let us return to the example of Figure 11.5 , but we focus on the single register type t_1, and neglect the other register type t_2. Initially, there are two reuse circuits with two costs $\mu_1 = \mu^{t_1}(u_1, u_1) = 3$ and $\mu_2 = \mu^{t_1}(u_3, u_3) = 2$. Thus, as shown in example 11.1, the initial unroll factor is equal to $lcm(3, 2) = 6$. It is easy to see that if we increment the reuse distance $\mu^{t_1}(u_3, u_3)$ from 2 to 3, then the cost of the reuse circuit (u_3, u_3) becomes equal to 3, and hence the unroll factor becomes equal to $lcm(3, 3) = 3$ instead of 6. The new number of allocated registers becomes equal to $RC^{t_1} = 3 + 3$ instead of 5 initially. A valid kernel code generation with 6 registers of type t_1 and an unroll factor equal to 3 is given in listing 11.2.

Algorithm 11.4. LCM-MIN algorithm

Require: k: the number of reuse circuits; μ_i: the weights of the reuse circuits; $\mathcal{R}^t$: the number of architectural registers; ρ: the initial loop unrolling degree

Ensure: the minimal loop unrolling degree ρ^* and a list $r_1, \ldots, r_k$ of added registers with $\sum_{i=1}^{k} r_i$ minimal

$R = \mathcal{R}^t - \sum_{1 \leq i \leq k} \mu_i$ {The remaining registers}

$\rho^* \leftarrow \mu_k$ {minimal value of loop unrolling ρ^*}

if $\rho = \rho^* \vee R = 0$ **then**

    if $R = 0$ **then**

        $\rho^* \leftarrow \rho$ {ρ nothing can be done, no remaining registers}

    end if

else

    $r_k \leftarrow 0$ {number of registers added to the reuse circuit μ_k}

    $\beta \leftarrow \mu_k$ {value of the first node in the set S}

    $j \leftarrow 1$ {line number j in the set S}

    $\tau \leftarrow \rho \; div \; \mu_k$ {total number of lines in the set S}

    $stop \leftarrow$ **false** {$stop = true$ if the minimal is found}

    $success \leftarrow$ **false** {predicate returned by Algorithm 11.1}

    while $\beta \leq \rho \wedge \neg stop$ **do**

        {Traversing the set S until we find the minimal loop unrolling factor}

        $success \leftarrow Fixed\_Unrolling\_Problem(k, \mu_i, \mathcal{R}^t, \beta)$ {Apply for each node the algorithm 11.1}

        if $\neg success$ **then**

            if $r_k < R$ **then**

                r_k++ {we go to the next node on the same line}

            else

                $r_k \leftarrow 0$ {we go to the first node of the next line}

                j++

            end if

            $\beta \leftarrow j \times (\mu_k + r_k)$ {compute the new value of the potential new unrolling factor β}

            if $\beta > \rho \wedge j < \tau$ **then**

                {ignore the dashed node}

                $r_k \leftarrow 0$ {dashed node, we go to the first node of the next line}

                j++

                 $\beta \leftarrow j \times \mu_k$

            end if

        else

            $\rho^* \leftarrow \beta$ {β may be the minimal loop unrolling degree}

            if $\rho^* \leq (j+1) \times \mu_k$ **then**

                $stop \leftarrow$ **true** {we are sure that ρ^* is the minimal loop unrolling degree}

            else

                $\rho \leftarrow \rho^*$ {we find a new value of ρ to minimize}

                $\tau \leftarrow \rho \; div \; \mu_k$

                $r_k \leftarrow 0$

                j++

                $\beta \leftarrow j \times \mu_k$

            end if

        end if

    end while

end if

```
FOR  i=0,   i<N,   i=i+3
  u_1(i)    :  R1  = ...
  u_2(i)    :
  u_3(i)    :  R4  = R3...
  u_4(i)    :  ...= R4...

  u_1(i+1): R2  = ...
  u_2(i+1):
  u_3(i+1): R5  = R1...
  u_4(i+1): ...= R5...

  u_1(i+2): R3  = ...
  u_2(i+2):
  u_3(i+2): R6  = R2...
  u_4(i+2): ...= R6...
ENDFOR
```

Listing 11.2. *Example of a sequential kernel code generation for the register type t_1*

EXAMPLE 11.3.– Let us consider a more complex example with a set of five reuse circuits with the respective weights: $\mu_1 = 3, \mu_2 = 4, \mu_3 = 5, \mu_4 = 7, \mu_5 = 8$. The initial number of allocated registers is equal to $RC = 3 + 4 + 5 + 7 + 8 = 27$. The loop unrolling degree ρ is their LCM ($\rho = lcm(3, 4, 5, 7, 8) = 840$). Let us assume that we have $\mathcal{R}^t = 32$ architectural registers in the target processor. Hence, we have $R = 32 - 27 = 5$ remaining registers. By applying algorithm 11.4, we find that the minimal numbers of registers added to each reuse circuits are $r_1 = 1, r_2 = 0, r_3 = 3, r_4 = 1, r_5 = 0$. The new reuse circuits' weights become $\mu_1 = 3 + 1 = 4$, $\mu_2 = 4 + 0 = 4$, $\mu_3 = 5 + 3 = 8, \mu_4 = 7 + 1 = 8, \mu_5 + 0 = 8$. The new number of allocated registers become equal to $4 + 4 + 8 + 8 + 8 = 32$. The new unroll factor becomes equal to $\rho^* = lcm(4, 4, 8, 8, 8) = 8$, which means that we reduced it by a $ratio = \frac{\rho}{\rho^*} = 105$.

The next section extends the algorithm of unroll factor minimization to the case of multiple register types.

11.5. Unroll factor minimization in the presence of multiple register types

In the presence of multiple register types, minimizing the loop unrolling degree of each type separately does not lead to the minimal loop unrolling degree for the whole loop, as illustrated in the following example.

EXAMPLE 11.4.– Let us return to the example in Figure 11.5 on page 201. We want to minimize the loop unrolling degree of the initial reuse graph in Figure 11.5(b), where two register types t_1, t_2 are considered. The initial kernel loop unrolling degree $\rho = 12$ is the LCM of $\rho^{t_1} = 6$ and $\rho^{t_2} = 12$ which are, respectively, the LCM of the different reuse circuits weights for each register type. In this configuration, let us assume that we have $\mathcal{R}^{t_j} = 8$ available architectural registers in the processor for each register type t_j. Hence, we have $R^{t_1} = 8 - 5 = 3$ (resp $R^{t_2} = 1$) remaining registers for register type t_1 (resp t_2). By applying the loop unrolling minimization for each register type separately as studied in section 11.4, the minimal loop unrolling degree for each register type becomes: $\rho^{t_1*} = 3$ for register type t_1 and $\rho^{t_2*} = 4$ for register type t_2, see Figure 11.8(a). However, the global kernel loop unrolling degree is not minimal $\rho' = lcm(\rho^{t_1*}, \rho^{t_2*}) = 12$. The minimal global kernel loop unrolling degree is computed below.

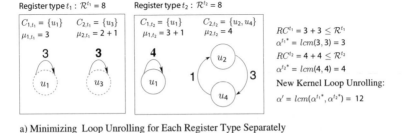

a) Minimizing Loop Unrolling for Each Register Type Separately

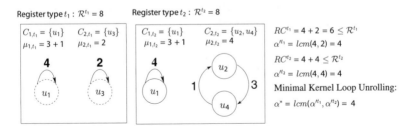

b) Minimizing Loop Unrolling for all Register Types Conjointly

Figure 11.8. *Modifying reuse graphs to minimize loop unrolling factor*

In Figure 11.8(b), we provide a solution where the minimal loop unrolling degree is $\rho^* = 4 < \rho'$. The unroll factor of t_1 is equal to 4, which is not its minimal value (equal to 3 as shown above). However, the global unroll factor that satisfies both t_1 and t_2 is minimal and equal to 4. The minimal number of registers added to each reuse circuit of each type are: $r_{1,t_1} = 1$, $r_{2,t_1} = 0$, $r_{1,t_2} = 1$, $r_{2,t_2} = 0$. Note that r_{i,t_j} is the number of registers added to the ith reuse circuit of the type t_j. Our method explained in the following sections guarantees that the new number of allocated registers will not exceed the number of architectural registers for each register type t_j.

Now, let us examine an example of a valid code generation associated to the reuse graphs of Figure 11.8(b), even though at this stage of compilation, the loop is not yet scheduled. Listing 11.3 shows a kernel code generation for the register type t_1 only: registers of type t_1 are given the prefix R. The number of allocated registers is $RC^{t_1} = 4 + 2 = 6$ and the unroll factor is equal to 4. Listing 11.4 shows a kernel code generation for the register type t_2 only: registers of type t_2 given the prefix S. The number of allocated registers is $RC^{t_2} = 4 + (1 + 3) = 8$ and the unroll factor is equal to 4. The kernel code generation that is correct for both t_1 and t_2 is given in listing 11.5 and the unroll factor is minimal and equal to 4: note that the statement u_1 has two destination registers of two distinct types, as previously illustrated in the DDG of Figure 11.5(a). As can be seen, the initial unroll factor was equal to 12, as computed in example 11.1 on page 202, we minimize it here to 4, which is the optimal value. We also guarantee that the number of extra registers used does not exceed the number of remaining registers.

```
FOR i=0,  i<N,  i=i+4
  u_1(i):  R1 =
  u_2(i):
  u_3(i):  R5 =   R4 +...
  u_4(i):  ...= R5 +...

  u_1(i+1):  R2 =
  u_2(i+1):
  u_3(i+1):  R6 = R1 +...
  u_4(i+1):...=  R6 +...

  u_1(i+2):  R3 =
  u_2(i+2):
  u_3(i+2):  R5= R2 +  ...
  u_4(i+2):...= R5 +...

  u_1(i+3):  R4=
  u_2(i+3):
  u_3(i+3):  R6 = R3 +...
  u_4(i+4):  ...= R6 +...
ENDFOR
```

Listing 11.3. *Kernel code generation for register type t_1*

```
FOR i=0,  i<N,  i=i+4
  u_1(i):  S1 =   S7 +...
  u_2(i):  S5 = S1 +...
  u_3(i):
```

```
u_4(i):  S6 = S8 + S5

u_1(i+1):  S2 = S8 +...
u_2(i+1):  S6 = S2 +...
u_3(i+1):
u_4(i+1):  S7= S5 + S6

u_1(i+2):  S3 = S5 +...
u_2(i+2):  S7 = S3 +...
u_3(i+2):
u_4(i+2):  S8 = S6 + S7

u_1(i+3):  S4 = S6 +...
u_2(i+3):  S8 = S4 +...
u_3(i+3):
u_4(i+4):  S5 = S7 + S8
ENDFOR
```

Listing 11.4. *Kernel code generation for register type t_2*

```
FOR i=0, i<N, i=i+4
 u_1(i):  R1,S1 =   S7
 u_2(i):  S5 = S1
 u_3(i):  R5 =   R4
 u_4(i):  S6 = S8 + S5 + R5

 u_1(i+1):  R2,S2 = S8
 u_2(i+1):  S6 = S2
 u_3(i+1):  R6 = R1
 u_4(i+1):  S7= S5 + S6 + R6

 u_1(i+2):  R3,S3 =  S5
 u_2(i+2):  S7 = S3
 u_3(i+2):  R5 =   R4
 u_4(i+2):  S8 = S6 + S7 + R5

 u_1(i+3):  R4,S4 =  S6
 u_2(i+3):  S8 = S4
 u_3(i+3):  R6 = R3
 u_4(i+4):  S5 = S7 + S8 + R6
ENDFOR
```

Listing 11.5. *Kernel code generation for the two register types conjointly*

The following section defines the search space S for the minimal kernel loop unrolling ρ^*.

11.5.1. *Search space for minimal kernel loop unrolling*

According to the properties of LCM and to the formulation of problem 11.1, the search space S for the minimal kernel loop unrolling ρ^* is bounded. In fact, three cases arise:

Case 1: No remaining registers for all the different register types. In this case, the initial loop unrolling degree cannot be minimized $\rho^* = \rho$.

Case 2: No remaining registers for some register types. Assume that ρ^j is the loop unrolling degree for the register type $t_j \in \mathcal{T}$. In this way, $\rho = lcm(\rho^1, \ldots, \rho^n)$. We define the subset $\mathcal{T}'$ which contains all the register types such that there are no remaining registers for these register types after periodic register allocation ($\mathcal{T}' \subset \mathcal{T}$ such that $\mathcal{T}' = \{t \in \mathcal{T} \mid R^t = 0\}$). If there are no registers left for these register types, we cannot minimize their loop unrolling degrees, see section 11.4. Therefore, the minimal global loop unrolling degree $\rho^* \geq \rho^j \ \forall \ t_j \in \mathcal{T}'$. By considering $\rho' = lcm_{t \in \mathcal{T}'}(\rho^t)$, we have the following inequality:

$$\rho' \leq \rho^* \leq \rho \tag{11.1}$$

In addition, from LCM properties:

$$\rho^* \text{ is multiple of } \rho' \tag{11.2}$$

From equations [11.1] and [11.2], the search space S is defined as follows:

$$S = \{\beta \in \mathbb{N} \mid \beta \text{ is multiple of } \rho' \ \wedge \ \rho' \leq \beta \leq \rho\}$$

Here, each value β can be a potential final loop unrolling degree.

Case 3: All register types have some remaining registers. From the associative property of LCM, we have:

$$\rho^* = lcm(lcm(\mu_{1,t_1} + r_{1,t_1}, \ldots, \mu_{k_1,t_1} + r_{k_1,t_1}), \ldots,$$
$$lcm(\mu_{1,t_n} + r_{1,t_n}, \ldots, \mu_{k_n,t_n} + r_{k_n,t_n}))$$
$$\Longrightarrow \rho^* = lcm(\mu_{1,t_1} + r_{1,t_1}, \ldots, \mu_{k_1,t_1} + r_{k_1,t_1}, \ldots, \mu_{1,t_n}$$
$$+ r_{1,t_n}, \ldots, \mu_{k_n,t_n} + r_{k_n,t_n})$$

The final loop unrolling factor ρ^* is a multiple of each updated reuse circuit weight ($\mu_{i,t_j} + r_{i,t_j}$) with the number of additional registers (r_{i,t_j}) varying from 0 (no added register for this circuit) to R^{t_j} (all the remaining registers are added to this reuse circuit).

Furthermore, if we assume that μ_{k_n,t_n} is the maximum weight of all the different circuits for all register types ($\mu_{k_n,t_n} = \max_{t_j} (\max_i \mu_{i,t_j})$) then ρ^* is a multiple of this specific updated circuit (ρ^* is a multiple of $(\mu_{k_n,t_n} + r_{k_n,t_n})$ with $0 \leq r_{k_n,t_n} \leq R^{t_n}$). We notice here that any reuse circuit satisfies this latter property, but it is preferable to consider the reuse circuit with a maximal weight because it decreases the cardinality of the search space S. Finally, the search space S can be stated as follows:

$$S = \{\beta \in \mathbb{N} \mid \beta \text{ is multiple of } (\mu_{k_n,t_n} + r_{k_n,t_n}),$$
$$\forall r_{k_n,t_n} = 0, R^{t_n} \wedge \mu_{k_n,t_n} \leq \beta \leq \rho\}$$

After describing the set S of all possible values of ρ^* (Case 2 and Case 3), the minimal kernel loop unrolling ρ^* is defined as follows:

$$\rho^* = \min\{\beta \in S | \forall t_j \in \mathcal{T}, \exists (r_{1,t_j}, \ldots, r_{k_j,t_j}) \in \mathbb{N}^{k_j} \text{ such that:}$$

β is the Common Multiple (CM) of the following updated reuse circuits weights:

$$\mu_{1,t_1} + r_{1,t_1}, \ldots, \mu_{k_1,t_1} + r_{k_1,t_1}, \ldots, \mu_{1,t_j} + r_{1,t_j}, \ldots, \mu_{k_j,t_j}$$
$$+ r_{k_j,t_j}, \ldots, \mu_{1,t_n} + r_{1,t_n}, \ldots, \mu_{k_n,t_n} + r_{k_n,t_n}$$
$$\wedge \sum_{i=1}^{k_j} r_{i,t_j} \leq R^{t_j}\}$$

Another problem arises here: how do we decide if the value β can be a potential new loop unrolling? Solving this problem is explained in the next section.

11.5.2. Generalization of the fixed loop unrolling problem in the presence of multiple register types

PROBLEM 11.4.– General fixed loop unrolling.– Let $\beta \in S$ be a fixed loop unrolling degree and let $\mathcal{T} = \{t_1, \ldots, t_n\}$ be the set of register types. β can be a potential new loop unrolling iff we find for each register type $t_j \in \mathcal{T}$, a minimal distribution of the remaining registers R^{t_j} between its reuse circuits (μ_{i,t_j}) such that this new loop unrolling degree β satisfies the following constraints:

1) $\beta = CM(\mu_{1,t_1} + r_{1,t_1}, \ldots, \mu_{k_1,t_1} + r_{k_1,t_1}, \ldots, \mu_{1,t_n} + r_{1,t_n}, \ldots, \mu_{k_n,t_n} + r_{k_n,t_n})$

2) $\forall t_j \in \mathcal{T} \; \sum_{i=1}^{k_j} r_{i,t_j} \leq R^{t_j}$: for each register type, the additional registers does not exceed the number of remaining registers.

In order to determine if β can be the new kernel loop unrolling, we propose generalizing the *fixed loop unrolling problem* solution to all register types. In fact, the different Constraints in problem 11.4 are the generalization of the *fixed loop unrolling problem* constraints which must be satisfied for all the register types.

In general, the *fixed loop unrolling problem* proposes to add to each reuse circuit μ_{i,t_j} of each register type t_j, a minimal number of registers r_{i,t_j} from the remaining R^{t_j} registers such that $\mu_{i,t_j} + r_{i,t_j}$ is the smallest divisor of the fixed loop unrolling β greater or equal to μ_{i,t_j}. In this way, if the additional registers, for each register type, do not exceed the number of remaining registers $\sum_{i=1}^{k_j} r_{i,t_j} \leq R^{t_j}$, then β can be the new loop unrolling degree.

By using the associative property of the common multiple, we have:

$$\beta = CM(\mu_{1,t_1} + r_{1,t_1}, \ldots, \mu_{k_1,t_1} + r_{k_1,t_1}, \ldots, \mu_{1,t_n} + r_{1,t_n}, \ldots, \mu_{k_n,t_n} + r_{k_n,t_n})$$

$$\Rightarrow \forall t_j \in \mathcal{T}, \ \beta \ \text{is a Common Multiple of} \ \mu_{1,t_j} + r_{1,t_j}, \ldots, \mu_{k_j,t_j} + r_{k_j,t_j}$$

Consequently, algorithm 11.5 implements our solution for problem 11.4 by reusing algorithm 11.1 previously defined.

The solution of the *general fixed loop unrolling problem* (problem 11.4) constitutes the basis of the solution for the *loop unrolling minimization problem* (problem 11.1) explained in the next section.

11.5.3. *Algorithmic solution for the loop unrolling minimization (LUM, problem 11.1)*

In order to compute the minimal kernel loop unrolling ρ^*, our solution consists of checking if each value β in the search space S can be a solution for the *fixed loop unrolling problem*: it is guaranteed that the minimum of all these values is the minimal loop unrolling degree.

Instead of computing all values β of S which satisfy the *general fixed loop unrolling problem* and finally taking the minimal one, we describe in Figure 11.9 an efficient way to find the minimal ρ^* depending on the construction of the lattice S. Figure 11.9 also illustrates the different cases of the construction of the solution space S. The value of each node represents a potential new loop unrolling degree and an arc between two nodes a, b $(a \rightarrow b)$ means that $a < b$. The absence of an arc between two nodes means that the order is unknown. The structure of the search space depends on the availability of the different types of registers:

Algorithm 11.5. General fixed loop unrolling problem

Require: $\beta \in S$ the fixed loop unrolling, $\mathcal{T} = \{t_1, \ldots, t_n\}$ the set of register types. For each register type t_j, we require the number k_j of reuse circuits, the different weights of reuse circuits μ_{i,t_j} the remaining register R^{t_j} and its initial loop unrolling degree ρ_j

Ensure: The Boolean $success$ and for each type t_j, the different added registers

$$r_{1,t_j}, \ldots, r_{k_j,t_j} \text{ with } \sum_{i=1}^{k_j} r_{i,t_j} \ minimal$$

$success \leftarrow$ **true** {defines if β can be the new kernel loop unrolling}

$j \leftarrow 1$ {represents the type t_j of T}

calculate the different divisors of β

while $j \leq n \wedge success$ **do**

  if $R^{t_j} = 0$ **then**

    if $\beta \mod \rho_j \neq 0$ **then**

      $success \leftarrow$ **false** {no optimization for the type t_j, the new unrolling degree must be a multiple of ρ_j}

    end if

  else

    $success \leftarrow Fixed\_Unrolling\_Problem(\beta, k_j, R^{t_j}, \mu_{1,t_j}, \ldots, r_{1,t_j}, \ldots)$

    {we don't calculate the different divisors of β inside the function}

  end if

  $j \leftarrow j + 1$

end while

– *Case 1 (no registers left for all the different register types)*: no loop unroll minimization is possible, $\rho^* = \rho$.

– *Case 2 (no registers left for some register types)*: ρ^* is multiple of ρ', we apply algorithm 11.5 to each node of Figure 11.9 until the predicate $success$ returned by this algorithm is **true** or until we reach the last node ρ.

– *Case 3: some registers left for all the different register types*: we traverse the set S in the same way as described in section 11.4. If we consider $\mu = \mu_{k_n,t_n}$ (maximum weight of all the different circuits for all register types) and $R = R^{t_n}$ (remaining registers for the register type t_n) then we traverse the set S by proceeding line by line. In each line, we apply algorithm 11.5 to each node in turn until the value of the predicate $success$ returned by this algorithm is **true** or until we arrive at the last line where $\beta = \rho$. If the value β of the node i of the line j verifies the predicate ($success = $ **true**), then we have two cases:

    a) If the value of this node is less than the value of the first node of the next line then we are sure that this value is optimal ($\rho^* = \beta$). This is because all the remaining nodes are greater than β (by construction of the set S).

b) Otherwise we have found a new value of unrolling degree which is less than the original ρ. We note this new value ρ" and we try once again to minimize it until we find the minimal (case a). The search space becomes smaller ($S' = \{\beta \in \mathbb{N} | \forall r = 0..R : \beta$ is multiple of $(\mu + r) \wedge (j + 1) \times \mu \leq \beta \leq \rho$"$\}$).

Case 1: No remaining registers for all register types

Case 2: No remaining registers for some register types

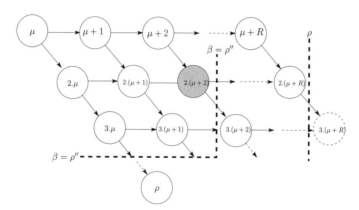

Case 3: Remaining registeres for all register types

Figure 11.9. *Loop unrolling values in the search space S*

After describing our solution for the LUM problem in the case of unscheduled loops, the next section studies the same problem but in the context of already scheduled loops.

11.6. Unroll factor reduction for already scheduled loops

When the SWP is fixed, circular lifetime intervals are known, and can be modelled using the meeting graph, as referred to in section 11.2.2.

If we base our unroll factor minimization method on the meeting graph rather than on the reuse graph, we lose in terms of generality of the unroll factor obtained, but we will see that we are able to reduce algorithmic complexity and the quality of the solution.

Figure 11.10 illustrates an example with a single register type. We want to reduce the loop unrolling degree of the five circuits of the meeting graph in Figure 11.10(b). The loop is already software pipelined with an $II = 5$ (the SWP is not drawn). According to the definition of the meeting graph, every node u corresponds to a variable (or to a dummy node to cover all the II period), and its weight $\omega(u)$ is simply its live range. For instance, $\omega(u_1 9) = 14$ means that it is alive during 14 clock cycles. As can be seen, this meeting graph has only one connected component, and MAXLIVE $= \frac{\sum_{\forall u} \omega(u)}{II} = 27$ (see Figure 11.10(a)). Then, the meeting graph is decomposed into elementary circuits (by following the different chords). Every elementary circuit C_i has a weight equal to $\mu_i = \frac{\sum_{u \in C_i} \omega(u)}{II}$. In the example of Figure 11.10(b), we have five elementary circuits with the following weights $\mu_1 = 3, \mu_2 = 4, \mu_3 = 5, \mu_4 = 7, \mu_5 = 8$. If we want to allocate exactly $RC =$ MAXLIVE $= 27$ registers, the kernel loop unrolling degree resulting from this decomposition is $\rho = lcm(\mu_1, \mu_2, \mu_3, \mu_4, \mu_5) = 840$, the LCM of the weights of the different circuits. However, this unroll factor is very large and it is impractical to allow the loop to be unrolled 840 times. The meeting graph proposes in this case to unroll the loop MAXLIVE times. This unroll factor is equal to 27, which is lower than 840 but is still too large. In order to reduce it, we apply the loop unrolling reduction for the meeting graph circuits. Let us assume that we have $\mathcal{R}^t = 32$ available architectural registers. Hence we have $R = \mathcal{R}^t - RC = 32 - 27 = 5$ remaining registers.

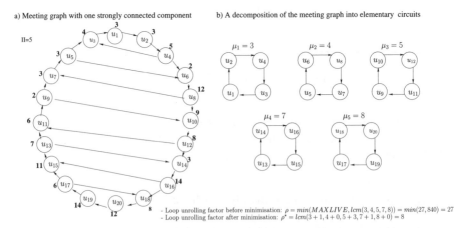

a) Meeting graph with one strongly connected component   b) A decomposition of the meeting graph into elementary circuits

- Loop unrolling factor before minimisation: $\rho = min(MAXLIVE, lcm(3,4,5,7,8)) = min(27,840) = 27$
- Loop unrolling factor after minimisation: $\rho^* = lcm(3+1, 4+0, 5+3, 7+1, 8+0) = 8$

Figure 11.10. *Example of loop unrolling reduction using meeting graph*

Once the meeting graph is decomposed into elementary circuits, this section aims to compute the minimal loop unrolling degree ρ^* for the software pipelined loop using the meeting graph framework. Here, the reader must be aware that this does not guarantee minimality for other possible decompositions of the meeting graph into elementary circuits. Computing the minimal unroll factor for any circuit decomposition of the meeting graph is a combinatorial open problem. So, in the context of this section, we consider a fixed decomposition of the meeting graph, we prefer to use the term *reduction* of unroll degree instead of minimization to avoid confusion.

As in the previous sections, we are willing to exploit the remaining registers, looking for a good distribution of these registers over all the different strongly connected components. In Figure 11.10(b), the final loop unrolling degree found with this method is $\rho^* = 8$ instead of 27 or 840. The minimal number of registers added to each circuit of the meeting graph are: $r_1 = 1$, $r_2 = 0$, $r_3 = 3$, $r_4 = 1$, $r_5 = 0$. Note that r_i is the number of registers added to the ith circuit of meeting graph.

The formal problem of loop unroll reduction in the context of meeting graph is almost the same as problem 11.1 (multiple register types) and problem 11.2 (single register types), except that MAXLIVE or MAXLIVE $+ 1$ are known to be valid unroll factors in the case of a single register type. In other words, if we have multiple register types, we are faced with problem 11.1 that we studied in section 11.5. If we have a single register type, then we have a unique defined MAXLIVE that we can use to improve the solution of problem 11.2. Consequently, the problem of unroll factor minimization in the context of scheduled loops can be stated as follows (for a single register type only).

PROBLEM 11.5.– LCM-RED in the Context of Meeting Graph.– Let R be the number of remaining registers after a periodic register allocation (PRA) performed by a meeting graph. Let be $\mu_1, \cdots, \mu_k \in \mathbb{N}$ be the weights of the different identified elementary circuits of the meeting graph used for PRA. Compute the added registers $r_1, \cdots, r_k$ such that:

- $\sum_{i \in [1,k]} r_i \leq R$ (validity constraint)

- $\rho^* = lcm(\mu_1 + r_1, \ldots, \mu_k + r_k)$ is minimal and

    - $\rho^* \leq$ MAXLIVE^t if the MG has a unique identified elementary circuits for PRA.

    - $\rho^* \leq$ MAXLIVE$^t + 1$ if the MG has multiple identified elementary circuits for PRA.

The next section explains our solution for problem 11.5.

11.6.1. *Improving algorithm 11.4 (LCM-MIN) for the meeting graph framework*

A meeting graph (MG) can have several strongly connected components of weight $\mu_1, \ldots, \mu_k \in \mathbb{N}$ (if there is only one connected component, its weight is $\mu_1 = \text{MAXLIVE}$). This leads to the upper bound of unrolling $\rho = lcm(\mu_1, \ldots, \mu_k)$. In addition, if $\rho > \text{MAXLIVE}$, the MG framework guarantees an upper bound of loop unrolling degree U_{max} equal to MAXLIVE or MAXLIVE $+ 1$. In fact, if the MG has one strongly connected component then the maximum loop unrolling degree is $U_{max} = \text{MAXLIVE}$. Otherwise, if it has several strongly connected components, Lelait *et al.* [EIS 95b] propose creating one strongly connected component by adding a complete circuit of unitary dummy intervals to the MG. One extra register is needed to achieve this, which yields to allocate MAXLIVE $+ 1$ registers by unrolling the loop $U_{max} = \text{MAXLIVE} + 1$. This one extra register is required to cyclically permute all the values in registers.

Moreover a possible lower bound for the unroll factor is computed by decomposing the MG into as many circuits as possible and then computing the LCM of their weights. However, in practice, the loop unrolling degree can be high even though the number of registers used is minimal.

Our result in this section consists in identifying a reduced loop unrolling degree ρ^* for a fixed periodic schedule using the MG technique. Given a fixed circuit decomposition of the MG, we use algorithm 11.4, looking for a good distribution of the remaining registers over all the different MG circuits. Having an upper bound for the loop unrolling degree (MAXLIVE or MAXLIVE $+ 1$), we reduce the search space S by computing all the possible new loop unrolling degrees β less than or equal to MAXLIVE or MAXLIVE $+ 1$, depending on whether the MG has one or more strongly connected components. Figure 11.11 describes the new search space S in the MG.

11.6.1.1. *Algorithmic complexity analysis for solving problem 11.5*

Our algorithm to solve problem 11.5 is very similar to algorithm 11.4, so we do not detail it here. The only difference resides in the fact that the solution space S of Figure 11.11 has shrunk compared to Figure 11.7. In the worst case, we visit each node in the set S. The set S has $R \times \frac{\text{MAXLIVE}}{\mu_k}$ nodes (respectively, $R \times \frac{\text{MAXLIVE}+1}{\mu_k}$). We know that MAXLIVE $\leq \mathcal{R}^t$ and $1 \leq \mu_k$. Thus, the maximal number of nodes is equal to $R \times \mathcal{R}^t$. Since we apply algorithm 11.1 on each node at most, the worst case complexity for solving problem 11.5 is equal to $O(R \times (\mathcal{R}^t)^3)$, which is better than the worst time complexity of algorithm 11.4 described in section 11.4.

11.7. Experimental results

All the algorithms presented in this chapter have been implemented and extensively tested, see Appendix 5. As explained in section 9.5, we followed two experimental scenarios: a stand-alone evaluation (independently from the compiler), and an integrated evaluation (inside a compilation flow). The stand-alone evaluation has been conducted on a single register type, while the integrated evaluation was done inside the st200cc compilation toolchain with multiple register types. This section presents our conclusions as follows:

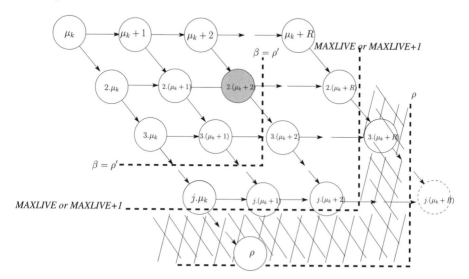

Figure 11.11. *The new search space S in the meeting graph*

– For stand-alone unscheduled DDG, with a single register type:

- While the maximal algorithmic complexity of algorithm 11.4 is exponential, its practical execution time on our benchmarks is fast enough to be considered inside a cross compiler. However, when we use randomly generated DDG, we found some rare case where the execution time is high (1,000 seconds).

- If the number of available registers is not fixed, and when we apply register minimization using SIRA, then the minimal unrolling degree is reached if we use only 12 additional registers in average. The harmonic average unrolling degree is then divided by two.

- If the number of available registers is fixed, and when we apply SIRA without register minimization (just bound the register requirement), then the harmonic average loop unrolling is divided by 1.41 on a machine with 32 registers, divided by 1.96 on a machine with 64 registers and divided by 2.71 on a machine with 128 registers. The average number of used additional registers is, respectively, 1, 3 and 14.

– For stand-alone scheduled DDG, with a single register type:

- Fixing a schedule of the loops helps to find lower unrolling degrees.

- After loop unroll degree minimization, we find that 75% of the scheduled loops do no longer require unrolling.

- The maximal minimized unroll factor was 63 if we have 64 available registers.

- The average minimized unroll factor is less than 1.5 in benchmarks, and for all the tested architectural configurations (the number of available registers was varied from 16 to 256).

– When we integrate loop unroll minimization inside st200cc with multiple register types:

- Minimizing the unroll degree of each register type separately leads to higher unrolling degree than if we tackle all the register types conjointly.

- The minimized unroll degree of half of the loops is under 3, and 75% of the loops has a minimized unroll degree less than 7.

- The maximal minimized loop unrolling factor is 50.

- Even if we apply loop unrolling for all loops, they all fit in the Icache capacity of the ST231 processor.

11.8. Related work

We review in this section some related work on code generation for periodic register allocation, that we did not deal with as part of the background in section 11.2. There is a very large body of literature on instruction scheduling, software pipelining, and register allocation. For instance, the authors in [PAR 91] already studied a suitable unrolling factor to produce rate-optimal SWP in data flow programs. That authors showed that the optimum loop unrolling factor is the least common multiple of the number of registers. In this section we review only research that deals specifically with register allocation and code generation of software pipelined loops.

11.8.1. *Rotating register files*

In order to generate a code for variables spanning multiple iterations, some processor architectures (Cydra, Itanium) provide hardware support called a *rotating register file* (RRF) [DEH 89, DEH 93]. RRF is a hardware mechanism to prevent successive lifetime intervals from being assigned to the same physical registers. Consider the following example:

LOOP
$$a[i + 2] = a[i] + 1$$
ENDLOOP

In this example, variable $a[i]$ spans three iterations (defined in iteration $i - 2$ and used in iteration i). Hence, at least 3 physical registers are needed to carry simultaneously $a[i]$, $a[i + 1]$ and $a[i + 2]$. A rotating register file R automatically performs the move operation at each iteration. R acts as a FIFO buffer. The major advantage is that instructions in the generated code see all live values of a given variable through a single operand, avoiding explicit register copying. Below $R[k]$ denotes a register with offset k from R.

$$\text{Iteration } i \quad \text{Iteration } i + 2$$
$$R = R[-2] + 1 \quad R[+2] = R + 1$$

Using an RRF avoids increasing code size due to loop unrolling, or to decrease the computation throughput due to the insertion of move operations.

11.8.2. *Inserting* move *operations*

This method is also called *register renaming*. Considering the previous example, we use 3 registers to allocate $a[i]$ and perform move operations at the end of each iteration [NIC 92a]: $a[i]$ in register $R1$, $a[i + 1]$ in register $R2$ and $a[i + 2]$ in register $R3$. Then we use move operations to shift registers across the register file at every iteration:

LOOP
$$R3 = a[i] + 1$$
$$a[i + 2] = R1 + 2$$
$$R1 = R2$$
$$R2 = R3$$
ENDLOOP

However, it is easy to see that if variable v spans d iterations, we have to insert $d - 1$ extra move operations *at each iteration*. In addition, this may increase the II and may require rescheduling the code if these move operations do not fit into the kernel. This is generally unacceptable as it negates most of the benefits of software pipelining.

11.8.3. *Loop unrolling after software pipelining*

Without RRF and inserting copy operations, loop unrolling is more suitable for maintaining II. The resulted loop body itself is bigger but no extra operations are executed in comparison with the original code. MVE has already been explained. Other work proposes to implement a generalized form of modulo expansion in [DIN 97c, HEN 92], but with the same limitation of MVE, that is $RC^t \geq \text{MAXLIVE}^t$ without proving a formal upper-bound on RC^t. Since we base our approach on reuse graphs and meeting graphs, we are able to guarantee that $\mathcal{R}^t \geq RC^t \geq \text{MAXLIVE}^t$.

11.8.4. *Code generation for multidimensional loops*

Instruction level parallelism (ILP) scheduling is a special case of the general k-periodic multidimensional scheduling problem. Indeed, SWP is the special case when the scheduling period is unique and integral. The case of multidimensional memory storage optimization is also interesting if we target regular loop nests for high performance codes [ALA 05]. Using registers instead of memory cells is a special case studied in [RON 08]. Multidimensional approaches are more appropriate for regular computer intensive codes: 1) our target loops are one-dimensional at the backend level, where the compiler has broken the multidimensional structure of the loop nest. 2) The exact mathematical relationship between MAXLIVE^t, II and the unrolling factor is not known yet in the case of multidimensional instruction scheduling. That is, the problem of optimal register allocation in multidimensional loops with minimal unroll factor is still an open problem; a sub-optimal heuristic for this problem is presented in [RON 08]. 3) The code size needed to optimally exploit ILP and registers in multidimensional loop nests is more complex to model with a single unroll factor. Indeed, code generation in this case uses multidimensional unroll factors [BAS 04, VAS 06], that may in theory create a larger code size than a one-dimensional innermost loop.

11.9. Conclusion on loop unroll degree minimization

In the absence of rotating register files, periodic register allocation asks to unroll the SWP kernel in order to generate spill-free or move-free code. Inside some compilers, the classical modulo variable expansion was used until recently because it generates low unrolling factors but with the risk of introducing unnecessary spill code. On the other hand, the meeting graph approach guarantees that the unrolled loop requires exactly MAXLIVE registers but with the risk of higher unroll factors.

This chapter shows how to solve this open dilemma. First, we guarantee that the number of required registers in the unrolled SWP kernel does not exceed the number of available registers. Second, we formalize the problem of minimal loop unrolling relying on the remaining registers after periodic register allocation. We provide an algorithm to compute the minimal unroll factor.

The problem of minimal unroll factor computation differs if we consider a single or multiple register types, or if we consider scheduled or unscheduled loops. We provided an algorithmic solution for all these variants, and we showed that all are based on a minimization problem of a least common multiple, called LCM-MIN. If the target architecture contains a single register type, then loop unroll minimization amounts to minimize a single least common multiple. If the processor contains multiple register types, then we proved that minimizing the unroll factor of each register type does not separately lead to a global minimum. Consequently we proposed an adapted algorithm based on LCM minimization that optimizes the global unroll factor. If the loops are not scheduled, then our minimization method is plugged as a postpass to SIRA. If the loops are scheduled, then our loop reduction method is plugged as a postpass to meeting graphs. Choosing between the two previous techniques depends on the compiler design flow (each compiler has its phase ordering decision).

The worst case performance of our LCM-MIN algorithm is exponential. However, our solution is fast in practice, and inputs that result in exponential running time are very rare: indeed, it did not happen in the standard benchmarks we experimented with, and seldom with random DDG generation. However, two open problems remain, despite numerous contacts with number theory and combinatorics experts: the first one is to prove that the problem is (or is not) computationally hard in the worst case; the second problem is to find the average case complexity of our current algorithm.

Concerning the experimental evaluation, we carefully studied the efficiency of our method in stand-alone and integrated context. For a stand-alone context, independently of the compiler and the architecture, we demonstrated that our unroll factor minimization is fast and the final resulted unrolling degrees are satisfactory in almost all cases. Nevertheless, we noticed that some loops still require high unrolling degrees even after our optimization. These occasional high unrolling degrees suggest that it may be worthwhile to consider combining the insertion of move operations with kernel unrolling.

For an integrated context, we plugged our solution inside st200cc compiler for ST231 VLIW processors. We compiled all C and C++ applications from FFMPEG, MEDIABENCH, SPEC2000 and SPEC2006. We demonstrated that: (1) our loop unrolling minimization is fast enough to be included inside an interactive commercial quality cross compiler. (2) The resulting loop unrolling factors are satisfactory. As a side-result of this work, we notice that the presence of rotating registers files is not really necessary, as loop unrolling seems to be a satisfactory solution to generate code after periodic register allocation. Nevertheless, we noticed that some loops still require high unrolling degrees even after our optimization.

PART 4

Epilog: Performance, Open Problems

Epilog: Performance Open Problems

12

Statistical Performance Analysis: The Speedup-Test Protocol

Numerous code optimization methods are usually experimented by doing multiple observations of the initial and the optimized execution times in order to declare a speedup. Even with a fixed input and execution environment, program execution times vary in general. Hence, different kinds of speedups may be reported: the speedup of the average execution time, the speedup of the minimal execution time, the speedup of the median, etc. Many published speedups in the literature are observations of a set of experiments. To improve the reproducibility of the experimental results, this chapter presents a rigorous statistical methodology regarding program performance analysis. We rely on well-known statistical tests (Shapiro–Wilk's test, Fisher's F-test, Student's t-test, Kolmogorov–Smirnov test and Wilcoxon–Mann–Whitney test) to study whether the observed speedups are statistically significant or not. By fixing $0 < \alpha < 1$ a desired risk level, we are able to analyze the statistical significance of the average execution time as well as the median. We can also check if $\mathbb{P}[X > Y] > \frac{1}{2}$, the probability that an individual execution of the optimized code is faster than the individual execution of the initial code. Our methodology defines a consistent improvement compared to the usual performance analysis method in high-performance computing as in [JAI 91, LIL 00]. The Speedup-Test protocol certifying the observed speedups with rigorous statistics is implemented and distributed as an open-source tool based on R software in [TOU 10] and published in [TOU 13b].

12.1. Code performance variation

The community of program optimization and analysis, code performance evaluation, parallelization and optimizing compilation has, for many decades, published numerous research and engineering articles in major conferences and journals. These articles study efficient algorithms, strategies and techniques to accelerate program execution times, or to optimize other performance metrics (MIPS, code size, energy/power, MFLOPS, etc.). The efficiency of a code optimization technique is generally published according to two principles, not necessarily disjoint. The first principle is to provide a mathematical proof given a theoretical model that the published research result is correct and/or efficient: this is the difficult part of research in computer science, since if the model is too simple, it would not represent the real world, and if the model is too close to the real world, the mathematics becomes too complex to digest. The second principle is to propose and implement a code optimization technique and to practice it on a set of chosen benchmarks in order to evaluate its efficiency. This chapter concerns the last point: how can we convince the community by rigorous statistics that the experimental study publishes fair and reproducible results.

Part of the non-reproducibility of the published experiments is explained by the fact that the observed speedups are sometimes "rare" events. It means that they are far from what we could observe if we redo the experiments multiple times. Even if we take an ideal situation where we use exactly the original experimental machines and software, it is sometimes difficult to reproduce exactly the same performance numbers again and again, experience after experience. Since some published performance numbers represent exceptional events, we believe that if a computer scientist succeeds in reproducing the performance numbers of his colleagues (with a reasonable error ratio), it would be equivalent to what rigorous probabilists and statisticians call a "surprise". We argue that it is better to have a lower speedup that can be reproduced in practice than a rare speedup that can be remarked by accident.

One of the reasons for the non-reproducibility of the results is the variation of execution times of the same program given the same input and the same experimental environment. With the massive introduction of multi-core architectures, we observe that the variations of execution times become exacerbated because of the complex dynamic features influencing the execution: affinity and threads scheduling policy, synchronization barriers, resource sharing between threads, hardware mechanisms for speculative execution, etc. Consequently, if you execute a program (with a fixed input and environment) n times, it is possible to obtain n really distinct execution times. To illustrate this, we consider the experiments published in [MAZ 10]. We use the violin plot[1] in Figure 12.1 to report the execution times of some SPEC OMP 2001 applications compiled with gcc. When we use thread-level parallelism (two or more threads), the execution time decreases overall but with a deep disparity. Consider, for instance, the case of swim. The version with two threads runs between 76 and 109 s, and the version with four threads runs between 71 and 90 s. This variability is also present when swim is compiled with icc (the Intel C compiler). The example of wupwise in Figure 12.1 is also interesting. The version with two threads runs between 376 and 408 s, and the version with six threads runs

---

1 The violin plot is similar to box plots, except that they also show the probability density of the data at different values.

between 187 and 204 s. This disparity between the distinct execution times of the same program with the same data input cannot be justified by accidents or experimental hazards because we can observe that the execution times are not normally distributed and frequently have a bias.

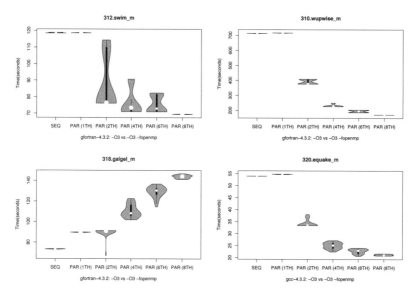

Figure 12.1. *Observed execution times of some SPEC OMP 2001 applications (compiled with gcc)*

What makes a binary program execution time vary, even if we use the same data input, the same binary and the same execution environment? Here are some factors:

1) factors intrinsic to the program itself: synchronization functions, OS calls, etc.;

2) factors related to the execution environment: loaded machine, starting stack address in the memory, variable CPU frequency, dynamic voltage scaling, thread pinning on cores, etc.;

3) factors related to the processor micro-architecture: cache effects, out of order execution, automatic data prefetching, speculative execution, branch prediction, etc.;

4) factors related to the performance measurement: noise of measuring, imprecision of the measurement, etc.

It is very difficult to control the complex combination of all the above influencing factors, especially on a supercomputer where the user is not allowed to have a root access to the machine. Consequently, if someone executes a program (with a fixed input and experimental environment) n times, it is possible to obtain n distinct execution times. The mistake is to assume that these variations are minor, and stable in general. The variations of execution times is something that we observe everyday, we cannot neglect them, but we can analyze them statistically with rigorous methodologies. Customary behavior in the community is to replace all the n execution times by a single value, such as the minimum, the mean, the median or the maximum, losing important data on variability and prohibiting the generation of statistics.

This chapter presents a rigorous statistical protocol to compare the performances of two code versions of the same application. While we consider that the performance of a program is measured by its execution time, our methodology is general and can be applied to other metrics of performance (energy consumption, for instance). It is important, however, to notice that our methodology applies for a *continuous* model of performance, not a discrete model. In a continuous model, we do not exclude integer values for measurements (that may be observed due to sampling), but we consider them as continuous data. We must also highlight that the name "Speedup-Test" does not rely on the usual meaning of statistical testing. Here, the term "test" in the "Speedup-Test" title is employed because our methodology makes intensive usage of proved statistical tests, and we do not define a new one.

This chapter is organized as follows: section 12.2 defines the background and notations needed for the chapter. Section 12.3 describes the core of our statistical methodology for the performance comparison between two code versions. Section 12.4 gives a quick overview on the free software we released for this purpose, called `SpeedupTest`. Section 12.5 shows how we can estimate the chance that the code optimization would provide a speedup on a program not belonging to the initial sample of benchmarks used for experiments. Section 12.6 describes some test cases and experiments using `SpeedupTest`. Section 12.7 discusses some related work before we conclude. In order to improve the fluidity and the readability of the chapter, we detail some notions in the appendix, making the chapter self-contained.

12.2. Background and notations

Let C be an initial code, let C' be a transformed version after applying the program optimization technique. Let I be a fixed data input for the programs C and C'. If we execute the program $C(I)$ n times, it is possible that we obtain n distinct execution times. Let X be the random variable representing the execution time of $C(I)$. Let $\mathcal{X} = \{x_1, \cdots, x_n\}$ be a sample of observations of X, i.e the set of the observed execution times when executing $C(I)$ n times. The transformed code C' can be executed m times with the *same* data input I producing m execution times too. Similarly, let Y be the random variable representing its execution time. Let $\mathcal{Y} = \{y_1, \cdots, y_m\}$ be a sample of observations of Y, it contains the m observed execution times of the code $C'(I)$.

The theoretical means of X and Y are denoted as μ_X and μ_Y, respectively. The theoretical medians of X and Y are denoted $\text{med}(X)$ and $\text{med}(Y)$. The theoretical variances are denoted as σ_X^2 and σ_Y^2. The cumulative distribution functions (CDF) are denoted $F_X(a) = \mathbb{P}[X \leq a]$ and $F_Y(a) = \mathbb{P}[Y \leq a]$, where $\mathbb{P}[X \leq a]$ is the notation used for the probability that $X \leq a$. The probability density functions are denoted as $f_X(x) = \frac{dF_X(x)}{dx}$ and $f_Y(y) = \frac{dF_Y(y)}{dy}$.

Since X and Y are two samples, their sample means are denoted as $\bar{X} = \frac{1}{n} \sum_{i=1}^{n} x_i$ and $\bar{Y} = \frac{1}{m} \sum_{i=1}^{m} y_i$, respectively. The sample variances are denoted as s_X^2 and s_Y^2. The sample medians of X and Y are denoted $\overline{\text{med}}(X)$ and $\overline{\text{med}}(Y)$.

After collecting X and Y (the sets of execution times of the codes $\mathcal{C}(I)$ and $\mathcal{C}'(I)$, respectively, for the same data input I), a simple definition of the speedup [HEN 02] sets it as $\frac{X}{Y}$. In reality, since X and Y are random variables, the definition of a speedup becomes more complex. Ideally, we must analyze the probability density functions of X, Y and $\frac{X}{Y}$ to decide whether an observed speedup is statistically significant or not. Since this is not an easy problem, multiple types of observed speedups are usually reported in practice to simplify the performance analysis:

1) The observed speedup of the minimal execution times:

$$\text{spmin}(\mathcal{C}, I) = \frac{\min_i x_i}{\min_j y_j}$$

2) The observed speedup of the mean (average) execution times:

$$\text{spmean}(\mathcal{C}, I) = \frac{\bar{X}}{\bar{Y}} = \frac{\sum_{1 \leq i \leq n} x_i}{\sum_{1 \leq j \leq m} y_j} \times \frac{m}{n}$$

3) The observed speedup of the median execution times:

$$\text{spmedian}(\mathcal{C}, I) = \frac{\overline{\text{med}}(X)}{\overline{\text{med}}(Y)}$$

Usually, the community publishes the best speedup among those observed, without any guarantee of reproducibility. In the below are our opinions on each of the above speedups:

– Regarding the observed speedup of the minimal execution times, we do not advise its use for many reasons. Appendix A of [TOU 10] explains why using the observed minimal execution time is not a fair choice regarding the chance of reproducing the result.

– Regarding the observed speedup of the mean execution time, it is well understood in statistical analysis but remains sensitive to outliers. Consequently, if the program under optimization study is executed a few times by an external user, the latter may not be able to observe the reported average. However, the average execution time is commonly accepted in practice.

– Regarding the observed speedup of the median execution times, it is the one that is used by the SPEC organization [STA 06]. Indeed, the median is a better choice for reporting speedups, because the median is less sensitive to outliers. Furthermore, some practical cases show that the distribution of the execution times are skewed, making the median a better candidate for summarizing the execution times into a single number.

The previous speedups are defined for a single application with a fixed data input $C(I)$. When multiple benchmarks are tested, we are sometimes faced with the need of reporting an *overall speedup* for the whole set of benchmarks. Since each benchmark may be very different from the other or may be of distinct importance, sometimes a weight $W(C_j)$ is associated with a benchmark C_j. After running and measuring the speed of every benchmark (with multiple runs of the same benchmark), we define $\texttt{ExecutionTime}(C_j, I_j)$ as the considered execution time of the code C_j having I_j as data input. $\texttt{ExecutionTime}(C_j, I_j)$ replaces all the observed execution times of $C_j(I_j)$ with one of the usual functions (mean, median and minimal), i.e. the mean or the median or the minimal of the observed execution times of the code C_j. The overall observed speedup of a set of b benchmarks is defined by the following equation:

$$S = \frac{\sum_{j=1,b} W(C_j) \times \texttt{ExecutionTime}(C_j, I_j)}{\sum_{j=1,b} W(C_j) \times \texttt{ExecutionTime}(C'_j, I_j)} \qquad [12.1]$$

This speedup is a global measure of the acceleration of the execution time. Alternatively, some users prefer to consider G the *overall gain*, which is a global measure of how much (in percentage) the overall execution time has been reduced:

$$G = 1 - \frac{\sum_{j=1,b} W(C_j) \times \texttt{ExecutionTime}(C'_j, I_j)}{\sum_{j=1,b} W(C_j) \times \texttt{ExecutionTime}(C_j, I_j)} = 1 - \frac{1}{S} \qquad [12.2]$$

Depending on which function has been used to compute $\texttt{ExecutionTime}(C_j, I_j)$, we speak about the overall speedup and gain of the average execution time, median execution time or minimal observed execution time.

All the above speedups are observation metrics based on samples that do not guarantee their reproducibility since we are not sure about their statistical significance. Section 12.3 studies the question for the average and median execution times. Studying the statistical significance of the speedup of the minimal execution time remains a difficult open problem in non-parametric statistical theory (unless the probability density function is known, which is not the case in practice).

12.3. Analyzing the statistical significance of the observed speedups

The observed speedups are performance numbers observed once (or multiple times) on a sample of executions. Does this mean that other executions would conclude with similar speedups? How can we be sure about this question if no mathematical proof exists, and with which confidence level? This section answers this question and shows that we can test if $\mu_X > \mu_Y$ and if med$(X) >$ med(Y). For the remainder of this section, we define $0 < \alpha < 1$ as the risk (probability) of error, which is the probability of announcing a speedup that does not really exist (even if it is observed on a sample). Conversely, $(1 - \alpha)$ is the usual confidence level. Usually, α is a small value (for instance, $\alpha = 5\%$).

The reader must be aware that in statistics, the risk of error is included in the model; therefore, we are not always able to decide between two contradictory situations (contrary to logic where a quantity cannot be true and false at the same time). Furthermore, the misuse of language defines $(1 - \alpha)$ as a confidence level, while this is not exactly true in the mathematical sense. Indeed, there are two types of risks when we use statistical tests; Appendix A7.2 describes these two risks and discusses the notion of the confidence level. We often say that a statistical test (normality test, Student's test, etc.) concludes favorably by a confidence level $(1 - \alpha)$ because it did not succeed in rejecting the tested hypothesis with a risk level equal to α. When a statistical test does not reject a hypothesis with a risk equal to α, there is usually no proof that the contrary is true with a confidence level of $(1 - \alpha)$. This way of reasoning is admitted for all statistical tests since in practice it works well.

12.3.1. *The speedup of the observed average execution time*

Having two samples $\mathcal{X}$ and $\mathcal{Y}$, deciding if μ_X the theoretical mean of X is higher than μ_Y, the theoretical mean of Y with a confidence level $1 - \alpha$ can be done due to the Student's t-test [JAI 91]. In our situation, we use the one-sided version of the Student's t-test and not the two-sided version (since we want to check whether the mean of X is greater than the mean of Y, not to test if they are simply distinct). Furthermore, the observation $x_i \in \mathcal{X}$ does not correspond to another observation $y_j \in \mathcal{Y}$; so we use the unpaired version of the Student's t-test.

12.3.1.1. *Remark on the normality of the distributions of X and Y*

The mathematical proof of the Student's t-test is valid for Gaussian distributions only [SAP 90, BRO 02]. If X and Y are not from Gaussian distributions (normal is synonymous to Gaussian), then the Student's t-test is known to stay robust for large samples (due to the central limit theorem), but the computed risk α is not exact [BRO 02, SAP 90]. If X and Y are not normally distributed and are small samples, then we cannot conclude with the Student's t-test.

12.3.1.2. *Remark on the variances of the distributions of X and Y*

In addition to the Gaussian nature of X and Y, the original Student's t-test was proved for populations with the same variance ($\sigma_X^2 \approx \sigma_Y^2$). Consequently, we also need to check whether the two populations X and Y have the same variance by using the Fisher's F-test, for instance. If the Fisher's F-test concludes that $\sigma_X^2 \neq \sigma_Y^2$, then we must use a variant of Student's t-test that considers Welch's approximation of the degree of freedom.

12.3.1.3. *The size needed for the samples X and Y*

The question now is to know what is a *large* sample. Indeed, this question is complex and cannot be answered easily. In [LIL 00, JAI 91], a sample is said to be large when its size exceeds 30. However, that size is well known to be arbitrary, it is commonly used for a numerical simplification of the test of Student[2]. Note that $n > 30$ is not a size limit needed to guarantee the robustness of the Student's t-test when the distribution of the population is not Gaussian, since the t-test remains sensitive to outliers in the sample. Appendix C in [TOU 10] gives a discussion on the notion of *large* sample. In order to set the ideas, let us consider that $n > 30$ defines the size of large samples: some books devoted to practice [LIL 00, JAI 91] write a limit of 30 between small ($n \leq 30$) and large ($n > 30$) samples.

12.3.1.4. *Using the Student's t-test correctly*

H_0, the null hypothesis that we try to reject (in order to declare a speedup) by using Student's t-test, is that $\mu_X \leq \mu_Y$, with an error probability (of rejecting H_0 when H_0 is true, i.e. when there is no speedup) equal to α. If the test rejects this null hypothesis, then we can accept H_a the alternative hypothesis $\mu_X > \mu_Y$ with a confidence level $1 - \alpha$ (Appendix A7.2 explains the exact meaning of the term *confidence level*). The Student's t-test computes a p-value, which is the smallest probability of error to reject the null hypothesis. If p-value$\leq \alpha$, then the Student's t-test rejects H_0 with a risk level lower than α. Hence, we can accept H_a with a confidence level $(1-\alpha)$. Appendix A7.2 gives more details on hypothesis testing in statistics, and on the exact meaning of the confidence level.

---

2 When $n > 30$, the Student distribution begins to be correctly approximated by the standard Gaussian distribution, making it possible to consider z values instead of t values. This simplification is out of date, it has been made in the past when statistics used to use precomputed printed tables. Nowadays, computers are used to numerically compute real values of all distributions, so we no longer need to simplify the Student's t-test for $n > 30$. For instance, the current implementation of the Student's t-test in the statistical software R does not distinguish between small and large samples, contrary to what is explained in [JAI 91, LIL 00].

As explained before, the correct usage of the Student's t-test is conditioned by:

1) If the two samples are large enough (say $n > 30$ and $m > 30$), use of the Student's t-test is admitted but the computed risk level α may not be preserved if the underlying distributions of X and Y are too far from being normally distributed ([HOL 73, p. 71]).

2) If one of the two samples is small (say, $n \leq 30$ or $m \leq 30$):

a) If X or Y does not follow Gaussian distribution with a risk level α, then we cannot conclude about the statistical significance of the observed speedup of the average execution time.

b) If X and Y follow Gaussian distributions with a risk level α, then:

- If X and Y have the same variance with a risk level α (tested with Fisher's F-test), then use the original procedure of the Student's t-test.

- If X and Y do not have the same variance with a risk level α, then use Welch's version of the Student's t-test procedure.

The detailed description of the Speedup-Test protocol for the average execution time is illustrated in Figure 12.2.

The problem with the average execution time is its sensibility to outliers. Furthermore, the average is not always a good indicator of the observed execution time felt by the user. In addition, the Student's test has been proved only for Gaussian distributions, while it is rare in practice to observe them for program execution times [MAZ 10]: the usage of the Student's t-test for non-Gaussian distributions is admitted for large samples but the risk level is no longer guaranteed.

The median is generally preferable to the average for summarizing the data into a single number. The next section shows how to check if the speedup of the median is statistically significant.

12.3.2. *The speedup of the observed median execution time, as well as individual runs*

This section presents the Wilcoxon–Mann–Whitney [HOL 73] test, a robust statistical test to check whether the median execution time has been reduced or not after a program transformation. In addition, the statistical test we are presenting also checks whether $\mathbb{P}[X > Y] > 1/2$, as is proved in Appendix D of [TOU 10, p. 35]: this is a very good information for the real speedup felt by the user ($\mathbb{P}[X > Y] > 1/2$ means that there is more chance that a single random run of the optimized program will be faster than a single random run of the initial program).

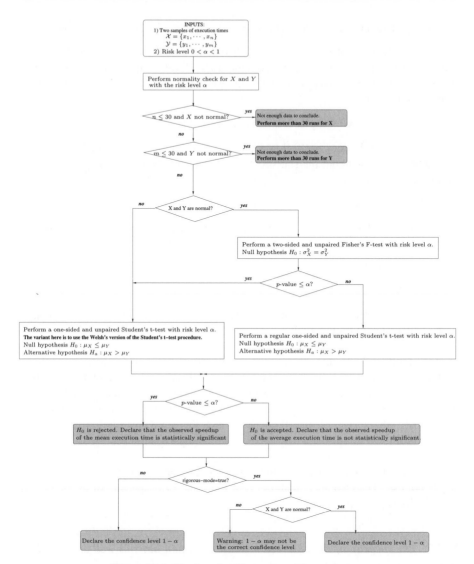

Figure 12.2. *The Speedup-Test protocol for analyzing the average execution time*

Contrary to the Student's t-test, the Wilcoxon–Mann–Whitney test does not assume any specific distribution for X and Y. The mathematical model [HOL 73,

p. 70] imposes that the distributions of X and Y differ only by a location shift Δ; in other words, that

$$F_Y(t) = \mathbb{P}\left[Y \leq t\right] = F_X(t + \Delta) = \mathbb{P}\left[X \leq t + \Delta\right] \quad (\forall t)$$

Under this model (known as the *location model*), the location shift equals $\Delta = \text{med}(X) - \text{med}(Y)$ (as well as $\Delta = \mu_X - \mu_Y$ in fact) and X and Y consequently do not differ in dispersion. If this constraint is not satisfied, then as admitted for the Student's t-test, the Wilcoxon–Mann–Whitney test can still be used for large samples in practice but the announced risk level may not be preserved. However, two advantages of this model is that the normality is no longer needed and that assumptions on the sign of Δ can be readily interpreted in terms of $\mathbb{P}\left[X > Y\right]$.

To check if X and Y satisfy the mathematical model of the Wilcoxon–Mann–Whitney test, a possibility is to use Kolmogorov–Smirnov's two-sample test [CON 71] as described below.

12.3.2.1. *Using the test of Kolmogorov–Smirnov at first step*

The objective is to test the null hypothesis H_0 of the equality of the distributions of the variables $X - \text{med}(X)$ and $Y - \text{med}(Y)$, using the Kolmogorov–Smirnov's two-sample test applied to the observations $x_i - \overline{\text{med}}(X)$ and $y_j - \overline{\text{med}}(Y)$. The Kolmogorov–Smirnov test computes a p-value: if p-value $\leq \alpha$, then H_0 is rejected with a risk level α. That is, X and Y do not satisfy the mathematical model needed by the Wilcoxon–Mann–Whitney test. However, as said before, we can still use the test in practice for sufficiently large samples but the risk level may not be preserved [HOL 73].

12.3.2.2. *Using the test of Wilcoxon–Mann–Whitney*

As done previously with the Student's t-test for comparing between two averages, here we want to check whether the median of X is greater than the median of Y, and if $\mathbb{P}\left[X > Y\right] > \frac{1}{2}$. This requires us to use the one-sided variant of the Wilcoxon–Mann–Whitney test. In addition, since the observation x_i from X does not correspond to an observation y_j from Y, we use the unpaired version of the test.

We set the null hypothesis H_0 of Wilcoxon–Mann–Whitney test as $F_X \geq F_Y$, and the alternative hypothesis as $H_a : F_X < F_Y$. As a matter of fact, the (functional) inequality $F_X < F_Y$ means that X tends to be greater than Y. In addition, note that under the location shift model, H_a is equivalent to the fact that the location shift Δ is > 0.

The Wilcoxon–Mann–Whitney test computes a p-value. If the p-value $\leq \alpha$, then H_0 is rejected. That is, we admit H_a with a confidence level $1 - \alpha$: $F_X > F_Y$.

This leads us to declare that the observed speedup of the median execution times is statistically significant, $\text{med}(X) > \text{med}(Y)$ with a confidence level $1 - \alpha$, and $\mathbb{P}[X > Y] > \frac{1}{2}$. If the null hypothesis is not rejected, then the observed speedup of the median is not considered to be statistically significant.

Figure 12.3 illustrates the speedup-test protocol for the median execution time.

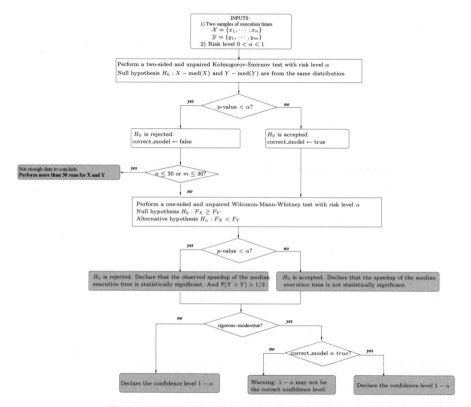

Figure 12.3. *The Speedup-Test protocol for analyzing the median execution time*

12.4. The Speedup-Test software

The performance evaluation methodology described in this chapter has been implemented and automated in a software called SpeedupTest. It is a command line software that works on the shell: the user specifies a configuration file, then the software reads the data, checks if the observed speedups are statistically significant and prints full reports. SpeedupTest is based on R [TEA 08]; it is available as a free software in [TOU 10]. The programming language is a script (R and bash), so the code itself is portable across multiple operating systems and hardware platforms. We have tested it successfully on Linux, Unix and Mac OS environments (other platforms may be used).

The input of the software is composed of:

– A unique configuration file in CSV format: it contains one line per benchmark under study. For each benchmark, the user has to specify the file name of the initial set of performance observations ($\mathcal{X}$ sample) and the optimized performances ($\mathcal{Y}$ sample). Optionally, a weight ($W(\mathcal{C})$) and a confidence level can be defined individually per benchmark or globally for all benchmarks. It is possible to ask SpeedupTest to compute the highest confidence level per benchmark to declare statistical significance of speedups.

– For each benchmark (two code versions), the observed performance data collected needs to be saved in two distinct raw text files: a file for the $\mathcal{X}$ sample and another for the $\mathcal{Y}$ sample.

The reason why we split the input into multiple files is to simplify the configuration of data analysis. Due to our choice, making multiple performance comparisons requires modifications in the CSV configuration file only, and the input data files remain unchanged.

SpeedupTest accepts some optional parameters in the command line, such as a global confidence level (to be applied to all benchmarks), weights to be applied on benchmarks and required precision for confidence intervals (not detailed in this chapter but explained in [TOU 10]).

The output of the software is composed of four distinct files:

1) a global report that prints the overall speedups and gains of all the benchmarks;

2) a file that details the individual speedup per benchmark, its confidence level and its statistical significance;

3) a warning file that explains for some benchmarks why the observed speedup is not statistically significant;

4) an error file that prints any misbehavior of the software (for debugging purposes).

The user manual of the software, sample data and demos are present in [TOU 10]. The next section presents an experimental use of the software and studies the probability of getting a significant statistical speedup on any program that does not necessarily belong to the initial set of tested benchmarks.

12.5. Evaluating the proportion of accelerated benchmarks by a confidence interval

Computing the overall performance gain or speedup for a sample of b programs does not allow us to estimate the quality or the efficiency of the code optimization technique. In fact, within the b programs, only a fraction of a benchmarks have a speedup, and $b - a$ programs have a slowdown. In this section, we want to analyze the probability p to get a statistically significant speedup if we apply a code transformation. If we consider a sample of b programs only, we could say that the chance to observe a speedup is $\frac{a}{b}$. But this computed chance $\frac{a}{b}$ is observed on a sample of b programs only. So what is the confidence interval of p? The following paragraphs answer this question.

In probability theory, we can study the random event {the program is accelerated with the code optimization under study}. This event has two possible values: true or false, so it can be represented by a Bernoulli variable. To compile accurate statistics, it is very important that the initial set of b benchmarks be selected randomly from a large database of representative benchmarks. If the set of b benchmarks are selected manually and not randomly, then there is a bias in the sample and the statistics we compute in this section are wrong. For instance, if the set of b programs are retrieved from well-known benchmarks (SPEC or others), then they cannot be considered as sufficiently random, because well-known benchmarks have been selected manually by a group of people, not selected randomly from a large database of programs.

If we randomly select a sample of b representative programs as a sample of benchmarks, we can measure the chance of getting the fraction of accelerated programs as $\frac{a}{b}$. The higher this proportion is, the better the quality of the code optimization would be. In fact, we want to evaluate whether the code optimization technique is beneficial for a large fraction of programs. The proportion $C = \frac{a}{b}$ has only been observed on a sample of b programs. There are many techniques for estimating the confidence interval for p (with a risk level α).

The simplest and most commonly used formula relies on approximating the binomial distribution with a normal distribution. In this situation, the confidence interval is given by the equation $C \mp r$, where

$$r = z_{1-\alpha/2} \times \sqrt{\frac{C(1 - C)}{b}}$$

In other words, the confidence interval of the proportion is equal to $[C - r, C + r]$. Here, $z_{1-\alpha/2}$ represents the value of the quartile of order $1 - \alpha/2$ of the standard normal distribution ($\mathbb{P}\left[N(0, 1) > z\right] = \frac{\alpha}{2}$). This value is available in a known precomputed table and in many softwares (Table A.2 in [JAI 91]). We should notice that the previous formula of the confidence interval of the proportion C is accurate only when the value of C are not too close from 0 or 1. A frequently cited rule of thumb is that the normal approximation works well as long as $a - \frac{a^2}{b} > 5$, as indicated, for instance, in [SAP 90] (section 2.7.2). However, in another contribution [BRO 01], that condition was discussed and criticized. The general subject of choosing appropriate sample size, which ensures an accurate normal approximation, was discussed in Chapter VII 4, example (h) of the reference book [FEL 68].

When the approximation of the binomial distribution with a normal one is not accurate, other techniques may be used, which will not be presented here. The R software has an implemented function that computes the confidence interval of a proportion based on the normal approximation of a binomial distribution, see the example below.

EXAMPLE (WITH R) 12.1.– Having $b = 30$ benchmarks selected randomly from a large set of representative benchmarks, we obtained a speedup on only $a = 17$ cases. We want to compute the confidence interval for p around the proportion C=17/30=0.5666 with a risk level equal to $\alpha = 0.1 = 10\%$. We easily estimate the confidence interval of C using the R software as follows:

```
> prop.test
(17, 30, conf. level = 0.90)

90 percent confidence interval: 0.4027157 0.7184049
```

Since $a - \frac{a^2}{b} = 17 - \frac{17^2}{30} = 7.37 > 5$, the computed confidence interval of the proportion is accurate. Note that this confidence interval is invalid if the initial set of $b = 30$ benchmarks was not randomly selected among a large number of representative benchmarks.

The above test allows us to say that we have a 90% chance that the proportion of accelerated programs is between 40.27% and 71.87%. If this interval is too wide for the purpose of the study, we can reduce the confidence level as an initial, and straightforward, solution. For instance, if I consider $\alpha = 50\%$, the confidence interval of the proportion becomes $[49.84\%, 64.23\%]$.

The next formula [JAI 91] gives the minimal number b of benchmarks to be selected randomly if we want to estimate the proportion confidence interval with a precision equal to $r\%$ with a risk level α:

$$b \geq (z_{1-\alpha/2})^2 \times \frac{C(1 - C)}{r^2}$$

EXAMPLE (WITH R) 12.2.– In the previous example, we obtained an initial proportion equal to $C = 17/30 = 0.5666$. If we want to estimate the confidence interval with a precision equal to 5% with a risk level of 5%, we put $r = 0.05$ and we read in the quartiles tables $z_{1-0.05/2} = z_{0.975} = 1.960$. The minimal number of benchmarks to observe is then equal to: $b \geq 1.960^2 \times \frac{0.566 \times (1 - 0.566)}{0.05^2} = 377.46$. We need to randomly select 378 benchmarks in order to assert that we have a 95% chance that the proportions of accelerated programs are in the interval $0.566 \mp 5\%$.

The following section presents our implementation of the performance evaluation methodology.

12.6. Experiments and applications

Let us first describe the set of program benchmarks; their source codes are written in C and Fortran:

1) SPEC CPU 2006: a set of 17 sequential applications. They are executed using the standard `ref` data input.

2) SPEC OMP 2001: a set of 9 parallel OpenMP applications. Each application can be run in a sequential mode, or in a parallel mode with 1, 2, 4, 6 or 8 threads, respectively. They are executed using the standard `train` data input.

From our experience, we consider that all the benchmarks have equal weight $(\forall k, W(\mathcal{C}_k) = 1)$. The binaries of the above benchmarks have been generated using two distinct compilers of equivalent release date: `gcc 4.1.3` and Intel `icc 11.0`. These compiler versions were the ones available when our experimental studies were carried out. Newer compiler versions may be available now and in the future. Other compilers may be used. A typical future project would be to make a fair performance comparison between multiple parallelizing compilers. Note that our experiments have no influence on the statistical methodology that we describe, since we base our work on mathematics, but not on experimental performance data. Any performance data can be analyzed, and the versions of the tools that are used to log performance data have no influence on the theory behind them.

We experimented multiple levels (compiler flags and options) of code optimizations carried out by both compilers. Our experiments were conducted on a Linux workstation (Intel Core 2, two quad-core Xeon processors, 2.33 GHz.). For each binary version, we repeated the execution of the benchmark 31 times and recorded the measurement. For a complete description of the experimental setup and environment used to collect the performance data, please refer to [MAZ 10]. The data are released publicly in [TOU 10]. This section focuses more on data analysis than data collection techniques. Next, we describe three possible applications of the `SpeedupTest` software. Note that applying the `SpeedupTest` in every section below requires less than 2 s of computation on a MacBook pro (2.53 GHz Intel Core 2 Duo).

The following section provides an initial set of experiments that compare the performances of different compiler flags.

12.6.1. *Comparing the performances of compiler optimization levels*

We consider the set of SPEC CPU 2006 (17 programs). Every source code is compiled using gcc 4.1.3 with three compiler optimization flags: -O0 (no optimization), -O1 (basic optimizations) and -O3 (aggressive optimizations). That is, we generate three different binaries per benchmark. We want to test whether the optimization levels -O1 and -O3 are really efficient compared to -O0. This requires us to consider 34 couples of comparisons: for every benchmark, we compare the performance of the binary generated by -O1 versus -O0 and the one generated by -O3 versus -O0.

The observed performances of the benchmarks reported by the tool are:

```
Overall gain (ExecutionTime=mean) = 0.464

Overall speedup (ExecutionTime=mean) = 1.865

Overall gain (ExecutionTime=median) = 0.464

Overall speedup (ExecutionTime=median) = 1.865
```

The overall observed gain and speedups are identical here because in this set of experiments, the observed median and mean execution times of every benchmark were almost identical (with three digits of precision). Such observations advocate that the binaries generated due to optimization levels -O1 and -O3 are really efficient compared to -O0. To be confident of such a conclusion, we need to rely on the statistical significance of the individual speedups per benchmark (for both median and average execution times). They have all been accepted with a confidence level equal to 95%, i.e. with a risk level of 5%. Our conclusions remain the same even if we reduce the confidence level to 1%, i.e. with a risk level of 99%.

The tool also computes the following information:

```
The observed proportion of accelerated benchmarks (speedup of the
mean) a/b = 34/34 = 1 The confidence level for computing proportion
confidence interval is 0.9. Proportion confidence interval (speedup
of the mean) = [0.901; 1] Warning: this confidence interval of
the proportion may not be accurate because the validity condition
{a(1-a/b)>5} is not satisfied.
```

Here, the tool states that the probability that the compiler optimization option -O3 would produce a speedup (versus -O1) of the mean execution time belongs to the interval [0.901; 1]. However, as noted by the tool, this confidence interval may not be accurate because the validity condition $a - \frac{a^2}{b} > 5$ is not satisfied. Recall that the computed confidence interval of the proportion is invalid if b the experimented set of benchmarks is not randomly selected among a huge number of representative benchmarks. Since we experimented selected benchmarks from SPEC CPU 2006, this condition is not satisfied; so we cannot advocate for the precision of the confidence interval.

Instead of analyzing the speedups obtained by compiler flags, one could obtain speedups by launching parallel threads. The next section studies this aspect.

12.6.2. *Testing the performances of parallel executions of OpenMP applications*

In this section, we investigate the efficiency of a parallel execution against a sequential application. We consider the set of 9 SPEC OMP 2001 applications. Every application is executed with 1, 2, 4, 6 and 8 threads, respectively. We compare every version to the sequential code (no threads). The binaries have been generated with the Intel icc 11.0 compiler using the flag -O3. So we have to conduct a comparison between 45 couples of benchmarks.

The observed performances of the benchmarks reported by the tool are:

```
Overall gain (ExecutionTime=mean) = 0.441

Overall speedup (ExecutionTime=mean) = 1.79

Overall gain (ExecutionTime=median) = 0.443

Overall speedup (ExecutionTime=median) = 1.797
```

These overall performance metrics clearly advocate that a parallel execution of the application is faster than a sequential execution. However, by analyzing the statistical significance of the individual speedups with a risk level of 5%, we find that:

– As expected, none of the single-threaded versions of the code were faster than the sequential version: this is because a sequential version has no thread overhead, and the compiler is better able to optimize the sequential code compared to the single-threaded code.

– Strange enough, the speedup of the average and median execution times has been rejected in five cases (with two threads or more). In other words, the parallel version of the code in five cases is not faster (in average and median) than the sequential code.

Our conclusions remain the same if we increase the risk level to 20% or if we use the gcc 4.1.3 compiler instead of icc 11.0.

The tool also computes the following information:

```
The observed proportion of accelerated benchmarks (speedup
of the mean) a/b = 31/45 = 0.689 The confidence level for
computing proportion confidence interval is 0.95. Proportion
confidence  interval (speedup of the mean) = [0.532; 0.814]
The minimal  needed number of randomly selected benchmarks
is 330 (in  order to have a precision r=0.05).
```

Here the tool indicates that:

1) The probability that a parallel version of an OpenMP application would produce a speedup (of the average execution time) against the sequential version belongs to the interval [0.532; 0.814].

2) If this probability confidence interval is not tight enough, and if the user requires a confidence interval with a precision of $r = 5\%$, then the user has to make experiments on a minimal number of randomly selected benchmarks $b = 330$.

Let us now make a statistical comparison between the program performance obtained by two distinct compilers. That is, we want to check whether the icc 11.0 produces more efficient codes compared to gcc 4.1.3.

12.6.3. *Comparing the efficiency of two compilers*

In this last section of performance evaluation, we want to answer the following question: which compiler (gcc 4.1.3 or Intel icc 11.0) is the best on an Intel Dell workstation? Both compilers have similar release dates and both are tested with aggressive code optimization level -O3.

A compiler or a computer architecture expert would say, clearly, that the Intel icc 11.0 compiler would generate faster codes. The reason for this is that gcc 4.1.3 is a free general purpose compiler that is designed for almost all processor architectures, while icc 11.0 is a commercial compiler designed for Intel processors only: the code optimizations of icc 11.0 are specially focused for the workstation on which the experiments have been conducted, while gcc 4.1.3 has less focus on Intel processors.

The experiments have been conducted using the set of nine SPEC OMP 2001 applications. Every application is executed in a sequential mode (without thread), or in parallel mode (with 1, 2, 4, 6 and 8 threads, respectively). We compare the performances of the binaries generated by icc 11.0 with the binaries generated by gcc 4.1.3. So, we make a comparison between 54 couples.

The observed performances of the benchmarks reported by the tool are:

```
Overall gain (ExecutionTime=mean) = 0.14

Overall speedup (ExecutionTime=mean) = 1.162

Overall gain (ExecutionTime=median) = 0.137

Overall speedup (ExecutionTime=median) = 1.158
```

These overall performance metrics clearly advocate that icc 11.0 generated faster codes than gcc 4.1.3. However, by analyzing the statistical significance of the individual speedups, we find that:

– With a risk level of 5%, the speedup of the average execution time is rejected in 14 cases among 54. If the risk is increased to 20%, the number of rejections decreases to 13 cases. With a risk of 99%, the number of rejections decreases to 11 cases.

– With a risk level of 5%, the speedup of the median execution time is rejected in 13 cases among 54. If the risk is increased to 20%, the number of rejections decreases to 12 cases. With a risk of 99%, the number of rejections remains at 12 cases among 54.

Here we can conclude that the efficiency of the gcc 4.1.3 compiler is not as bad as thought, however is still under the level of efficiency for a commercial compiler such as icc 11.0.

The tool also computes the following information:

```
The observed proportion of accelerated benchmarks (speedup of the
median) a/b = 41/54 = 0.759. The confidence level for computing
proportion confidence interval is 0.95. Proportion confidence
interval (speedup of the median) = [0.621; 0.861]. The minimal
number of  randomly selected benchmarks needed is 281 (in order
to have a precision  r = 0.05).
```

Here the tool says that:

1) The probability that icc 11.0 beats gcc 4.1.3 (produces a speedup of the median execution time) on a randomly selected benchmark belongs to the interval [0.621; 0.861].

2) If this probability confidence interval is not tight enough, and if the user requires a confidence interval with a precision of $r = 5\%$, then the user has to make experiments on a minimal number of randomly selected benchmarks $b = 281$!

12.6.4. *The impact of the Speedup-Test protocol over some observed speedups*

In this section, we give a synthesis of our experimental data to show that some observed speedups (that we call "hand made") are not statistically significant. In each benchmark family, we counted the number of non-statistically significant speedups among those that are "hand made". Table 12.1 gives a synthesis. The first column describes the benchmark family, with the compiler used and the number of observed speedups (pairs of samples). The second column provides the number of non-statistically significant speedups of the average execution times. The last column provides the number of non-statistically significant speedups of the median execution times.

As observed in the table, we analyzed 34 pairs of samples for the SPEC CPU 2006 applications compiled with icc. All the observed speedups are statistically significant. When the program execution times are less stable, such as in the case of SPEC OMP 2006 (as highlighted in [MAZ 10]), some observed speedups are not statistically significant. For instance, 14 speedups of the average execution times (among 45 observed ones) are not statistically significant (see the third line of Table 12.1). Also, 13 observed speedups of the median execution times (among 45 observed ones) are not statistically significant (see the last line of Table 12.1).

Benchmark family	Average execution times	Median execution times
SPEC CPU 2006 (icc, 34 pairs) (icc)	0	0
SPEC OMP (icc, 45 pairs)	14	14
SPEC OMP (gcc, 45 pairs)	13	14

Table 12.1. *Number of non-statistically significant speedups in the tested benchmarks*

12.7. Related work

12.7.1. *Observing execution times variability*

The literature contains some experimental research highlighting that program execution times are sometimes increasingly variable or unstable. In the article of *raced profiles* [LEA 09], the performance optimization system is based on observing the execution times of code fractions (functions, and so on). The mean execution time of such code fractions is analyzed due to the Student's t-test, aiming to compute a confidence interval for the mean. The previous article does not fix the data input of each code fraction: indeed, the variability of execution times when the data input varies cannot be analyzed with the Student's t-test. The reason is that when data input varies, the execution time varies inherently based on the algorithmic complexity, and not on the structural hazards.

Program execution time variability has been shown to lead to wrong conclusions if some execution environment parameters are not kept under control [MYT 09]. For instance, the experiments on sequential applications reported in [MYT 09] show that the size of Unix shell variables and the linking order of object codes both may influence the execution times.

Recently, we published in [MAZ 10] an empirical study of performance variation in real-world benchmarks with fixed data input. Our study concludes three points: (1) The variability of execution times of long-running sequential applications (SPEC CPU 2000 and 2006) is marginal. (2) The variability of execution times of long-running parallel applications such as SPEC OMP 2001 is important on multi-core processors, such variability cannot be neglected. (3) Almost all the samples of execution times do not follow a Gaussian distribution, which means that the Student's t-test, as well as mean confidence intervals, cannot be applied to small samples.

12.7.2. *Program performance evaluation in presence of variability*

In the field of code optimization and high-performance computing, most of the published articles declare observed speedups as defined in section 12.2. Unfortunately, few studies based on rigorous statistics are really conducted to check whether the observations of the code performance improvements are statistically significant or not.

Program performance analysis and optimization may rely on two well-known books that explain digested statistics to our community [JAI 91, LIL 00] in an accessible way. These two books are good introductions for compiling fair statistics for analyzing performance data. Based on these two books, previous work on statistical program performance evaluation has been published [GEO 07]. In the later article, the authors rely on the Student's t-test to compare between two average execution times (the two-sided version of the student t-test) in order to check whether $\mu_X \neq \mu_Y$. In our methodology, we improve the previous work in two directions. First, we conduct a *one-sided* Student's t-test to validate that $\mu_X > \mu_Y$. Second, we check the normality of small samples and the equivalence of their variances (using the Fisher F-test) in order to use the classical Student's t-test instead of the Welch variant.

In addition, we must note that [JAI 91, LIL 00, GEO 07] focus on comparing the mean execution times only. When the program performances have some extrema values (outliers), the mean is not a good performance measure (since the mean is sensitive to outliers). Consequently, the median is usually advised for reporting performance numbers (such as for SPEC scores). Consequently, we rely on more academic books on statistics [SAP 90, BRO 02, HOL 73] for comparing two medians. Furthermore, these fundamental books help us to mathematically understand some common mistakes and statistical misunderstandings that we report in [TOU 10].

A limitation of our methodology is that we do not study the variations of execution times due to changing the program's input. The reason is that the variability of execution times when the data input varies cannot be analyzed with the statistical tests as we did. This is simply because when the data input varies, the execution time varies inherently based on the algorithmic complexity (intrinsic characteristic of the code), and not based on the structural hazards of the underlying machine. In other words, observing distinct execution times when varying data input of the program cannot be considered a hazard, but as an inherent reaction of the program under analysis.

12.8. Discussion and conclusion on the Speedup-Test protocol

Program performance evaluation and their optimization techniques suffer from the non-reproducibility of published results. It is, of course, very difficult to reproduce exactly the experimental environment since we do not always know all the details or factors influencing it [MYT 09]. This document treats a part of the problem by defining a rigorous statistical protocol allowing us to consider the variations of program execution times if we set the execution environment. The variation of program execution times is not a chaotic phenomenon to neglect or to smooth; we should keep it under control and incorporate it inside the statistics. This would allow us to assert with a certain level of confidence that the performance data we report are reproducible under similar experimental environments. The statistical protocol that we propose to the scientific community is called the *Speedup-Test* and is based on clean statistics as described in [SAP 90, HOL 73, BRO 02].

Compared to [LIL 00, JAI 91], the Speedup-Test protocol analyzes the median execution time in addition to the average. Contrary to the average, the median is a better performance metric, because it is not sensitive to outliers and is more appropriate for skewed distributions. Summarizing the observed execution times of a program with their median allows us to evaluate the chance of having a faster execution time if we do a single run of the application. Such a performance metric is closer to the feeling of the users in general. Consequently, the Speedup-Test protocol is more rigorous than the protocol described in [LIL 00, JAI 91], based on the average execution times. Additionally, the Speedup-Test protocol is more cautious than [LIL 00, JAI 91] because it checks the hypothesis on the data distributions before applying statistical tests.

The Speedup-Test protocol analyzes the distribution of the observed execution times. For declaring a speedup for the average execution time, we rely on the Student's t-test under the condition that X and Y follow a Gaussian distribution (tested with Shapiro–Wilk's test). If not, using the Student's t-test is permitted for large samples but the computed risk level α may still be inaccurate if the underlying distributions of X and Y are too far from being normally distributed. For declaring a speedup for the median execution time, we rely on the Wilcoxon–Mann–Whitney test. Contrary to the Student's t-test, the Wilcoxon–Mann–Whitney test does not assume any specific distribution of the data, except that it requires that X and Y differ only by a shift location (that can be tested with the Kolmogorov–Smirnov test).

According to our experiments detailed in [TOU 10], the size limit $n > 30$ is not always sufficient to define a large sample: by large sample, we mean a sample size that allows us to observe the central limit theorem in practice. As far as we know, there is no proof defining the minimal valid size to be used for arbitrary sampling. Indeed, the minimal sample size depends on the distribution function, and cannot be fixed for any distribution function (*parametric statistics*). However, we noticed that for SPEC CPU 2006 and SPEC OMP 2001 applications, the size limit $n > 30$ is reasonable (but not always valid). Thus, we use this size limit as a practical value in the Speedup-Test protocol.

We conclude with a short discussion about the risk level we should use in this type of statistical study. Indeed, there is no unique answer to this crucial question. In each context of code optimization, we may be asked to be more or less confident in our statistics. In the case of hard real-time applications, the risk level must be low enough (less than 5%, for instance). In the case of soft real-time applications (multimedia, mobile phone, GPS, etc.), the risk level can be less than 10%. In the case of desktop applications, the risk level may not necessarily be too low. In order to make a fair report of a statistical analysis, we advise that all the experimental data and risk levels used for statistical tests are made public.

Conclusion

C.1. Some open problems in backend optimizing compilation

C.1.1. *Problem of instruction selection*

One of the most interesting problems in backend code optimization is instruction selection, which we did not address in this book because we think that the problem is still open when instruction schedules are not fixed.

Instruction selection allows us to transform a low-level intermediate code into the assembly code of the target machine. We think that the classical model based on pattern matching (rewriting rules and trees [AHO 07]) does not exactly describe the problem of instruction selection. Indeed, such syntactic rules allow us to transform m intermediate instructions into a single assembly instruction, using a static cost model [AHO 07]. We think that a more accurate model must be based on code semantics. That is, the general problem is transforming m low-level intermediate instructions into n assembly instructions computing the same result, and this could be modeled by algorithm recognition as studied in [ALI 05]. The reason is that, with the advance of reconfigurable computing and heterogeneous architectures, some sophisticated assembly instructions (with complex semantics) may be introduced in the instruction set: mathematical functions, vector instructions, domain-specific instructions, etc. Rewriting rules based on pattern matching are fragile techniques that may not detect opportunities for transforming m low-level three address instructions into sophisticated instructions. More advanced code analysis based on program semantics should be used.

Another open question for instruction selection is its phase ordering. Indeed, it is not clear where the best place to introduce the instruction selection step inside a backend compiler flow is. Usually, instruction selection is applied before register allocation and instruction scheduling. In this case, the cost model used to select an instruction among others is not exact, since the instruction-level parallelism (ILP) extracted afterward may hide or increase a cost: think about the case of multiply-add that may be favored by the instruction selection step, while it is not exactly the best candidate to enhance ILP if a single functional unit exists for executing it.

Contrary to instruction scheduling and register allocation, we think that instruction selection suffers from a lack of fundamental knowledge that helps us to design elegant and robust heuristics. For all these reasons, we think that instruction selection remains an interesting problem to study in backend compilation.

C.1.2. *Code optimization for multi-core and many-core processors*

Putting multiple processors inside the same microchip (including network on chips) does not fundamentally change the problems of parallel programming. The programming paradigms used for multiprocessors are exactly the same for multi-cores: shared memory (OpenMP), distributed memory (MPI), threads and process, multi-agents, bio-inspired parallelism, can all be used to program multi-core processors. Furthermore, parallel algorithms would not change simply because a multiprocessor machine is transformed into a multi-core processor. In addition, the performance of a parallel program always remains limited by its sequential part: contrary to the Moore's law which hits its practical limit, Amdhal's law remains valid forever. Consequently, the importance of the optimization of sequential codes is not reduced by the multi-core era; it remains a complementary research activity.

We think that the introduction of multi-core processors brings us new application domains for parallelism (not a new paradigm). Indeed, parallelism used to be an expert domain mainly tackled for scientific computing and simulation. Automatic parallelization was initially thought for regular codes (static control programs) such as Fortran programs executing on supercomputers. With multi-cores, parallelism becomes a *cheap* technology that brings high-performance computing at home, opening a new market for semiconductor industry. Consequently, the applications that must be optimized for multi-cores are general purpose ones, clearly distinct from regular scientific codes. Such applications are executed on desktops, programmed with languages such as java/C/C++, where the programmer makes an extensive usage of data pointers, data structures, while-loops, if-then-else construct, external libraries, indirect array accesses and function pointers. Automatic parallelization in this context becomes very limited in practice.

The future trend of the number of cores inside a microchip is not clear today. Maybe the number of cores will increase for many years, or it may hit a physical limit quickly, or maybe the technology will focus on heterogeneous architectures, with specialized cores surrounding a subset of general-purpose cores. As usual, the question is how to optimize the usage of all these cores through enough parallelism.

Our personal view is to design the applications in parallel from the beginning if possible, though not all problems can be solved with parallel algorithms. For the huge amount of existing irregular sequential codes, they should be parallelized with semiautomatic tools. For this purpose, we may need some advanced data flow analysis methods that consider irregular program structures.

Finally, we think about the aspect of the performance instability on multi-cores. We think that the notion of speedups usually used for summarizing a code performance with a single number must be analyzed carefully with a rigorous statical method, as explained in this book. In addition, general-purpose codes have performances sensitive to input data, contrary to scientific regular codes, which are sensitive to the size of the input data. The chosen input data may favor one execution path among others; so the notion of a single speedup per program becomes questionable.

C.2. Summary

We present here our impressions after a long-term research effort in backend code optimization. As research methodology, we favored formal computer science when the objective to optimize was clear at the architectural level. For instance, the number of registers, ILP and code size are clearly defined objectives, which can be observed in the final code. We believe that optimizing for architecturally visible objectives should be formal because: (1) the architecture of a processor does not change quickly, so it allows more time for investing in fundamental studies; (2) formal research allows us to make connection with other computer science areas and benefit from their vision (algorithmic theory, complexity, discrete applied mathematics and combinatorial optimization); (3) formal results in code optimization allow us to verify the correctness of the generated code; and (4) investing in a compilation step is a hard and costly effort; it should be done under strong basis.

As architecturally visible objectives, we showed how to efficiently tackle the phase ordering problem between register optimization and instruction scheduling. We demonstrate that is better to first satisfy register constraints to guarantee the absence of spilling before instruction scheduling. Our processor model is general enough to be used for most of the existing superscalar, very long instruction word (VLIW) and explicitly parallel instruction computing (EPIC) processors. We provided theorems to understand, and designed efficient heuristics. Our methods have been implemented and tested as stand-alone tools inside a real compiler. We demonstrated that the quality of the codes generated due to our register optimization methods is better. We also released our software that is independent of an existing compiler, allowing its future integration inside code optimization or analysis tools.

Another architecturally visible objective is code size, more precisely the relationship between loop unrolling factor, the number of allocated registers and the

ILP. Our fundamental knowledge on the relationship between these three metrics allows us to design an optimal (exponential but efficient) algorithm that minimizes the unrolling factor without degrading ILP while guaranteeing the absence of spill code. The application of this research result is devoted to the embedded VLIW area. We showed then that code size and code performance are not necessarily two antagonistic optimization objectives, and trade-off is not always necessary between code compaction and code performance.

Concerning the optimizing compilation in general, we studied the problem of phase ordering. We proved that iterative compilation is not fundamentally better than static compilation. If we consider the long compilation time used in iterative approaches, we believe that it can be used for more aggressive static approaches. First, because static compilation does not favor a program input. Second, in static compilation, we can use abstract performance models that may help to design efficient phase ordering strategies in the future. Third, static code optimization methods can be combined with code verification to certify that the final generated codes are correct.

When we optimize objectives for micro-architectural mechanisms, we favored practical research with stress on experimental observations. The reason is that micro-architectures are too complex to model, and may change quickly, so we do not have time to invest in fundamental research. Furthermore, we think that a compiler backend should not be patched with *ad hoc* optimization methods that focus on a specific micro-architectural problem. For such types of backend optimizations, we think that they are more appropriate in separate tools for semiautomatic code optimization. For instance, we demonstrated that the memory disambiguation mechanisms in superscalar processors do not make full memory address comparisons, and may sequentialize the execution of independent operations. To solve this problem, we designed an *ad hoc* load/store vectorization strategy. In another research effort devoted to VLIW processors, we showed how to combine data preloading and prefetching to optimize some irregular embedded codes. All these methods are efficient in practice because they optimize the interaction between the ILP and the micro-architecture.

As cache mechanisms have been considered constant micro-architectural enhancements for a long time, we think that there is room for abstracting the problem in order to study it from the scheduling theory point of view. Ideally, the scheduling problem must consider variable memory instruction latencies: a memory instruction has a latency that depends on the placement of the data inside the cache. Inversely, the placement of the data inside the cache depends on the schedule of the memory instructions. This cyclic relationship defines an interesting open problem for scheduling theory.

The current advance in reconfigurable computing, and the possible future emergence of heterogeneous computing, would introduce complex instruction sets with rich semantics. This would put special stress on instruction selection in backend compilation, a problem that we did not tackle in this current book. Indeed, the implemented instruction selection heuristics inside compilers are mainly based on syntactic pattern matching (rewriting rules) that cannot capture all the semantics of low-level instructions. We think that more sophisticated algorithm recognition methods must be used to build efficient automatic instruction selection phases.

Finally, readers must be aware that code optimization using sophisticated compilation methods is one of the multiple processes needed for improving program performances. In order to observe a real code performance improvement, the user must combine multiple optimizing compilation methods by considering detailed hardware characteristics. In addition, he/she may also need to deal with the operating system and machine workload (modify the configuration and optimize some operating system parameters). Optimizing a code by compilation does not necessarily yield observed performance improvement. And an observed code performance improvement does not necessarily result from an applied code optimization method. Sometimes, applying a code optimization method transforms the program and alters its interaction with the hardware with a new execution scenario which is completely different from the one assumed by the compiler.

Appendix 1

Presentation of the Benchmarks
used in our Experiments

This appendix describes the benchmarks and the data dependence graphs (DDG) that we used in our experiments. The DDGs have been generated by the st200cc compiler from STmicroelectronics, using the option -03. Superblock formation and loop unrolling are enabled, and instruction selection has been performed for the ST231 VLIW processor.

The ST231 processor used for our experiments executes up to four operations per clock cycle with a maximum of one control operation (goto, jump, call, return), one memory operation (load, store, prefetch) and two multiply operations per clock cycle. All arithmetic instructions operate on integer values with operands belonging either to the general register (GR) file (64×32 bit) or to the branch register (BR) file (8×1 bit). Floating-point computations are emulated by software. In order to eliminate some conditional branches, the ST200 architecture also provides conditional selection. The processing time of any operation is a single clock cycle, while the latencies between operations range from 0 to 3 clock cycles.

Note that we make our DDG public for helping the research community to share their data and to reproduce our performance numbers.

A1.1. Qualitative benchmarks presentation

We consider a representative set of applications for both high performance and embedded benchmarks. We chose to optimize the set of the following collections of well-known applications programmed in C and C++.

1) FFMPEG is the reference application benchmark used by STMicroelectronics for their compilation research and development. It is a representative application for

the usage of ST231 (video mpeg encoder/decoder). The application is a set of 119 C files, containing 112,997 lines of C code.

2) MEDIABENCH is a collection of 10 applications for multimedia written in C (encryption, image and video processing, compression, speech recognition, etc.). In its public version, MEDIABENCH is not portable to any platform because some parts are coded in assembly language of some selected workstation targets (excluding very lng instruction word (VLIW) targets). Our used MEDIABENCH collection has first been ported to ST231 VLIW platform. The whole MEDIABENCH application has 1,467 C files, containing 788,261 lines of C code.

3) SPEC2000 is a collection of applications for high-performance computing and desktop market (scientific computing, simulation, compiler, script interpreters, multimedia applications, desktop applications, etc.). It is a group of 12 big applications of representative integer programs and 4 big applications of floating-point programs. The whole collection contains 469 C files and 151 C++ files (656,867 lines of C and C++ code).

4) SPEC CPU2006 is the last collection of applications for scientific computing, intensive computation and desktop market. Compared to SPEC2000, SPEC2006 has larger code size and data sets (2386 C file, 528 C++ files and 3,365,040 C/C++ lines).

Both FFMPEG and MEDIABENCH collections have been successfully compiled, linked and executed on the embedded ST231 platform. For SPEC2000 and SPEC CPU2006, they have been successfully compiled and statically optimized but not executed because of one of the three following reasons:

1) Our target embedded system does not support some required dynamic function libraries by SPEC (the dynamic execution system of an embedded system is not as rich as a desktop workstation).

2) The large code size of SPEC benchmarks does not fit inside small embedded systems based on ST231.

3) The amount of requested dynamic memory (heap) cannot be satisfied at execution time on our embedded platform.

Consequently, our experiments report static performance numbers for all benchmark collections. The dynamic performance numbers (executions) are reported only for FFMPEG and MEDIABENCH applications.

The next section provides some useful quantitative metrics to analyze the complexity of our benchmarks.

A1.2. Quantitative benchmarks presentation

In order to gain a precise idea on problem sizes handled by our register optimization methods, we report six metrics using histograms (the x-axis represents the values and the y-axis represents the number of loops of the given values):

1) The numbers of nodes (loop statements) are depicted in Figure A1.1 for each benchmark collection. The whole median[1] is equal to 24 nodes; the maximal value is 847. FFMPEG has the highest median of nodes numbers (29).

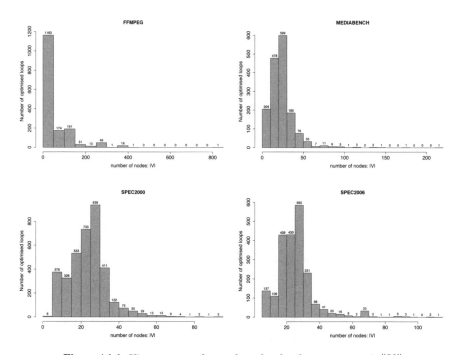

Figure A1.1. *Histograms on the number of nodes (loop statements): $\|V\|$*

2) The numbers of nodes writing inside GRs are depicted in Figure A1.2. The whole median is equal to 15 nodes; the maximal value is 813 nodes. FFMPEG has the highest median (21 nodes).

3) The numbers of nodes writing inside BRs are depicted in Figure A1.3. The whole median is equal to 3 nodes; the maximal value is 35 nodes. Both FFMPEG and MEDIABENCH have a median of 1 node, meaning that half of their loops have

---

1 We deliberately choose to report the median value instead of the mean value because the histograms show a skewed (biased) distribution [JAI 91].

a unique branch instruction (the regular loop branch). It can be noted that our model considers loops with multiple branch instructions inside their bodies.

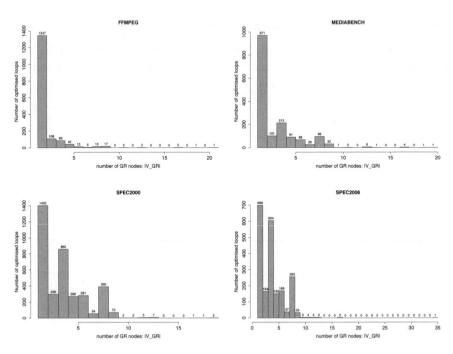

Figure A1.2. *Histograms on the number of statements writing inside general registers* $\left\|V^{R,GR}\right\|$

4) The numbers of edges (data dependences) are depicted in Figure A1.4 for each benchmark collection. The whole median is equal to 73 edges; the maximal value is 21,980 edges. The highest median is FFMPEG one (99 edges).

5) the MinII values are depicted in Figure A1.5. We recall that $MinII = \max(MII, MII_{res})$, where MII_{res} is the minimal II imposed by the resource constraints of the ST231 processor. The whole median of MinII values is equal to 12 clock cycles; the maximal value is 640 clock cycles. The highest median is that of FFMPEG (20 clock cycles);

6) The numbers of strongly connected components are depicted in Figure A1.6. The whole median is equal to nine strongly connected components, which means that, if needed, half of the loops can be split by loop fission into nine smaller loops; the maximal value is equal to 295. FFMPEG has the smallest median (seven strongly connected components).

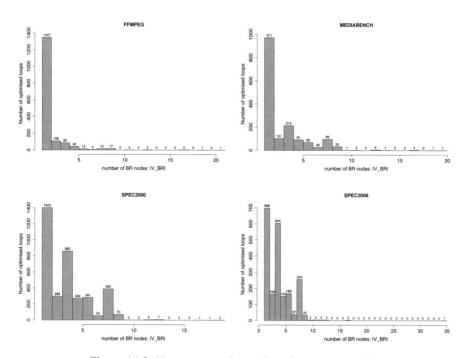

Figure A1.3. *Histograms on the number of statements writing inside branch registers* $\left\| V^{R,BR} \right\|$

These quantitative measures show that the FFMPEG application brings *a priori* the most difficult and complex DDG instances for code optimization. This analysis is confirmed by our experiments below.

A1.3. Changing the architectural configuration of the processor

The previous section shows a quantitative presentation of our benchmarks when we consider the ST231 VLIW processor with its architectural configuration. In order to emulate more complex architectures, we configured the st200cc compiler to generate DDG for a processor architecture with three register types $\mathcal{T} = \{FP, GR, BR\}$ instead of two. Consequently, the distribution of the number of values per register type becomes the following.[2]

---

2 MIN stands for MINimum, FST stands for FirST quantile (25% of the population), MED stands for MEDian (50% of the population), THD stands for THirD quantile (75% of the population) and MAX stands for MAXimum.

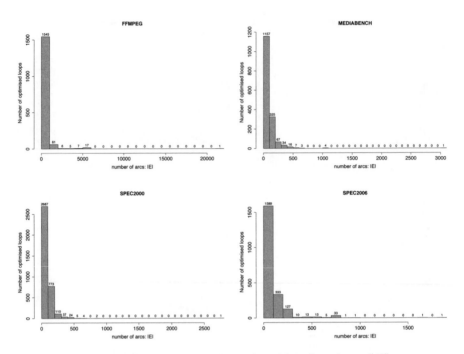

Figure A1.4. *Histograms on the number of data dependences* $\|E\|$

Type			MEDIABENCH	SPEC2000	SPEC2006	FFMPEG
		MIN	1	1	1	1
		FST	2	3	3	2
FP		MED	4	6	4	5
		THD	8	14	12	8
		MAX	68	72	132	32
		MIN	1	1	1	2
		FST	6	7	8	12
GR		MED	9	12	12	29
		THD	16	17	18	105
		MAX	208	81	74	749
		MIN	1	1	1	1
		FST	1	1	1	1
BR		MED	1	3	3	1
		THD	3	5	4	1
		MAX	21	27	35	139

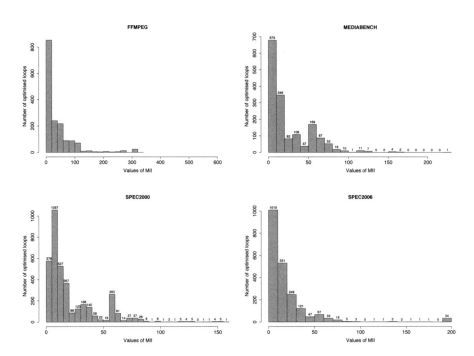

Figure A1.5. *Histograms on MinII values*

We also considered various configurations for the number of architectural registers. We considered three possible configurations named small, medium and large architectures, respectively:

Name of the architecture	$\mathcal{R}^{FR}$: FP registers	$\mathcal{R}^{GR}$: GR registers	$\mathcal{R}^{BR}$: BR registers
Small architecture	32	32	4
Medium architecture	64	64	8
Large architecture	128	128	8

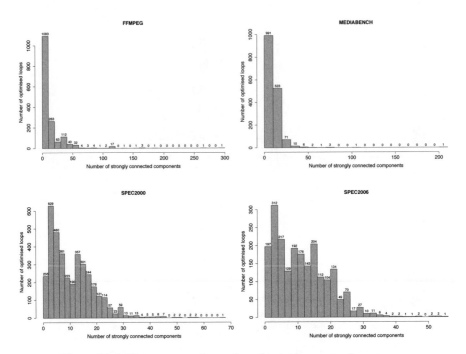

Figure A1.6. *Histograms on the number of strongly connected components*

Appendix 2

Register Saturation Computation on Stand-alone DDG

This appendix summarizes our full experiments in [BRI 09a].

A2.1. The cyclic register saturation

Our experiments were conducted on a regular Linux workstation (Intel Xeon, 2.33 GHz and 9 GB of memory). The data dependency graphs (DDGs) used for experiments come from SPEC2000, SPEC2006, MEDIABENCH and FFMPEG sets of benchmarks, all described in Appendix 1. We used the directed acyclic graph (DAG) of the loop bodies, and the configured set of register types is $\mathcal{T} = (FP, BR, GR)$. Since the compiler may unroll loops to enhance instruction-level parallelism (ILP) scheduling, we have also experimented the DDG after loop unrolling with a factor of 4 (so the sizes of DDGs are multiplied by a factor of 5). The distribution of the sizes of the unrolled loops may be computed by multiplying the initial sizes by a factor of 5.

A2.1.1. *On the optimal RS computation*

Since computing register saturation (RS) is NP-complete, we have to use exponential methods if optimality is needed. An integer linear program was proposed in [TOU 05, TOU 02], but was extremely inefficient (we were unable to solve the problem with a DDG larger than 12 nodes). We replaced the integer linear program with an exponential algorithm to compute the optimal RS [BRI 09a]. The optimal values of RS allow us to test the efficiency of GREEDY-K heuristics. From our experiments in [BRI 09a], we conclude that the exponential algorithm is usable in practice with reasonably medium-sized DAGs. Indeed, we successfully computed floating point (FP), general register (GR) and branch register (BR), RS of more than 95% of the original loop bodies. The execution time did not exceed 45 ms in 75% of the cases. However, when the size of the DAG becomes critical, performance of optimal RS computation dramatically drops. Thus, even if we managed to compute the FP and BR saturation of more than 80% of the bodies of the loops unrolled four times, we were able to compute the GR saturation of only 45% of these bodies. Execution times also literally exploded, compared to the ones obtained for initial loop bodies: the slowdown factor ranges from 10 to over 1,000.

A2.1.2. *On the accuracy of Greedy-k heuristic versus optimal RS computation*

In order to quantify the accuracy of the GREEDY-K heuristic, we compared its results to the exponential (optimal) algorithm: for these experiments, we put a time-out of 1 h for the exponential algorithm and we recorded the RS computed within this time limit. We then counted the number of cases where the returned value is lesser than or equal to the optimal register saturation. The results are shown on the boxplots[1] of Figure A2.1 for both the initial DAG and the DDG unrolled four times.

Furthermore, we estimate the error ratio of the GREEDY-K heuristic with the formula $1 - \dfrac{\sum RS^{t'}(G)}{\sum RS^{t}(G)}$ for $t \in \mathcal{T}$, where $RS^{t'}(G)$ is the approximate register saturation computed by GREEDY-K. The error ratios are shown in Figure A2.2.

The experiments highlighted in Figures A2.1 and A2.2 show that GREEDY-K is good for approximating the RS. However, when the DAGs were large, as the particular case of bodies of loops unrolled four times, the GR saturation was underestimated in more than half of the cases as shown in Figure A2.1(d). To balance this, first, we need to remind ourselves that the exact GR saturation was unavailable for more than half of the DAGs (the optimality is not reachable for large DAG, and we have put a time-out of resolution time of 1 h); hence, the size of the sample is clearly smaller than for the other statistics. Second, as shown in Figure A2.2, the error ratio remains low, since it is lower than 12%–13% in the worst cases.

In addition to the accuracy of GREEDY-K, the next section shows that it has a satisfactory speed.

---

1 Boxplot, also known as a *box-and-whisker diagram*, is a convenient way of graphically depicting groups of numerical data through their five-number summaries: the smallest observations (min), lower quartile ($Q1 = 25\%$), median ($Q2 = 50\%$), upper quartile ($Q3 = 75\%$) and largest observations (max). The min is the first value of the boxplot and the max is the last value. Sometimes, the extrema values (min or max) are very close to one of the quartiles. This is why we sometimes do not distinguish between the extrema values and some quartiles.

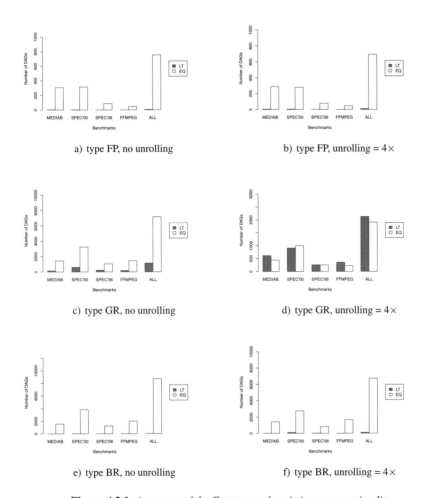

Figure A2.1. *Accuracy of the* GREEDY-K *heuristic versus optimality*

A2.1.3. GREEDY-K *execution times*

The computers used for the experiments were Intel-based PCs. The typical configuration was Core 2 Duo PC at 1.6 GHz, running GNU/Linux 64 bits (kernel 2.6), with 4 GB of main memory.

Figure A2.3 shows the distribution of the execution times using boxplots. As can be remarked, we note that GREEDY-K is reasonably fast to be included inside an interactive compiler. If faster RS heuristics are needed, we invite the readers to study a variant of GREEDY-K in [BRI 09a].

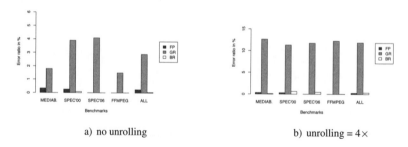

a) no unrolling   b) unrolling = 4×

Figure A2.2. *Error ratios of the* GREEDY-K *heuristic versus optimality*

This section shows that the acyclic RS computation is fast and accurate in practice. The following section shows that the periodic RS is more computation intensive.

A2.2. The periodic register saturation

We have developed a prototype tool based on the research results presented in section 8.3. It implements the integer linear program that computes the periodic register saturation of a DDG. We use a PC under linux, equipped with a dual-core Pentium D (3.4 GHz), and 1 GB of memory. We did thousands of experiments on several DDGs with a single register type extracted from different benchmarks (SPEC, Whetstone, Livermore, Linpac and DSP filters). Note that the DDGs we use in this section are not those presented in Appendix 1, but they come from previous data. The size of our DDG ranges from 2 nodes and 2 edges to 20 nodes and 26 edges. They represent the typical small loops intended to be analyzed and optimized using the periodic register saturation (PRS) concept. However, we also experimented larger DDGs produced by loop unrolling, resulting in DDGs with size $\|V\| + \|E\|$ reaching 460.

A2.2.1. *Optimal PRS computation*

From the theoretical perspective, PRS is unbounded. However, as shown in Table A2.1, the PRS is bounded and finite because the duration L is bounded in practice: in our experiments, we took $L = \sum_{e \in E}$, which is a convenient upper bound. Figure A2.4 provides some plots on maximal periodic register need versus initiation intervals of many DDG examples. These curves have been computed using optimal intLP resolution using CPLEX. The plots neither start nor end at the same points because the parameters MII (starting point) and L (ending point) differ from one loop to another. Given a DDG, its PRS is equal to the maximal value of RN for any II. As can be seen, this maximal value of RN always holds for $II = MII$. This result is intuitive, since the lower the II, the higher ILP degree, and consequently, higher the register need. The asymptotic plots of Figure A2.4 show that maximal PRN versus II describes non-increasing functions. Indeed, the maximal RN is either a constant or a decreasing function. Depending on $\mathcal{R}^t$ the number of available registers, PRS computation allows us to deduce that register constraints are irrelevant in many cases (when $PRS^t(G) \leq \mathcal{R}^t$).

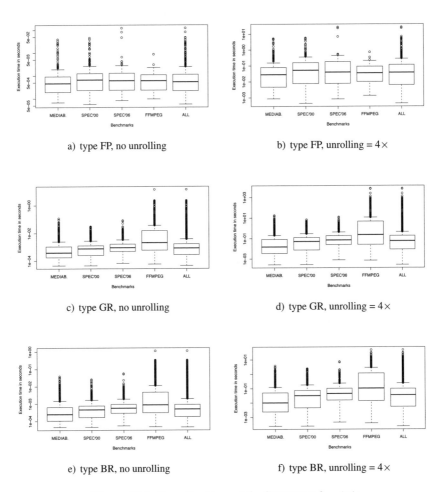

a) type FP, no unrolling   b) type FP, unrolling $= 4\times$

c) type GR, no unrolling   d) type GR, unrolling $= 4\times$

e) type BR, no unrolling   f) type BR, unrolling $= 4\times$

Figure A2.3. *Execution times of the* GREEDY-K *heuristic*

Optimal PRS computation using intLP resolution may be intractable because the underlying problem is NP-complete. In order to be able to compute an approximate PRS for larger DDGs, we use a heuristics with the CPLEX solver. Indeed, the operational research community provides efficient ways to deduce heuristics based on exact intLP formulation. When using CPLEX, we can use a generic branch-and-bound heuristics for intLP resolution, tuned with many CPLEX parameters. In this chapter, we choose a first satisfactory heuristic by bounding the resolution with a real-time limit (say, 5 or 1 s). The intLP resolution stops when time goes out and returns the best feasible solution found. Of course, in some cases, if the given time limit is not sufficiently high, the solver may not find a feasible solution (as in any heuristic targeting an NP-complete problem). The use of such CPLEX generic heuristics for intLP resolution avoids the need for designing new heuristics. Table A2.1 shows the results of PRS computation in the case of both optimal PRS and approximate PRS (with time limits of 5 and 1 s). As can be seen, in most cases, this simple heuristic computes the optimal results. The more time we give to CPLEX computation, the closer it will be to the optimal one.

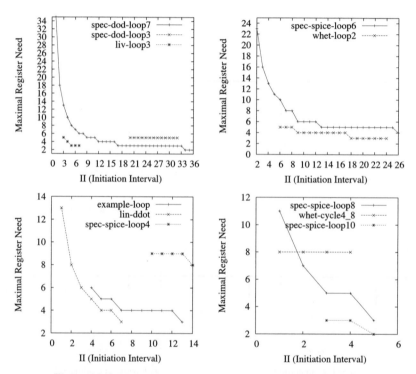

Figure A2.4. *Maximal periodic register need vs. initiation interval*

We will use this kind of heuristics in order to compute approximate PRS for larger DDGs in the next section.

Benchmark	Loop	PRS	PRS (5 s)	PRS (1 s)
SPEC - SPICE	loop1	4	4	4
	loop2	28	28	28
	loop3	2	2	2
	loop4	9	9	NA
	loop5	1	1	1
	loop6	23	23	23
	loop8	11	11	11
	loop9	21	21	NA
	loop10	3	3	3
	tom-loop1	11	NA	NA
SPEC - DODUC	loop1	11	NA	NA
	loop2	6	6	5
	loop3	5	5	5
	loop7	35	35	35
SPEC - FPPP	fp-loop1	4	4	4
Linpac	ddot	13	13	NA
Livermoore	loop1	8	8	NA
	loop5	5	5	5
	loop23	31	NA	NA
Whetstone	loop1	6	5	NA
	loop2	5	5	5
	loop3	4	4	4
	cycle4-1	1	1	1
	cycle4-2	2	2	2
	cycle4-4	4	4	4
	cycle4-8	8	8	8
Figure 1 DDG	loop1	6	6	6
TORSHE	van-Dongen	10	10	9
DSP filter	WDF	6	6	6

Table A2.1. *Optimal versus approximate PRS*

A2.2.2. *Approximate PRS computation with heuristic*

We use loop unrolling to produce larger DDGs (up to 200 nodes and 260 edges). As can be seen in some cases (spec-spice-loop3, whet-loop3 and whet-cycle-4-1), the PRS remains constant, irrespective of the unrolling degrees, because the cyclic data dependence limits the inherent ILP. In other cases (lin-ddot, spec-fp-loop1 and spec-spice-loop1), the PRS increases as a sublinear function of unrolling degree. In other cases (spec-dod-loop7), the PRS increases as a superlinear function of unrolling degree. This is because unrolling degree produces bigger durations L, which increase the PRS with a factor greater than the unrolling degree.

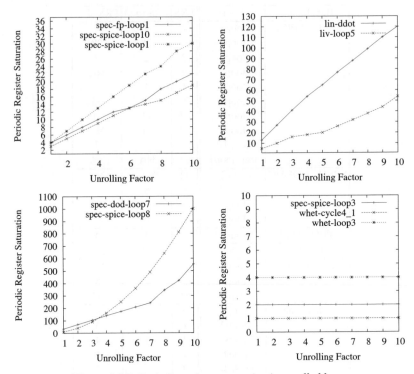

Figure A2.5. *Periodic register saturation in unrolled loops*

Appendix 3

Efficiency of SIRA on the Benchmarks

A3.1. Efficiency of SIRALINA on stand-alone DDG

This section summarizes our full experiments in [BRI 09b]. SIRALINA can be used to optimize all register types conjointly, as explained in section 9.4, or to optimize each register type separately. When register types are optimized separately, the order in which they are processed is of importance, since optimizing a register type may influence the register requirement of another type (because the statements are connected by data dependences). This section studies the impact of SIRALINA on register optimization with multiple register types (separate or conjoint) in the context of three representative architectures (small, medium and large, see section A1.3).

The computers used for the stand-alone experiments were Intel-based PCs. The typical configuration was Core 2 Duo PC at 1.6 GHz, running GNU/Linux 64 bits (kernel 2.6), with 4 GB of main memory.

A3.1.1. *Naming conventions for register optimization orders*

In this appendix, we experiment with many configurations for register optimization. Typically, the order of register types used for optimization is a topic of interest. For $\mathcal{T} = \{t_1, \ldots, t_n\}$ a set of register types, and $p : [\![1; n]\!] \rightarrow [\![1; n]\!]$ a permutation; we note $\mathcal{O} = t_{p(1)}; t_{p(2)}; \ldots; t_{p(n)}$ the register-type optimization order consisting of optimizing the registers sequentially for the types $t_{p(1)}, t_{p(2)}, \ldots, t_{p(n)}$ in this order. We note $\mathcal{O} = t_1 t_2 \ldots t_n$ (or indifferently any other permutation) when no order is relevant (i.e. types $\{t_1, \ldots, t_n\}$ altogether): for sake of brevity, we also call this a register optimization order.

EXAMPLE A3.1.– Assume that $\mathcal{T} = \{FP, GR, BR\}$. Then:

– Floating point (FP), general register (GR) and branch register (BR) is the register optimization order which focuses first on the FP type, then on the GR type and, finally, on the BR type;

– FP, BR and GR is the register optimization order that focuses first on the FP type, then on the BR type and, finally, on the GR type;

– FP, GR and BR is the register optimization order where all the types are solved simultaneously. It is equivalent to FP BR GR, to GR FP BR, etc.

A3.1.2. *Experimental efficiency of SIRALINA*

For each architectural configuration, and for each register type order, Figure A3.1 illustrates the percentage of solutions found by SIRALINA and the percentage of data dependence graphs (DDGs) that need spilling: we say that SIRALINA finds a solution for a given DDG if it finds a value for MII (which is the value of II in the SIRALINA linear program) such that all the register requirements of all register types are below the limit imposed by the processor architecture: $\forall t \in \mathcal{T}, \sum_{e_r \in E^{\text{reuse},t}} \mu^t(e_r) \leq \mathcal{R}^t$. Each bar of the figure represents a register optimization order as defined in section A3.1.1. Figure A3.1 also shows, in the case where a solution exists, whether the critical circuit (MII) has been increased or not compared to its initial value.

We note that most of the time, SIRALINA found a solution that satisfied the architectural constraints. Of course, the percentage of success increases when the number of architectural registers is greater. Thus, SIRALINA succeeds find a solution for the small architecture about 95% of the time and almost 100% of the time for large architecture.

We also observe that the proportion of cases for which a solution was found for II = MII is between 60% and 80%, depending on the benchmark family and the SIRALINA register optimization order. Thus, the performance of the software pipelining would not suffer from the extension of the DDG made after applying SIRALINA.

Finally, the simultaneous register optimization order FPGRBR gives very good results, often better than the results obtained with the sequential orders.

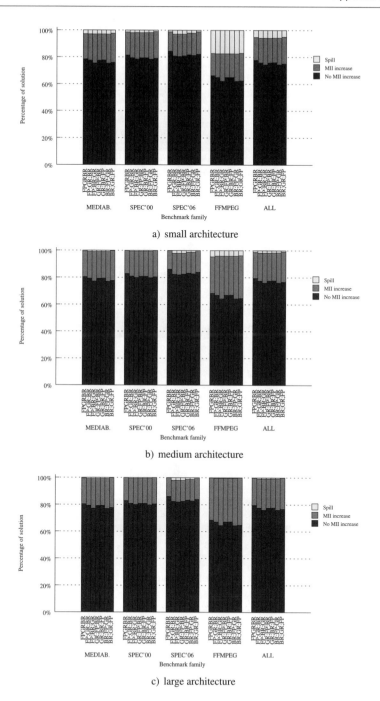

a) small architecture

b) medium architecture

c) large architecture

Figure A3.1. *Percentage of DDG treated successfully by SIRALINA and the impact on the MII*

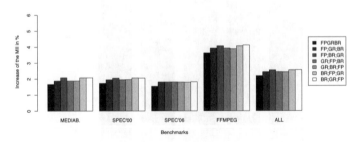

a) small architecture

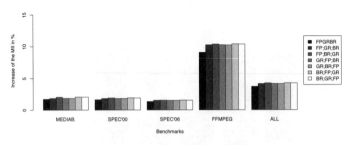

b) medium architecture

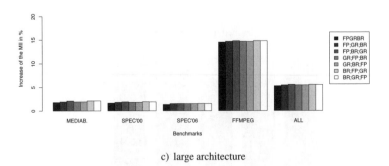

c) large architecture

Figure A3.2. *Average increase of the MII*

A3.1.3. *Measuring the increase of the MII*

The previous section shows that most of the DDGs do not end up with an increase in MII. Still we need to quantify the overall MII increase. Figure A3.2 shows the increase of the MII when SIRALINA found a solution for a DDG. The figure plots the results for each register optimization order and for each benchmark family. This increase is computed overall on all DDGs by the formula $\dfrac{\sum MII(G')}{\sum MII(G)} - 1$, where $MII(G')$ is the new critical circuit constructed after applying SIRALINA on the DDG G, while $MII(G)$ is its initial value.

We observe that the global increase of the MII is relatively low (about 15% in the worst case). More precisely, the increase is negligible for MEDIABENCH, SPEC2000 and SPEC2006 benchmarks whereas it cannot be neglected on FFMPEG benchmarks. The reason is that the FFMPEG benchmark contains much more complex and difficult DDG instances compared to the other benchmarks.

A3.1.4. *SIRALINA execution times*

Figure A3.3 shows the boxplot[1] of execution times of SIRALINA, depending on the register optimization order. We measured the execution time taken by SIRALINA to find a solution for a DDG, given an architectural configuration. All execution times are reported, including the cases where SIRALINA did not find a solution.

We observed that simultaneous SIRALINA register optimization order clearly outperforms the sequential register optimization orders, since it is almost twice as fast as the latter.

A close examination (not clear from Figure A3.3) of the execution times also shows that the speed of sequential register optimization orders is highly dependent on the order in which register types are treated. This is not surprising since a search for a solution (iterating on II) may continue unnecessarily if a subset of the constraints can be satisfied but not the entire set. For instance, imagine a (hypothetical) architecture with GR=FP=∞ and BR=0, then depending on the order in which types are treated, a sequential search procedure will fail more or less quickly on any DDG that has at least one BR value.

---

1 Boxplot, also known as a *box-and-whisker diagram*, is a convenient way of graphically depicting groups of numerical data through their five-number summaries: the smallest observations (min), lower quartile ($Q1 = 25\%$), median ($Q2 = 50\%$), upper quartile ($Q3 = 75\%$) and largest observations (max). The min is the first value of the boxplot, and the max is the last value. Sometimes, the extrema values (min or max) are very close to one of the quartiles. This is why we sometimes do not distinguish between the extrema values and some quartiles.

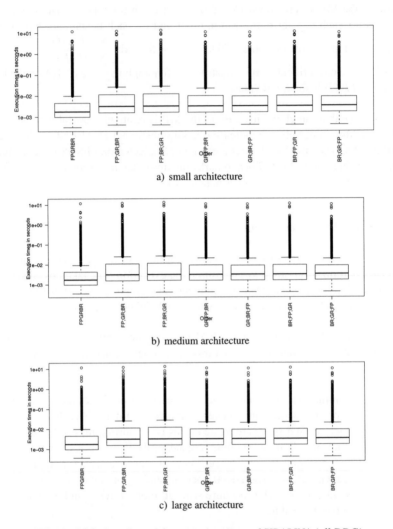

Figure A3.3. *Boxplots of the execution times of SIRALINA (all DDG)*

A3.2. Efficiency of SIRALINA plugged with an industrial compiler

This section presents our experimental results when SIRA is plugged inside a compiler.

Our experimental setup is based on st200cc, a STMicroelectronics production compiler based on the Open64 technology (www.open64.net), whose code generator has been extensively rewritten in order to target the STMicroelectronics ST200 Very Long Instruction Word (VLIW) processor family. These VLIW processors implement a single cluster derivative of the Lx architecture [FAR 00], and are used in several successful consumer electronics products, including DVD recorders, set-top boxes and printers.

The ST231 processor used for our experiments executes up to four operations per clock cycle with a maximum of one control operation (goto, jump, call, return), one memory operation (load, store, prefetch) and two multiply operations per clock cycle. All arithmetic instructions operate on integer values with operands belonging either to the GR file (64 × 32 bit) or to the BR file (8 × 1 bit). FP computation is emulated by software. In order to eliminate some conditional branches, the ST200 architecture also provides conditional selection. The processing time of any operation is a single clock cycle, while the latencies between operations range from 0 to 3 clock cycles.

The st200cc compiler augments the Open64 code generator with super-block instruction scheduling optimizations, including a software pipelining (SWP). We inserted the SIRA optimizer that preconditions the dependence graph before software pipelining in order to bound MAXLIVE for any subsequent schedule (see Figure A3.4).

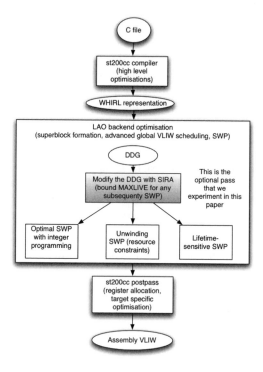

Figure A3.4. *Plugging SIRA into the ST231 compiler toolchain (LAO backend)*

Three subsequent software pipelining methods are experimented in conjunction with SIRA:

1) SWP under resource constraints only. The SWP heuristic is called *unwinding* [DIN 01];

2) optimal SWP under resource constraints, based on integer linear programming. Since the optimal solution may be intractable in practice, a time-out of 10 s is enabled for each integer linear program. The solver used was CPLEX version 10;

3) a lifetime-sensitive SWP under resource constraints [DIN 97b].

The present register allocator inside st200cc is named after SWP. It is a heuristic based on Chow's priority-based method, which is known not to be optimal. Consequently, even though the SIRA framework guarantees the absence of spilling whether register allocation optimal methods are used [WER 99], the current register allocation heuristic inside the st200cc compiler may still introduce a spill code.

The st200cc compiler has the capability of compiling variants of the ST200 VLIW architecture, including changes in the instruction latencies, the issue width and the number of allocatable registers. When we configure the processor to have 64 GRs and 8 BRs, we find that the register pressure is not problematic in most of the applications (only few spill instructions are generated): when register pressure is low, any weak register optimization method would work fine and it is not necessary to use a more clever method as we experiment in this research result. In order to highlight the efficiency of a register optimization method such as ours, we must experiment harder constraints by compiling for smaller processors with less registers. For this work, we configured the compiler to assume the embedded VLIW processors to have 32 general-purpose registers (GR) and 4 BRs. Experiments with fewer registers have been published in [TOU 11].

Both FFMPEG and MEDIABENCH C applications have successfully been compiled, linked and executed on the embedded ST231 platform. For the C applications of SPEC2000, they have been successfully compiled and statically optimized but not executed because of one of the three following reasons:

1) Our target embedded system does not support some required dynamic function libraries by SPEC (the dynamic execution system of an embedded system is not as rich as a desktop workstation).

2) The large code size of SPEC benchmarks does not fit inside small embedded systems based on ST231.

3) The amount of requested dynamic memory (heap) cannot be satisfied at execution time on our embedded platform.

Consequently, our experiments report static performance numbers for all benchmark collections (FFMPEG, MEDIABENCH and SPEC2000). The dynamic performance numbers (executions) are only reported for FFMPEG and MEDIABENCH applications. This is not a restriction of the study because SPEC2000 are representative of the embedded applications we target; we statically optimize SPEC2000 applications simply to check and demonstrate at compile time that our spill optimization method also works well for these kinds of large applications.

As highlighted in the previous section, and demonstrated in [TOU 11], it is better to optimize the register types conjointly. Here we report on this situation only.

A3.2.1. *Static performance results*

A3.2.1.1. *Spill code reduction and IIdecrease*

We statically measure the amount of spill code reduced due to our SIRALINA method. The spill code decrease is computed for all SWP loops. It is measured on all loops as $\frac{\text{InitialSpill Count} - \text{ReducedSpillCount}}{\text{InitialSpillCount}}$. Figure A3.5(a) illustrates our results. As can be seen, for any SWP scheduler used in combination with SIRA, spill code reduction is impressive, including if we add SIRA to the lifetime-sensitive SWP.

We could think that introducing additional edges inside the DDG before software pipelining would also restrict the instruction-level parallelism (ILP) scheduling, since extra constraints are added. So we measured the variation of II resulted from the integration of SIRA inside the compilation tool-chain. We measured II variation as $\frac{\sum II_2 - II_1}{\sum II_1}$, where II_2 corresponds to the II computed after software pipelining of the constrained DDG (when applying SIRALINA), and II_1 corresponds to the II computed after software pipelining of the initial DDG (without applying SIRALINA). Surprisingly, Figure A3.5(b) illustrates that SIRA is beneficial for II. This can easily be explained by two factors: (1) less spill induces lower II; (2) adding new edges actually helps the schedulers, since they are not optimal in practice[2].

A3.2.1.2. *Decoupling Register Constrains from SWP*

In this section, we study the impact of using SIRA combined with SWP (unwinding) versus a lifetime sensitive SWP. We measured the static spill count reduction and the II variation as defined in the previous section. Figure A3.5(a) illustrates that spill code is better reduced thanks to combining SIRA with SWP, instead of a lifetime sensitive SWP. Regarding II reduction, the situation is subject to debate. Figure A3.5(b) shows that II is reduced for SPEC2000 applications.

---

2 Remember that the exact scheduler using CPLEX has a time-out of 10s, which does not allow to compute optimal schedules in practice.

However, it is increased for FFMPEG and MEDIABENCH. Since the static II is computed with fixed memory latencies (three clock cycles) at compile time, the increase of the static II should be less problematic than a cache miss resulted from spill code.

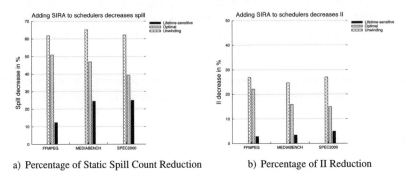

a) Percentage of Static Spill Count Reduction   b) Percentage of II Reduction

Figure A3.5. *The impact of SIRA on static code quality*

A3.2.1.3. *Does SIRA definitely remove spill code?*

In this section, we count the number of loops that no longer have spill once SIRA is used. Remember that SIRA guarantees, in theory, that any SWP will not require more registers than the available ones. If an optimal cyclic register allocation is done after SWP, such as [WER 99], then we guarantee the absence of spilling. Unfortunately, the register allocation heuristic present inside the st200cc compiler is a variant of Chow's priority-based algorithm, which is not optimal. It is then possible that unnecessary spilling is introduced.

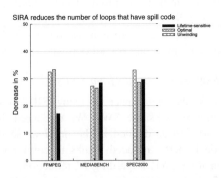

Figure A3.6. *Loops where spill code disappears completely*

Figure A3.6 shows the percentage of the loops that no longer have spill once SIRA is reduced. As can be seen, for any scheduler used in combination with SIRA, the percentage is significant.

A3.2.2. *Execution time performance results*

This section provides performance numbers when we execute the binary code generated on an ST231 VLIW processor, all compiled with -O3 optimization level. Since ST231 is an embedded processor (so we have no access to a workstation based on it), we use the precise simulator of STmicroelectronics. We warn the reader to remember that some optimized loops may or may not belong to hot execution paths, depending on the application and the chosen program input. This section plots the performance using the standard input of MEDIABENCH and FFMPEG. Other input data sets may exist, bringing distinct speedups for the same applications. Also, depending on the application, software pipelining (SWP) may or may not bring a significant speedup; all depends on the time fraction spent in the software pipelined loops, and the interactions with the microarchitectures mechanisms and other code optimization passes. Nowadays, it is really difficult to isolate the benefit of a single code optimization method such as SIRA.

We made a profiling to capture the percentage of the execution times spent in the SWP loops. In all MEDIABENCH applications, the percentage is really low. For example, the percentage of execution times spent in SWP loops was 1.7% for adpcm-decode, 2.23% for adpcm-encode epic, 2.9% for g721, 0% for gsm, 4.9% for jpeg-decode and only 10.8% for FFMPEG; the latter application is considered as the most representative of the usage of the ST231. From these profile data, we clearly see that we cannot expect *a priori* a significant speedup for the overall application execution times. We still made experiments to study the impact of SIRA on the execution times, presented in the next section.

A3.2.2.1. *Speedups*

In this section, we report the speedup of the whole application, not the speedups of the individual loops or code kernels optimized by SIRA combined with the three SWP schedulers. In addition, we experimented with an option of SIRA, called saturate, that allows us to not minimize the register pressure to the lowest possible level; due to this option, SIRA stops register optimization as soon as it reaches the number of available registers. This requires us to bound the periodic register saturation instead of minimizing the register requirement.

Figure A3.7 illustrates all the speedups obtained using the standard input. As expected when analyzing the profiling data (where the percentage of the execution times spent in SWP is low), we remark that the overall execution times do not vary in most of the applications, even if static spill count and II was reduced significantly.

However, we noticed some important overall speedups, from 1.1 for `adpcm-encode` in Figure A3.7(a) up to 2.45 for `g721-encode` in Figure A3.7(b). We unfortunately got some slowdowns; the worst one was 0.81 for `mesa-texgen` shown in Figure A3.7(c).

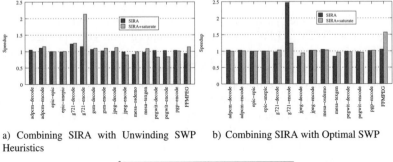

a) Combining SIRA with Unwinding SWP Heuristics   b) Combining SIRA with Optimal SWP

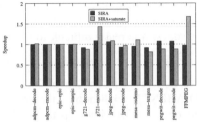

c) Combining SIRA with Lifetime-Sensitive SWP

Figure A3.7. *Speedups of the whole application using the standard input*

We carried out a deeper performance characterization to understand the real reasons for these speedups and slowdowns; it is seen that Icache effects are mainly responsible for these dynamic performances. These are studied in the following section.

A3.2.2.2. *Impact on instruction cache effects*

Nowadays, with numerous code optimization methods implemented inside optimizing compilers, inserting a new code optimization inside an existing complex compiler suffers from the phase ordering problem and from the interaction between complex phenomena [TOU 06]. For instance, register allocation seems to be a code optimization that alters spill code (Dcache effects) and instruction scheduling (ILP extraction). But it also influences the instruction cache behavior since the instruction schedule is altered. While reducing the amount of spill code reduces the code size, and should in theory improve Icache phenomena, this is not really the case. The reason is that Icache in our embedded VLIW processors is direct mapped.

Consequently, Icache conflicts account for a large fraction for Icache misses: depending on the code layout in memory, multiple hot functions and loops may share the same Icache lines, even if their size fits inside the Icache capacity [GUI 05]. If Icache is fully associative, capacity Icache conflicts could benefit from the reduction of code size, but this is not what happens with direct mapped caches. At our level of optimization, we have no control on Icache effects when we do register allocation. Other code optimization methods could be employed to improve the interaction with direct mapped Icache [GUI 05].

To illustrate our discovery, we present the performance characterization of the two applications that resulted in the highest speedup (2.45 for g721-encode) and the lowest slowdown (0.81 for mesa-texgen). We measured the execution time in clock cycles using precise simulation, and we characterize it into the five main categories of stalls on ST231: computation + Dcache stalls + Icache stalls + interlock stalls + branch penalties. Figure A3.8 illustrates the five categories of execution times. The first bar corresponds to the execution time of the code generated without using SIRA. The second bar shows the execution time of the code generated when we use SIRA, optimizing all register types conjointly. The last bar shows the execution time when we apply SIRA with the saturate option. We can clearly see that the Icache effects explain the origin of the observed slowdowns and the speedups.

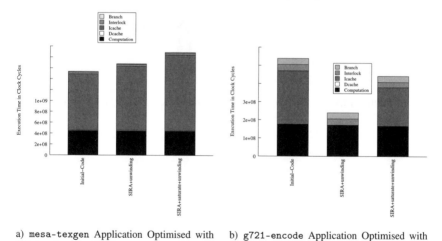

a) mesa-texgen Application Optimised with Lifetime Sensitive SWP

b) g721-encode Application Optimised with Optimal SWP

Figure A3.8. *Performance characterization of some applications*

However, in certain situations spill code reduction improves DCache effects. The following section presents a case study.

A3.2.2.3. *Impact on data cache effects*

As previously stated, FFMPEG is the most complex code to optimize, and represents the typical application for ST231 processor. Figure A3.9 illustrates its performance characterization when we apply SIRA before optimal SWP. The first bar corresponds to the execution time of the code generated without using SIRA. The second bar shows the execution time of the code generated when we use SIRA, optimizing all register types conjointly. The third bar shows the execution time of the code generated when we use SIRA, optimizing GR registers before BR registers. The last bar shows the opposite order (BR followed by GR). While the second bar shows improvement in Icache penalties, the last bar clearly shows that Dcache stalls reduced due to the application of SIRA.

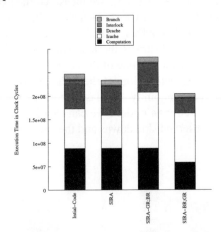

Figure A3.9. *Performance characterization of the FFMPEG application*

Appendix 4

Efficiency of Non-Positive Circuit Elimination in the SIRA Framework

A4.1. Experimental setup

These experiments were conducted by Sébastien Briais on the stand-alone data dependence graph (DDG) described in Appendix 1. We assume $\mathcal{T} = \{GR, BR, FP\}$. We used a regular Linux workstation (Intel Xeon, 2.33 GHz, 9 GB of memory).

A4.1.1. *Heuristics nomenclature*

Our methods to avoid the creation of non-positive circuits are of three types:

1) UAL is the (pessimistic) naive heuristic that consists of applying SIRALINA with unit-assumed-latencies (UAL) semantics only. That is, we do not consider non-unit-assumed-latencies (NUAL) code semantics from the beginning.

2) CHECK is the reactive strategy that consists of first applying SIRALINA with NUAL semantics. If a non-positive circuit is detected, we apply a second pass, which applies SIRALINA but with a UAL semantics.

3) SPE is the proactive strategy, based on shortest paths equations (SPE). If $n(n \geq 1)$ is the bound on the maximal number of iterations used, we write SPE_n.

A4.1.2. *Empirical efficiency measures*

For each heuristic of non-positive circuit elimination, for each DDG and for each initiation interval II between MII and L (L is a fixed upper bound on the admissible values for II), we measured the execution time taken by each heuristic (listed above) to minimize the register requirement; we also recorded the number of registers computed by the three methods (UAL,CHECK and SPE). We are going to examine these results in the next sections.

We have also considered three possible target architectures (small, medium and large) as described in A1.3. When the number of available registers is fixed in the architecture, we may need to iterate on multiple values for II in order to get a solution below the processor capacity; that is, since register minimization is applied for a fixed II, we may need to iterate on multiple values of II if the minimized register requirement is still above the number of available registers. The strategy for iterating over II for one of our heuristics (here, any of the three methods previously described can be used: UAL, CHECK, SPE) is the following:

– check whether the heuristic produces a solution that satisfies the register constraints for II = MII;

- if yes, stop and return the solution;

- if no, check whether the method gives a solution that satisfies the constraints for II = L (maximal allowed value for II):

- if yes (II = L gives a solution), search linearly the smallest II > MII such that the heuristic computes a solution that satisfies the register constraints;

- if no (II = L does not give a solution), then fail (no solution found, spilling is required).

For each architecture and for each DDG G, we determined whether the heuritic (UAL, CHECK or SPE) is able to find a solution that satisfies the architectural constraints. We thus measured:

– the elapsed time needed to determine whether a solution exists;

– the smallest II for which a solution exists (when applicable).

Regarding the iterative heuristic of non-positive circuit elimination (SPE), we arbitrarily fixed the maximal number of iterations to 3 and 5. In order to get an idea of how many iterations the iterative methods could take in the worst case before reaching a fixed point (convergence), we conducted the experiments by setting the maximum number of iterations allowed to 1,000 and recorded the number of iterations reached. Remember that if a fixed point (convergence) is detected, the iterative algorithm stops before reaching 1,000 iterations.

A4.2. Comparison between the heuristics execution times

In this section, we compare and discuss the execution times of the heuristics of non-positive circuits elimination.

A4.2.1. *Time to minimize register pressure for a fixed II*

In this section, we apply the three methods with all values of II. Figure A4.1 shows the distribution of execution times of UAL heuristic: MIN is the minimal value, FST is the value of first quartile (25% of the values are less than or equal to the FST value), THD is the value of the third quartile (75% of the values are less than or equal to the THD value) and MAX is the maximal value. We also use boxplot to graphically depict the values of MIN, FST, MEDIAN, THD and MAX.

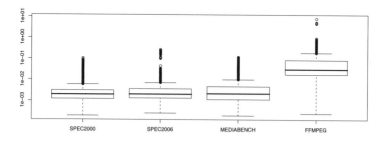

	SPEC2000	SPEC2006	MEDIABENCH	FFMPEG
MIN	0.000194	0.000254	0.000194	0.000244
FST	0.00121	0.001309	0.00114	0.017507
MEDIAN	0.001954	0.002007	0.002158	0.031229
THD	0.003092	0.003601	0.004682	0.08647
MAX	0.102878	0.267225	0.118746	7.97499

Figure A4.1. *Execution times of UAL (in seconds)*

Figure A4.2 shows the distribution of CHECK heuristic execution times.

Figure A4.3 shows the distribution of SPE_n heuristic execution times for $n \in \{5, 1000\}$.

From the above results, we found that, as expected, UAL is the fastest heuristic. CHECK is between one and three times slower than UAL, which was also expected because it consists of running SIRALINA, performing a check and in the worst case running SIRALINA a second time.

Regarding our proactive heuristic, SPE heuristic seems to have quite a reasonable running time, but is still more expensive than UAL or CHECK (about 10 times slower).

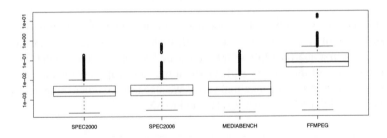

	SPEC2000	SPEC2006	MEDIABENCH	FFMPEG
MIN	0.000211	0.00028	0.000215	0.00026
FST	0.001517	0.001556	0.00137	0.040792
MEDIAN	0.002499	0.002673	0.003029	0.073375
THD	0.004925	0.005263	0.007788	0.202154
MAX	0.183653	0.636804	0.268994	17.8744

Figure A4.2. *Execution times of CHECK (in seconds)*

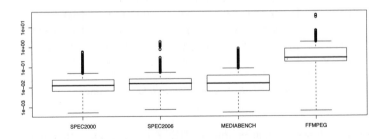

	SPEC2000	SPEC2006	MEDIABENCH	FFMPEG
MIN	0.000534	0.000747	0.000536	0.000627
FST	0.006597	0.007188	0.006236	0.176632
MEDIAN	0.012591	0.015273	0.015129	0.275262
THD	0.024067	0.025851	0.037576	0.793465
MAX	0.587562	1.84686	0.834527	37.7923

a) 5 iterations

Figure A4.3. *a) Execution times of SPE (in seconds)*

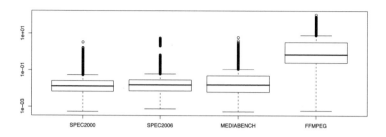

	SPEC2000	SPEC2006	MEDIABENCH	FFMPEG
MIN	0.000544	0.000766	0.00054	0.00061
FST	0.006702	0.007244	0.00633	0.257014
MEDIAN	0.013011	0.015423	0.015643	0.716324
THD	0.02542	0.028811	0.048997	3.3835
MAX	3.35579	5.67563	6.17455	106.426

b) 1000 iterations

Figure A4.3. *b) Execution times of SPE (in seconds)*

A4.3. Convergence of the proactive heuristic (iterative SIRALINA)

In this section we study the speed of convergence (in terms of number of iterations) of SPE heuristic. Recall that *SPE* is said to *converge* when it reaches a fixed point, i.e. when the set of reuse edges does not change between two consecutive iterations of algorithm 10.1. All the values of II are tested; so the experiments we consider in this section are for all DDG and for all II values.

Figure A4.4 shows the distribution of the number of iterations of SPE heuristic (truncated at 1,000). We observe that on a small number of DDGs, the upper bound of 1,000 iterations has been reached by SPE heuristic. It is indeed well possible that the iterative process does not terminate in the general case. Note, finally, that this information may be used to set the upper bound in an industrial compiler on the maximal number of iterations: five iterations seems to be a satisfactory practical choice since it allows the convergence in 75% of the cases for SPEC2000, SPEC2006 and MEDIABENCH benchmarks.

A4.4. Qualitative analysis of the heuristics

In this section, we study the quality of the solution produced by the heuristics. The qualitative aspects include the number of registers needed to schedule the DDG and the loss of parallelism due to an increase of the MII resulted from * UAL, CHECK and SPE.

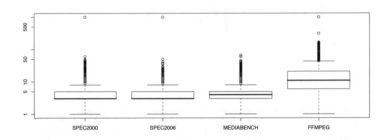

	SPEC2000	SPEC2006	MEDIABENCH	FFMPEG
MIN	1	1	1	1
FST	3	3	3	6
MEDIAN	3	3	4	11
THD	5	5	5	21
MAX	1000	1000	66	1000

Figure A4.4. *Maximum observed number of iterations for SPE*

A4.4.1. *Number of saved registers*

In this section, we analyze the number of registers each heuristic manages to optimize. Our tests are for all DDG, for all II values. We graphically compare the heuristics: for each set of benchmarks, and each register type, we construct a partial order (lattice) as follows:

– the vertices are labeled with the name of the heuristic;

– a directed edge links an heuristic A to an heuristic B iff the number of registers (of considered type) computed by heuristic B is statistically greater (worse) than the number of registers (of the same type) computed by heuristic A: by statistically greater, we mean that we applied a one sided Student's t-test between the alternatives A and B, and we report the risk level of this statistical test (between brackets in the edges). The edge is also labeled with the ratio $\dfrac{\sum_{G,II} R_B}{\sum_{G,II} R_A}$ where R_B is the number of registers (of considered type) computed by heuristic B and R_A is the number of registers computed by heuristic A.

The lattices are given in Figures A4.5, A4.6, A4.7 and A4.8.

For instance, we read in Figure A4.5 that the number of registers of type branch register (BR) computed by UAL heuristic is 1.069, which is greater than the number of registers of type BR computed by CHECK heuristic.

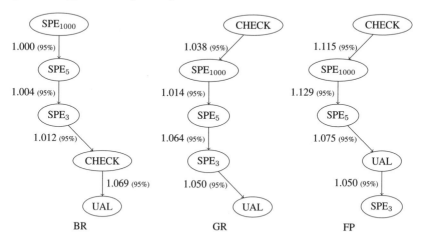

Figure A4.5. *Comparison of the heuristics' ability to reduce the register pressure (SPEC2000)*

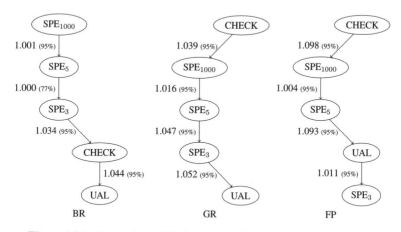

Figure A4.6. *Comparison of the heuristics' ability to reduce the register pressure (MEDIABENCH)*

First, from these results, we observe that the ordering of the heuristics depends on the register type. Indeed, since the heuristics try to reduce register pressure of all types simultaneously, it happens that some perform better on one type that on the others.

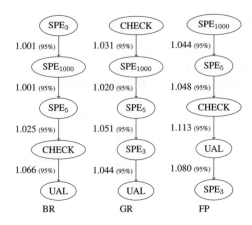

Figure A4.7. *Comparison of the heuristics' ability to reduce the register pressure (SPEC2006)*

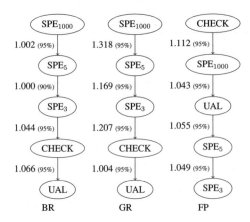

Figure A4.8. *Comparison of the heuristics' ability to reduce the register pressure (FFMPEG)*

Second, we see that UAL is the worst heuristic regarding register requirements. This is not surprising since this is the most naive way to eliminate non-positive circuits.

Finally, we observe that CHECK is sometimes the best heuristic (in particular for general register (GR) and floating point (FP) types on all benchmarks except FFMPEG). We can explain this by the fact that the proportion of DDG with non-positive circuits on SPEC2000, SPEC2006 and MEDIABENCH is low (less than 40%). Consequently, the reactive strategy (CHECK) is appropriate, since more than 60% of the DDG did not get a non-positive circuit from the beginning (so they did not require a correction step).

A4.4.2. *Proportion of success when looking for a solution that satisfies the register constraints*

In this section, we do not analyze the amount of registers needed as in the previous section. We assume an architecture with a fixed number of available registers, and we count the number of solutions that have a register requirement below the processor capacity. We decompose the solutions into three families: the DDGs that have been solved without MII increase, the DDGs that have been solved with MII increase and the DDG that was not solved with the heuristic (spilled). All the results are present in [BRI 10].

We noted that most of the time our heuristics found a solution that satisfies the register constraints. Of course, the percentage of success increased while the architecture constraints were relaxed. Apart from the FFMPEG benchmarks under the small architecture constraints (where the number of available registers is very small, so the constraints on register pressure are harder to satisfy), the percentage of success is above 95%. In these cases, all the heuristics give comparable results.

For the FFMPEG benchmarks, we see that SPE_5 and SPE_{1000} give slightly better results than the naive UALheuristic (1%–3% better). We observe that in most cases of success, the MII has not been increased at all.

A4.4.3. *Increase of the MII when looking for a solution that satisfies the register constraints*

We count the MII increase by the formula $\dfrac{\sum MII_h(G)}{\sum MII(G)} - 1$, where $MII_h(G)$ is the MII of the associated DDG computed by heuristic h. In other words MII_h is the smallest period II that satisfies the register constraints when we use heuristic h, where $h \in \{\text{UAL, CHECK, SPE}_n\}$. All the results are present in [BRI 10].

These results show that the increase of the MII is very low (less than 6% in the worst case). It is clearly negligible on SPEC2000, SPEC2006 and MEDIABENCH benchmarks. On FFMPEG benchmarks, we see that when dealing with small architecture, SPE heuristics tend to increase the MII more than UAL or CHECK heuristics, whereas for bigger architecture, SPE_5 and SPE_{1000} give slightly better results than UAL or CHECK.

A4.5. Conclusion on non-positive circuit elimination strategy

The conclusions we can take from this extensive experimental study are contrasted. On the one hand, the results show that the proactive heuristic SPE allows us to save a little more registers than the two naive heuristics UAL and CHECK. On the other hand, these results also show that our proactive heuristic is more expensive regarding the execution times than the reactive one.

Thus, we advise the following policy: if the target architectures are embedded systems, where compilation time does not need to be interactive and where register constraints are strong, we recommend the use of the SPE proactive heuristic. As we have seen, it optimizes registers better than the reactive heuristic while still being quite cheap. On the contrary, if the target architecture is a general purpose computer (workstation, desktop or supercomputer), where register constraints are not too strong, it is probably sufficient to use the reactive heuristic CHECK, as it already gives good results in practice and it is only between one and three times slower than the UAL heuristic.

Appendix 5

Loop Unroll Degree Minimization: Experimental Results

All our benchmarks have been cross-compiled on a regular Dell workstation, equipped with Intel(R) Core(TM)2 CPU of 2.4 GHz and Linux operating system (kernel version 2.6, 64 bits).

A5.1. Stand-alone experiments with single register types

This section presents full experiments on a stand-alone tool by considering a single register type only. Our stand-alone tool is independent of the compiler and processor architecture. We will demonstrate the efficiency of our loop minimization method for both unscheduled loops (as studied in section 11.4) and scheduled loops (as studied in section 11.6).

A5.1.1. *Experiments with unscheduled loops*

In this context, our stand-alone tool takes a data dependence graph (DDG) as input, just after a periodic register allocation done by SIRA, and applies a loop unrolling minimization (LUM).

A5.1.2. *Results on randomly generated data dependence graphs*

First, our stand-alone software generates the number of distinct reuse circuits k and their weights $(\mu_1, \ldots, \mu_k)$. Afterwards, we calculate the number of remaining registers $R = \mathcal{R}^t - \sum_{i=1}^{k} \mu_i$ and the loop unrolling degree $\rho = lcm(\mu_1, \ldots, \mu_k)$. Finally, we apply our method for minimizing ρ.

We did extensive random generations on many configurations: we varied the number of available registers $\mathcal{R}^t$ from 4 to 256, and we considered 10,000 random instances containing multiple hundreds of reuse circuits. Each reuse circuit can be arbitrarily large. That is, our experiments are done on random DDGs with an unbounded number of nodes (as large as one wants). Only the number of reuse circuits is bounded.

Figure A5.1 is a two-dimensional (2D) plot representing the code size compaction ratio obtained thanks to our method. The code size compaction is counted as the ratio between the initial unrolling degree and the minimized one ($ratio = \frac{\rho}{\rho^*}$). The x-axis represents the number of available hardware registers (going from 4 to 256) and the y-axis represents the code compaction ratio. As can be seen, our method allows us to have a code size reduction ranging from 1 to more than 10,000. In addition, we note in Figure A5.1 that the ratio is very important when the $\mathcal{R}^t$ is greater. For example, the ratio of some minimization exceeds 10,000 when $\mathcal{R}^t = 256$. Figure A5.2 summarizes all the ratio numbers with their harmonic and geometric means. As observed, these average ratios are significant and increase with the number of available registers.

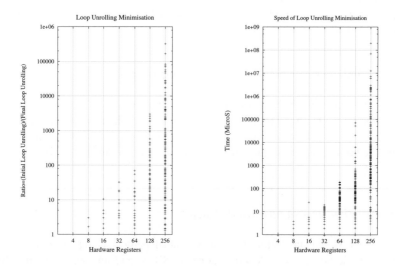

Figure A5.1. *Loop unrolling minimization experiments (random DDG, single register type)*

Furthermore, our method is very fast. Figure A5.1 plots the speed of our method on a dual-core 2 GHz Linux PC, ranging from 1 microsecond to 10 seconds. This speed is satisfactory for optimizing compilers devoted to embedded systems (not to interactive compilers like gcc or icc). We also note that the speed of extremely rare minimization (when $\mathcal{R}^t = 256$) can reach 1,000 s.

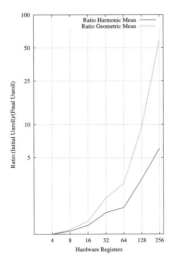

Figure A5.2. *Average code compaction ratio (random DDG, single register type)*

A5.1.3. *Experiments on real DDG*

The DDGs we use here are extracted from various real benchmarks, either from the embedded domain or from the high-performance computing domain: DSP-filters, Spec, Lin-ddot, Livermore, Whetstone, etc. The total number of experimented DDGs is 310, their sizes range from 2 nodes and 2 arcs up to 360 nodes and 590 arcs. Afterwards, we performed experiments on these DDGs, depending on the considered number of registers. We considered the following three configurations:

1) a machine with an unbounded number of registers;

2) a machine with a bounded number of registers varying from 4 to 256;

3) a machine with a bounded number of registers varying from 4 to 256 with the option `continue` (described later).

A5.1.3.1. *Machine with an unbounded number of registers*

Theoretically, the best result for the *LCM-MIN problem* (section 11.4) is $\rho^* = \mu_k$ the greatest value of μ_i, $\forall i = 1, k$. Hence, with these experiments we aim to calculate the mean of the added registers ($\sum_{i=1}^{k} r_i$) required to obtain an unrolling degree of

μ_k. Recall that μ_k is the weight of the largest circuit, so the smallest possible unrolling degree is μ_k.

In order to interpret all the data resulting from the application of our method to all DDGs, we present some statistics. Indeed, we have looked for an arithmetic mean to represent the average of the added registers $(AVR^{ar}(\sum_{i=1}^{k} r_i))$ needed to obtain μ_k. Moreover, we calculate the harmonic mean of all the ratio $(AVR^{har}(\frac{\rho}{\mu_k}))$.

Our experiments show that using 12.1544 additional registers on average is sufficient to obtain a minimal loop unrolling degree with $\rho^* = \mu_k$. We also note that we have a high harmonic mean for the ratio $(AVR^{har}(\frac{\rho}{\mu_k}) = 2.10023)$. That is, our LUM pass is very efficient regarding code size compaction.

A5.1.3.2. *Machine with a bounded number of registers*

We consider a machine with a bounded number of architectural registers $\mathcal{R}^t$. We varied $\mathcal{R}^t$ from 4 to 256 and applied our code optimization method on all DDGs. For each configuration, we looked for an arithmetic mean to represent the average of number of added registers $(AVR^{ar}(\sum_{i=1}^{k} r_i))$. Moreover, we calculate the weighted harmonic mean of all the ratios described as $AVR^{har}(\frac{\rho}{\rho^*})$, as well as the geometric mean described as $AVR^{GM}(\frac{\rho}{\rho^*})$. Finally, we also calculate the arithmetic mean of the remaining registers $(AVR^{ar}(R))$ after the register allocation step given by our backend compilation framework.

Table A5.1 shows that our solution finds the minimum unrolling factor in all configurations except when $\mathcal{R}^t = 4$. On average, a small number of added registers are sufficient for having a minimal loop unrolling degree (ρ^*). For example, in the configuration with 32 registers, we find the minimal loop unrolling degree, if we add on average 1.07806 registers among 9.72285 remaining registers. We also note that we have, in many configurations, a high harmonic and geometric mean for the ratio $(AVR^{har}(ratio))$. For example, in the machine with 256 registers, $AVR^{har}(ratio) = 2.725$ and $AVR^{har}(ratio) = 5.61$. Note that in practice, if we have more architectural registers, then we have more remaining registers. Consequently, we can minimize the unrolling factors in lower values. This explains, for instance, why the minimum unrolling degree uses more remaining registers when there are 256 architectural registers than when there are 8 (see Table A5.1), with the advantage of a better loop unroll minimization ratio on average.

Figure A5.3 shows the harmonic mean of the minimized (final) and the initial loop unrolling weighted by the number of nodes of different DDGs. We calculate this weighted harmonic mean on different configurations. We give a generic very long instruction word (VLIW) processor with an issue width of four instructions per clock cycle, where all the DDGs are pipelined with $II = MII = \max(MII_{\text{ress}}, MII_{\text{dept}})$. In all configurations, the average of the final unrolling degree of pipelined loops is below 8, which is a significant improvement over the initial unrolling degree. For example, in the configuration where $\mathcal{R}^t = 64$, the minimized loop unrolling is, on average, equal to 7.78.

$\mathcal{R}^t$	$AVR^{ar}(\sum_{i=1}^{k} r_i)$	$AVR^{har}(ratio)$	$AVR^{GM}(ratio)$	$AVR^{ar}(R)$
4	0	1	1	0.293562
8	0.0151163	1.00729	1	0.818314
16	0.250158	1.10463	1.16	2.72361
32	1.07806	1.4149	1.73	9.72285
64	3.07058	1.96319	3.34	29.0559
128	14.0731	2.71566	5.54	79.6419
256	15.2288	2.72581	5.61	207.118

Table A5.1. *Machine with bounded number of registers*

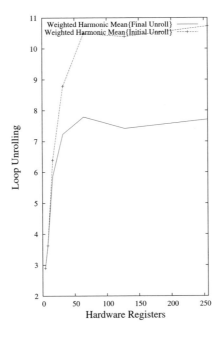

Figure A5.3. *Weighted harmonic mean for minimized loop unrolling degree*

A5.1.3.3. *Machine with bounded number of registers and option* `continue`

In these experiments, we use the `continue` option of our periodic register allocation. Without this option, SIRA computes the first periodic register allocation which verifies $\sum \mu_i \leq \mathcal{R}^t$ (not necessarily minimal). If we use the option `continue`, SIRA generates the periodic register allocation that minimizes $\sum \mu_i$, leaving more remaining registers to the LUM process. In order to compare these two configurations (a machine with a bounded number of registers versus a machine with bounded number of registers using option `continue`), we reproduce the statistics of the previous experiments using this additional option. The results are provided in Table A5.2.

$\mathcal{R}^t$	$AVR^{ar}(\sum_{i=1}^{k} r_i)$	$AVR^{har}(ratio)$	$AVR^{GM}(ratio)$	$AVR^{ar}(R)$
4	0	1	1	0.33412
8	0.015841	1.00774	1.01	0.885657
16	0.253726	1.10477	1.16	2.79591
32	1.09681	1.42146	1.74	9.96854
64	3.25124	2.02749	3.59	31.1405
128	9.40373	2.28922	4.32	81.7739
256	15.1959	2.71729	5.58	207.394

Table A5.2. *Machine with bounded registers with option* `continue`

By comparing Table A5.1 and Table A5.2, we notice that some configurations yield a better harmonic mean for the code compaction ratio with the `continue` option, when $\mathcal{R}^t \leq 64$. Conversely, the ratio without the `continue` option is better when $\mathcal{R}^t \geq 128$. These strange results are side effects of the reuse circuits generated by SIRA, which differ depending on the number of architectural registers. In addition, increasing the number of remaining registers (by performing minimal periodic register allocation) does not necessarily imply a maximal reduction of loop unrolling degree.

A5.1.4. *Experiments with scheduled loops*

We integrated our loop unrolling reduction method as a postpass of the meeting graph technique. Since SWP has already been computed, the loop unrolling reduction method is applied when meeting graph finds that MAXLIVE $\leq \mathcal{R}^t$. Otherwise, the meeting graph (MG) does not unroll the loop and proposes a heuristic to introduce spill code.

Table A5.3 shows the number of DDGs when the MG finds periodic register allocation without spilling among 1,935 DDGs and the number of DDGs where spill codes are introduced.

$\mathcal{R}^t$	Unrolled loop with MG	Spilled loops with MG
16	1, 602	333
32	1, 804	131
64	1, 900	35
128	1, 929	6
256	1, 935	0

Table A5.3. *Number of unrolled loops compared to the number of spilled loops resulted (by using meeting graphs)*

In order to highlight the improvements of our loop unrolling reduction method on DDG where MG found a solution (no spill), we show in Figure A5.4 a boxplot[1] for each processor configuration. We remark that the final (reduced) loop unrolling of half of the DDG is under 2 and that the minimized loop unrolling of 75% of applications is less than or equal to 3, while the upper quartile of initial loop unrolling is less than or equal to 6. We note also that the maximum loop unrolling degree is improved in each processor configuration. For example, in the machine with 128 registers, the maximum loop unrolling degree is reduced from 21, 840 to 41.

In addition, we looked for an arithmetic mean to represent the average of the initial loop unrolling ρ, the final loop unrolling ρ^* and $ratio = \frac{\sum \rho}{\sum \rho^*}$. Table A5.4 shows that on average the final loop unrolling degree is greatly reduced compared to the initial loop unrolling degree.

For each configuration, we also computed the number of loops where the reduced loop unrolling degree is less than MAXLIVE. In Table A5.5, we produce the different results. It shows that in each configuration, the minimal loop unrolling degree obtained using our method is significantly less than MAXLIVE. Only a very small number of loops are unrolled MAXLIVE times.

We also measured the running time of our approach using instrumentation with gettimeofday function. On average, the execution time of loop unrolling reduction in the meeting graph is about 5 microseconds. The maximum run-time is about 600 microseconds.

---

1 Boxplot, also known as a *box-and-whisker diagram*, is a convenient way of graphically depicting groups of numerical data through their five-number summaries: the smallest observations (min), lower quartile ($Q1 = 25\%$), median ($Q2 = 50\%$), upper quartile ($Q3 = 75\%$) and largest observations (max). The min is the first value of the boxplot, and the max is the last value. Sometimes, the extrema values (min or max) are very close to one of the quartiles. This is why sometimes we do not distinguish between the extrema values and some quartiles.

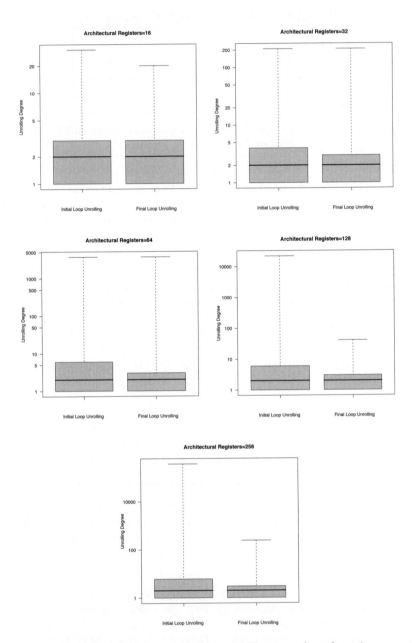

Figure A5.4. *Initial versus final loop unrolling in each configuration*

$\mathcal{R}^t$	Average initial loop unrolling factors	Average reduced loop unrolling factors	Average arithmetic ratio
16	2.743	2.207	1.242
32	4.81	2.569	1.872
64	25.86	11.02	2.346
128	236.6	2.852	82.959
256	525.7	3.044	172.7

Table A5.4. *Arithmetic mean of initial loop unrolling, final loop unrolling and ratio*

$\mathcal{R}^t$	Minimal loop unrolling < MAXLIVE	number of loops unrolled MAXLIVE times	Total number of loops
16	1,601	1	1,602
32	1,801	3	1,804
64	1,893	7	1,900
128	1,929	0	1,929
256	1,935	0	1,935

Table A5.5. *Comparison between final loop unrolling factors and MAXLIVE*

A5.1.4.1. *Loop unrolling of scheduled versus unscheduled loops*

In order to compare the final loop unrolling using the MG (scheduled loops) and SIRA (unscheduled loops), we conducted experiments on larger DDGs from both high performance and embedded benchmarks: SPEC2000, SPEC2006, MEDIABENCH and LAO (internal STMicroelectronics codes). We applied our algorithm to a total of 9,027 loops. We consider a machine with a bounded number of architectural registers $\mathcal{R}^t$. We varied $\mathcal{R}^t$ from 16 to 256.

The experiments show that final loop unrolling degrees computed by MG are lower than those computed by SIRA. The minimal unrolling degree for 75% of SIRA optimized loops is less than or equal to 7. In contrast, MG does not require any unrolling at all (unroll degree equal to 1) for 75% of loops.

We highlight in Table A5.6 some of the other results. We report the arithmetic mean of final loop unrolling and the maximum final loop unrolling. It shows that in each configuration, the average of minimal loop unrolling degree obtained due to our method is small when using MG compared with the average of final loop unrolling in SIRA. We also show that the maximum final loop unrolling degrees are low in MG compared to those in SIRA. The main exception is LAO where the unrolling degree for the meeting graph on a machine with 16 registers is actually slightly higher. In the first line of Table A5.6, we see that the value 30 exceeds MAXLIVE+1, while our method should result in an unrolling factor equal to at most MAXLIVE+1, if enough remaining registers exist. This extreme case is due to the fact that there are no registers left to apply our loop unrolling reduction method.

$\mathcal{R}^t$	Benchmarks	Average final loop unrolling		Maximum final loop unroll	
		MG	SIRA	MG	SIRA
16	LAO	1.127	2.479	30	28
	MEDIABENCH	1.175	2.782	12	26
	SPEC2000	1.113	2.629	9	28
	SPEC2006	1.085	2.758	9	16
32	LAO	1.219	3.662	9	57
	MEDIABENCH	1.185	3.032	9	84
	SPEC2000	1.118	2.823	9	28
	SPEC2006	1.09	2.966	9	26
64	LAO	1.3	6.476	9	72
	MEDIABENCH	1.426	3.225	63	84
	SPEC2000	1.119	2.881	9	45
	SPEC2006	1.09	3.001	9	26
128	LAO	1.345	9.651	9	88
	MEDIABENCH	1.215	3.338	14	84
	SPEC2000	1.119	2.916	9	45
	SPEC2006	1.09	3.063	9	275
256	LAO	1.345	9.733	9	88
	MEDIABENCH	1.214	3.384	14	84
	SPEC2000	1.119	2.946	9	45
	SPEC2006	1.09	3.256	9	27

Table A5.6. *Optimized loop unrolling factors of scheduled versus unscheduled loops*

The choice between the two techniques depends on whether the loop is already software pipelined or not. If periodic register allocation should be done for any reason before software pipelining, then SIRA is more appropriate; otherwise, MG followed by LUM provides lower loop unrolling degrees.

In the following section, we study the efficiency of our method when integrated inside a real industrial compiler.

A5.2. Experiments with multiple register types

Our experimental setup is based on st200cc compiler, which target the VLIW ST231 processor. We followed the methodology described in Appendix A3.2.

First, regarding compilation times, our experiments show that the runtime of our SIRA register allocation followed by LUM is less than 1 s per loop on average. So, it is fast enough to be included inside an industrial cross-compiler such as st200cc.

A5.2.1. *Statistics on minimal loop unrolling factors*

Figure A5.5 shows numerous boxplots representing the initial loop unrolling degree and the final loop unrolling degree of the different loops per benchmark application. In each benchmark family (LAO, MEDIABENCH, SPEC2000 and SPE2006), we note that the loop unrolling degree is reduced significantly from its initial value to its final value.

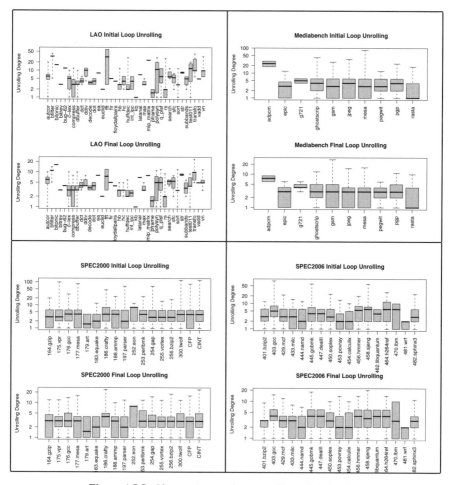

Figure A5.5. *Observations on loop unrolling minimization*

To highlight the improvements of our LUM method, we show in Figure A5.6 a boxplot for each benchmark family (LAO, SPEC2000, SPEC2006 and MEDIABENCH). We can remark that the final loop unrolling of half of the applications is under 3 and that the final loop unrolling of 75% of applications is less than or equal to 5. This compares favorably with the loop unrolling degrees calculated by minimizing each register type in isolation. Here, the final loop unrolling degree of half of the applications is under 5 and the final loop unrolling of 75% of the applications is under 7, the final loop unrolling for the remaining loops can reach 50. These numbers demonstrate the advantage of minimizing all register types concurrently. Of course, if the code size is a hard constraint, we do not generate the code if the loop unrolling factor is prohibitive and we backtrack from SWP. Otherwise, if the code size budget is less restrictive, our experimental results show that by using our minimal loop unrolling technique, all the unrolled loops fit in the Icache of the ST321 (32 kbytes size).

Final Loop Unrolling

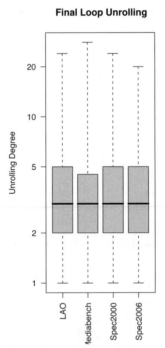

Figure A5.6. *Final loop unrolling factors after minimization*

Appendix 6

Experimental Efficiency of Software Data Preloading and Prefetching for Embedded VLIW

For our experimentation, we used a cycle-accurate simulator provided by STmicroelectronics. The astiss simulator offers the possibility of considering a non-blocking cache. We fixed the number of misinformation status hold registers (MSHR) (the pending loads queue) at 8. We made the choice of eight MSHR, because during experimentation, we observed that the instruction-level parallelism (ILP) and register pressure reach a limit when MSHR is set to eight; a larger MSHR does not yield more performance. We use a simulator for our experiments for many reasons:

– It is not easy to have a physical machine based on a very long instruction word (VLIW) ST231 processor. These processors are not sold for workstations, and are part of embedded systems such as mobile phones, DVD recorders, digital TV, etc. Consequently, we do not have direct access to a workstation for our experiments.

– The ST231 processor has a blocking cache architecture, while we conduct our experimental study on a non-blocking cache. Only simulation allows us to consider a non-blocking cache.

– Our experimental study requires precise performance characterization that is not possible with direct measurement on executions: the hardware performance counters of the ST231 do not allow to characterize processor stalls we are focusing on (stalls due to Dcache misses). Only simulation allows us to precisely measure the reasons of the processor stalls.

Concerning the compilation phase, we use the -O3 compilation option for all tested benchmarks with the st200cc compiler. The data preloading technique has been implemented (by STmicroelectronics) inside this compiler to set the load latencies at different granularity levels: loops, functions, application. The compiler does not insert prefetch instructions, so we insert them manually inside the assembly code following our methodology explained in section 6.2.

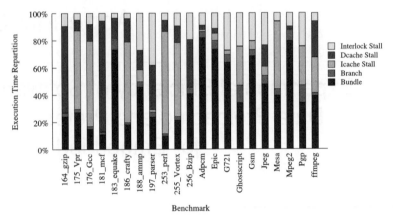

Figure A6.1. *Execution time repartition for Spec benchmarks*

We make experiments on SPEC2000 and MEDIABENCH. Furthermore, we use the vendor benchmark called FFMPEG used for their internal research. The first time, we made a precise performance characterization of all these benchmarks. For each executed application, we decomposed its execution times using the following formula: $T = Calc + DC + IC + InterS + Br$, where T is the total execution time in processor clock cycles, $Calc$ is the effective computation time in cycles, DC is the number of stall cycles due to Dcache misses, IC is the number of stall cycles due to instruction cache misses, $InterS$ is the number of stall cycles due to the interlock mechanism and finally Br is the number of branch penalties. Figure A6.1 plots the performance characterization of the used benchmarks. As can be seen for MEDIABENCH applications, only small fraction of the execution time is lost due to Dcache penalties, except in the case of jped. So, most of the MEDIABENCH applications will do not take advantage from Dcache optimization techniques on ST231. The best candidates for our low-level cache optimization method are the benchmarks, which contain large Dcache penalty fractions. As shown in Figure A6.1, Mcf and Gzip seem to be the best candidates for Dcache improvement. Indeed, Mcf has more than 76% of Dcache penalty, and Gzip has more than 56% of Dcache penalty. Other benchmarks have smaller fractions of Dcache penalties, between 10% and 20% depending on the benchmark. However, these benchmarks have enough Dcache misses to expect some positive results. The benchmarks that have negligible fraction due to Dcache stalls are ignored for our optimization strategy.

For each optimized benchmark, we made a precise trace analysis to determine the regularity of the delinquent loads. We apply the prefetching and preloading techniques described previously and we compare the results to the performance of the generated code with the -O3 compiler optimization level. Figure A6.2 illustrates our experimental results (performance gain). As shown, the prefetch technique allows us to have positive overall performance gain up to 9.12% (mcf). Due to prefetching, some cache misses are eliminated. However, prefetching requires regular data streams to be applied efficiently. If the data stream is not regular (non-constant strides), the preloading technique is more efficient. While it requires a compilation trade-off between register pressure and load latencies, the produced performance gain is satisfactory in practice: we can obtain up to 6.83% overall performance gain for bzip. The preloading technique gives good results except in the crafty benchmark. After a deep study of crafty, we observed that specifying larger latencies for load instructions has a negative impact on a critical loop. This loop causes a slowdown due to the instructions' cache penalty because the memory layout of the codes changed, creating conflict misses. Note that we can obtain higher speedup when we combine the two techniques conjointly. As shown in Figure A6.2, jpeg gains more than 14% of the execution time.

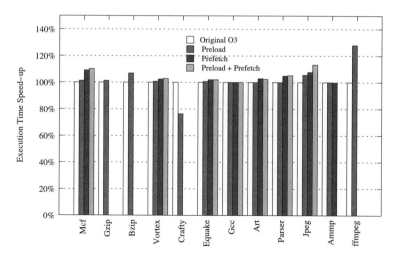

Figure A6.2. *Efficiency of data prefetching and preloading. Note that prefetching is not applicable to all applications*

Regarding code size, our prefetching technique does not introduce any extra code in practice; we succeed in scheduling all prefetch instructions inside free VLIW slots. However, the preloading technique may induce some negligible code size growth (3.9% in extreme case of mcf) (see Figure A6.3).

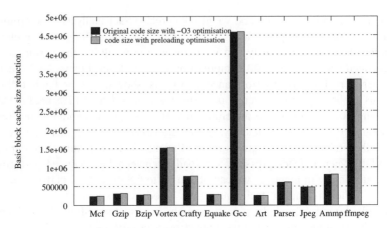

Figure A6.3. *Initial and modified codes sizes*

Appendix 7

Appendix of the Speedup-Test Protocol

A7.1. Why is the observed minimal execution time not necessarily a good statistical estimation of program performances?

Considering the minimum value of the n observed execution times is sometimes used in the literature but can be discussed:

– Nothing guarantees that this minimum execution time is an *ideal* execution of the program.

– Nothing guarantees that the minimum execution time over multiple runs represents the run with the least noise.

– Nothing guarantees that this minimum execution time is a consequence of the optimization technique under study. Maybe this minimum execution time is an accident, or a consequence of dynamic voltage scaling, or anything else.

– If this minimal execution time is a rare event, all the statistics based on the minimum describe rare speedups. So, they easily become non-reproducible.

In addition to the above arguments, there is a mathematical argument against using the minimal execution time. Indeed, contrary to the sample average or the sample median, the sample minimum does not necessarily follow a normal distribution. That is, the sample minimum does not necessarily converge quickly toward its theoretical value. The variance of the sample minimum may be pretty high for an arbitrary population. Formally, if θ is the theoretical minimal execution time, then the sample $\min_i x_i$ may be far from θ; everything depends on the distribution function of X. For an illustration, see Figure A7.1 for two cases of distributions, explained below:

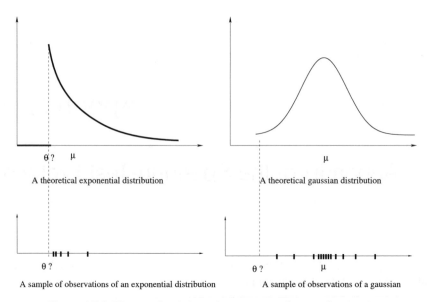

Figure A7.1. *The sample minimum is not necessarily a good estimation of the theoretical minimum*

A7.1.1. *Case of exponential distribution function shifted by θ*

If X follows an exponential distribution function shifted by θ, it has the following density function:

$$f_x = \begin{cases} e^{-(x-\theta)} & \text{if } x \geq \theta \\ 0 & \text{if } x < \theta \end{cases}$$

θ is the unknown theoretical minimum. If $X = \{x_1, \cdots, x_n\}$ is a sample for X, then $\min_i x_i$ is a natural estimator for θ. In this situation, this estimator would be good, since its value would be very close to θ.

A7.1.2. *Case of normal populations*

If X follows a Gaussian distribution function $N(\mu, \sigma^2)$ ($\mu > 0$ and $\theta > 0$), then the theoretical minimum θ does not exist (because the Gaussian distribution does not have a theoretical minimum). If we consider a sample $\mathcal{X} = \{x_1, \cdots, x_n\}$, the minimum value $\min_i x_i$ is not a very reliable parameter of position, since it still has a high variance when the sample size n is quite large.

To illustrate this fact, let us consider a simulation of a Gaussian distribution function. We use a Monte Carlo estimation of the variance of $\bar{X}$ and $\min_i x_i$ as a function of n the sample size. The number of distinct samples is $N = 10,000$. The simulated Gaussian distribution has a variance equal to 1. Table A7.1 presents the results of our simulation, and demonstrates that the variance of the sample minimum remains high when we increase the sample size n.

Value of n	20	50	100	1,000	10,000
Standard deviation of $\bar{X}$	0.22	0.14	0.10	0.03	0.01
Standard deviation of $\min_i x_i$	0.53	0.47	0.43	0.35	0.30

Table A7.1. *Monte Carlo simulation of a Gaussian distribution: we see that when the sample size n increases, the sample mean converges quickly to the theoretical mean (the variance reduces quickly). However, we observe that the sample minimum still has a high variance when the sample size n increases*

From all the above analyses, we clearly see that depending on the distribution function, the sample minimum may be a rare observation of the program execution time.

A7.2. Hypothesis testing in statistical and probability theory

Statistical testing is a classical mechanism to decide between two hypotheses based on samples or observations. Here, we should note that almost all statistical tests have proved $0 < \alpha < 1$ risk level for rejecting a hypothesis only (called the null hypothesis H_0). The probability $1-\alpha$ is the confidence level of not rejecting the null hypothesis. It is not a proved probability that the alternative hypothesis H_a is true with a confidence level $1 - \alpha$.

In practice we say that if a test rejects H_0 a null hypothesis with a risk level α, then we *admit* H_a the alternative hypothesis with a confidence level $1 - \alpha$. But this confidence level is not a mathematical one, except in rare cases.

For further hints on hypothesis testing, we invite the reader to study section 14.2 from [SAP 90] or section B.4 from [BRO 02]. We can, for instance, understand that statistical tests have in reality two kinds of risks: a primary α risk, which is the probability to reject H_0 while it is true, and a secondary $0 < \beta < 1$ risk which is the probability to accept H_0 while H_a is true, see Table A7.2. So, intuitively, the confidence level, sometimes known as the *strength* or *power* of the test, could be defined as $1 - \beta$. All the statistical tests we use (normality test, Fisher's F-test, Student's t-test, Kolmogorov–Smirnov's test and Wilcoxon–Mann–Whitney's test) have only proved α risks levels under some hypothesis.

To conclude, we must say that hypothesis testing in statistics usually does not confirm a hypothesis with a confidence level $1 - \beta$, but in reality it rejects a hypothesis with a risk of error α. If a null hypothesis H_0 is not rejected with a risk α, we say that we admit the alternative hypothesis H_a with a confidence level $1 - \alpha$. This is not mathematically true, because the confidence level of accepting H_a is $1 - \beta$, which cannot be computed easily.

Truth / Decision of the statistical test	H_0	H_a
H_0	$1 - \alpha$	β
H_a	α	$1 - \beta$

Table A7.2. *The two risk levels for hypothesis testing in statistical and probability theory. The primary risk level ($0 < \alpha < 1$) is generally the guaranteed level of confidence, while the secondary risk level ($0 < \beta < 1$) is not always guaranteed*

In this appendix, we use the deviating term "confidence level" for $1 - \alpha$ because it is the definition used in the R software to perform numerous statistical tests.

A7.3. What is a *reasonable* large sample? Observing the central limit theorem in practice

Even reading the rigorous texts on statistics and probability theory [SAP 90, HOL 73, KNI 00, BRO 02, VAA 00], we would not find the answer to the golden question of *how large should a sample be?* Indeed, there is no general answer to this question. It depends on the distributions under study. For instance, if the distribution is assumed Gaussian, we know how to compute the minimal sample size to perform a precise Student's t-test.

Some books devoted to practice [LIL 00, JAI 91] write a limit of 30 between small ($n \leq 30$) and large ($n > 30$) samples. However, this limit is arbitrary, and does not correspond to a general definition of large samples. The number 30 has been used for a long time because when $n > 30$, the values of the Student's distribution become close to the values of normal distributions. Consequently, by considering z values instead of t values when $n > 30$, the manual statistical computation becomes easier. For instance, the Student's test uses this numerical simplification. Nowadays, computers are used everywhere; hence, these old simplifications become out of date.

However, we still need to have an idea about the size of a large sample if we want a general (non-parametric) practical statistical protocol that is common to all benchmarks. For the purpose of defining such arbitrary size for the Speedup-Test, we conducted extensive experiments that lasted many months. We considered two well-known benchmarks families:

1) The set of SPEC OMP2001 benchmarks with various numbers of threads (from one thread to eight). The number of distinct applications is 36.

2) The set of SPECCPU2006 applications (CFP and CINT). The number of distinct applications is 29.

We generated binaries using the flags -O3 --fno-strict-aliasing. The version of gcc and gfortran is 4.3 under Linux. All the applications have been executed with the train input data on two distinct execution environments:

1) *Low overhead environment:* dynamic voltage scaling is inactive, reduced OS services, no background applications, the machine executes a unique application at a time, applications are executed back-to-back.

2) *High overhead environment:* For SPEC OMP2001 applications, they are executed on a machine with a high background workload and overhead (the machine used was executing many other applications during the experiments).

Let us check if the central limit theorem is observable in such practice, and for which sample size. Our methodology is as follows:

1) Consider n the size of a sample. n is the number of runs of a benchmark. n varies between 5 and 100.

2) Consider N the number of distinct samples. Consequently, each application runs $n \times N$ times. N varies between 10 and 500. We have put a limit $n \times N = 1000$.

3) Consider the vector $\{\bar{x}_1, \cdots, \bar{x}_N\}$, the N observations of the sample mean: $\bar{x}_i$ is the sample mean of the ith sample.

4) According to the central limit theorem, if X is continuous with finite theoretical variance, and if $\bar{X}$ denotes the sample mean of a sample of size n of the distribution of X, then $\bar{X}$ should have an approximately Gaussian distribution when n is sufficiently large. Thus, here we have a sample of size N of the distribution of $\bar{X}$, which will help us to decide for which n this distribution can be considered Gaussian.

5) We do the same normality analysis for the sample median $\overline{\text{med}}(X)$, which should follow a normal distribution when n is also sufficiently large.

We used the Shapiro-Wilk normality test with a risk level $\alpha = 5\%$. For the low overhead environment, Tables A7.3 and A7.4 illustrate the number of cases that are not of Gaussian distribution if we consider samples of size n. As can be seen, it is difficult in practice to observe the central limit theorem for all sample sizes. There may be multiple reasons for that:

– The normality check test has an intrinsic error level equal to α.

– The observations x_i from X may not be totally independent observations.

– The sample size is not sufficiently large.

However, we can see that for $n > 30$, the situation is more acceptable than for $n \leq 30$. This experimental analysis shows that it is not possible to decide for a fixed value of n that distinguishes between small samples and large samples. For each program, we may have a specific distribution function for its execution times. So, in theory, we should make a specific statistical analysis for each program. Since the purpose of the speedup test is to have a common statistical protocol for all situations, we accept that the arbitrary value $n > 30$ would make a frontier between small and large samples. Other values for n may be decided for specific contexts.

Tables A7.5 and A7.3 illustrate the results of the same experiments but conducted on a high overhead environment. As can be seen, the central limit theorem is much less observable in this chaotic context. These tables strongly suggest that we should always make measurements on a low-workload environment.

n	5	10	15	20	25	30	35	40	45	50	55	60	65	70	75	80	85	90	95	100
$\bar{X} \not\sim N$	19	16	13	7	6	7	6	6	8	5	3	3	4	5	3	4	3	2	3	2
$\overline{\text{med}}(X) \not\sim N$	23	13	13	10	10	9	9	4	6	5	5	5	5	5	4	4	6	2	4	7

Table A7.3. *SPEC OMP2001 on low-overhead environment: the number of applications among 36 where the sample mean and the sample median do not follow a Gaussian distribution in practice as a function of the sample size (risk level $\alpha = 5\%$). These measurements have been conducted on an isolated machine with low background workload and overhead*

n	5	10	15	20	25	30	35	40	45	50	55	60	65	70	75	80	85	90	95	100
$\bar{X} \not\sim N$	24	17	8	11	8	6	4	6	7	6	5	9	5	5	3	3	4	5	3	5
$\overline{\text{med}}(X) \not\sim N$	17	8	7	9	1	5	4	5	4	2	4	3	2	3	4	3	1	3	3	1

Table A7.4. *SPECCPU2006 executed on low overhead environment: the number of applications among 29 where the sample mean and the sample median do not follow a Gaussian distribution in practice as a function of the sample size (risk level $\alpha = 5\%$). These measurements have been conducted on an isolated machine with low background workload and overhead*

n	5	10	15	20	25	30	35	40	45	50	55	60	65	70	75	80	85	90	95	100
$\bar{X} \not\sim N$	26	24	23	19	19	18	18	18	15	14	16	15	16	16	14	15	15	14	14	12
$\overline{\text{med}}(X) \not\sim N$	27	24	23	23	21	21	21	20	20	19	17	17	18	16	17	13	14	11	12	15

Table A7.5. *SPEC OMP2001 on high-overhead environment: the number of applications among 36 where the sample mean and the sample median do not follow a Gaussian distribution in practice as a function of the sample size (risk level $\alpha = 5\%$)*

n	5	10	15	20	25	30	35	40	45	50	55	60	65	70	75	80	85	90	95	100
$\bar{X} \not\sim N$	23	23	21	20	20	21	20	20	19	20	21	20	20	19	18	16	16	14	14	15
$\overline{\mathrm{med}(X)} \not\sim N$	23	22	22	21	21	21	20	20	21	20	20	20	21	19	19	16	18	15	15	15

Table A7.6. *SPECCPU2006 on high-overhead environment: the number of applications among 29 where the sample mean and the sample median do not follow a Gaussian distribution in practice as a function of the sample size (risk level $\alpha = 5\%$)*

Bibliography

[AAR 97] AARTS B., BARRETEAU M., BODIN F., *et al.*, "OCEANS: optimizing compilers for embedded applications", *Proceedings of EuroPar '97*, Lecture Notes in Computer Science, Springer-Verlag, 1997.

[ABR 93] ABRAHAM S.G., SUGUMAR R.A., WINDHEISER D., *et al.*, "Predictability of load/store instruction latencies", *Proceedings of the 26th Annual International Symposium on Microarchitecture (MICRO)*, IEEE Computer Society Press, Los Alamitos, CA, USA, pp. 139–152, 1993.

[ABR 98] ABRAHAM S.G., KATHAIL V., DIETRICH B.L., "Meld scheduling: a technique for relaxing scheduling constraints", *International Journal on Parallel Programming*, vol. 26, no. 4, pp. 349–381, 1998.

[ABR 00] ABRAHAM S.G., Efficient backtracking instruction schedulers, Report no. HPL-2000-56, Hewlett-Packard Laboratories, May 2000.

[AHO 07] AHO A.V., LAM M.S., SETHI R., *et al.*, *Compilers: Principles, Techniques, and Tools*, Pearson/Addison Wesley, Boston, MA, USA, 2007.

[AHU 93] AHUJA R.K., MAGNANTI T.L., ORLIN J.B., *Network Flows: Theory, Algorithms, and Applications* Prentice Hall, 1993.

[AIK 95] AIKEN A., NICOLAU A., NOVACK S., "Resource-constrained software pipelining", *IEEE Transactions on Parallel and Distributed Systems*, vol. 6, no. 12, pp. 1248–1270, 1995.

[AKK 98] VAN DEN AKKER J.M., HURKENS C.A.J., SAVELSBERGH M.W.P., "Time-indexed formulations for single-machine scheduling problems: column generation", *INFORMS Journal on Computing*, vol. 12, no. 2, pp. 2000–2029, 1998.

[ALA 05] ALAIN D., ROBERT S., GILLES V., "Lattice-based memory allocation", *IEEE Transactions on Computers*, vol. 54, no. 10, pp. 1242–1257, October 2005.

[ALE 93] ALEXANDER T., Performance prediction for loop restructuring optimization, Masters Thesis, Physics/Computer Science Department, University of Carnegie Mellon, July 1993.

[ALI 05] ALIAS C., Program optimization by template recognition and replacement, PhD Thesis, University of Versailles Saint-Quentin en Yvelines, December 2005.

[ALL 95] ALLAN V.H., JONES R.B., LEE R.M., et al., "Software pipelining", ACM Computing Surveys, vol. 27, no. 3, pp. 367–432, 1995.

[ALL 02] ALLEN R., KENNEDY K., Optimizing Compilers for Modern Architectures, Morgan and Kaufman, 2002.

[ALM 04] ALMAGOR L., COOPER K.D., GROSUL A., et al., "Finding effective compilation sequences", Proceeding of the Conference on Languages, Compilers, and Tools for Embedded Systems (LCTES'04), ACM, Washington, DC, June 2004.

[ALS 06] AL-SUKHNI H., HOLT J., CONNORS D.A., "Improved stride prefetching using extrinsic stream characteristics", Proceeding of the International Symposium on Performance Analysis of Systems and Software (ISPASS), IEEE Computer Society, pp. 166–176, 2006.

[ALT 95] ALTMAN E., Optimal software pipelining with functional units and registers, PhD Thesis, McGill University, Montreal, October 1995.

[AMB 94] AMBROSCH W., ERTL M.A., BEER F., et al., "Dependence-conscious global register allocation", Lecture Notes in Computer Science, vol. 782, pp. 125–136, 1994.

[AMM 08] AMMENOUCHE S., TOUATI S.-A.-A., JALBY W., "Practical precise evaluation of cache effects on low level embedded VLIW computing", High Performance Computing and Simulation Conference (HPCS), Nicosia, Cyprus, ECMS, June 2008.

[AMM 09] AMMENOUCHE S., TOUATI S.-A.-A., JALBY W., "On instruction-level method for reducing cache penalties in embedded VLIW processors", The 11th IEEE International Conference on High Performance Computing and Communications (HPCC), Seoul, South Korea, June 2009.

[BAC 13] BACHIR M., TOUATI S.-A.-A., BRAULT F., et al., "Minimal unroll factor for code generation of software pipelining", International Journal of Parallel Programming, Springer, vol. 41, no. 1, pp. 1–58, 2013.

[BAL 95] BALA V., RUBIN N., "Efficient instruction scheduling using finite state automata", MICRO 28: Proceedings of the 28th Annual International Symposium on Microarchitecture, pp. 46–56, 1995.

[BAS 04] BASTOUL C., "Code generation in the polyhedral model is easier than you think", International Conference on Parallel Architecture and Compilation Techniques (PACT '13 IEEE), Juan-les-Pins, France, pp. 7–16, September 2004.

[BER 89] BERNSTEIN D., JAFFE J.M., RODEH M., "Scheduling arithmetic and load operations in parallel with no spilling", SIAM Journal on Computing, vol. 18, no. 6, pp. 1098–1127, December 1989.

[BEY 07] BEYLER J.C., CLAUSS P., "Performance driven data cache prefetching in a dynamic software optimization system", Proceedings of the 21st Annual International Conference on Supercomputing (ICS), ACM, New York, pp. 202–209, 2007.

[BID 04] BIDAULT T., GUILLON C., BOUCHEZ F., *et al.*, "Procedure placement using temporal ordering information: dealing with code size expansion", *2004 International Conference on Compilers, Architectures and Synthesis of Embedded Systems (CASES '04)*, Washington, DC, 2004.

[BOD 90] BODIN F., CHAROT F., "Loop optimization for horizontal microcoded machines", *Proceedings of the 1990 International Conference on Supercomputing*, Amsterdam, Netherlands, 1990.

[BOU 06] BOUCHEZ F., DARTE A., GUILLON C., *et al.*, "Register allocation: what does the NP-completeness proof of CHaitin *et al.* really prove?", *International Workshop on Languages and Compilers for Parallel Computing (LCPC '06)*, Springer Verlag, pp. 283–298, November 2006.

[BOU 07a] BOUCHEZ F., DARTE A., RASTELLO F., "On the complexity of register coalescing", *International Symposium on Code Generation and Optimization (CGO '07)*, IEEE Computer Society Press, pp. 102–114, March 2007.

[BOU 07b] BOUCHEZ F., DARTE A., RASTELLO F., "On the complexity of spill everywhere under SSA form", *ACM SIGPLAN/SIGBED Conference on Languages, Compilers, and Tools for Embedded Systems (LCTES '07)*, ACM, pp. 103–112, June 2007.

[BRA 95] BRASIER T.S., SWEANY P.H., BEATY S.J., *et al.*, "CRAIG: a practical framework for combining instruction scheduling and register assignment", *Parallel Architectures and Compilation Techniques (PACT '95)*, Springer Verlag, pp. 11–18, 1995.

[BRI 94] BRIGGS P., COOPER K.D., TORCZON L., "Improvements to graph coloring register allocation", *ACM Transaction Programming Languages and Systems.*, vol. 16, no. 3, pp. 428–455, 1994.

[BRI 09a] BRIAIS S., TOUATI S.-A.-A., Experimental study of register saturation in basic blocks and super-blocks: optimality and heuristics, Report no. HAL-INRIA-00431103, Available at http://hal.archives-ouvertes.fr/inria-00431103, University of Versailles Saint-Quentin en Yvelines, October 2009.

[BRI 09b] BRIAIS S., TOUATI S.-A.-A., Schedule-sensitive register pressure reduction in innermost loops, basic blocks and super-blocks, Report no. HAL-INRIA-00436348, Available at http://hal.archives-ouvertes.fr/inria-00436348, University of Versailles Saint-Quentin en Yvelines, November 2009.

[BRI 10] BRIAIS S., TOUATI S.-A.-A., DESCHINKEL K., Ensuring Lexicographic-Positive Data Dependence Graphs in the SIRA Framework, Report no. HAL-INRIA-00452695, available at http://hal.archives-ouvertes.fr/inria-00452695, University of Versailles Saint-Quentin en Yvelines, February 2010.

[BRO 01] BROWN L.D., CAI T., DASGUPTA A., "Interval estimation for a binomial proportion", *Statistical Science*, vol. 16, no. 2, pp. 101–133, 2001.

[BRO 02] BROCKWELL P.J., DAVIS R.A., *Introduction to Time Series and Forecasting*, Springer, 2002.

[BRU 99] BRUCKER P., DREXL A., MÖHRING R., *et al.*, "Resource-constrained project scheduling: notation, classification, models, and methods", *European Journal of Operational Research*, vol. 112, no. 1, pp. 3–41. 1999.

[BRU 04] BRUCKER P., *Scheduling Algorithms*, 4th ed., Springer Verlag, 2004.

[CAL 88] CALLAHAN D., COCKE J., KENNEDY K., "Estimating interlock and improving balance for pipelined architectures", *Journal of Parallel and Distributed Computing*, vol. 5, no. 4, pp. 334–358, August 1988.

[CAL 90] CALLAHAN D., CARR S., KENNEDY K., "Improving register allocation for subscripted variables", *Proceedings of the SIGPLAN '90 Conference on Programming Language Design and Implementation (PLDI '90)*, June 1990.

[CHA 82] CHAITIN G.J., "Register allocation and spilling via graph coloring", MCKINLEY K.S., (ed.), *Best of PLDI*, ACM, pp. 66–74, 1982.

[CHA 95] CHANG P.P., LAVERY D.M., MAHLKE S.A., *et al.*, "The importance of prepass code scheduling for superscalar and superpipelined processors", *IEEE Transactions on Computers*, vol. 44, no. 3, pp. 353–371, March 1995.

[CHE 92] CHEN T.-F., BAER J.-L., "Reducing memory latency via non-blocking and prefetching caches", *Proceedings of the 5th International Conference on Architectural Support for Programming Languages and Operating Systems (ASPLOS-V)*, ACM, New York, pp. 51–61, 1992.

[CHR 87] CHRISTOFIDES N., ALVAREZ-VALDÉS R., TAMARIT J.M., "Project scheduling with resource constraints: a branch and bound approach", *European Journal of Operational Research*, vol. 29, pp. 262–273, 1987.

[CHR 98] CHRYSOS G., EMER J., "Memory dependence prediction using store sets", *Proceedings of the 25th Annual International Symposium on Computer Architecture (ISCA '98)*, of *ACM Computer Architecture News*, ACM, New York, vol. 26, no.3, pp. 142–154, June 1998.

[CLI 95] CLICK C., COOPER K.D., "Combining analyses, combining optimizations", *ACM Transactions on Programming Languages and Systems*, vol. 17, no. 2, pp. 181–196, 1995.

[COH 04] COHEN A., GIRBAL S., TEMAM O., "A polyhedral approach to ease the composition of program transformations", *Proceedings of Euro-Par (Euro-Par '04)*, August 2004.

[CON 71] CONOVER W.J., *Practical Nonparametric Statistics*, John Wiley, New York, 1971.

[COO 98] COOPER K., SCHIELKE P., SUBRAMANIAN D., An experimental evaluation of list scheduling, TR98-326, Department of Computer Science, Rice University, September 1998.

[COO 02] COOPER K.D., SUBRAMANIAN D., TORCZON L., "Adaptive optimizing compilers for the 21st century", *The Journal of Supercomputing*, vol. 23, no. 1, pp. 7–22, 2002.

[COR 01] CORMEN T.H., LEISERSON C.E., RIVEST R.L., *et al.*, *Introduction to Algorithms*, 2nd ed., The MIT Press and McGraw-Hill Book Company, 2001.

[COR 08] CORNERO M., COSTA R., PASCUAL R.F., *et al.*, "An experimental environment validating the suitability of CLI as an effective deployment format for embedded systems", *International Conference on High Performance Embedded Architectures and Compilers*, 2008.

[DAR 00] DARTE A., HUARD G., "Loop shifting for loop compaction", *International Journal of Parallel Programming*, vol. 28 no. 5, pp. 499–534, October 2000.

[DAR 07] DARTE A., QUINSON C., "Scheduling register-allocated codes in user-guided high-level synthesis", *IEEE International Conference on Application Specific Systems, Architectures and Processors (ASAP)*, pp. 140–147, 9–11 2007.

[DAS 99] DASDAN A., IRANI S.S., GUPTA R.K., "Efficient algorithms for optimum cycle mean and optimum cost to time ratio problems", *ACM IEEE Design Automation Conference (DAC '99)*, 1999.

[DAV 95] DAVIDSON J.W., JINTURKAR S., "Improving instruction-level parallelism by loop unrolling and dynamic memory disambiguation ", *Proceedings of the 28th Annual International Symposium on Microarchitecture (MICRO-28)*, December 1995.

[DEH 89] DEHNERT J.C., HSU P.Y.-T., BRATT J.P., "Overlapped loop support in the Cydra 5", *ASPLOS-III: Proceedings of the 3rd International Conference on Architectural Support for Programming Languages and Operating Systems*, ACM, New York, pp. 26–38, 1989.

[DEH 93] DEHNERT J.C., TOWLE R.A., "Compiling for the Cydra 5", *Journal of Supercomputing*, vol. 7, nos. 1–2, pp. 181–227, 1993.

[DEM 01] DEMASSEY S., ARTIGUES C., MICHELON P., "Comparing lower bounds for the RCPSP under a same hybrid constraint-linear programming approach", *International Conference on Constraint Programming – (CP '01), Proceedings of the Workshop on Cooperative Solvers in Constraint Programming (CoSolv '01)*, 2001.

[DEM 05] DEMASSEY S., ARTIGUES C., MICHELON P., "Constraint-propagation-based cutting-planes: an application to the resource-constrained project scheduling problem", *INFORMS Journal on Computing*, vol. 17, no. 1, pp. 52–65, 2005.

[DES 08] DESCHINKEL K., TOUATI S.-A.-A., "Efficient method for periodic task scheduling with storage requirement minimization", *Proceedings of Annual International Conference on Combinatorial Optimization and Applications (COCOA)*, Lecture Notes in Computer Science, Springer-Verlag, Saint Johns, Newfoundland, Canada, August 2008.

[DES 11] DESCHINKEL K., TOUATI S.-A.-A., BRIAIS S., "SIRALINA: efficient two-steps heuristic for storage optimisation in single period task scheduling", *Journal of Combinatorial Optimization*, vol. 22, nos. 819–844, 2011.

[DIN 94] DE DINECHIN B.D., An introduction to simplex scheduling, IFIP PACT, pp. 327–330, 1994.

[DIN 95] DE DINECHIN B.D., "Insertion scheduling: an alternative to list scheduling for modulo schedulers", *8th International Workshop on Languages and Compilers for Parallel Computing (LCPC '95)*, Colombus, OH, August 1995.

[DIN 96] DE DINECHIN B.D., "Parametric computation of margins and of minimum cumulative register lifetime dates", *9th International Workshop on Languages and Compilers for Parallel Computing (LCPC '96)*, pp. 231–245, 1996.

[DIN 97a] DE DINECHIN B.D., "A unified software pipeline construction scheme for modulo scheduled loops", *4th International Conference on Parallel Computing Technologies, (PaCT '97)*, September 1997.

[DIN 97b] DE DINECHIN B.D., "Parametric computation of margins and of minimum cumulative register lifetime dates", *Proceedings of the 9th International Workshop on Languages and Compilers for Parallel Computing, (LCPC '96)*, Springer-Verlag, London, UK, pp. 231–245, 1997.

[DIN 97c] DE DINECHIN B.D., "A unified software pipeline construction scheme for modulo scheduled loops", *Proceedings of the 4th International Conference on Parallel Computing Technologies, (PaCT '97)*, Springer-Verlag, London, UK, pp. 189–200, 1997.

[DIN 97d] DING C., CARR S., SWEANY P.H., "Modulo scheduling with cache reuse information", *Proceedings of the 3rd International Euro-Par Conference on Parallel Processing (Euro-Par)*, Springer-Verlag, London, UK, pp. 1079–1083, 1997.

[DIN 99] DE DINECHIN B.D., "Extending modulo scheduling with memory reference merging", *8th International Conference on Compiler Construction (CC '99)*, March 1999.

[DIN 00] DE DINECHIN B.D., DE FERRIÈRE F., GUILLON C., *et al.*, "Code generator optimizations for the ST120 DSP-MCU core", *International Conference on Compilers, Architectures, and Synthesis for Embedded Systems (CASES)*, November 2000.

[DIN 01] DE DINECHIN B.D., Modulo scheduling with regular unwinding, Mines ParisTech, CRI, 2001.

[DIN 04a] DE DINECHIN B.D., "From machine scheduling to VLIW instruction scheduling", *ST Journal of Research*, vol. 1, no. 2, 2004.

[DIN 04b] DE DINECHIN B.D., "Modulo scheduling with regular unwinding", *Discrete Optimization Methods in Production and Logistics (DOM)*, 2004.

[DIN 07] DE DINECHIN B.D., "Scheduling monotone interval orders on typed task systems", *26th Workshop of the UK Planning and Scheduling Special Interest Group (PlanSIG)*, 2007.

[ECK 03] ECKER K., Scheduling Theory, Slides, 2003.

[EEC 03] EECKHOUT L., VANDIERENDONCK H., BOSSCHERE K.D., "Quantifying the impact of input data sets on program behavior and its applications", *Journal of Instruction-Level Parallelism*, vol. 5, pp. 1–33, 2003.

[EIC 95a] EICHENBERGER A.E., DAVIDSON E.S., "Stage scheduling: a technique to reduce the register requirements of a modulo schedule", *Proceedings of the 28th Annual Symposium on Microarchitecture (MICRO-28)*, 1995.

[EIC 95b] EICHENBERGER A.E., DAVIDSON E.S., ABRAHAM S.G., "Optimum modulo schedules for minimum register requirements", *International Conference on Supercomputing (ICS)*, 1995.

[EIC 96] EICHENBERGER A.E., DAVIDSON E.S., ABRAHAM S.G., "Minimizing register requirements of a modulo schedule via optimum stage scheduling", *International Journal of Parallel Programming*, vol. 24, no. 2, pp. 103–132, April 1996.

[EIC 97] EICHENBERGER A.E., DAVIDSON E.S., "Efficient formulation for optimal modulo schedulers", *SIGPLAN Notice*, vol. 32, no. 5, pp. 194–205, 1997.

[EIS 93] EISENBEIS C., WINDHEISER D., "Optimal software pipelining in presence of resource constraints", *Proceedings of the International Conference on Parallel Computing Technologies (PaCT '93)*, 1993.

[EIS 95a] EISENBEIS C., GASPERONI F., SCHWIEGELSHOHN U., "Allocating registers in multiple instruction-issuing processors", *Proceedings of the IFIP WG 10.3 Working Conference on Parallel Architectures and Compilation Techniques (PACT '95)*, ACM Press, pp. 290–293, 27–29 June 1995.

[EIS 95b] EISENBEIS C., LELAIT S., MARMOL B., *et al.*, "The meeting graph: a new model for loop cyclic register allocation", *Proceedings of the IFIP WG 10.3 Working Conference on Parallel Architectures and Compilation Techniques (PACT)*, BIC L., BÖHM W., EVRIPIDOU P., (eds.), ACM, Limassol, Cyprus, pp. 264–267, June 1995.

[FAR 94] FARKAS K.I., JOUPPI N.P., "Complexity/performance tradeoffs with non-blocking loads", *21st Annual Symposium on Computer Architecture (ISCA)*, April 1994.

[FAR 00] FARABOSCH G., FISHER J.A., DESOLI G., *et al.*, "Lx: a technology platform for customizable VLIW embedded processing", *Proceedings of the 27th Annual International Symposium on Computer Architecture (ISCA)*, ACM, New York, NY, pp. 203–213, 2000.

[FEA 94] FEAUTRIER P., "Fine-grain scheduling under resource constraints", *Languages and Compilers for Parallel Computing (LCPC '94)*, 1994.

[FEL 68] FELLER W., *An Introduction to Probability Theory and its Applications*, 3rd ed., vol. 1, John Wiley and Sons, Inc., 1968.

[FER 98] FERNANDES M.M., A clustered VLIW architecture based on queue register files, PhD Thesis, University of Edinburgh, 1998.

[FIM 00] FIMMEL D., MÜLLER J., "Optimal software pipelining under register constraints", *Proceedings of the International Conference on Parallel and Distributed Processing Techniques and Applications (PDPTA)*, Las Vegas, NV, vol. 5, June 2000.

[FIM 01] FIMMEL D., MULLER J., "Optimal software pipelining under resource constraints", *International Journal of Foundations of Computer Science (IJFCS)*, vol. 12, no. 6, pp. 697–718, 2001.

[FIM 02] FIMMEL D., MÜLLER J., "Optimal software pipelining with rational initiation interval", *Proceedings of the International Conference on Parallel and Distributed Processing Techniques and Applications (PDPTA)*, Las Vegas, NV, vol. 2, June 2002.

[FIN 02] FINKE G., GORDON V., PROTH J.-M., "Scheduling with due dates (annotated bibliography of complexity and algorithms)", *Les cahiers du laboratoire Leibniz*, January 2002.

[FIS 05] FISHER J.A., FARABOSCHI P., YOUNG C., *Embedded Computing: A VLIW Approach to Architecture, Compilers and Tools*, Morgan Kaufmann Publishers, 2005.

[FRE 92] FREUDENBERGER S.M., RUTTENBERG J.C., "Phase ordering of register allocation and instruction scheduling", *Code Generation – Concepts, Tools, Techniques, Proceedings of the International Workshop on Code Generation*, Springer-Verlag, London, pp. 146–172, 1992.

[FRI 99] FRIGO M., "A fast Fourier transform compiler", *Proceedings of Programing Language Design and Implementation*, 1999.

[GAS 94] GASPERONI F., SCHWIEGELSHOHN U., "Generating close to optimum loop schedules on parallel processors", *Parallel Processing Letters,* vol. 4, pp. 391–403, 1994.

[GEO 07] GEORGES A., BUYTAERT D., EECKHOUT L., "Statistically rigorous java performance evaluation", *Proceedings of the 22nd ACM SIGPLAN Conference on OOPSLA*, ACM SIGPLAN Notices, Montreal, Canada, vol. 42, no. 10, pp. 57–76, October 2007.

[GOL 91] GOLDFARB D., HAO J., KAI S.-R., "Shortest path algorithms using dynamic breadth-first search", *Networks*, vol. 21, pp. 29–50, 1991.

[GOO 88a] GOODMAN J.R., HSU W.-C., "Code scheduling and register allocation in large basic blocks", *Proceedings of the International Conference on Supercomputing (ICS '88)*, 1988.

[GOO 88b] GOODMAN J.R., HSU W.-C., "Code scheduling and register allocation in large basic blocks", *Proceedings of 1988 International Conference on Supercomputing*, St. Malo, France, pp. 442–452, July 1988.

[GOV 94] GOVINDARAJAN R., ALTMAN E.R., GAO G.R., "Minimizing register requirements under resource-constrained rate-optimal software pipelining", *Proceedings of the 27th Annual International Symposium on Microarchitecture (MICRO-27)*, December 1994.

[GOV 03] GOVINDARAJAN R., YANG H., AMARAL J.N., *et al.*, "Minimum register instruction sequencing to reduce register spills in out-of-order issue superscalar architecture", *IEEE Transactions on Computers*, vol. 1, no. 52, pp. 4–20, 2003.

[GUI 05] GUILLON C., RASTELLO F., BIDAULT T., *et al.*, "Procedure placement using temporal-ordering information: dealing with code size expansion", *Journal of Embedded Computing*, vol. 1, no. 4, pp. 437–459, 2005.

[GUP 79] GUPTA U.I., LEE D.T., LEUNG J.Y.-T., "An optimal solution for the channel-assignment problem", *IEEE Transactions on Computers*, vol. C–28, pp. 807–810, 1979.

[HAN 93] HANK R., MAHLKE S., BRINGMANN R., *et al.*, "Superblock formation using static program analysis", *26th International Symposium on Micro-architecture (MICRO-26)*, 1993.

[HAN 94] HANEN C., MUNIER A., "Cyclic scheduling on parallel processors: an overview", *Scheduling Theory and its Applications,* Wiley & Sons, 1994.

[HAN 95] HANEN C., MUNIER A., "A study of the cyclic scheduling problem on parallel processors", *DAMATH: Discrete Applied Mathematics and Combinatorial Operations Research and Computer Science,* vol. 57, nos. 2–3, pp. 167–192, 1995.

[HEN 92] HENDREN L.J., GAO G.R., ALTMAN E.R., *et al.*, "A register allocation framework based on hierarchical cyclic interval graphs", *Lecture Notes in Computer Science*, vol. 641, pp. 176–191, 1992.

[HEN 93] HENDREN L.J., GAO G.R., ALTMAN E.R., *et al.*, "A register allocation framework based on hierarchical cyclic interval graphs", *The Journal of Programming Languages,* vol. 1, no. 3, pp. 155–185, September 1993.

[HEN 02] HENNESSY J.L., PATTERSON D.A., GOLDBERG D., *Computer Architecture: A Quantitative Approach*, Morgan Kaufmann, 2002.

[HOL 73] HOLLANDERAND M., WOLFE D.A., *Nonparametric Statistical Methods*, Wiley-Interscience, 1973.

[HOW 01] HOWGRAVE-GRAHAM N., "Approximate integer common divisors", *Cryptography and Lattices, International Conference (CaLC)* of Lecture Notes in Computer Science, vol. 2146, pp. 51–66, 2001.

[HUA 01] HUARD G., Algorithmique du décalage d'Instructions, PhD Thesis, Ecole Normale Supérieure, Lyon, France, December 2001.

[HUF 93a] HUFF R.A., "Lifetime-sensitive modulo scheduling", *SIGPLAN Conference on Programming Language Design and Implementation (PLDI '93)*, June 1993.

[HUF 93b] HUFF R.A., "Lifetime-sensitive modulo scheduling", *ACM SIGPLAN Notices*, vol. 28, no. 6, pp. 258–267, June 1993.

[JAI 91] JAIN R., *The Art of Computer Systems Performance Analysis: Techniques for Experimental Design, Measurement, Simulation, and Modeling*, John Wiley and Sons, Inc., New York, 1991.

[JAL 06] JALBY W., LEMUET C., TOUATI S.-A.-A., "An efficient memory operations optimization technique for vector loops on itanium 2 processors", *Concurrency and Computation: Practice and Experience*, vol. 11, no. 11, pp. 1485–1508, 2006.

[JAN 01] JANSSEN J., Compilers strategies for transport triggered architectures, PhD Thesis, Delft University, Netherlands, 2001.

[JOH 91] JOHNSON M., *Superscalar Microprocessor Design*, Prentice Hall, Englewood Cliffs, NJ, 1991.

[KEN 92] KENNEDY K., MCINTOSH N., MCKINLEY K., Static performance estimation in a parallelizing compiler, Center for Research on Parallel Computation, Rice University, May 1992.

[KES 98] KESSLER C., "Scheduling expression DAG for minimal register need", *Computer Languages,* vol. 24, no. 1, pp. 33–53, 1998.

[KNI 99] KNIES A., FANG J., LI W., "Tutorial: IA64 architecture and compilers", IEEE (Ed.), *Hot Chips 11: Stanford University, Stanford, California*, IEEE Computer Society Press, August 1999.

[KNI 00] KNIGHT K., *Mathematical Statistics*, Texts in Statistical Science Series, Chapman & Hall/CRC Press, Boca Raton, FL, 2000.

[KOG 81] KOGGE P.M., *The Architecture of Pipelined Computers*, McGraw-Hill, New York, 1981.

[KOL 96] KOLISCH R., "Serial and parallel resource-constrained project scheduling methods revisited: theory and computation", *European Journal of Operational Research,* vol. 90, no. 2, pp. 320–333, 1996.

[KOL 99] KOLISCH R., HARTMANN S., "Heuristic algorithms for solving the resource-constrained project scheduling problem: classification and computational analysis", *Project Scheduling: Recent Models, Algorithms and Applications,* Kluwer, 1999.

[KOR 11] KORDON A.M., "A graph-based analysis of the cyclic scheduling problem with time constraints: schedulability and periodicity of the earliest schedule", *Journal of Scheduling*, vol. 14, no. 1, pp. 103–117, February 2011.

[KRO 81] KROFT D., "Lockup-free instruction fetch/prefetch cache organization", *Proceedings of the 8th Annual Symposium on Computer Architecture (ISCA)*, IEEE Computer Society Press, Los Alamitos, CA, pp. 81–87, 1981.

[KUH 55] KUHN H.W., "The Hungarian method for the assignment problem", *Naval Research Logistics Quarterly*, vol. 2, pp. 83–97, 1955.

[LAM 88a] LAM M., "Software pipelining: an effective scheduling technique for VLIW machines", *SIGPLAN Conference on Programming Language design and Implementation (PLDI '88)*, June 1988.

[LAM 88b] LAM M., "Software pipelining: an effective scheduling technique for VLIW machines", *Proceedings of the ACM SIGPLAN 1988 Conference on Programming Language design and Implementation (PLDI)*, ACM, New York, pp. 318–328, 1988.

[LAV 95] LAVERY D.M., HWU W.-M.W., "Unrolling-based optimizations for modulo scheduling", *Proceedings of the 28th Annual Symposium on Microarchitecture (MICRO-28)*, 1995.

[LEA 09] LEATHER H., O'BOYLE M., WORTON B., "Raced profiles: efficient selection of competing compiler optimizations", *Conference on Languages, Compilers, and Tools for Embedded Systems (LCTES '09)*, ACM SIGPLAN/SIGBED, June 2009.

[LEI 91] LEISERSON C.E., SAXE J.B., "Retiming synchronous circuitry", *Algorithmica*, vol. 6, pp. 5–35, 1991.

[LEM 04] LEMUET C., JALBY W., TOUATI S.-A.-A., "Improving load/store queues usage in scientific computing", *International Conference on Parallel Processing (ICPP)*, Montreal, Canada, August 2004.

[LEU 01] LEUNG A., PALEM K.V., PNUELI A., Scheduling time-constrained instructions on pipelined processors, ACM TOPLAS, vol. 23, no. 1, pp. 73–103, January 2001.

[LIL 00] LILJA D.J., *Measuring Computer Performance: A Practitioner's Guide*, Cambridge University Press, 2000.

[LLO 95] LLOSA J., VALERO M., AYGUADÉ E., *et al.*, "Hypernode reduction modulo scheduling", *28th International Symposium on Microarchitecture (MICRO-28)*, December 1995.

[LLO 96] LLOSA J., GONZÁLEZ A., AYGUADÉ E., *et al.*, "Swing modulo scheduling: a lifetime-sensitive approach", *Conference on Parallel Architectures and Compilation Techniques (PACT '96)*, October 1996.

[LLO 02] LLOSA J., FREUDENBERGER S.M., "Reduced code size modulo scheduling in the absence of hardware support", *Proceedings of the 35th Annual ACM/IEEE International Symposium on Microarchitecture (MICRO-35)*, 2002.

[LOW 93] LOWNEY P.G., FREUDENBERGER S.M., KARZES T.J., *et al.*, "The multiflow trace scheduling compiler", *The Journal of Supercomputing*, vol. 7, pp. 1–2, 1993.

[LU 03] LU J., CHEN H., FU R., *et al.*, "The performance of runtime data cache prefetching in a dynamic optimization system", *Proceedings of the 36th Annual IEEE/ACM International Symposium on Microarchitecture (MICRO)*, IEEE Computer Society, Washington, DC, p. 180, 2003.

[MAH 95] MAHLKE S.A., HANK R.E., McCORMICK J.E., *et al.*, "A comparison of full and partial predicated execution support for ILP processors", *Proceedings of the 22nd International Symposium on Computer Architecture (ISCA '95)*, June 1995.

[MAN 92] MANGIONE-SMITH W., ABRAHAM S.G., DAVIDSON E.S., "Register requirements of pipelined processors", ACM (ed.), *Proceedings of 1992 International Conference on Supercomputing, Washington, DC*, ACM, New York, NY, pp. 260–271, 19–23 July 1992.

[MAN 93] MANGIONE-SMITH W., SHIH T.-P., ABRAHAM S., *et al.*, "Approaching a machine-application bound in delivered performance on scientific code", *Proceedings of the IEEE*, vol. 81, no. 8, pp. 1166–1178, 1993.

[MAT 04] MATIYASEVICH Y., "Elimination of quantifiers from arithmetical formulas defining recursively enumerable sets", *Mathematics and Computers in Simulation*, vol. 67, nos. 1–2, pp. 125–133, 2004.

[MAZ 10] MAZOUZ A., TOUATI S.-A.-A., BARTHOU D., "Study of variations of native program execution times on multi-core architectures", *International Workshop on Multi-Core Computing Systems (MuCoCoS)*, Krakow, Poland, February 2010.

[MEL 01] MELEIS W.M., "Dural-issue scheduling for binary trees with spills and pipelined loads", *SIAM Journal on Computing*, vol. 30, no. 6, pp. 1921–1941, March 2001.

[MUC 04] MUCHNICK S.S., GIBBONS P.B., "Best of PLDI 1979 – 1999: efficient instruction scheduling for a pipelined architecture", *SIGPLAN Notices*, vol. 39, no. 4, pp. 167–174, 2004.

[MUN 98] MUNIER A., QUEYRANNE M., SCHULZ A.S., "Approximation bounds for a general class of precedence constrained parallel machine scheduling problems", *6th International Integer Programming and Combinatorial Optimization (IPCO)*, 1998.

[MYT 09] MYTKOWICZ T., DIWAN A., HAUSWIRTH M., *et al.*, "Producing wrong data without doing anything obviously wrong!", *Proceeding of the 14th International Conference on Architectural Support for Programming Languages and Operating Systems (ASPLOS)*, ACM, New York, pp. 265–276, 2009.

[NAG 07] NAGARAKATTE S.G., GOVINDARAJAN R., "Register allocation and optimal spill code scheduling in software pipelined loops using 0-1 integer linear programming formulation", *Compiler Construction (CC)*, of Lecture Notes in Computer Science, Springer, Braga, Portugal, vol. 4420, pp. 126–140, March 2007.

[NAT 95] NATARAJAN B., SCHLANSKER M.S., "Spill-free parallel scheduling of basic blocks", *Proceedings of the 28th Annual International Symposium on Microarchitecture (MICRO-28)*, 1995.

[NIC 92a] NICOLAU A., POTASMAN R., WANG H., "Register allocation, renaming and their impact on fine-grain parallelism", *Proceedings of the 4th International Workshop on Languages and Compilers for Parallel Computing*, Springer-Verlag, London, UK, pp. 218–235, 1992.

[NIE 99] NIELSON F., NIELSON H.R., HANKIN C., *Principles of Program Analysis*, Springer-Verlag, New York, Inc., 1999.

[NIN 93b] NING Q., GAO G.R., "A novel framework of register allocation for software pipelining", *Conference Record of the 20th ACM SIGPLAN-SIGACT Symposium on Principles of Programming Languages*, ACM, Charleston, SC, pp. 29–42, January 1993.

[NOR 94] NORRIS C., POLLOCK L.L., "Register Allocation over the Program Dependence Graph", *SIGPLAN Notices*, vol. 29, no. 6, pp. 266–277, June 1994.

[ÖNE 93] ÖNER K., DUBOIS M., "Effects of memory latencies on non-blocking processor/cache architectures", *Proceedings of the 7th international conference on Supercomputing (ICS)*, ACM, New York, USA, pp. 338–347, 1993.

[OND 02] ONDER S., "Cost Effective Memory Dependence Prediction using Speculation Levels and Color Sets", *International Conference on Parallel Architectures and Compilation Techniques (PACT)*, Virginia, IEEE, September 2002.

[OSG 13] OSG, "Open64 Compiler Tools", http://open64.sourceforge.net/, 2013.

[PÜS 05] PÜSCHEL M., MOURA J. M. F., JOHNSON J., *et al.*, "SPIRAL: code generation for DSP transforms", *Proceedings of the IEEE special issue on Program Generation, Optimization and Adaptation*, vol. 93, no. 2, pp. 232–275, 2005.

[PAL 93] PALEM K.V., SIMONS B., "Scheduling time-critical instructions on RISC machines", *ACM Transactions on Programming Languages and Systems (TOPLAS)*, vol. 15, no. 4, pp. 632–658, September 1993.

[PAL 04] PALPANT M., ARTIGUES C., MICHELON P., "LSSPER: solving the resource-constrained project scheduling problem with large neighborhood search", *Annals of Operations Research*, vol. 131, pp. 237–257, 2004.

[PAP 79] PAPADIMITRIOU C., YANNAKAKIS M., "Scheduling interval-ordered tasks", *SIAM Journal of Computing*, vol. 8, no. 3, pp. 405–409, 1979.

[PAR 91] PARHI K.K., MESSERSCHMITT D., "Static rate-optimal scheduling of iterative data-flow programs via optimum unfolding", *Transactions on Computers*, vol. 40, no. 2, pp. 178–195, 1991.

[PAR 03] PARK I., OOI C.L., VIJAYKUMAR T.N., "Reducing design complexity of the load/store Queue", *Proceedings of the 36th International Symposium on Microarchitecture (MICRO-36 2003)*, San Diego, CA, December 2003.

[PAT 94] PATTERSON D.A., HENNESSY J.L., *Computer Organization and Design The Hardware-Software Interface*, Morgan Kaufmann Publishers, 1994.

[PET 90] PETTIS K., HANSEN R.C., "Profile guided code positioning", *Proceedings of the ACM SIGPLAN 90 Conference onProgramming Language Design and Implementation (PLDI '90)*, June 1990.

[PIN 93] PINTER S.S., "Register allocation with instruction scheduling: a new approach", *SIGPLAN Notices*, vol. 28, no. 6, pp. 248–257, June 1993.

[PRI 69] PRITSKER A.A.B., WATTERS L.J., WOLFE P.M., "Multi-project scheduling with limited resources: a zero-one programming approach", *Management Science,* vol. 16, no. 1, 93–108, 1969.

[PRO 94] PROEBSTING T.A., FRASER C.W., "Detecting pipeline structural hazards quickly", *POPL '94: Proceedings of the 21st Symposium on Principles of Programming Languages*, ACM, pp. 280–286, 1994.

[RAJ 00] RAJAGOPALAN S., VACHHARAJANI M., MALIK S., "Handling irregular ILP within conventional VLIW schedulers using artificial resource constraints", *International Conference on Compilers, Architectures, and Synthesis for Embedded Systems (CASES)*, November 2000.

[RAJ 01] RAJAGOPALAN S., RAJAN S.P., MALIK S., *et al.,* "A re-targetable VLIW compiler framework for DSPs with instruction level parallelism", *IEEE Transactions on Computer-Aided Design,* vol. 20, no. 11, pp. 1319–1328, November 2001.

[RAU 81] RAU B.R., GLAESER C.D., "Some scheduling techniques and an easily schedulable horizontal architecture for high performance scientific computing", *14th Annual Workshop on Microprogramming (MICRO-14)*, December 1981.

[RAU 92a] RAU B.R., LEE M., TIRUMALAI P., *et al.,* "Register allocation for software pipelined loops", *Proceedings of the ACM SIGPLAN 1992 Conference on Programming Language Design and Implementation (PLDI '92)*, June 1992.

[RAU 92b] RAU B.R., SCHLANSKER M.S., TIRUMALAI P.P., "Code generation schemas for modulo scheduled loops", *Proceedings of the 25th Annual International Symposium on Microarchitecture (MICRO-25)*, December 1992.

[RAU 92c] RAU B.R., LEE M., TIRUMALAIAND P.P., *et al.*, "Register allocation for software pipelined loops", *Proceedings of the ACM SIGPLAN 1992 Conference on Programming Language Design and Implementation (PLDI)*, ACM, New York, pp. 283–299, 1992.

[RAU 92d] RAU B.R., SCHLANSKER M.S., TIRUMALAI P.P., "Code generation schema for modulo scheduled loops", *SIGMICRO Newsletter*, vol. 23, nos. 1–2, pp. 158–169, 1992.

[RAU 93a] RAU B.R., FISHER J.A., "Instruction-level parallel processing: history, overview, and perspective", *Journal of Supercomputing*, vol. 7, nos. 1–2, pp. 9–50, May 1993.

[RAU 93b] RAU B.R., FISHER J.A., "Instruction-level parallel processing: history, overview, and perspective", *Journal of Supercomputing*, vol. 7, pp. 9–50, May 1993.

[RAU 94] RAU B.R., "Iterative modulo scheduling: an algorithm for software pipelining loops", *Proceedings of the 27th Annual International Symposium on Microarchitecture (MICRO)*, ACM, New York, pp. 63–74, 1994.

[RAU 96] RAU B.R., "Iterative modulo scheduling", *The International Journal of Parallel Processing,* vol. 24, no. 1, pp. 63–74, February 1996.

[RAV 91] RAVINDRA R.K.A., MAGNANTI T.L., ORLIN J.B., *Network Flows: Theory, Algorithms, and Applications*, John Wiley and Sons, New York, 1991.

[RON 08] RONG H., DOUILLET A., GAO G.R., "Register allocation for software pipelined multidimensional loops", *ACM Transactions on Programming Languages and Systems*, vol. 30, no. 4, pp. 1–68, 2008.

[RUT 96b] RUTTENBERG J., GAO G.R., STOUTCHININ A., *et al.*, "Software pipelining showdown : optimal vs. heuristic methods in a production compiler", *Proceedings of the ACM SIGPLAN Conference on Programming Language Design and Implemantation*, ACM, New York, pp. 1–11, May 1996.

[SAP 90] SAPORTA G., *Probabilités, Analyse des Données et Statistique*, Editions Technip, Paris, France, 1990.

[SAV 98] SAVELSBERGH M.W.P., UMA R.N., WEIN J., "An experimental study of LP-based approximation algorithms for scheduling problems", *Proceedings of the 9th Annual ACM-SIAM Symposium on Discrete Algorithms*, 1998.

[SAW 97] SAWAYA A., Pipeline logiciel: découplage et contraintes de registres, PhD Thesis, University of Versailles Saint-Quentin-En-Yvelines, April 1997.

[SCH 87] SCHRIJVER A., *Theory of Linear and Integer Programming*, John Wiley and Sons, New York, 1987.

[SCH 91] SCHWIEGELSHOHN U., GASPERONI F., EBCIOGLU K., "On optimal parallelization of arbitrary loops", *Journal of Parallel and Distributed Computing*, vol. 11, pp. 130–134, 1991.

[SCH 94] SCHLANSKER M., RAU B., MAHLKE S., Achieving high levels of instruction-level parallelism with reduced hardware complexity, Hewlett Packard, 1994.

[SCH 00] SCHLANSKER M.S., RAU B.R., "EPIC: explicitly parallel instruction computing", *Computer*, vol. 33, no. 2, pp. 37–45, February 2000.

[SHA 98] SHAW P., "Using constraint programming and local search methods to solve vehicle routing problems", *Proceedings of 4th International Conference Principles and Practice of Constraint Programming (CP '98)*, October 1998.

[SIL 97] SILVERA R., WANG J., GAO G.R., *et al.*, "A register pressure sensitive instruction scheduler for dynamic issue processors", *Proceedings of the 1997 International Conference on Parallel Architectures and Compilation Techniques (PACT '97)*, IEEE Computer Society Press, San Francisco, CA, pp. 78–89, November 1997.

[SIL 99] SILC J., BOBIC B., UNGERER T., *Processor Architecture: From Dataflow to Superscalar and Beyond*, 1st edition, Springer, 1999.

[SPR 95] SPRECHER A., KOLISCH R., DREXL A., "Semi-active, active, and non-delay schedules for the resource-constrained project scheduling problem", *European Journal of Operational Research*, vol. 80, pp. 94–102, 1995.

[STA 06] STANDARD PERFORMANCE EVALUATION CORPORATION, SPEC CPU, 2006.

[SUC 06] SUCHA P., HANZÁLEK Z., "Scheduling of tasks with precedence delays and relative deadlines - framework for time-optimal dynamic reconfiguration of FPGAs", *IPDPS*, IEEE, pp. 1–8, 2006.

[TAN 06] TANG V., SIU J., VASILEVSKIY A., *et al.,* "A framework for reducing instruction scheduling overhead in dynamic compilers", *CASCON '06: Proceedings of the 2006 Conference of the Center for Advanced Studies on Collaborative Research*, p. 5, 2006.

[TEA 08] TEAM R. D.C., *R: A Language and Environment for Statistical Computing*, R Foundation for Statistical Computing, Vienna, Austria, 2008.

[THE 92] THEOBALD K.B., GAO G.R., HENDREN L.J., "On the limits of program parallelism and its smoothability", W.M. HWU (ed.), *Proceedings of the 25th Annual International Symposium on Microarchitecture*, IEEE, Portland, OR, pp. 10–19, December 1992.

[TOU 01] TOUATI S.-A.-A., "Optimal acyclic fine-grain schedule with cache effects for embedded and real time systems", *Proceedings of the 9th International Symposium on Hardware/Software Codesign*, ACM, Copenhagen, Denmark, April 2001.

[TOU 02] TOUATI S.-A.-A., Register pressure in instruction level parallelism, PhD Thesis, University of Versailles Saint-Quentin en Yvelines, June 2002.

[TOU 03] TOUATI S.-A.-A., EISENBEIS C., "Early control of register pressure for software pipelined loops", *Proceedings of International Conference on Compiler Construction (CC)*, Lecture Notes in Computer Science, Springer-Verlag, Warsaw, Poland, April 2003.

[TOU 04] TOUATI S.-A.-A., EISENBEIS C., "Early periodic register allocation on ILP processors", *Parallel Processing Letters*, vol. 14, no. 2, pp. 287–313, June 2004.

[TOU 05] TOUATI S.-A.-A., "Register saturation in instruction level parallelism", *International Journal of Parallel Programming*, vol. 33, no. 4, pp. 393–449, August 2005.

[TOU 06] TOUATI S.-A.-A., BARTHOU D., "On the decidability of phase ordering problem in optimizing compilation", *Proceedings of the International Conference on Computing Frontiers*, ACM, Ischia, Italy, May 2006.

[TOU 07] TOUATI S.-A.-A., "On the periodic register need in software pipelining", *IEEE Transactions on Computers*, vol. 56, no. 11, pp. 1493–1504, November 2007.

[TOU 09] TOUATI S.-A.-A., Cyclic task scheduling with storage requirement minimisation under specific architectural constraints: case of buffers and rotating storage facilities, Avialable at http://hal.archives-ouvertes.fr/inria-00440446, University of Versailles Saint-Quentin en Yvelines, December 2009.

[TOU 10] TOUATI S.-A.-A., WORMS J., BRIAIS S., "The speedup-test", Avialable at http://hal.archives-ouvertes.fr/inria-00443839, University of Versailles Saint-Quentin en Yvelines, January 2010.

[TOU 11] TOUATI S.-A.-A., BRAULT F., DESCHINKEL K., *et al.,* "Efficient spilling reduction for software pipelined loops in presence of multiple register types in embedded VLIW processors", *ACM Transactions on Embedded Computing Systems*, vol. 10, no. 4, pp. 1–47, November 2011.

[TOU 13a] TOUATI S.-A.-A., BRIAIS S., DESCHINKEL K., "How to eliminate non-positive circuits in periodic scheduling: a procative strategy based on shortest path equations", *RAIRO-Operations Research*, vol. 47, no. 3, pp. 223–249, 2013.

[TOU 13b] TOUATI S.-A.-A., WORMS J., BRIAIS S., "The speedup-test: a statistical methodology for program speedup analysis and computation", *Journal of Concurrency and Computation: Practice and Experience*, vol. 25, no. 10, pp. 1410–1426, 2013.

[TRI 05] TRIANTAFYLLIS S., VACHHARAJANI M., AUGUST D.I., "Compiler optimization-space exploration", *Journal of Instruction-Level Parallelism*, vol. 7, pp. 1–25, January 2005.

[TUC 75] TUCKER A., "Coloring a family of circular arcs", *SIAM Journal on Applied Mathematics*, vol. 29, no. 3, pp. 493–502, November 1975.

[VAA 00] VAN DER VAART A.W., *Asymptotic Statistics*, Cambridge University Press, June 2000.

[VAS 06] VASILACHE N., BASTOUL C., COHEN A., "Polyhedral code generation in the real world", *Proceedings of the International Conference on Compiler Construction (ETAPS CC '06)*, Springer-Verlag, Vienna, Austria, pp. 185–201, March 2006.

[VEL 02] VELDHUIZEN T.L., LUMSDAINE A., "Guaranteed optimization: proving nullspace properties of compilers", *9th International Symposium on Static Analysis (SAS 2002), Lecture Notes in Computer Science*, Springer, vol. 2477, pp. 263–277, 2002.

[VER 02] VERBRUGGE C., Fast local list scheduling, Report no. SABLE-TR-2002-5, School of Computer Science, McGill University, March 2002.

[WAH 03] WAHLEN O., HOHENAUER M., BRAUN G., *et al.*, "Extraction of efficient instruction schedulers from cycle-true processor models", *Proceedings of the 7th International Workshop on Software and Compilers for Embedded Systems (SCOPES 2003)*, of Lecture Notes in Computer Science, Springer, vol. 2826, pp. 167–181, 2003.

[WAN 94a] WANG J., EISENBEIS C., JOURDAN M., *et al.*, "Decomposed software pipelining: a new perspective and a new approach", *International Journal of Parallel Programming*, vol. 22, no. 3, pp. 351–373, June 1994.

[WAN 94b] WANG J., KRALL A., ERTL M.A.,*et al.*, "Software pipelining with register allocation and spilling", *Proceedings of the 27th Annual International Symposium on Microarchitecture*, San Jose, CA, pp. 95–99, November 1994.

[WAN 94c] WANG K.-Y., "Precise compile-time performance prediction for superscalar-based computers", *ACM SIGPLAN Notices*, vol. 29, no. 6, pp. 73–84, June 1994.

[WAN 95] WANG J., KRALL A., ERTL M.A., "Decomposed software pipelining with reduced register requirement", *Proceedings of the IFIP WG10.3 Working Conference on Parallel Architectures and Compilation Techniques (PACT '95)*, Limassol, Cyprus, pp. 277–280, June 1995.

[WER 99] DE WERRA D., EISENBEIS C., LELAIT S., *et al.*, "On a graph-theoretical model for cyclic register allocation", *Discrete Applied Mathematics*, vol. 93, nos. 2–3, pp. 191–203, July 1999.

[WHA 01] WHALEY R., PETITET A., DONGARRA J., "Automated empirical optimizations of software and the ATLAS project", *Parallel Computing*, vol. 27, nos. 1–2, pp. 3–25, 2001.

[WHI 97] WHITFIELD D., SOFFA M.L., "An approach for exploring code-improving transformations", *ACM Transactions on Programming Languages and Systems*, vol. 19, no. 6, pp. 1053–1084, 1997.

[WIL 00] WILKEN K., LIU J., HEFFERNAN M., "Optimal instruction scheduling using integer programming", *Proceedings of the ACM SIGPLAN 2000 Conference on Programming Language Design and Implementation (PLDI '00)*, 2000.

[WOL 98] WOLF M.E., MAYDAN D.E., CHEN D.-K., "Combining loop transformations considering caches and scheduling", *International Journal of Parallel Programming*, vol. 26, no. 4, pp. 479–503, 1998.

[WU 02] WU Y., "Efficient discovery of regular stride patterns in irregular programs and its use in compiler prefetching", *ACM SIGPLAN Notices*, vol. 37, no. 5, pp. 210–221, May 2002.

[YOA 99] YOAZ A., EREZ M., RONEN R., *et al.*, "Speculation techniques for improving load related instruction scheduling", *26th Annual International Symposium on Computer Architecture (26th ISCA '99), Computer Architecture News*, ACM SIGARCH, vol. 27, pp. 42–53, May 1999.

[ZAL 01] ZALAMEA J., LLOSA J., AYGUADÉ E., *et al.*, "MIRS: modulo scheduling with integrated register spilling", *Proceedings of the 14th Annual Workshop on Languages and Compilers for Parallel Computing (LCPC '01)*, August 2001.

[ZHA 05] ZHAO M., CHILDERS B.R., SOFFA M.L., "A model-based framework: an approach for profit-driven optimization", *ACM SIGMICRO International Conference on Code Generation and Optimization (CGO '05)*, San Jose, CA, March 2005.

Lists of Figures, Tables and Algorithms

LIST OF FIGURES

INTRODUCTION

I.1. Pipelined vs. simultaneous execution xxi
I.2. Superscalar execution xxii
I.3. Simple superscalar pipelined steps xxiii
I.4. VLIW processors xxv
I.5. Block diagram of a TTA xxvii

CHAPTER 1

1.1. Classes of phase-ordering problems 17
1.2. Classes of best-parameters problems 20

CHAPTER 2

2.1. The ST220 cumulative resource availabilities and resource class
requirements 28
2.2. Source code and the inner loop body code generator representation . . 29
2.3. The block scheduled loop body and the block schedule resource table 30
2.4. The software pipeline local schedule and the
software pipeline resource table 30

CHAPTER 3

3.1. The time-indexed dependence inequalities of Christofides *et al.* [CHR 87] 48

CHAPTER 4

4.1. Original dependence graph 52
4.2. Augmented dependence graph 52
4.3. A reservation table, a regular reservation table and a reservation vector   55
4.4. Counted loop software pipeline construction with and without
preconditioning 61
4.5. While-loop software pipeline construction without and with modulo
expansion 62
4.6. The st200cc R3.2 compiler performances on the HP benchmarks . .   63
4.7. Definition of the contributions v_i^t to the register pressure   65
4.8. Sample cyclic instruction scheduling problem   69

CHAPTER 5

5.1. Sample schedules for a two-resource scheduling
problem (horizontal time)   80
5.2. Scoreboard Scheduling within the time window (window_size = 4) . .   84
5.3. Scoreboard Scheduling and moving the time window
(window_size = 4)   84
5.4. Benchmark basic blocks and instruction scheduling results   88
5.5. Time breakdown for cycle scheduling and scoreboard scheduling . . .   89

CHAPTER 6

6.1. Example of Alpha 21264 processor   97
6.2. Example of Power 4 processor   98
6.3. Cache behavior of Itanium 2 processor   99
6.4. Vectorization on Itanium 2   102
6.5. Stride patterns classification   112

CHAPTER 7

7.1. DAG example with acyclic register need   124
7.2. Periodic register need in software pipelining   127
7.3. Circular lifetime intervals   129
7.4. Relationship between the maximal clique and the width of a
circular graph   132
7.5. Examples of DDG with unique possible killer per value   138

CHAPTER 8

8.1. DAG model 145
8.2. Valid killing function and bipartite decomposition 148
8.3. Example of computing the acyclic register saturation 152

CHAPTER 9

9.1. Example for SIRA and reuse graphs 162

CHAPTER 10

10.1. Linear program based on shortest paths equations (SPE) 187

CHAPTER 11

11.1. Minimal unroll factor computation depending on phase ordering . . . 193
11.2. Example to highlight the short-comings of the MVE technique 197
11.3. SWP kernel unrolled with MVE 198
11.4. Example to explain the optimality of the meeting graph technique . . 199
11.5. Example for SIRA and reuse graphs 201
11.6. Graphical solution for the fixed loop unrolling problem 207
11.7. How to traverse the lattice S 211
11.8. Modifying reuse graphs to minimize loop unrolling factor 214
11.9. Loop unrolling values in the search space S 221
11.10. Example of loop unrolling reduction using meeting graph 222
11.11. The new search space S in the meeting graph 225

CHAPTER 12

12.1. Observed execution times of some SPEC OMP 2001 applications
(compiled with gcc) 235
12.2. The Speedup-Test protocol for analyzing the average execution time . 242
12.3. The Speedup-Test protocol for analyzing the median execution time . 244

APPENDIX 1

A1.1. Histograms on the number of nodes (loop statements): $\|V\|$ 265

A1.2. Histograms on the number of statements writing inside general registers $\|V^{R,GR}\|$ 266

A1.3. Histograms on the number of statements writing inside branch registers $\|V^{R,BR}\|$ 267

A1.4. Histograms on the number of data dependences $\|E\|$ 268

A1.5. Histograms on MinII values 269

A1.6. Histograms on the number of strongly connected components 270

APPENDIX 2

A2.1. Accuracy of the GREEDY-K heuristic versus optimality 273

A2.2. Error ratios of the GREEDY-K heuristic versus optimality 274

A2.3. Execution times of the GREEDY-K heuristic 275

A2.4. Maximal periodic register need vs. initiation interval 276

A2.5. Periodic register saturation in unrolled loops 278

APPENDIX 3

A3.1. Percentage of DDG treated successfully by SIRALINA and the impact on the MII 281

A3.2. Average increase of the MII 282

A3.3. Boxplots of the execution times of SIRALINA (all DDG) 284

A3.4. Plugging SIRA into the ST231 compiler toolchain (LAO backend) . 285

A3.5. The impact of SIRA on static code quality 288

A3.6. Loops where spill code disappears completely 288

A3.7. Speedups of the whole application using the standard input 290

A3.8. Performance characterization of some applications 291

A3.9. Performance characterization of the FFMPEG application 292

APPENDIX 4

A4.1. Execution times of UAL (in seconds) 295

A4.2. Execution times of CHECK (in seconds) 296

A4.3. Execution times of SPE (in seconds) 296

A4.3. Execution times of SPE (in seconds) 297

A4.4. Maximum observed number of iterations for SPE 298

A4.5. Comparison of the heuristics ability to reduce the register pressure (SPEC2000) 299

A4.6. Comparison of the heuristics ability to reduce the register pressure (MEDIABENCH) 299

A4.7. Comparison of the heuristics ability to reduce the register pressure (SPEC2006) 300

A4.8. Comparison of the heuristics ability to reduce the register pressure (FFMPEG) 300

APPENDIX 5

A5.1. Loop unrolling minimization experiments (random DDG, single register type) 304

A5.2. Average code compaction ratio (random DDG, single register type) . 305

A5.3. Weighted harmonic mean for minimized loop unrolling degree 307

A5.4. Initial versus final loop unrolling in each configuration 310

A5.5. Observations on loop unrolling minimization 313

A5.6. Final loop unrolling factors after minimization 314

APPENDIX 6

A6.1. Execution time repartition for Spec benchmarks 316

A6.2. Efficiency of data prefetching and preloading. Note that prefetching is not applicable to all applications 317

A6.3. Initial and modified codes sizes 318

APPENDIX 7

A7.1. The sample minimum is a not necessarily a good estimation of the theoretical minimum 320

LIST OF TABLES

INTRODUCTION

I.1. Other contributors to the results presented in this book xix

CHAPTER 3

3.1. Polynomial-time solvable parallel machine scheduling problems . . . 41
3.2. NP-hard parallel machine scheduling problems 42
3.3. Performance guarantees of the GLSA with arbitrary priority 44
3.4. Performance guarantees of the GLSA with a specific priority 45
3.5. Problems solved by the algorithm of Leung,
Palem and Pnueli [LEU 01] steps 1 and 2 45

CHAPTER 6

6.1. Examples of measured performance degradation factors 100
6.2. Worst-case performance gain on Alpha 21264 101
6.3. Worst-case performance gain on Itanium 2 102
6.4. Examples of code and data regularity/irregularity 108
6.5. Examples of prefetch: simple case and using extra register case 114

CHAPTER 12

12.1. Number of non-statistically significant speedups in the tested
benchmarks 253

APPENDIX 2

A2.1. Optimal versus approximate PRS 277

APPENDIX 5

A5.1. Machine with bounded number of registers 307
A5.2. Machine with bounded registers with option continue 308
A5.3. Number of unrolled loops compared to the number of spilled loops
resulted (by using meeting graphs) 309
A5.4. Arithmetic mean of initial loop unrolling, final loop
unrolling and ratio 311
A5.5. Comparison between final loop unrolling factors and MAXLIVE . . 311
A5.6. Optimized loop unrolling factors of scheduled versus unscheduled
loops 312

APPENDIX 7

A7.1. Monte Carlo simulation of a Gaussian distribution 321
A7.2. The two risk levels for hypothesis testing in statistical and probability
 theory. 322
A7.3. SPEC OMP2001 on low-overhead environment 324
A7.4. SPECCPU2006 executed on low overhead environment 324
A7.5. SPEC OMP2001 on high-overhead environment 324
A7.6. SPECCPU2006 on high-overhead environment 325

LIST OF ALGORITHMS

CHAPTER 1

1.1. Computing a good compilation sequence in the compilation cost model   14
1.2. Optimize_Node(n)   15

CHAPTER 8

8.1. GREEDY-K heuristic 150

CHAPTER 10

10.1. The algorithm $IterativeSIRALINA$ 185
10.2. The function $UpdateReuseDistances$ 187

CHAPTER 11

11.1. Fixed loop unrolling problem 208
11.2. DIV_NEAR 208
11.3. DIVISORS 209
11.4. LCM-MIN algorithm 212
11.5. General fixed loop unrolling problem 220

Index

A

absolute register sufficiency, 133
acyclic lifetime interval, 123
    register saturation, 145
    scheduling, 123
α, risk level, 233, 321
$\alpha \mid \beta \mid \gamma$, notation of machine scheduling
    problems, 40
anti-dependence, 164, 165
augmented dependence graph, 52

B

best-parameters problem in phase
    ordering, 18
β, secondary risk level, 321
birth date, 127
blocking cache, 109
boxplot, 272
bundles, 54

C

C_{max} (maxspan), 40
$\overline{\mathcal{CG}}(G)$, 130
$chains$, 40
carried dependences, 33
central scheduling problem, 43
$\mathcal{CG}(G)$, 128
circular fractional interval, 130
    lifetime interval, 128
CM, 206

column number, 72
connected bipartite component, 149
$Cons(u^t)$, 122
critical circuit, 126
cyclic machine scheduling problem, 29
    register need, 125
    scheduling, 125

D

d_i for deadlines, 40
DAG, directed acyclic graph, 123
data preloading, 114
DDG associated to reuse graph, 164
DDG, data dependence graph, 122
delinquent load, 111
dependence record, 82
descendant values, 148
disjoint value DAG, 148
$\delta_{r,t}$, 123
due dates, d_i, 39
$DV^k(G)$, 148
$\delta_{w,t}$, 123

E

E_{dep}, 47, 49
E^k, 165
$E^{k,t}$, 165
E^μ, 165
$E^{\mu,t}$, 165
$E^{\text{reuse},t}$, 163
$E^{\text{reuse},t}_{(i)}$, 185

$E^{R,t}$, 122
excessive set, 125
    value, 125
extended DAG associated with k, 147

F

feasible schedule, 40
fixed loop unrolling problem, 206
flow edges, 122
fractional circular graph, 130

G

$\gamma^t(u,v)$, 186
$G = (V, E)$, 122
$G^{\to k}$, 147
general fixed loop unrolling, 218
Graham list scheduling, 43
$G^{\text{reuse},t}$, 163
$G^{\text{reuse},t} = (V^{R,t}, E^{\text{reuse},t})$, 163, 202

H, I

H_0, null hypothesis, 321
H_a, alternative hypothesis, 321
Hungarian algorithm, 173
II, initiation interval, 125
$inTree$, 40
insertion scheduling, 56
instruction, 122
    selection, 257
inter-region scheduling problem, 84
interval-order, 45
intLP, 153
$intOrder(mono\ l_i^j)$, 40
iterative compilation, 3
iterative modulo scheduling, 33

J, K

job-based list scheduling, 43
K, 165
K-periodic schedules, 31
kernel, 126
k_{u^t}, 147, 164
killing function, 147
    nodes, 164

L

L, the duration, 126
L_{max} (maximum lateness), 40
$\lambda(C)$, 179
large neighborhood search (LNS), 74
$lat(u)$, 122
left-end of the cyclic interval, 128
lexicographic-positive circuit, 179
    DDG, 179
lifetime, 127
    node, 53
lifetime-sensitive instruction scheduling
    problems (LSISP), 27
    modulo schedule, 51
linear assignment problem, 172
list scheduling, 43
load/store vectorization, 100
loop unwinding, 33

M

$\mu^t(C)$, 163
$\mu^t(e_r)$, 163, 201
$\widehat{\mu}^t_{(i)}$, 185
MA^k, 149
MAXLIVE, 125
MAXLIVE^t, 195
MCRL, 52
meeting graph, 197
memory disambiguation mechanism, 91
MG, 197
MII, Minimum Initiation Interval, 126
$\widehat{\mu^*}^t(u,v)$, 184
MISP, 33
modulo instruction scheduling problem, 33
    scheduling, 32
    variable expansion, 196
monotone interval-order, 46
miss information status hold registers
    (MSHR), 109
MVE, 196

N

node, 122
non-blocking cache, 109
non-positive circuit, 180
NUAL, 122

O

$outTree$, 40
$\{O_i\}_{1 \leq i \leq n}$, 29
operation, 122
overall gain, 238
 speedup, 238

P

$\Phi(e_r)$, 165
$PK(G) = (V, E^{PK})$, 146
$p_i = 1$, 40
$p_i = p$, 40
$prec(l_i^j)$, 40
$prec(l_i^j = l)$, 40
Pm, parallel processors, 40
partial modulo schedule, 56
pending load queue, 109
periodic register need, 125, 128
 saturation, 153
 sufficiency, 132
 schedules, 30
 scheduling, 125
periods around the circle, 128
phase ordering problem, 8, 9
$pkill_G(u)$, 146
potential killing DAG, 146
 operation, 146
preloading, 114
$\prec$, 148
preemptive and non-preemptive
 scheduling, 39
$PRF^t(G)$, 132
$PRN_\sigma^t(G)$, 129, 130
producer node, 53
PRS, 153
ψ_t, 186

R

r_i for release dates, 40
$\downarrow_R (u)$, 148
RCISP, 64
RCMSP, 70, 72, 74
RC^t, 196
RC^t, 202
RCPSP, 47
read after write (RAW), 79

register allocation instruction scheduling
 problems (RAISP), 27
 class, 122
 need, 123
 pressure instruction scheduling
 problems (RPISP), 27
 renaming, 227
 type, 122
register-constrained instruction scheduling
 problems (RCISP), 27
$\mathcal{R}^t$, 122
$\mathcal{R}$, 205
relaxation (scheduling), 42
release dates r_i, 39
reservation table, 55
 vectors, 55
resource-constrained project scheduling
 problems (RCSP), 42
reuse circuit, 163
 distance, 163, 201
 distances, 159
 edges, 159, 163
 graphs, 163
ρ, unroll factor, 199, 202
ρ^t, unroll factor, 202
right-end of the cyclic
 interval, 128
risk level, 233
$RN_\sigma^t(G)$, 125, 145
rotating register files, 226
row number, 72
RPISP, 48
R^t, 204
$RS^t(G)$, 145
RSlib, 151

S

σ, 123
$\{\sigma_i^k\}_{0 \leq i \leq n+1}^{k>0}$, 30
$\{\sigma_i\}_{1 \leq i \leq n}$, 40
$\sigma_{k_u t}{}^*$, 184
$\sigma_u{}^*$, 184
$\Sigma_L(G)$, 126
saturating acyclic schedule, 145
 killing function, 149
 SWP schedule, 153
 values, 145, 149

schedulable DDG, 179
  problem, 170
scoreboard scheduling, 80
serial edges, 122
SIRA, 162
SIRAlib, 174, 187
SIRALINA, 169
speedup, 237
speedup-Test, 236
spmean$(\mathcal{C}, I)$, 237
spmedian$(\mathcal{C}, I)$, 237
spmin$(\mathcal{C}, I)$, 237
$src(e)$, 122
stage scheduling, 134
statement, 122
steady state, 126
software pipelining (SWP), 125

T, U

θ_i^j, latency, 33
θ_i^j, dependence latency, 41
temporal constraints, 39

$tgt(e)$, 122
u^t, 122
UAL, 122
uniform dependence, 30

V

v, 146
valid killing function, 147
values simultaneously alive, 125
variable expansion, 191
vertice, 122
$V^{k,t}$, 164
$V^{R,t}$, 122, 163

W

ω_i^j, 33
  distance, 33
ω^t, 168
$\omega(u)$, 198
write after read (WAR), 79
write after write (WAW), 79